AMERICAN JUDAISM

JOHN A. HARDON, s.j.

Bellarmine School of Theology
Loyola University, Chicago

LOYOLA UNIVERSITY PRESS

Chicago   60657

© 1971 Loyola University Press

Library of Congress Catalog Card Number: 72-148264

ISBN 0-8294-0199-7

Printed in the United States of America

CONTENTS

About this book

American Judaism was designed by William Nicoll of
Edit, Inc. It was set in the composing room of
Loyola University Press. The type face is 10/13 and 9/11
Caledonia. The display type is 36 and 48 Baskerville
and 48 Baskerville Old Style.

It was printed by Photopress, Inc., on
Warren's 60-pound English Finish paper and
bound by The Engdahl Company.

FOREWORD

One of the most fascinating pursuits of man is his attempt to understand not only how and why he lives, but how and why his neighbor lives. Despite the fact that Jews and Christians have been living side by side for close to two thousand years, it would seem they really do not know much about one another, let alone understand one another. On the one hand, to the Christian, the Jew was always living in error and blindness, refusing to see the "light" of the Christian message; and on the other hand, to the Jew, the Christian was always regarded with suspicion, if not outright hostility. By and large many attempts at "dialogue" had at least the implicit assumption of an attempt to convert the Jew to the truth, and bring him under the wings of Mother Church. The Jewish reaction was predictable and understandable.

However, by the mid-twentieth century (no doubt in part due to the Holocaust and the establishment of the State of Israel) there seems to be a concerted effort on the part of some to understand the Jewish way of life as an entity in itself. Realizing that the Judaeo-Christian tradition is a rather nebulous and tenuous association, what one really finds are two rather distinct religious traditions based on quite different foundations of faith and historical experiences leading to different faith systems and life styles.

This new book, *American Judaism*, by the Jesuit scholar John A. Hardon, is a thoroughgoing attempt to bring to the Christian, particularly Catholic, audience an understanding of this Jewish way of life. While the title is about American Jews and Judaism, Father Hardon usually does not limit his exposition to Jews in America only. He correctly realizes that American Jewry is only one example of Jewish life in a particular historical and social context. He therefore brings into focus the entire gamut of Jewish history and law, starting from the biblical period. Where one often finds a rather negative view of the Pharisaic and Rabbinic Jerusalem, Father Hardon attempts, successfully, to see the continuing value of Judaism in an unbroken line from the Bible until today. His analysis of the various schools of Judaic, religious thought is particularly perceptive, as also his discussion of the principles of Jewish law in its developing traditions throughout the centuries.

This is not so much a book on the particular American Jewish experience, but on the whole spectrum of Judaism as a religion and a community of the Covenant, using the American Jew as an example. The assessment of the current status of the American Jewish community is not only interesting reading, but a valuable contribution to the study of how an ancient tradition attempts to integrate itself into an entirely new social and political constellation. Professor Hardon is to be commended for his effort and is to be wished a "ye yasher kochacha," may your strength be encouraged.

MOSHE DAVIDOWITZ

Spertus College of Judaica
Chicago, Illinois

INTRODUCTION

Few aspects of our national life have been treated more extensively than American Judaism. Every phase of the subject has been explored from every possible angle. Jewish history and culture, religion and philosophy, politics and education have been covered in such profusion that another book on Judaism in America must seem like arrogant effrontery—as though something significant could still be added to the library of American Judaica.

Yet, I wrote this book with confidence that it would not repeat the obvious but have a message for those who may be very vocal in talking about the Jews but not so well informed about the faith and deep religious inspiration on which Judaism is built. America needs this faith and inspiration as never before in its history, because it is one foundation on which the nation stands. Judaism and Christianity are the two pillars that support the structure of American society. Each has contributed to the national ethos.

Those who are professed Christians should learn that their religion is based on the prophets and sages of Israel. These pages have been written mainly in the hope that the present drive for Christian unity might develop into the wider movement for a united Judaeo-Christianity.

As I see it, Christians have three things to learn about the Jews: that Judaism is a living faith and not a religion that somehow stopped growing with the rise of Christianity; that this faith has more in common with the Christian philosophy of life than any other religious culture of mankind; and that Jews and Judaism are not the same thing, no more than Christians are all that Christianity is or should be.

I spent several months thinking how best to present an adequate and accurate picture of American Judaism to Christian readers. Years of personal and professional relationship with Jews told me that, whatever the book contains, it should not presume on anything. Consequently much of what I have to say is already known by those who really know Judaism. But how many people qualify and would honestly claim such knowledge? This was the informative purpose that I set myself: to tell my fellow Christians what they ought to know about those from whose heritage their own religious loyalties are derived.

More important, however, than information, is to see a living religion with centuries of past history in some kind of synthesis. There is a basic unity in modern Judaism that needs to be better known. It is often belied by the variety and contrariety of forms which it takes in profession of faith, ritual custom, and ethical perspective which have made America the most denominational country in the world. American freedom has affected every religious tradition, including the Jewish, with results that no one denies. The popular division of Orthodox, Conservative, and Reform Jews is only a convenient way of designating what is actually a spectrum of religious belief and practice among the Jews in America. They reflect both extremes to a degree not found in other religions. They also prove that such extremes are possible without destroying their basic identity. It was my intention to search out this identity which underlies all Judaism, no matter how many differences it may show.

Information and synthesis are available elsewhere and alone would not have justified writing another book on the Jews in America. Others have done this as well and, I am sure, better than I. What I felt was still needed was to say all that needs saying factually, objectively, and sympathetically but also as seen by a Christian theologian who is also interpreting what he sees. I quickly add that the interpretation has not been filtered through any other judgment than the fundamental one of trying to evaluate for others as I would want my own beliefs and practices to be evaluated by them.

For too long have the followers of Abraham and Jesus been strangers to one another in the land where they have both found such liberty as no other country provides. Yet liberty to practice one's own religion is not enough. It should mean the liberty to respect the religion of others and cooperate with them in the pursuit of common goals.

Respect is impossible without knowing whom to respect and why. It was especially to offer those who are not Jews themselves an easy access to this kind of knowledge that the present volume was written. If it helps in any way to make Judaeo-Christianity a living reality and not only a hyphenated word, the research and reflection given to its writing will have been more than worth the effort expended.

Special thanks are due to Mrs. Carl Berg and Mrs. Warren Joyce for their painstaking secretarial services, without which this book could not have been published; and to Rev. John Keenan, S.S.S., and Rev. Sebastian Pagano, O.M.I., for editorial assistance. My gratitude to Moshe Davidowitz for reading the manuscript and writing his generous Foreword.

Spertus College of Judaica (Chicago), the National Film Board of Canada, and the Proulx Brothers (Ottawa) kindly furnished the photographs pictured in the volume.

Rabbi Simon L. Echstein of Ottawa Beth Shalom gave invaluable advice on interpreting Jewish synagogue customs and ritual.

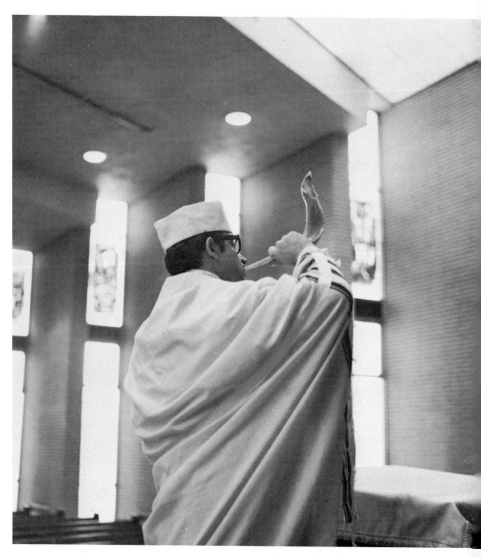

Blowing the Shofar (ram's horn). Symbol of the Jewish people since Isaac was a child. Sounded a hundred times at Rosh Ha-Shanah (New Year).

I

SACRED WRITINGS

American Judaism has a religious ancestry that must be seen, if only cursorily, if Jews are to be understood as something more than an ethnic minority or a national segment of American society. Their history belongs to the essence of their nature.

This is more easily said than done, because Jews themselves dispute on what exactly is a Jew. Etymologically there is no problem. The name comes from Judah, one of the twelve tribes of Israel. Later it came to apply to anyone belonging to the Hebrew race, and finally to those who profess the Jewish religion.

The unsolved question is whether Judaism is mainly ethnic or religious, since there are many Jews who are not direct descendants of Abraham, and many others who may be so descended but do not profess the Jewish faith.

Perhaps the best definition is to see Judaism as the heart and Jewry as the body of a permanent moral tradition, which has its roots in the prophets of Israel and its hopes in a forthcoming Messianic era.

This root and hope is deeply religious and also very distinctive. Too many Americans are satisfied to think of Judaism as the parent of Christianity and Islam—and no more. They forget that Judaism is a living faith whose vital elements have remained substantially unchanged and yet, paradoxically, the Jewish people have greatly changed over the centuries.

The main burden of this book is to see Judaism as a religious culture in present-day America. But we must first look back at the sources from which this culture is derived.

THE BIBLE

Any discussion of Jewish belief must begin with the Bible. Hebrews call it *Tanakh*, from the initial letters of the words *Torah*, *Neviim*, *Ketuvim*, meaning "Pentateuch," "Prophets," and "Hagiographa." They prefer this designation.

The Pentateuch contains the first five (Greek=*pente*) books, whose Hebrew names are taken from the first significant word in each book. Genesis tells the story of creation, of man's history until the time of Abraham—father of the Jews—and the tales of the patriarchs. Exodus describes the departure from Egypt, still symbolic of Jewish migrations; the giving of the Law (Torah) to Moses on Mount Sinai, and the construction of the Tabernacle to house the ark of the covenant with its tables of the Law. Leviticus, formerly known as *Torat Kohanim* (the priestly code), contains the legislation given to Moses after the Tabernacle was built and covers mainly the laws of sacrifice and impurity together with such moral and social directives as are not found in Exodus. Numbers recounts the wandering of the Israelites in the desert and gives still further legislation. Deuteronomy, also known as *Mishnah Torah* (Repetition of the Law), recapitulates the laws of Sinai, with variations, and records the last sermons of Moses.

Since the First Temple played such an important role in Jewish history, the prophetic books are divided on this basis. The Former

Prophets relate Israel's history from the conquest of Canaan to the destruction of the First Temple (586 B.C.). They cover the book of Joshua, telling of the conquest and division of Canaan; Judges continues the story until after the time of Samson, who exemplifies the Jewish desire for freedom; Samuel gives the biography of Samuel the prophet and the first two kings of Israel, Saul and David; and Kings spans the period from the reign of Solomon to the destruction by Nebuchadnezzar of the Temple in Jerusalem.

Among the Latter Prophets, Isaiah, Jeremiah, and Ezekiel are major. Isaiah is regarded as the seer of eternal peace at the end of days when the Lord's Anointed will judge the nations. Jeremiah remains a constant reminder to the Jews to keep the covenant their forefathers had made with God. Ezekiel is the great prophet of Jewish Messianism, who promises through Israel a final reestablishment in the world of the rule of peace.

The twelve Minor Prophets are regarded as a single book. According to rabbinic teaching, the prophetic spirit ceased with the last of the Minor Prophets. Since their time, the role of teachers in Israel has been assumed by the "Men of the Great Synagogue" and the wise men who succeeded them. They received the faculty of interpreting the biblical prophecies. Indeed, according to the Talmud, "a Sage is higher than a prophet,"[1] because without the sage a prophet might not be understood. Once the Messianic age appears, however, the ability to prophesy will return to Israel.

Hagiographa (*Ketuvim*=writings) have twelve books, or eleven if Ezra and Nehemiah are treated as a single work. The Psalms are a collection of prayers and hymns of which many were taken from the ancient Temple service; they are today the principal part of Jewish liturgy. Proverbs gather together numerous parables and statements of wise counsel. Their theme is mainly addressed to the young, and postulates a belief that due reward will ultimately come to the good (synonymous with the wise) and retribution to the wicked (identified with the foolish). Job is a religious dialogue concerned with the mystery of suffering in its relationship to sin.

Following Job are five scrolls (*megillot*) that are commonly read in most synagogues on special occasions. The idyllic story of Ruth deals with the period of the Judges and is recited for Pentecost.

The Canticle of Canticles is a series of love poems used at Passover. Lamentations recall the tragedy that befell the Temple and Jerusalem under the Babylonians; they are prayed on the day of fast (ninth of Av) commemorating the destruction of the First and Second Temples. Ecclesiastes meditates on the passing nature of human life on earth and is reserved for the Feast of Tabernacles. The Esther story of persecution under the Persian King Ahasuerus is read annually at Purim.

Finally the Hagiographa contain the Daniel narrative from the Babylonian Exile and the prophet's apocalyptic visions; Ezra-Nehemiah spans the events after the return of the Jews from Babylon; and Chronicles, now in two parts, summarizes the history of Israel down to the end of the exile in Babylon with special attention to the kingdom of Judah.

Immediately a distinction should be made between the Bible of the Jews and the Old Testament of Christianity. Seven books of the Old Testament, as received by Roman Catholics and the Eastern Orthodox, are considered Apocrypha by the Jews.

While some Jewish scholars believe there were originally two independent canons of the Hebrew Bible, others defend their original unity because of the intimate relationship between the various pre-Christian Jewish communities. The two canons have come to be known as the Palestinian, used by the Jews in and around Palestine, and the Alexandrian, followed by Jews who were dispersed in other lands.

The Alexandrian canon was available in the well-known Greek version, the Septuagint, completed about 132 B.C. It differed from the Palestinian in the order of the biblical books and in its greater extent. The threefold grouping into the Law, Prophets, and Writings was absent, and several other books, not found in the Hebrew Bible of Palestine, were included. They were Wisdom, Ecclesiasticus, Judith, Tobit, and Baruch, and in most manuscripts, the first two books of Maccabees.

By the end of the first century of the Christian era, the Pharisees of Palestine decided against the Alexandrian canon on the basis of four criteria, which are still invoked by Jewish authors in determining the revealed word of God: (1) the book in question had to conform to the Pentateuch, (2) it could not have been written after the time of Ezra, (3) it had to be written in Hebrew, and (4) it must have been written in Palestine.

Since the book of Baruch and the epistle of Jeremiah were not of Palestinian origin; the book of Sirach (Ecclesiasticus) and First Maccabees were written after the time of Ezra; Tobit and parts of Esther and Daniel were composed originally in Aramaic and also probably outside of Palestine; Judith was likely written in Aramaic, while Wisdom and Second Maccabees were done originally in Greek—they were all expunged from the biblical canon.

This canonization of the sacred scriptures was completed by the academy of the Sanhedrin, which met in Jabneh (Jamnia), a city of Palestine south of Jaffa. After the destruction of the Second Temple (A.D. 70), Rabbi Johann ben Zakkai reestablished the Sanhedrin at Jabneh until the Bar Kokba revolt (A.D. 135). Somewhere between these two dates, the Hebrew Bible was formally determined and, as the Sanhedrin concluded, "made a fence around it."

When speaking of the Apocrypha, Jews are careful to refer the term to noncanonical Jewish literature written during the period of the Second Temple and up to the Bar Kokba revolt. They freely admit that it contains works similar to those in the Bible and actually found in the Septuagint, but excluded from the canon for the reasons given. They further distinguish these writings from the Pseudepigrapha which are commonly rejected by the Catholic Church as apocryphal, like the book of Jubilees and the Third and Fourth books of Maccabees.

The Protestant Reformers in the sixteenth century reverted to the Jewish canon of the Old Testament, on the same principles invoked by the Sanhedrin of Jabneh.

TALMUD

If pre-Christian Judaism is unintelligible without the Bible—Torah, Neviim, and Ketuvim—the Jewish faith since the Christian era is unexplainable without the Talmud, which is the main repository of Judaic tradition. As a collective name, *Talmud* means "instruction" and comprehends two sets of writings: the third-century Mishnah, compiled by Rabbi Judah about A.D. 215, and the fourth to sixth centuries' Gemara, which has come down in two forms, the Babylonian in Eastern Aramaic and the Palestinian in Western Aramaic.

Mishnah has a double meaning, either "study by repetition" or "second" because considered second to the Pentateuch. It is a codification of Jewish laws, *Halakoth*, from the time of the Restoration until the end of the second century. Originally oral, the laws were later reduced to written form.

From the early third century the Mishnah supplanted the numerous earlier collections and so put an end to much controversy, notably between the schools of Shammai and Hillel. Rabbi Judah was a lineal descendant of Hillel, who upheld the liberal and lenient interpretation of the law and whose followers were conciliatory in all controversies. The Mishnah, therefore, is not an original work but a redaction of earlier material and it is written in the Hebrew typical of Jewish scholars at that time.

Each of the six divisions—Seeds (laws on agriculture), Festivals and Women (marriage laws), Injuries (civil and criminal regulations), Holy Things (worship and ritual), and Purifications—is divided into two parts or Tractates, which are further subdivided into chapters, and the chapters into paragraphs or precepts.

As a sectarian law-code, the Mishnah builds on the principle of precedent, giving the sayings of learned Rabbis, in quotation or paraphrase, and often only a sentence in length. No effort is made to classify the statements beyond a general assembly of similar material under a single heading.

Most of the legislation is extremely minute. Thus, "an egg laid on a festival may be eaten on the same day. So say the school of Shammai; the school of Hillel, however, say it must not. The school of Shammai say that leaven the size of an olive and browned bread the size of a date are to be removed before the Passover; but the school of Hillel say that both must be removed when the size of an olive only."[2] Then follow thirteen pages of commentary, pro and con, discussing the two opinions on the foregoing and the allied subject of burying wild game or fowl on festival days.

Among numerous prohibitions for dealing with heathen non-Israelites are several referring to the latter's religious holidays. Thus "three days before the festival of the heathen it is forbidden to have any business with them. One must not lend them anything which can be useful to them, nor borrow such from them. And the same is the case with cash money, even to pay or to receive payment is forbidden. Rabbi Jehuda, however, maintains: To receive payment is allowed, because it is a displeasure to the payers. And he was answered: Although it is now a displeasure, it pleases them in the future."[3] Again a long commentary of eleven pages evaluates the different interpretations.

Indicative of the high regard in which the Talmudic tradition was held, a Mishnah in the treatise *Sanhedrin* decrees that "the punishment of him who transgresses the decision of the Scribes is more rigorous than for that which is plainly written in the Scriptures."[4] The example given is that of a person who claims, against the Scribes, that the Jewish phylactery (or leather case containing vellum strips with four passages, from Exodus and Deuteronomy) should have five strips instead of four. One explanation of this "strange passage" is that some Jewish Christians were adding a fifth text, from the prologue of St. John's Gospel.[5]

However not all the Mishnah is so rabbinical. The treatise *Aboth*, on the Fathers of the Synagogue, is a collection of wise epigrams and homely counsels that are very quotable. One statement follows another with no logical correlation.

> Rabbi Tarphon was in the habit of saying, "The day is short, the work is great, the workmen are slothful, the reward is rich, the Master is urgent."[6]
>
> Rabbi Ishmail said, "Be obedient to a superior, affable to a petitioner, and friendly to all mankind."[7]
>
> Rabbi Jannai said, "It is beyond our power to explain either the prosperity of the wicked or the afflictions of the righteous."[8]
>
> Rabbi Jacob used to say, "This world is only a vestibule of the world to come. So prepare yourself in the vestibule to be admitted into the banquet hall." He also said, "Better is one hour of repentance and good deeds in this world than all the life of the world to come, though one hour of bliss in the future is better than a lifetime in this world."[9]

A great deal of Jewish tradition on the meaning of various aspects of religious ritual and practice prescribed by the Bible derives from the Gemara, whose lengthy interpretations form the quantitative bulk of the Talmud.

The treatise *Pesachim* (Passover) covers almost three hundred pages in a standard edition, divided into twelve sections or sets of regulations: concerning the removal of leaven from the house on the eve of the Passover and the exact time when this must be accomplished; the time for eating leavened bread on the eve of the Passover; what material is to be used for making unleavened bread and bitter herbs; articles which cause transgression of the law prohibiting leaven to be seen or found in the house of an Israelite; work which may and such as must not be performed on the day preceding the festival of Passover; the sacrifice of the Paschal Lamb; acts which supersede the due observance of the Sabbath; sacrifice of the Paschal offering and what is to be done if one sacrifice is confounded with another; the roasting of the Paschal Lamb, the manner and procedure if the Paschal Lamb becomes defiled, which parts of the lamb are eaten; those obligated to eat the Paschal sacrifice, where it is to be eaten, companies appointed to eat it, and the difference between the first and second Passover; the second Passover, concerning cases where the Paschal sacrifice had become mixed; and regulations about the meal on the eve of the Passover and the four cups of wine to be drunk with the meal.

With rare exception, the Gemara expands on the Mishnah, clarifies obscurities, and offers as many as a dozen opinions on what the Mishnah states as a single prescription. According to the Mishnah, for example, the duty of eating bitter herbs on the Passover may be acquitted with lettuce, wild endive, bitter coriander, and horseradish, if fresh or dry, but not pickled or cooked in any way. On which the Gemara offers variant interpretations, including the general one that, "all herbs emitting white juice may serve to satisfy the duty of eating bitter herbs on the Passover." In fact Rabbi Johann ben Berokah allowed even such as when cut should become a shade paler. "Anonymous teachers, however, say that all bitter herbs emit white juice, and become a shade paler when cut," so that any herb showing this quality may be used.[10]

Commentators on the Talmud sometimes mistakenly leave the impression that no distinction is recognized between scriptural and rabbinical prescriptions, and certainly there has been enough to warrant this judgment in the case of some Jewish leaders. But the Talmud itself occasionally distinguishes between the two levels of obligation, as in the same context on the use of herbs and unleavened bread at the Paschal supper. The Hillel referred to was the contemporary of Christ, whose followers opposed the school of Shammai as the more liberal and tolerant interpreters of the Law.

> Rabhina said, "Rabbi Mesharshia the son of Rabbi Nathan told me, that so said Hillel, quoting a tradition: A man should not place the bitter herbs between unleavened cakes and eat them in that manner. Why not? Because the eating of unleavened cakes is a biblical commandment, while the eating of bitter herbs in this day is only a rabbinical ordinance. Now if the two be eaten together, the bitter herbs might destroy the taste of the cakes, and thus a rabbinical ordinance would supersede a biblical commandment. And even according to those who hold that one commandment cannot nullify another when both are fulfilled at the same time, such is only the case when both are biblical or both rabbinical. But when one is a biblical and the other a rabbinical commandment, the rabbinical nullifies the other, and hence their joint fulfillment is not allowed."[11]

Other passages in the Talmud which place rabbinical tradition on the same level as the Bible should be read in the light of this more modest rabbinization.

The same treatise has a series of fours: types among men, temperaments, disciples, and almsgivers.

> There are four types of men: The ordinary one says, "What is mine is mine and what is yours is yours." The queer one says, "What is mine is yours, and what is yours is mine." The saintly one says, "What is mine is yours and what is yours is yours." The wicked one says, "What is mine is mine, and what is yours is mine."[12]

Occasionally the title "Rabbi" is omitted from a sage's name, as with Elisha ben Abuya (born about A.D. 80). Elisha had been a Talmudic scholar but eventually turned freethinker. More often no author of a statement is given, but only the title, "Mishnah."

Gemara is the commentary on the Mishnah, and both are now included in the Talmud, with interpretation following rabbinic tradition. Jewish authorities in Babylonia organized those laws which had developed from the close of the Mishnah down to their own times; their commentaries together with the Mishnah received the name Babylonian Talmud. It represents the final codification of Jewish law. In Palestine the law was less well organized, mostly because of the unsettled conditions under the Roman Empire. What exists, however, has the name of Jerusalem or Palestinian Talmud.

If the Mishnah is detailed, the Gemara is minute in the extreme. This is specially true of the treatise *Sabbath*, which discusses in a single chapter such varied items as permissible and forbidden oils and wicks for lamps on the Sabbath, legitimate balsams, whether broken vessels may be used for fuel, practical laws regarding eggshells, and whether chairs may be dragged on the Sabbath either for fear of accident or to afford rest for the sick.

Tosephtha is still a further element in the Talmud, literally meaning "supplement," which corresponds roughly to the Mishnah in structure, but is shorter, drawn from ancient and more recent Judaic schools, and lacks the subtlety and precision of the standard Mishnah. Some scholars claim the Tosephtha represents the Palestine Mishnah, and that our Mishnah was reedited in Babylonia. Normally verbose, a sample exception is a triad of terms. "A prophet is called by ten different names. They are: ambassador, faithful, servant, messenger, seer, watchman, man of scrutiny, dreamer, prophet, and man of God. There are ten names for the Holy Spirit, namely, proverb, metaphor, riddle, words, saying, calling, commandment, prophecy, sacred speech and vision. Joy has ten different expressions: gladness, joy, rejoicing, joyfulness, pleasure, relish, satisfaction, complacency, delight and cheer."[13]

A Talmudic eccentricity is the penchant for numbers: three, four, six, seven, and ten of anything. Rabbi Nathan's Tosephtha discusses, in sequence, the meaning of three crows, charitable men, scholars, kinds of sweat, advantages of an earthen vessel—to which he adds six kinds of tears. Of charitable men, he says, "He who gives in charity may be blessed, but if he gives in the form of a loan it is still better; but he who gives one money to do business with, on the understanding that he shall pay him half the profits, is best of all."[14]

Running as a theme through the Mishnah, Gemara, and To-sephtha is the value of studying the Torah (Mosaic law), which is to be prized above wealth, honor, and life itself; and the wicked-ness of profaning the Holy Name, for which "there is no repentance pending, and the Day of Atonement does not forgive." The precept of justice is repeated under a hundred forms, and always a respect for the wise men whose "thought concerning this world is: All that is in the world is of no importance to me, for this world is not mine. They are occupied in teaching others, and no one can see in their teaching anything wrong. Their questions are to the point and their answers according to the law."[15]

Targum is the Hebrew for "interpretation" and the name given to the Aramaic translations or paraphrases of the Old Testament, made when Hebrew had ceased to be the normal medium of speech among the Jews. They were the outcome of the explanatory oral matter which for a long time had been unofficially added to the Scripture readings in the worship of the synagogue. The Mishnah has extensive directions on how and how much of the Targum was to be given and forbade that it be written down. But this regulation very likely did not apply to private use or study, since Targumic literature seems to have existed from the first century after Christ. While the oldest extant Targums are not earlier than the fifth century, their theological content certainly goes back to Old Testa-ment times.

Whatever else it is, the Talmud makes no pretense of being a code or catechism, laying down in summary categorical form what the Jewish obligations are. It is rather the record of a process, the actual process by means of which the Mosaic law is made clear. This explains the tensions it preserves: different views in conflict, argument advancing and receding, contradictions reconciled only by the subtlest dialectic, disparate subjects somehow unified by means of the association of religious ideas, and the succession of generations of Talmudic scholars seeking for new insights to meet new situations that are sanctioned by the old laws.

In spite of this variety and movement, however, the Talmud leaves the general impression of unbending rigidity, where the main concern is to preserve the ancient traditions. But that is only one phase of the Jewish religious literature.

Officially approved Targums were produced first in Babylon and later in Palestine, the most famous being the Targum of Onkelos on the Pentateuch, and the Targum of Jonathan on the Prophets, both of which were in use in the third century after Christ. All of the books of the Old Testament had their Targums, with the exception of Ezra, Nehemiah, and Daniel, which already contained large sections in Aramaic.

What is highly significant about the Targums is the degree of freedom they show in interpreting the Bible, by way of paraphrase, circumlocution, legendary additions, and rhetorical digressions that point up the nonrestrictive doctrinal content of Judaism, already in the first centuries after the "great schism." Otherwise than Christianity, its stress has not been on definite dogmatic teaching and still less on mandatory creeds. The Targums also help to explain the present status of the Jewish religion on its dogmatic side.

Midrashim are the rabbinical commentaries on the Hebrew Scriptures. Technically the singular *Midrash* refers to the general study or explanation of the Old Testament, whereas the plural *Midrashim* are free interpretations made by the ancients, which were later collected into formal commentaries on the Bible.

Etymologically the term *Midrash* is the Hebrew for "investigation," and refers to the Jewish method of biblical exegesis which aimed at discovering in the sacred text a meaning deeper than the literal one, not unlike the "spiritual sense" in the Christian Bible. The unexpressed basis of the Midrashim was a belief that every detail of the text is important because it is all of divine origin. Two kinds of commentaries exist: *Midrash Halacha* which deal with the derivation of the Oral Law (*Halacha*) from the Scriptures; and *Midrash Haggadah* as an exposition of the nonlegal parts of the sacred text for purposes of edification.

Midrashim are not really distinct from the Talmud, but rather make it up, from the viewpoint of rabbinical exegesis. Less conspicuous in the Mishnah, the Gemara and Tosephtha portions are filled with biblical quotations around which the Talmudic commentary revolves as its center.

Not untypical of the Midrashic method is a Gemara from the treatise *Sabbath*.

> Rabbi Elazar Hakappur said, "A man should always pray for deliverance from poverty, although if he himself will not eventually come to poverty, his children or his grandchildren will, as it is written (Deuteronomy 15:11), 'There will not be wanting poor in the land where you dwell, therefore do I command you to open your hand to your needy and your brother.' The Hebrew term 'therefore' is *Biglal* and the school of Ishmael taught that *Biglal* is the equivalent of *Galgal*, meaning a 'wheel' thus inferring, from that word, that poverty is like a wheel, always turning from one to the other."[16]

Not only are the Midrashim indispensable evidence of the authentic Jewish mentality, but they serve as guideposts on the Judaic attitude toward Christianity, at least obliquely by their interpretation of classic Messianic passages in the prophetic books of the Old Law.

MOSES MAIMONIDES

Comparable to the Talmud in authority and in many respects more influential in shaping the mind of Judaism are the writings of the rabbinic sage Moses ben (son of) Maimon, known commonly as Moses Maimonides.

It is no exaggeration to say that Maimonides stands next to the prophet Moses in the estimation of many Jews as their greatest religious leader and the man whose wisdom produced the Judaism of modern times, even as Moses had shaped the religion of Israel centuries before Christ. "From Moses unto Moses," it was said, "there was none like Moses," meaning that in the twenty-five hundred intervening years (and since), from the prophet Moses, no one has more clearly assessed the genius of his people or more accurately expressed its spirit than Maimonides. He is the nearest to a prophet since the prophetic age of Israel.

Born at Cordova, Spain, in 1135, Maimonides received a comprehensive education from his father, a learned Talmudist. During an anti-Jewish persecution by the Moslem Alhomades (1149), his family fled into exile and settled at Fez, the capital of Morocco, where he wrote the "Letter of Consolation" to strengthen his coreligionists in their trials. He concluded with a prayer.

> When misfortunes overtake us, and there is no king to order our affairs, and no advisor to guide us, and no place of safety where we can flee, and no army wherewith we may be protected, and no power even to speak, when we are deprived of every resource, and when every refuge is cut off and all our hopes are frustrated, there is no escape but to You. We call and You come to our aid, we cry and You answer, for You are our refuge.[17]

When a purist Jewish writer charged that all Jews who compromised in the least with Islam, even externally, were apostates, Maimonides defended their action as licit because under duress, but had to flee Morocco on account of the religious antagonism he aroused. After a brief stay in Palestine, he settled at Fostat (Cairo) where he became the head of a flourishing Jewish community.

In 1168 he finished his commentary on the Mishnah known as the *Luminary*. But a mind as original as his could not be satisfied with mere comment. He often boldly differed from the Talmud and especially rapped at errors and superstitions. When commenting on the Mishnah passage which enumerates those unbelievers who are excluded from a share in the world to come, Maimonides stressed that Judaism is a religion at once exclusive because it embodies a set of revealed doctrines and inclusive because others than Jews, provided they believe in these truths, have assurance of salvation. His list of thirteen articles of faith is a synthesis of the Jewish religion and to this day is a convenient standard of orthodoxy. Within a century of his death, this précis of belief was employed as a theme for synagogue poems in all countries of Jewish habitation. Altogether some ninety poetic versions are to be counted, of which the most popular is the *Yigdal*, the liturgic verse which has been the inspiration of numerous musical creations.

In prose form the articles are a condensation of the Bible and Talmud, and of ten centuries of Judaic faith.

I believe with perfect faith that the Creator, praised be He, is the Creator and Guide of all creation, and that He alone has made, does make, and will make all things.

I believe with perfect faith that the Creator, praised be He, is a Unity, and that there is no unity like His in any manner, and that He alone is our God, who was, is, and will be.

I believe with perfect faith that the Creator, praised be He, is not a body, and that He is free from all attributes of a body, and that He has no form whatsoever.

I believe with perfect faith that the Creator, praised be He, is the first and the last.

I believe with perfect faith that to the Creator, praised be He, and to Him alone is it proper to pray, and that it is not proper to pray to any besides Him.

I believe with perfect faith that all the words of the prophets are true.

I believe with perfect faith that the prophecy of Moses our great teacher, may he rest in peace, was true, and that he was the father of the prophets, both those who preceded and who followed him.

I believe with perfect faith that the entire Torah now in our possession is the same that was given to Moses our teacher, may he rest in peace.

I believe with perfect faith that this Torah will never be replaced, and that there will never be another Torah from the Creator, praised be He.

I believe with perfect faith that the Creator, praised be He, knows every deed of men and all their thoughts, as it is written, "He fashions the hearts of them all and observes all their deeds." (Psalm 33:15).

I believe with perfect faith that the Creator, praised be He, rewards those who keep His commandments and punishes those that transgress His commandments.

I believe with perfect faith in the coming of the Messiah, and though he tarry I will wait daily for him.

I believe with perfect faith that there will be a revival of the dead at a time when it shall please the Creator, praised be He, and exalted His fame for ever and ever.[18]

According to Maimonides only that person is a true Jew who recognizes the validity of these articles without analysis. Anyone who denies even one of them should have no part in the Jewish community.

Maimonides chose thirteen principles because, he said, God possesses thirteen fundamental attributes (*shalot-esreh middot*), by which the universe was created and continues under divine guidance. Consequently, to question any of the articles would be, in effect, to deny God's basic attributes, through which alone the elements of the world have their being.

This elenchus of dogmas gave stability to historic Judaism as a way of life. Particularly the first five, on the existence and nature of God, helped to create modern Jewish theology. No such clear statements on the person of the Deity had been given in the Synagogue before. No doubt the divine attributes were in the Bible and Talmud, and in the rabbinical commentaries, but the average Jew was not equipped to make the necessary distinctions. Maimonides distinguished the essence from the accidentals, notably the unique character of the Torah in God's plan of communicating his truth to the world. Historically he was specially concerned to assure the eternal validity of the Judaic Law against two forces which derived from it: to insure its sufficiency in answer to the Christian claim that the Law must now be supplemented by the Gospel, and to safeguard its permanence against Islam which said the Koran replaces the writings of Moses.

About ten years after the *Luminary*, Maimonides brought out his *Mishnah Torah* (Second Law) in Hebrew, a Talmudic code in fourteen parts arranged by subject matter. It consists of a classification of Jewish religious doctrines, their interpretation by the masters, and their moral and philosophical implications. Among its surprising features is the inclusion of non-Jewish authorities in support of Maimonides' judgments.

In 1190 appeared his principal Arabic treatise, *The Guide for the Perplexed,* which scholars in every tradition consider a part of world literature. Through the *Guide* not only Maimonides but Judaism entered the orbit of Christian and Islamic thought. The work of the "Egyptian Moses" was studied assiduously by Albertus Magnus and Thomas Aquinas, who quoted him often.

The purpose of the *Guide* was to achieve a working harmony between reason and revelation. Its three sections treat of the idea of God; the arguments for God's existence, his manifestations, the world of spirits, the creation of the world in time, and prophecy; the interpretation of Ezekiel's vision, the problem of evil, the end of creation, divine providence, and divine knowledge. Maimonides' aim was to achieve a synthesis of the data of Jewish revelation and the speculation of human reason found in Aristotle. With all his devotion to Aristotle, however, Maimonides was too much a believer not to differ with the man he called "the chief of philosophers" and from whom he imbibed many ideas. In so doing he became the stumbling block for generations of Jews to the present day—some of whom admire Maimonides but speak of "the unsure weapon of the naive faith" with which he faced the problems of existence, whereas others see in him the great exemplar of human wisdom acknowledging its own limitations.

His significance for American Judaism is prominent beyond anything outside the Talmud. Maimonides' thirteen articles of faith are recited in every synagogue in America. His strong intellectualism is respected more than that of any other Jewish authority, except the Bible. His knowledge of Christianity and sympathy with its faith made his approach acceptable to American Christians, and his broad outlook paved the way for that congenial pluralism which is so typical of religion in the United States.

MYSTICISM AND THE CABALA

The main stream of Judaism has always had its competing or schismatic elements. Long before Christ there were Samaritans, the ancient "fundamentalists," worshipers of the letter of the Pentateuch, who still survive at Nabus in West Jordan. In the eighth century appeared the Karaites whose schism is indicated in their

Hebrew name, "Sons of the text," and the motto of their leader Anan, "search the Scriptures." But these and like schismatic movements have practically died out, or been absorbed in the main body of Jewry. It was otherwise with the rise of Jewish mysticism, stabilized in the Cabalistic renascence of the thirteenth century.

Literally *Cabala* means "oral tradition" and implies the tradition of the mystical schools. It was a development of tendencies similar to Gnosticism, and reached the height of its influence in the later Middle Ages, although Cabalism is still active today, in a greatly modified form as Hasidism.

It is difficult to trace the beginnings of Cabala, which is often the Hebrew equivalent for mysticism. According to the Cabalists, Moses on Mount Sinai and the prophets all received the Cabala. Actually we know that Ben Sira in the second century before Christ warned against preoccupation with "secret things," and the Jewish apocalyptic writings before and after Christ taught a good measure of Cabala. The Essenes, Alexandrian Jews, and the early Rabbis who favored the Pythagorean theory of numbers were forerunners of classic Cabalism.

Two types of Jewish mysticism became manifest early: the speculative or theosophic and the practical or theurgic. Practical mysticism stressed the wonder-working of controlling nature through a knowledge of the names and functions of angels; speculative mysticism held that all things exist as a result of ten emanations which graduate from God to the universe and serve as mediators.

After centuries of extravagances, the two types were combined, if not fused, by the thirteenth-century Spanish Jew, Moses de Leon in the *Zohar*, an esoteric commentary on the Pentateuch which became the sacred handbook of Jewish mysticism. The *Zohar* was historically a reaction against the rationalistic spirit of Maimonides. Yet in its effort to recapture "authentic Judaism" by reemphasizing the spiritual, it went to the opposite extreme. It drew heavily on Persian and Hindu sources and seriously tried to read into the five books of Moses what the Hindu Upanishads read into the four Vedas. The result is a curious mixture of Oriental stress on ecstatic union with God, and Judaic concern for the service of mankind.

On its speculative side, the most characteristic feature of classic Cabalism is the theory of the fulfillment of God. According to the Cabalists, the supreme and central mystery of religion is the Holy Union or "sacred marriage" between two aspects of the divine, the male with its creative dynamism and the female or receptive counterpart.

What is true of the Deity is equally true of man. For Cabalism, neither God nor man reaches the totality of perfection except in the union of the two sexes. A layer of mythology, borrowed from Hinduism, was thus laid on the foundations of Judaism—to the effect that perfection is possible only in the married state. In fact, the Cabala was the first system in the West to develop a mystical metaphysics of the sexual act, which bears more than superficial resemblance to the later theories of Sigmund Freud (1856-1939), Austrian Jew and founder of the theory of sexual psychoanalysis.

More serious, however, than its overstress on marriage, Cabalism shifted the whole center of Judaism from God to man. Its root conception represented God as being in need of man, and depending on man for the maintenance, or restoration of his divinity. Where the Pentateuch says, "Be holy as I your Lord am holy," and the trend of valid Jewish tradition teaches that God is Master of creation, the Cabala replaces the biblical theme with an esoteric but nonetheless emphatic pantheism, wherein the future destiny of God is bound up with the perfection of human society, mediated, as the Cabalist Isaac Luria explained, through the Jewish people.

Modern Judaism is unsympathetic with Cabalistic meanderings in the realm of numbers, or invoking the names of angels by way of incantation. Yet compromises have been made with its theory on the fulfillment of God and the need which the Deity has of man, although this has been against the main body of Judaic thought. Most Jewish writers tell the faithful to repudiate Cabalism as a form of idolatry; others are not so intransigent.

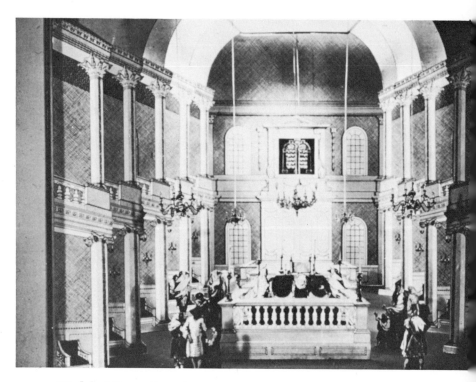

Model of Touro Synagogue,
Newport, Rhode Island

II

ORIGINS
AND
DEVELOPMENT
IN AMERICA

The origins of American Judaism are traceable to the fateful expulsion of the Jews from Spain in 1492. On March 21 of that year Ferdinand and Isabella issued a decree that gave the Spanish Jews an option of either becoming Christians or being expelled from the country. While many were baptized, including Ferrand Perez Coronel, chief rabbi of Castile, the majority preferred exile to renouncing their Jewish faith.

Ostensibly the reason for the edict was a desire to preserve the purity of the Christian faith, since many of the former converts remained secret Jews or Marranos as they were called. Actually the dominant motive was political, as Pope Sixtus IV suggested in a letter to Queen Isabella, protesting against the excesses of the Spanish Inquisition.

About 160,000 Jews left Spain on August 2, 1492, the final date set for their departure. It was the day before Columbus set sail from Palos to cross the Atlantic in search of the Indies.

Some of the exiles went as far as the Balkans and some found refuge with Pope Alexander VI in Rome. To his credit the pope turned down an appeal of the Roman Jews urging him to refuse admission to the Spanish refugees. Sometime later, Alexander could write that in Rome, Jews "are permitted to lead their life, free from interference from Christians, to continue their own rites, to gain wealth, and to enjoy many other privileges."[1] But Rome was not Spain.

A large number of the exiles wandered to Portugal, France, and Turkey, looking for a home where they might remain Jews. Their descendants remained loyal to the ancient faith, and the Jewish colonies they formed are still vigorous in cities like Lisbon, Marseilles, and the coastal towns of Northern Africa.

The royal decree had immediate consequences after the discovery of America. For a while laws were made against the Marranos going to the colonies. Yet as early as 1502 a Jewish convert, Juan Sanchez of Saragossa, was given royal permission to trade with the New World. Juan was the nephew of Gabriel Sanchez, chief treasurer of Aragon, friend and adviser of Columbus.

In a short time, others obtained similar permission, until the growing influence of the Marranos tradesmen in Latin America aroused the government to repressive measures against them, under the guise of religion. According to Jewish historians, the attachment of these immigrants to Judaism was so strong that they risked everything to keep even a few of the old religious customs of their fathers. Thus "men and women whose grandparents or great-grandparents had been unwilling converts to Christianity still taught their children the Shema, still gathered secretly to fast on the Day of Atonement, still married according to the Jewish law and still rested on the Sabbath Day. Even though they went to church and pretended to be Christians, they kept the feasts and fasts of Judaism in the secrecy of their homes."[2]

Unlike Spain, Portugal from the beginning encouraged Marranos to migrate to the New World, but like Spain it suspected the converts of Judaizing. Portuguese laws against them, however, were less severe, with the result that Brazil became a favorite settlement for Jewish Conversos, most of whom were tradesmen or engaged in commerce.

When Holland gained its freedom from Spain, it opened the doors to the Jews. They, in turn, helped the Dutch against Spain and Portugal, partly in Europe but mainly in Latin America. In 1631 the Dutch captured Recife, then the capital of Brazil, now called Pernambuco. Once the Dutch took over, many of the secret Jews both there and in other parts of South America took advantage of the situation and began openly to profess Judaism. It appears certain that Recife became the first Jewish community on American soil.

Within less than one generation, this community grew to about five thousand, supplemented regularly by newcomers from Amsterdam. They formed a congregation, named Kahal Kodesh, The Holy Congregation; they built sugar mills, developed an extensive trade with Holland, and were on their way to permanent tenure when war broke out again. This time, in spite of zealous assistance from the Jews, the Dutch lost their holdings and Portugal once more occupied Brazil.

When Recife fell in 1654, most of the Jews returned to Holland, among them Joseph Velosino, the first Hebrew author born in America. Others went to different Dutch colonies, notably Curacao (Netherlands West Indies), Surinam (formerly Dutch Guiana), and New Amsterdam (now New York).

JEWISH HISTORY IN COLONIAL TIMES

In September 1654, a small company of Jewish men, women, and children entered the harbor of New Amsterdam and asked for admission to the colony. But the governor, Peter Stuyvesant, was unhappy with the arrivals. He had already complained to his directors in the Dutch West Indies Company about the unequal competition with Jewish merchants living in the British colonies. This time he wrote for approval to bar the Brazilian refugees from settling in North America; and he might have succeeded except that the newcomers were backed by their confreres in Holland.

The directors' reply to Stuyvesant symbolizes the trials faced by the Jews for years to come. They agreed with the governor on principle, but felt he should permit the Jews to settle in his territory.

> We would like to agree to your wishes and request that the new territories should not be further invaded by people of the Jewish race, for we foresee from such immigration the same difficulties which you fear, but, after having further weighed and considered this matter, we observe that it would be unreasonable and unfair, especially because of the considerable loss sustained by the Jews in the taking of Brazil, and also because of the large amount of capital which they have invested in shares of the Company.
>
> After many consultations we have decided and resolved upon a certain petition made by said Portuguese Jews, that they shall have permission to sail to and trade in New Netherland and to live and remain there, provided the poor among them shall not become a burden to the Company or to the community but be supported by their own nation. You will govern yourself accordingly.[3]

Evidently Stuyvesant's fears were not resolved, because the next year he got another letter from Holland, this time on the subject of religion. The directors told him the permission they gave referred only to civil and political rights. It did not grant the Jews "the privilege of exercising their religion in a synagogue or a gathering." Practically speaking, therefore, "so long as you receive no request for granting them this liberty of religious exercise," his worries about the question were premature.[4] If and when he is pressed on the point, he must refer the matter to Holland and await further instructions.

The governor must have taken things into his own hands and restricted Jewish business beyond the rules set for him by the Company. A year later he was rebuked by the directors for prohibiting the Portuguese migrants from trading in New Amsterdam and from buying real estate. He should be guided by the norms in Holland where these privileges are "granted to them without difficulty here in this country." The same holds for the practice of their faith. They may "exercise in all quietness their religion within their houses, for which end they must without doubt endeavor to build their houses close together in a convenient place on one or the other side of New Amsterdam—at their choice—as they have done here."[5]

Finally Stuyvesant gave in and allowed the Jews to engage in trade—but not retail; to worship in private—but not build a synagogue. There were other limitations on their activity, as seen in the effort to drive them out of the colony when a Jew had kept his shop open on Sunday. But these were petty annoyances, and American Jews look upon the directives of the Dutch West Indies Company as the Magna Charta of religious liberty in the Western world.

Given their choice, the settlers chose to establish the community at the very tip of Manhattan Island, and slowly began to consolidate. In 1655 they asked for the right to have their own cemetery, which was granted them from the colony lands, outside the village, near the present location of Chatham Square, on the New Bowery. The inscriptions on the tombstones can still be read, in Hebrew and Spanish or Portuguese, which indicates that these Jews used the vernacular as their mother tongue but were also strictly orthodox because they used Hebrew on their tombstones.

New Amsterdam was a Dutch colony from 1625 to 1664. When the English took over in 1664, they changed the name to New York but did not substantially change the status of the Jews living there.

As toleration increased in England, however, it was also extended to the colonies. By 1682 the Jewish residents had rented a house for holding public services, and a synagogue is known to have existed in the city by 1695. It was between Broadway and Broad Street and was the first in North America. Its congregation Shearith Israel (the Remnant of Israel) was founded on the basis of a liberal decree of the Duke of York, allowing freedom of worship not only to Christians but "for any persons whatsoever," including the Jews.

Part of the structure of the American colonies was the duty of swearing allegiance to Great Britain. In 1727 the general assembly of New York amended the oath for Jews, permitting them to omit the words, "on the true faith of a Christian." One effect was to enable Jews to become naturalized and also to remove, by one more step, the control over religion then held by the Established Church of England.

Gradually the example of New York spread to other colonies. A synagogue was opened in Newport, Rhode Island, in 1763, now a national monument as the oldest surviving Jewish house of worship in the United States. The Newport Jewish cemetery is also the oldest still in existence, which occasioned Longfellow's famous lines: "How came they here? What burst of Christian hate, what persecution, merciless and blind, drove o'er the sea—that desert desolate— these Ishmaels and Hagars of mankind?"[6]

Conditions differed in different colonies. In Massachusetts, the Puritans seem to have specially favored the Jews because of their own predilection for the Old Testament. More than once in Puritan writings of that period, New England is described as "the new Canaan." Consistent with this tolerance, Hebrew was early studied at Harvard and a nonconverted Jew was granted a M.A. there in 1720, although no similar degree was given Jews at Oxford until 1870.

South Carolina reflected the same kind of freedom, for another reason. The constitution of 1669 was due mainly to John Locke's influence. As an avowed Deist, he urged that everyone be required to have a religion, but any religion would do. So Jews in that colony were naturalized as early as 1697, although the concession was later repealed. In 1774, Francis Salvador was chosen to the First Provincial Congress, reputedly the first Jew in modern history to serve in an elective office.

In Georgia, the charter of 1735 gave liberty of conscience to everyone "except Papists." Jews were given some of the earliest land grants, and Savannah became a Hebrew center where minor public offices were filled by Jews by 1765, and where, in 1801, David Emmanuel became the first Jewish governor in the new republic of the United States.

Pennsylvania followed the spirit of its Quaker founder, allowing residence to all "who confess and acknowledge the one Almighty and Eternal God, to be the Creator, Upholder, and Ruler of the world."[7] Jews were therefore admitted to the colony, although voting and officeholding were restricted to Christians, and gener-

ally to Protestants. A Jewish burial ground was permitted in Philadelphia in 1738, but there is no record of a synagogue until after
the Revolution.

With minor exceptions, the same situation obtained throughout
the colonies: residence permitted, franchise commonly denied, but
a steady progress in religious liberty as America approached its independence of England.

The internal life of the Jewish people in colonial times reflected
a pioneer mentality and a ready adjustment to the dominant culture
that sowed the seeds of tension for the crisis that finally came in the
nineteenth century.

American Sephardim

Most Jews of this period were of Sephardic stock. The term
Sepharad first referred to an Asiatic region, probably north of Palestine, to which exiles from Jerusalem were deported at the destruction of the First Temple (Obadiah 1:2). Gradually the name
Sephardi was applied to the Jews in Spain and to their descendants,
no matter where they migrated. By 1500 Sephardi communities included the Jews from Spain and Portugal who settled in Amsterdam, London, the West Indies, and North America.

More important, however, than their national origin was the
characteristic ritual and religious tradition which they inherited.
Their counterparts are the *Ashkenazim*, a biblical people (Genesis
10:3), whose name has been applied to the Germans since the ninth
century of the Christian era. Whereas the Ashkenazim tended to
migrate to East European countries, and favored Yiddish, the
Sephardim went south, north, and westward, and preferred Judaeo-
Spanish or Ladino in which a considerable literature had grown up.
The Ashkenazim are believed to be closer to ancient Palestinian
Judaism; the Sephardim going back ultimately to Babylonian Jewry.

The Sephardim still have a distinctive synagogue ritual, social
habits, and other features that distinguish them from the Ashkenazim. These differences will be examined in a later context. It may
be noted here that until well into the nineteenth century the majority of American Jews (about 15,000) were Sephardim. By 1880 the
number rose to a quarter million, mainly Ashkenazim immigrants

from Germany and Eastern Europe. While the Spanish Jews had been largely rich and cultured people, with a proud history, the Ashkenazim were the rank and file, poor or middle-class workmen and merchants, with rarely a professional among them.

Typical of Sephardim customs, which also affected the scattered Ashkenazim in colonial times, was the role of the *Parnas*, or chief of the community. Along with his associates, the Parnas set the schedule of hours for religious services, distributed the "honors" among the congregation, and authorized such important functions as weddings. There is the story of a prominent rabbi, Morris Raphall, who, as late as 1862, was obliged to ask permission from the Parnas to officiate at the marriage of his own daughter.

Besides supervision of the community in practical matters, the Parnas had the right to pass judgment on ritual law and fix the sanctions for unaffiliated and religiously wayward members. The provisions of two synagogues illustrate the severity of those days.

According to the Rodeph Shalom Congregation in Philadelphia, the synagogue could dictate even the residence privileges of Jewish believers.

> This Committee, after much deliberation, found it advisable, that when a married Yahudi (Jew), with family comes to live in the State of Pennsylvania, such Yahudi be allowed to remain in this state six months and should during this time declare himself willing to join Rodeph Shalom. When such a family has in the eyes of the congregation been found well behaving and when it should, may God forbid, be in need or in trouble, then the congregation should come to its help. But in case the family has not declared itself as desiring to affiliate with us, no help should be forthcoming to it.[8]

In view of the different circumstances, financial and social, in which many Jews found themselves in those days, this option of either affiliating or being cut off from Jewish assistance was a powerful motive to keep the people close to the synagogue.

Equally demanding were the rules of the historic Shearith Israel in New York, whose rules warned transgressors that "whosoever . . . continues to act contrary to our Holy Law by breaking any of the principles commanded will not be deem'd a member of our Congregation, have none of the Mitzote of the Synagogue conferred on him and when Dead, will not be buried according to the manner of our brethren."[9]

The threat of exclusion from burial among his brethren was feared by all believing Israelites and partly explains the prevalence of Jewish cemeteries in every locality—no matter how small—where Jews lived in colonial America.

These strict regulations also suggest some laxity of observance and the beginnings of community differences even before the heavy immigrations from Europe. Small infractions were punished by petty fines, but there was no redress for such grave offenses as inter-marriage with someone not Jewish; this was considered apostasy.

The synagogue and the community

Through colonial days and before the large migrations began, the center of Jewish life in North America was the synagogue. If the Jews in a given locality sometimes waited several years before open-ing a synagogue, it was not because they did not want one but be-cause the circumstances (mainly political) prevented them from setting up a permanent place of worship. As religious freedom in-creased, so also did the multiplication of synagogues, which came to symbolize and centralize Judaism along the Atlantic seaboard, before the westward march shortly after the War of Independence.

As originally conceived by the Sephardim, the synagogue was to be the focus of Jewish life for the whole community. Every Jew was expected to belong to it and every Jewish interest was hope-fully to flow from it. Each synagogue had its Parnas (as described) or president with his board of trustees, a treasurer, and a *hazzan* or cantor. Situations differed, but normally the cantor had his regular business and volunteered services for the synagogue. When a con-gregation became too large for gratis personnel, the people engaged a professional Hebrew scholar, who could chant the service, teach some Hebrew, preach in English, and slaughter the cattle according to prescribed ritual.

Although the Jews were primarily settled in seaport cities and involved in commerce and trade, their religious and social life maintained its traditional character. Synagogues were the mainstay of this tradition. They were houses of worship and assembly, of education, and of communal recreation. As far as the records show, the order of service followed the ancient Spanish *Minhag* and was observed down to the smallest detail. Members of the congregation were subject to community opinion and community sanction that finally derived from a central authority.

Most synagogues provided for the Jewish education of children. Shearith Israel, for example, had organized a Hebrew school in 1731 and by 1755 it became a regular parochial day school, where the hazzan taught the pupils Hebrew, Spanish, and English, writing and arithmetic. Those were charged tuition who could afford it; children of the poor were educated without cost.

Synagogue authorities also controlled social welfare for the people. When Peter Stuyvesant demanded that the Jews take care of their own indigent as a condition for admittance to New Amsterdam, he was already aware of the practice in Europe. But he had nothing to fear about the immigrants he was accepting.

The minute books of the New York settlement have been published, and they reveal how zealously those in want were cared for. The Tzedakah (righteousness) was imposed as a tax to help support every human need. Travelers could get money for their journey; funds were provided for lodging; the sick and the poor were supported by the synagogue; and, in some places, the directives for the practice of charity were read twice a year from the pulpit to remind the congregation of its duty. The New York regulations were extremely clear.

> If any poor person happen to come to this place and should want the assistance of the Synagog, the Parnaz is hereby impowered to allow every poor person for his maintenance the sum of eight shillings per week and no more—not exceeding the term of twelve weeks. And the Parnaz is also to use his utmost to despatch them to sum othere place as soon as possible; assisting them with necessarys for their voyage, that is, for a single person fourty shillings. But if it be a family, then the Parnaz shall call his assistants and consult with them both for their maintenance whilst ashore and also for their necessarys

when they depart. Those poor of the Congregation that shall apply for Sedaea shall be assisted with as much as the Parnaz and his assistants shall think fit.[10]

This practice of Tzedakah was inherited from their ancestors. In biblical times the regulations were intended for an agricultural society, for example, reserving a corner of the field for reaping by the needy.

During the Talmudic period, the institution was also made to cover education, since this was considered one of the essentials of Judaism. Rabbinic legislation extended the concept beyond the limits of an agrarian society, as in the case of the Sephardim colonials. The Talmud provided that a Tzedakah box (Kuphah) be kept in every community, out of which the poor were to be given funds for fourteen meals a week. Transient poor were to be given a daily allowance. Any person who stayed thirty days in the community automatically became obliged to contribute to the Tzedakah box, which a passage in the Talmud describes as one of the three foundations on which the world is built.

In all these enterprises the synagogue was the recognized organ of activity to the end of the eighteenth century. Closely knit, generally confined to coastal towns, and greatly dependent on England, the synagogue reflected in Jewish terms what New England Congregationalism meant to the Puritans: local autonomy based on a covenanted fellowship that neither wanted nor sought a wider ecclesiastical structure.

FROM THE AMERICAN REVOLUTION TO REFORM

With the founding of the American Republic, Judaism entered a new phase of its history. This was due partly to the new status of minorities in the country and partly to the rising immigration from Europe. But the complete explanation must be sought in a variety of factors that defy analysis and that can best be described as the Jewish spirit developing in an atmosphere of religious liberty.

Symbolic of the future was the exchange of letters between the Hebrew congregation in Newport, Rhode Island, and George Washington, occasioned by the president's visit to the city in 1790.

After referring to Washington as another Daniel, for whom they asked divine assistance "to discharge the arduous duties of chief magistrate of these States," the Jews expressed their gratitude for what they were confident would be a haven of peace.

> Deprived, as we have hitherto been, of invaluable rights of free citizens, we now—with a deep sense of gratitude to the Almighty Disposer of all events—behold a government erected by the majesty of the people, a government which gives no sanction to bigotry and no assistance to persecution, but generously affording to all liberty of conscience and immunities of citizenship, deeming every one, of whatever nation, tongue or language equal parts of the great governmental machine. This so ample and extensive Federal Union, whose base is philosophy, mutual confidence and public virtue, we cannot but acknowledge to be the work of the great God, who rules the armies of the heavens and among the inhabitants of the earth, doing whatever deemeth to Him good.[11]

Washington's reply is quoted in every history of American Judaism and is memorized by Jewish children in their synagogue classes. After referring to the "Liberty to Conscience" which they had a right to expect from the new United States, he expressed the wish and the prayer that "the children of the stock of Abraham, who dwell in this land, continue to merit and enjoy the good will of the other inhabitants. . . . May the Father of all mercies scatter light and not darkness in our paths and make us all in our several vocations useful here and, in His own due time and way, everlastingly happy."[12] The religious tone of Washington's letter shows how clearly he recognized the issue facing the Jews on the eve of the new republic as a test case of the freedom guaranteed not only to Christians by their coreligionists but, outside Christianity, to the sons of Abraham.

Jefferson and Madison reflected the same spirit of toleration shown by Washington. In several letters they wrote to congregations in New York and Savannah, they assured the Jews that, whatever had been their experience in other countries, America was different. Jefferson was especially incisive in saying this. He told the

Jews in New York that, "Your sect, by its sufferings, has furnished a remarkable proof of the universal spirit of religious intolerance inherent in every sect, disclaimed by all while feeble, and practiced by all when in power." American laws, he promised, were designed as the only antidote to this vice, "by putting all men on an equal footing."[13]

In another communication, this time to the synagogue in Savannah, Jefferson rejoiced over the presence of Jews in the country because they would insure that religious diversity which, in his judgment, was the best protector of liberty. The maxim of good civil government, he felt, must be reversed in the case of religion, "where its true form is 'divided we stand, united we fall.' "[14] By this he meant, as did Madison after him, that a multiplicity of religious bodies first creates the demand for independence of worship and practice, and then becomes the best security for religious liberty in any society. For when there is a variety of religions, and the more diverse the better, there cannot be a majority of any one group to oppress and persecute the rest.

Once religious freedom became established, the influx of Jews to America increased beyond anything in previous colonial history. Two waves of immigration, following the Spanish Sephardim, are commonly distinguished: the German to about 1880 and the Russian (with Central European) to the end of the First World War. Our concern now is mainly with the German because it was mainly responsible for the massive change in American Jewish religion from conservative to the extremely liberal. No single phenomenon in our national culture is more easily traceable than the sudden rise of Reform Judaism, whose ideas were transplanted from Europe but whose structure was occasioned by American democracy.

German origins of the Reform

Adaptations of Judaism to prevalent conditions and liberalization of its faith and practice were familiar since the beginning of the Christian era, and before that among the Sadducees who favored Hellenistic tendencies, repudiated oral tradition, and, among other doctrines, denied retribution in an afterlife, resurrection of the body, and the existence of angelic spirits.

The high-water mark of rationalization in the early Middle Ages occurred under Maimonides, whose principles of reform were less radical than might seem at first glance, since the basic dogmas he proposed are still professed by Orthodox Jews.

More sweeping were the liberal ideas of Moses Mendelssohn (1729-1786), the German scholar whose ideas transformed Judaism more completely than anything else since the fixation of the canon of the Jewish Bible at Jamnia, in Asia Minor, about thirty years after the destruction of Jerusalem.

Mendelssohn introduced among his people a new concept of their religion, born of the twin necessity, as he saw it, of adjustment and loyalty. The adjustment seemed to be demanded by the recent liberation of the Jews from their former ghetto existence, while loyalty was dictated by the demands of the Jewish faith.

Mendelssohn's theory was not new with him, but he gave it precision and zealous promotion that soon extended beyond the confines of his own country. He distinguished three elements in the Jewish religion, doctrines, historical truths, and ceremonial prescriptions. Among these he considered the first two accessible to all men, and therefore no cause of conflict with the then prevalent German rationalism. Only ritual laws were revealed to Israel. Since these were uniquely communicated to the sons of Abraham, they should be strictly observed.

In his original position, Mendelssohn was very clear. Judaism knows no revelation of eternal truths, comparable to the Christian belief in the Trinity, the Incarnation, or the Real Presence in the Eucharist. "I hold this to be an essential point in the Jewish religion, and I believe that this doctrine represents a characteristic difference between the Jewish and the Christian faiths. To put it briefly: I believe that Judaism recognizes no revealed religion in the sense understood by Christians."[15] On this first level, according to him, Jewish doctrines are such as may be considered "revealed by the Almighty," but only in the sense that they are made known "to all rational creatures through concepts and things themselves, written into the soul with a clarity that remains legible and understandable at all times and in all places."[16] He, therefore, opted for a kind of Jewish deism.

Historical truths also, for Mendelssohn, were not in the same category as in the Christian Scriptures where Jesus of Nazareth is believed to have himself been a revelation of the Father, and his actions, along with his teachings, were therefore supernatural manifestations.

Only Jewish ceremonials could be said to be revealed. God was, therefore, the lawgiver, "not in the sense of God as creator and preserver of the universe, but rather as God, protector and confederate of their (the Israelites') ancestors, liberator, founder and commander-in-chief, king and sovereign of this people; and He bestowed the most solemn sanction upon these laws, publicly and in an unheard-of, wondrous way."[17]

Yahweh was preeminently legislator for the Jewish nation, and to that extent it may rightly be called theocratic, since it has only him as its preceptor.

What Mendelssohn did was partially to satisfy both segments of the Jews, who were being split by the call for conformity to their surrounding culture. Traditionalists, who generally anathematized the ghetto-born philosopher, nevertheless were happy to accept his position that ceremonial laws were revealed. Reformers, on the other hand, looked at his basic theory, regarding doctrines and historical truths, which he claimed were naturally available without special revelation. They applied this principle to the whole body of Judaism, including ceremonial practice and rituals.

The seed had been sown and the guiding norms were thus laid for transportation to the United States.

Why the German migration?

It is impossible accurately to understand today's American Judaism without seeing something of the change that took place, quite abruptly, with the second German emigration from the Continent. Where the Spanish Jews came to America in small numbers, the Germans arrived in thousands. The Jewish population in the States increased from about 15,000 (mostly Spanish Sephardim) to more than 250,000 in 1880 (mostly German Ashkenazim). Why the sudden transfer of whole colonies and villages, established for generations in the Old World?

The reasons for the movement are to be found in Germany. After the Napoleonic Wars, Germany was reduced to great poverty, with few opportunities for maintaining any more than bare subsistence. Coupled with poverty was the unsettled condition of the government; there was a number of small, separate states, without central authority. Each principality became a tiny autocracy and passed or revised laws that discriminated against the Jews.

More important, however, than political factors was the reaction that followed the wave of liberation of the Jews under Napoleon and his imitators in France, England, Italy, and especially Germany. Although his motives were mainly dictated by statecraft, the French emperor radically changed the status of the Jews in Western and Central Europe. Jewish historians speak of this period of less than a hundred years, ending about 1870, as the "era of emancipation." More drastic adaptation to the environment and integration into the life of the times took place in this quarter-century than during any comparable period since the diaspora in A.D. 70.

The progress of assimilation, which previously had affected only the wealthier classes, now extended to the mainstream of Jewish society. In one country after another Jews became fully integrated, in customs, language, and social habits. Gradually the synagogue service came to resemble in external features the accepted norms of the religious life of the country as a whole. A vernacular literature sprang up to explain Judaism to those who could not read Hebrew. Rabbinical seminaries were built to prepare spiritual leaders in a more modern tradition, the first being established in Padua, in 1829.

In order to further the process more effectively, the "Reform" movement began speaking of Jews in adjectival, instead of substantive, terms. "The Jew was presented as an Englishman, Frenchman or German, of the 'Jewish' or even to avoid the despised word, 'Mosaic' persuasion."[18]

Assimilation led to acceptance, and acceptance soon gave the Jews an opportunity for leadership which they had not enjoyed since the Middle Ages. The roster of Jewish names in the highest positions of the land reads like a history of nineteenth-century Europe. Adolphe Cremieux (1796-1880) became minister of justice in

France, Eduard Lasker (1829-1884) led the National Party in the German Reichstag, Isaac Artom (1829-1900) was a confidant of Cavour and one of the architects of the Italian Risorgimento, and the baptized (though Jewish-inclined) Benjamin Disraeli (1804-1881) became prime minister of England.

The preeminence of the English and French branches of the House of Rothschild began with Mayer Amshel Rothschild (1743-1812), who was financial agent to the landgrave of Hesse-Cassel during the revolutionary war with France. By the late nineteenth century, the Rothschilds became a byword in European finance.

Moreover, in the popular mind, the names of Karl Marx, Heinrich Heine, Georg Brandes, Felix Mendelssohn were associated with Judaism, even when (as with Marx) the religion of his ancestors had been rejected.

All of this development of Jewish achievement ran parallel with a rising jealousy and suspicion, above all in those countries where the Jews had shown themselves most influential.

The focus of trouble was in Germany, where the participation of the Jews in the life of the people was more complete, and correspondingly more impressive. It was aggravated by the rise of a protest movement, popularly called "Young Germany," that waged a continual literary polemic against German racial nationalism and counted among its leading spirits such Jewish intellectuals as Ludwig Börne, originally Löb Baruch (1786-1837), and Heinrich Heine (1797-1856).

Börne was reared in the ghetto of Frankfurt am Main. He suffered all the disabilities of being a Jew, and became a rebel spirit. His *Briefe aus Paris*, pungent and bitter in their attack on the German despots, made him a hero for the group of German radicals. "The poor Germans!" he wrote, "Living in the lowest floor, oppressed by the seven floors of the upper classes, their anxiety is made lighter by speaking of people who are still lower than they are and who live in the cellar. Not being a Jew provides them with consolation at not being a state councillor." To those who attacked him as a Jew and accused him of being hostile to German patriotism, Börne replied, "Because I was a bondsman, I therefore love liberty more than you. Yes, because I have known slavery, I therefore love liberty more than you."[19] He was identifying himself with all his people.

If these sentiments evoked sympathy among those who favored a more democratic Germany, they aroused strong opposition among those who were already distrustful of Jewish influence.

Heine, like Börne, had been reluctantly baptized. As Heine put it, he embraced Christianity mainly to acquire "an entrance card to European culture." His prose writings became classics of modern German literature, and his poems were translated into almost all European languages and many of them set to music by Schubert, Mendelssohn, and Brahms. Nietzsche thought he was unequaled "through the kingdoms of all ages." But this only added fuel to the fire of animosity, especially when Heine became enamored of French liberty and disparaged what he considered German enslavement. "Paris," he once said, "is the New Jerusalem and the Rhine is the Jordan which divides the land of freedom from the country of the Philistines."[20]

If men like Börne and Heine were exceptional and, in fact, not typical of their Jewish contemporaries, they became symbols in the popular mind for a countermovement which began in the middle of the nineteenth century and found its full vent in the martyrdom of five million Jews in Nazi Germany exactly a hundred years later.

Anti-Semitism was thus born in the fertile soil of envy at seeing Jewish leadership in so many fields of German culture, and nationalism that seemed under attack by a few radicals who were known to be of Jewish blood. By 1881 a full-scale Anti-Semitic League was founded, emphasizing racial rather than religious antipathies and thus avoiding the charge of perpetuating the fanaticism of earlier days. It sent a solid block of deputies to the Reichstag, where inflammatory speeches against the Jews began to be heard.

It was during this period of unrest that Germany sent to the United States the largest contingent of Jews ever to leave their country. Their goal was the liberty which America promised them in a spate of books and periodicals, comparing the oppression suffered in Germany with the emancipation awaiting the Jewish people overseas. The novelist Leopold Kompert (1822-1886) was only one of a score of German Jewish writers who urged all the Jews of Central Europe to emigrate to America. They responded with enthusiasm.

One more feature of the Reform movement in Germany has practical bearing on the emigration to the States, and its consequent impress on American Judaism. The option that even the most liberal Jews in Germany understandably feared was abandonment of the ancestral religion and conversion to Christianity. When even the children of Moses Mendelssohn became Christians, the prospects of religious survival must have seemed extraordinarily difficult to the average German Jew. Many argued that Reform might serve to check the wave of conversions. Others felt that Reform alone was not enough; it had to be supplemented by emigration.

Yiddish influences

One aspect of the Jewish immigration during the nineteenth century is commonly overlooked. The Jews who came to America brought with them something more than racial pride or religious fervor. They also imported a written heritage that was almost unknown as long as the majority of Jews in this country were of Sephardic stock.

The Sephardim had developed a language all their own. Known as Ladino, it was a Judaeo-Spanish dialect first spoken by Mediterranean Jews and written in Hebrew letters. Its basis was medieval Castilian, along with other Spanish dialects, Portuguese, Hebrew, and fragments of Turkish and Greek.

The Ashkenazim produced an entirely different language, called Yiddish (German *jüdisch*=Jewish). Four main elements entered the formation of Yiddish: Hebrew, Loez, that is, the Jewish equivalent of Old French and Old Italian, German and Slavic. The most important of these was medieval German spoken in the Middle Rhine region. To this day it supplies about eighty-five percent of the vocabulary and grammatical structure.

Centuries of migration gradually dissipated interest in Ladino for all but those Jews who remained on the southern and eastern shores of the Mediterranean. Until recently the center for Ladino was Salonika, far from the great population centers of world Jewry.

Yiddish had a different history. Also written in Hebrew characters, except in some regions like the Soviet Union, it remains the "native" language of the Jewish people whenever they wish to express themselves with the fullness of their Judaic ancestry.

No doubt the Bible and the Talmud enjoy an objective value that nothing can replace. Yet for the average Jew in America today the Yiddish literature of the last seven hundred years has made an impress on his personality that rivals in subjective importance even the sacred Torah. The psychological impact of a library of classics that reveal the innermost thoughts of the Jewish soul is incalculable; and the fact that this influence is seldom recognized by non-Jewish commentators only highlights the subtle forces that have been at work for centuries.

Old Yiddish was spoken since the early twelve hundreds. But the first significant literary works were not produced until the sixteenth century. They included Arthurian romances, of which the best known was the *Bovo-Buch* or *Bovo-Maase*, a masterful epic that described the adventures of Prince Bovo of Antona (originally Sir Bevis of Hampton), written by Elijah Levita (1468-1549).

Elijah Levita symbolizes the degree to which Christianity has affected the Judaism with which it has lived in friendly cohabitation since the rise of Islam. Levita earned his living by teaching Hebrew to Christian humanists. These included Cardinal Egidio da Viterbo, who was his chief patron, and from whom he inherited not a few of his religious insights.

Yiddish writings have been specially conscious of the role of women in sustaining the Jewish way of life. The *Tzenah u-Reenah* ("Go forth and see, you daughters of Jerusalem," *Song of Songs* 3:11) by Jacob Ashkenazi (1550-1626) was an attractive commentary on the Pentateuch that wove biblical teaching and popular folklore into a collection that Jewish mothers still pass on to their children. An anthology of devotional prayers, the *Tekhines*, was also composed for women and is still in vogue.

Closer to modern times, Yiddish was used by Haskalah writers as a means of advancing the Enlightenment. Men like Solomon Ettinger (1801-1856), Abraham Ber Gottlober (1810-1899), and Isaac Meir Dick (1807-1893) started a tradition that has been carried on to the present day. Their poignant description of the sufferings of the Jews created a literary genre that has since become an integral part of Judaism. The names of Mendele Mocher Sephorim, Isaac Leib Peretz, and Sholem Aleichem are commonplace. Aleichem (1859-1916) was a gentle reformer whose leading characters are indelibly stamped on the contemporary Jewish mind, for example, *Tevye der Milchiger* (Tevye the Milkman), a lighthearted pauper who drove his rickety wagon in search of a few coins but whose thoughts soared across the world and reached up to God. The visits that Aleichem made to the United States enabled him to write with penetrating accuracy about the Jewish immigrants on American soil.

Twentieth-century Yiddish writers have already left their mark on European and American letters, but always mainly on the Jews themselves. The dramatists Jacob Gordin and Leon Kobrin, the lyric poets Simon Frugg and Solomon Bloomgarden, the socialists Morris Winchevsky and Abraham Liessin, the anarchists David Edelstadt and Joseph Bovshover are only examples of men whose prodigious writings have shaped present-day Jewish culture on both sides of the Atlantic.

When the Nazi tragedy befell the Jews in Germany, followed by the Soviet repression, many of the centers of creative Yiddish literature went out of existence. In the meantime new centers arose elsewhere, notably in America, to carry on what some historians believe is the literary mainstay of modern Judaism. Some would even say that Yiddish, as a living language, is the principal cohesive force in present-day Jewish culture.

Since the Second World War, the Institute for Jewish Research (*Yidisher Visenshaftlikher Institut*=YIVO) was moved from Vilna, in Lithuania, to New York City. One of its functions is to promote a better understanding and wider dissemination of Yiddish literature in the English-speaking world. Over fifty volumes have already been published, and more are planned for the future.

It would be impossible to do justice to the riches and depth of Yiddish writing in a volume of commentary, let alone in a few words. One feature of this language, however, is its tendency to express ideas in epigrams and proverbs. Even a small sampling of these may reveal something of the Yiddish spirit.

God waits long, but pays with interest.

God strikes with one hand and heals with the other.

Man strives and God laughs.

If thou intend a thing, God will help thee.

One path leads to paradise, but a thousand to hell.

The world can be changed by neither scolding nor laughing.

Give thine ear to all, thy hand to thy friends, but thy lips only to thy wife.

A third person may not interfere between two that sleep on the same pillow.

Women persuade men to good as well as to evil; but they always persuade.

Fools generally have pretty wives.

Love tastes sweet, but only with bread.

If a Jew breaks his leg, he says, "Praised be God that I did not break both legs"; if he breaks both, he says, "Praised be God that I did not break my neck."

When a Jew is hungry, he sings; when the master (Polish nobleman) is hungry, he whistles; when the peasant is hungry, he beats his wife.

If the Jew be right, he is beaten all the more.

The master (nobleman) thinks of his horse and dog, the Jew of his wife and child.

The angel of death always finds an excuse.

Better ruined ten times than dead once.

No man dies before his time.

Every man knows that he must die, but no one believes it.

Better a noble death than a wretched life.[21]

Yiddish writers have often come from among the poor and those suffering for their loyalty to Jewish ideals. Most of them never visited America. But their outlook and ideology reached this country in a literary migration that made as significant a contribution to American Judaism as any group of immigrants from Germany or Czarist Russia. They gave Jews in the United States a sense of ancestry and a kinship of spirit with people whose trials in other lands somehow made possible the enjoyment of freedom in America.

ORIGINS OF REFORM IN THE UNITED STATES

As originally conceived in Germany, the Reform movement maintained that to meet contemporary needs, changes had to be introduced in traditional Jewish thought and practices. One of the first changes was the formation of small synagogues by laymen who shortened the service, introduced the vernacular, utilized an organ, made the vernacular sermon a regular feature, and began the ceremony of group confirmation.

The first immigrants from Germany were from the more impoverished and less educated members of the Jewish community, who were hardly affected by the battle over reform in the upper strata of society. By the 1840s, however, the newcomers included many of the more sophisticated Reform Jews, along with some rabbis who had already played a leading role in updating their religion in Europe. Their influence not only turned the tide in favor of a more liberalized Judaism in America, but also set the pace for Jewish religious culture even to the present day.

They were, in a sense, the first real rabbis to labor among their people in the United States. They had received regular ordination and the best of education in German universities. It was not surprising, then, that their influence, almost from the start, was dominant. Except for a few leaders of the old Sephardic and Ashkenazic synagogues, of whom the chief was Isaac Leeser (1806-1868) of Philadelphia, no one of consequence opposed the Reform zeal of the German rabbis.

By 1850 they were able to band together small groups of their own nationals in *Reform Vereine*, which would in time become "temples," as the Reformers preferred to call their synagogues. Distinguished rabbis from Germany, or already in America, would be invited to take over these temples. In Baltimore, Har Sinai was the first congregation formed in this way (1842). Others soon followed, like Emmanuel in New York (1845), Sinai in Chicago (1858).

Some of the older synagogues might come under the aegis of an energetic rabbi who would convert his congregation to the Reform or, if he failed, he might secede to form a new temple community.

The case of Isaac Mayer Wise (1819-1900), father of Reform Judaism in the United States, is a perfect example of how effectively a strong leader could change the religious patterns of his people. When he came to America in 1846 he became rabbi of Congregation Bethel in Albany, New York, where he promptly started to change the Orthodox form of service. When opposition arose, the congregation split; one group followed Wise and another continued in its Orthodox tradition.

Eight years later, Wise became minister of the Orthodox synagogue Bene Yeshurun in Cincinnati. Soon after he installed an organ and slowly modified the ritual, without causing a schism. Before long, this congregation became one of America's leading Reform temples. With the sympathetic backing of the temple community, he went on to found two Jewish newspapers, in English and German; publish bilingual prayer books, and lay the foundation for Hebrew Union College, which is still the principal seminary in America for the training of the Reform rabbinate.

In Germany there had been many restrictions on the Reform movement, notably the existing structure that resisted change. But in America about the only limitation was the time and zeal of the rabbi and, as with Isaac Wise, his shrewdness in dealing with reactionary elements in the congregation.

Yet there were conflicts, often over matters that would look trivial to anyone who does not know the temper of religious Jewry. Around such questions as the installation of an organ, the use of mixed choirs of men and women, or of Jews and Gentiles, the amount of Hebrew in the ceremonial, the arrangement of family pews instead of putting the women in a balcony upstairs—heated battles were reported, as one group challenged another and even resorted to the civil courts.

As the number of Jews increased and synagogues multiplied, the structure of the Jewish community was visibly altered. New York had seventeen distinct "temples" by 1854. An immediate effect was to make the synagogue less relevant, if for no other reason at least because it was insufficient (or inefficient) to meet the customary needs. The ritual slaughter of animals and the baking of *matzoth* was soon taken over by commercial butchers and bakers.

So, too, with education. As the public school became more secular, synagogue instruction declined. This happened in New York almost overnight when, in 1853, the city took over the Public School Society and applied the state law of 1842 which forbade religious instruction in tax-supported institutions. For some time, the Jews had encouraged the application of such a law because they feared the teaching of Christianity in schools conducted by Christians. A century later the same attitude became operative on a national scale.

Other phases of Jewish life followed the same pattern. Financial aid for the needy faithful, the administration of cemeteries, provisions for social and cultural development, became gradually dissociated from the synagogue and more dependent on other agencies. It was a dramatic shift from century-old Jewish community life in the direction of a service-centered structure. American Judaism took on more and more the features of the rest of society, where organizations with specific functions replaced, in fact if not in theory, the role of the synagogue as the heart of a Jewish community.

Men like Wise promoted a Reform that was mainly practical, and that concerned itself especially with adjustment to the culture and the times. Other reformers were less pragmatic. They looked to a Jewish Reformation that completely revamped the Judaism of former days, yet remained essentially faithful to the spirit of Moses and the prophets. Under the leadership of David Einhorn (1809-1879), they wanted the Reform firmly established on theoretical principles and were impatient with such "minor" items as a vernacular ritual. If they favored these alterations on principle, they were also suspicious of their value. Instead of fostering a genuine Reform, concessions to American customs, including the vernacular, might inhibit the radical changes within the religion that were really necessary.

As might be expected of Einhorn, he wanted the vernacular, of course, but for the time being it should be German and not English. Writing in the paper he published for six years (to 1862), he felt, "It takes little familiarity with the condition of American Jewish religious life to recognize that the English element under present circumstances is a brake to Reform strivings. German research and science are the heart of the Jewish Reform idea, and German Jewry has the mission to bring life and recognition to this thought on American soil."[22] Einhorn was determined to reshape American Judaism with such philosophical depth as only the product of nineteenth-century German scholarship could insure.

Einhorn and companions were concerned with two questions above all others: the status of Jewish law, whether it was unchangeable or progressive; and the position of Jews in European and American society. The first question was easily settled and became a premise on which to build, namely that the Torah, although divine, was indeed subject to change with the changing times. But the second posed a problem which they never solved. If the Jews were a *people*, were they exiles in whatever country they lived, and did they hope one day to return to Palestine? If the Jews were a *religion*, were they only another denomination, and therefore not also a people?

Basically the issue behind both questions was how far should the Reform go. Nothing but a radical transformation of Judaism, as Einhorn had known it in Europe, could save either the people or the religion from absorption by an alien culture.

Accordingly a conference, urged by Einhorn, was held in Philadelphia in 1869 to draft the first set of principles that seemed to be necessary before genuine progress was possible. With Samuel Hirsch (1815-1889) as chairman, the Eastern rabbis decided among other items, that "the messianic aim of Israel is not the restoration of the old Jewish state under a son of David, nor the continued separation from other nations, but the union of all men as children of God acknowledging His unity, and the oneness of all rational beings and their call to moral sanctification."[23]

Written in German, the Philadelphia Resolutions paved the way for a more doctrinal position fifteen years later. They stressed the idea that the fall of the second Jewish commonwealth was not due to a divine visitation, in punishment for the people's sins. On the contrary, it was God's providential way of preparing his Chosen Race to go "to all parts of the earth so that they may fulfill their high priestly task to lead the nations in the true knowledge and worship of God."[24]

On the crucial issue of what happened to the Jewish priest-hood, the rabbis decided that both the service of the Aaronites and the Mosaic sacrifice were only preparatory "for the true priestly service of the whole people, which in fact began with the dispersion of the Jewish nation" in the first century of the Christian era.[25]

In the spirit of the ancient Sadducees, the Philadelphia Conference declared that "the belief in bodily resurrection has no religious foundation." Yet it may be said that "immortality is to be expressed exclusively in relation to continued spiritual existence."[26] This was a historic departure from the traditional Jewish belief, expressed by Maimonides (1135-1204), that the bodies of the just will rise from the dead on the last day.

Almost as soon as they were written, the Resolutions met with criticism, mainly that they were not sufficiently clear on matters of doctrine and too concerned with the status of the Jewish people in the land of their adoption. Though criticized, the Philadelphia document remains an authentic interpretation of the Reform, mostly on the practical side of ritual, language, and role in American society.

Immediately plans were made to supply the deficiency and produce a document that would express in clear, even theological terms, the genius of Neo-Judaism as understood by the inheritors of the German Enlightenment.

In the fall of 1885, the Pittsburgh Platform was written to meet the obvious need. No other document had as profound an effect on Jewish Americanization as this product of fifteen rabbis who were convinced that the future lay on the side of drastic change. It is still a valid formulation of the liberal tradition even though some of its present-day exponents go far beyond the revision of Hirsch and Einhorn, who seem almost reactionary by comparison.

One event in the progress of Reform had much to do with the strong reaction it aroused almost the day the Pittsburgh Platform was made public. It is not generally known that the Ethical Culture movement was a direct offspring of Jewish rationalism and its rise awakened the Jews of America to the crisis in their history posed by the Reform.

Felix Adler (1851-1933) is commonly regarded as the founder of Ethical Culture. But he received the inspiration for the movement from his father, Samuel, a German immigrant who became rabbi of Temple Emmanuel in New York. When Samuel was asked by a group of Jews for advice on building a new Reform synagogue in Chicago, he replied in a letter that has since become famous. It was brutally frank.

> I would state that the first and most important step for such a congregation to take is to free its service of shocking lies, to remove from it the mention of things and wishes which we would not utter if it had to be done in an intelligible manner. Such are, the lamentations about oppression and persecution, the petition for the restoration of the sacrificial cult, for the restoration of Israel to Palestine, the hope for a personal Messiah, and the resurrection of the body. In the second place, to eliminate fustian and exaggeration; and in the third place, to make the service clear, intelligible, instructive and inspiring.[27]

His son did not wait long to carry this spirit into practice. He was "converted," he said, from traditional Judaism once it dawned on him that he could no longer accept certain premises of his religion. In the Sabbath service, the officiating minister opens the Pentateuch scroll with the words, "This is the law which Moses set before the people of Israel." Felix Adler had just returned from studies in Palestine and he had become convinced that "the Mosaic religion is, so to speak, a religious mosaic," with hardly a single stone that could be traced directly to Moses.

He started Ethical Culture in 1876 in New York City, after turning down the prospect of succeeding his father in the rabbinate. Among the formative factors to which Adler attributed his discovery of Ethical Culture, the moral teachings of Jesus of Nazareth were of paramount importance.

Christian ethics, he explained, has promoted the moral development of mankind in a thousand ways, notably in emphasizing the inner springs of conduct. However, like every product of the mind and aspirations of man, it exhibits the limitations of the time and social conditions under which it arose, the conditions that have since changed.

It was Adler's contention that, with the help of Christianity, a philosophy of life could be developed that would dispense with the theology of the Gospels and bring up to date the ethical ideals of Jesus. Adler believed that Christian morality had quite supplanted the Jewish Torah. Similarly Ethical Culture would improve on the New Testament.

The single doctrine of the ethical aim as the supreme purpose of life became the basis of Ethical Culture. It emphasized the fact that such questions as God's existence and immortality are secondary. Theists, atheists, and agnostics have ever since been equally welcome in Ethical Societies. Following Immanuel Kant, Ethical Culture discarded the principle of priority of mind and the objective order of truth, in favor of a voluntarism which holds that the only good thing in the world is a well-disciplined will. Adler went further. He vaguely identified humanity with the Deity and his followers have since spoken of the "potentially divine nature in man," which needs only actuation, through ethical conduct, to be brought into fullness of being.

Although Ethical Culture now has a wide following that cuts across the spectrum of religious affiliation (or disbelief), it is still popularly associated with Judaism and represents the most extreme form of Jewish liberalism ushered in by the Reform.

RISE OF CONSERVATISM AND RUSSIAN MIGRATION

A reaction against the Reform began with the earliest published writings of Isaac Wise and David Einhorn. Among the first to react was Isaac Leeser, also a German immigrant, who founded the first Jewish congregational Hebrew school and the Maimonides training school for rabbis. As editor of *The Occident and Jewish Advocate*, he influenced Jewish communities throughout the United States and is generally held to be the spiritual father of Conservative Judaism. He was the first to introduce English in the American synagogue.

Leeser drew the important distinction between external forms and internal faith, which the Reform was charged with ignoring. His successor as rabbi in the old Sephardic synagogue of Philadelphia, Sabato Morais (1823-1897), carried into effect Leeser's hopes of adjustment to American culture without compromise of Jewish principles.

With the support of rabbis and laymen in about a dozen congregations he formed in 1885 the Jewish Theological Seminary Association. As expressed in the preamble to its constitution, the society was to foster loyalty to authentic Judaism.

> The necessity has been made manifest for associated and organized effort on the part of the Jews of America faithful to Mosaic Law and ancestral traditions, for the purpose of keeping alive the true Judaic spirit; in particular by the establishment of a seminary where the Bible shall be impartially taught and rabbinical literature faithfully expounded, and more especially where youths, desirous of entering the ministry, may be thoroughly grounded in Jewish knowledge and inspired by the precept and example of their instructors with the love of the Hebrew language and a spirit of devotion and fidelity to the Jewish law.[28]

Unfortunately for the cause of conservatism, Morais' efforts met with only scanty support. By 1900, six of the eleven synagogues that signed the original charter for the new seminary went over to the Reform. When Morais died, the future of his plans for preserving "the Mosaic law" was in doubt and might have vanished for want of interest except for a new phenomenon in the history of his people—the huge migration from Eastern and Central Europe.

The reasons behind the mass migration were similar to those which brought the Germans to the United States, with one major exception: oppression of the Jews in Czarist Russia was far beyond anything that occurred in Germany.

Historians agree that the policy of the Czarist government had been anti-Semitic in the extreme. Jews were generally excluded from the state service, were forbidden to acquire land, and were subjected to a quota system of admission to the universities and higher schools. Apart from these legal discriminations, the Jews were constantly fearful of pogroms, or outbursts of mob violence, accompanied by murder, outrage, and looting. Such outbreaks were not, as a rule, severely repressed by the authorities. Sometimes, especially during the 1905 Revolution, pogroms were even encouraged as a means of diverting the rage of the masses away from the government against the Jews.

The resentment which this created among the oppressed may be seen in the number who joined Lenin in his opposition to the Czarist tyranny. Commenting on the Second Congress of the Russian Socialist Democratic Labor Party (1903), he remarked that one third of the delegates present at the Congress were Jews. In fact, "by the beginning of the twentieth century this high proportion of Jewish leaders and followers had become characteristic of the entire gamut of Russian revolutionary movements; it was as true of the peasantist Social Revolutionaries as of their great opponents the Social Democrats."[29] Under stress of persecution, some worked for independence within Russia, others migrated to America.

All through the second half of the nineteenth century, and into the twentieth, the plight of the Russian Jews was publicized in the United States and evoked a sympathy in this country that has become legendary. Among the sympathizers who have made history was Emma Lazarus (1849-1887), an accomplished poetess whose Jewish consciousness was stirred by the trials of her people and their search for freedom overseas. Her sonnet "The New Colossus" was inscribed on the Statue of Liberty, New York, and symbolizes the sufferings of the Jews and the promise of freedom for all who come to America.

> Not like the brazen giant of Greek fame,
> With conquering limbs astride from land to land;
> Here at our sea-washed sunset gates shall stand
> A mighty woman with a torch, whose flame
> Is the imprisoned lightning, and her name
> Mother of Exiles. From her beacon-hand
> Glows world-side welcome; her mild eyes command
> The air-bridged harbor that twin cities frame,
> "Keep ancient lands, your storied pomp," cries she
> With silent lips, "Give me your tired, your poor,
> Your huddled masses yearning to breathe free.
> The wretched refuse of your teeming shore.

Send these, the homeless, tempest-tost to me,
I lift my lamp beside the golden door."[30]

Persons like Emma Lazarus typified the feeling of kinship between Jews in America and their coreligionists from overseas. This sense of solidarity played a large role in the encouragement of East European emigration, in spite of occasional outbreaks of feeling to the contrary. In 1884 the State of New York passed restrictive immigration laws and the *American Israelite* suggested that these laws be used to check the influx of Russian refugees.

This was an exception, however, since the mainstream of American Jewry was pleased with the coming of so many of its people and dedicated to the task of assimilating them to the American way of life. But the problem of assimilation was gigantic, and its roots touched deeply into the whole complex of Judaism as a religion or a nationality.

In order to understand something of the issues involved, it should be pointed out that the Enlightenment affected the Russian Jews much differently than it did the German Jews. Those in Germany were stimulated either to assimilation and conversion to contemporary thought or to create Reform Judaism. In Eastern Europe, the response was different. With minor exceptions, East European Jews did not convert nor assimilate, nor did they try at first to change their traditional religious beliefs.

Unlike the situation in Germany where the main impact was cultural and philosophical, the pressure in Russia was political and social. The very term *pogrom*, now a common noun which means "an organized massacre of helpless people," originated in Russia, where it meant "destruction," and provoked defensive and offensive reaction that has literally changed the course of world civilization. The rise of Russian Marxism cannot be understood without taking into account the inhuman pogroms initiated by the Czarist regime against the Jews.

Understandably, therefore, when the East European Jews came to America, they represented quite a different strain of Judaism than did the Germans who preceded them. Whereas the latter were more homogeneous in character and more commonly sympathetic to the Reform as a religious adaptation, the Russians were heterogeneous in the extreme. For one thing they were far more numerous. And among their hundreds of thousands could be found every color and shade of belief and unbelief conceivable.

Back in Russia, Poland, and the Balkans, their status—and almost condition of survival—had been to be considered a nation or a people among many of the ethnic groups in Eastern Europe. Moreover, the fierce anti-Semitism of those lands rapidly transformed them into a proletariat that felt it had to resist oppression to remain physically alive, let alone ethnically, and the result for many Russian Jews was to produce socialism, Zionism, and other radical but secular movements in their ranks.

Yet with all this ferment away from Orthodox Judaism and even from an organized religion, many Jews in Eastern Europe remained more firm than ever in the faith of their fathers. Between the two ends of the spectrum were the majority, struggling to be loyal to Moses and the prophets and trying to do something to ameliorate their nearly enslaved condition.

Both extremes and the middle crossed the Atlantic in search of freedom. They came in such droves that, as one Jewish chronicler described it, "To the established, middle-class, Americanized German Jews of the 1880's, the East European immigrants were a frightening apparition."[31] They were a stark contrast to the Ashkenazim who had migrated a generation before. They were more desperately poor, more intensely pious, more violently irreligious, and more radically extreme—with such diversity as the German Jews had never dreamed possible.

Articles and news items in the Jewish American papers reflected the bewilderment this mass migration produced. It defied classification, even when it aroused fear or inspiration, depending on whether the phenomenon was the Marxist Socialism of an Abraham Cahan or the scholarly Orthodoxy of a Rabbi Jacob Joseph.

If the newcomers were at first viewed with suspicion and even alarm, their dire needs soon evoked a responsive help from the Jewish establishment in America. Part of the motivation, no doubt, was a feeling that the crude religion and the extreme radicalism of the immigrants might affect their own solid middle-class position. Would not the average Gentile American lump all of them together,

Germans and East Europeans, and pass critical judgment on all without discrimination? But the strongest reason for assistance was the simple fact that the Slavs were Jews who looked to other Jews for help in time of distress.

Since most of the Russians were Orthodox, they needed synagogues. By 1900 there were no less than one hundred thirty of them in New York alone, made possible in large measure through the cooperation of Jewish residents in the state. The immigrants needed education, especially the children, and facilities were hopelessly inadequate. Schools had to be built and teachers trained to give the rising generation a love for their heritage. Financial aid, legal counsel, social direction—were all necessary and supplied by the Americans with a generosity that only those who have witnessed Jewish loyalty would appreciate.

It was not enough, however, to meet the crisis, in particular for the young immigrants who were faced with the dilemma of choosing between a rigid Orthodoxy and a complete rejection of the Jewish faith.

Abraham Cahan told the story of a young Russian Jewish yeshivah student who represented thousands. On the boat, David Levinsky ate no forbidden food and said the prescribed prayers daily. In America he searched out and found a synagogue like the one he knew back home. But he also began slipping away. First his earlocks were cut off, then he shaved, pretty soon he stopped going to the synagogue so he could attend night school and learn some English. Finally nothing was left, not even a stricken conscience over what happened to his religion.

David Levinsky symbolized the tragic lot of the Jews, first the German and later the Russian, who had been brought up to keep the commandments and regulations, but who lacked a solid religious knowledge of their Jewish practice and ritual. As their own commentators explain, these people often had nothing else than a set of religious observances surrounding them like armor. Once this armor was pierced by the simple question, Why? it often fell away and left nothing behind but a set of habits. For some these habits were so ingrained that they might believe nothing of the Torah and still less of the Talmud, and yet, from habit, follow the dietary laws, attend synagogue periodically and, if their training in Russia was good, they knew the prayers by heart.

An abortive attempt was made in 1888 to cope with the problem by organizing a large-scale organization to which synagogues would belong and under which the Jews could be federated in a kind of community. The project fell through because of internal rivalry, opposition by the radicals, and indifference of "uptown" Jewish elements.

More successful was the venture that soon developed into a third force in American Jewry, when Cyrus Adler (1863-1940) decided to restore the Jewish Theological Seminary. His decision was the culmination of years of planning on how to meet the double challenge that faced the Jews: the avowed rejection of Torah-true Judaism by the Reform and the loss of faith by the immigrants, mainly the youth from Russia and Eastern Europe.

A campaign for collecting funds for the theological seminary made it possible to hire a new faculty and bring Solomon Schechter (1847-1915) from Romania to head the institution. Under Schechter, Jewish Conservatism came to new life, as without him it might have passed out of history as an unattainable mirage.

Born in Romania, he studied in Vienna and Berlin, lectured on the Talmud at Cambridge, and was invited in 1901 to become president of the Jewish Theological Seminary of America in New York.

Under his direction, the seminary became an academic institution of the first rank. He worked to develop the seminary and its associated organizations, such as the United Synagogue of America, into the leading institutions of Conservative Judaism, whose philosophy he elaborated in a series of books and addresses that are classic in their field. He edited important scholarly texts, like *Documents of Jewish Sectaries*, and published several works in English, including *Studies in Judaism* (three volumes) that combined scholarship with popular appeal.

Schechter's thesis was that the mind alone cannot save Judaism from absorption by the dominant environment. Nothing less than mystical piety must be infused into the life of a modern Jew if he wants to remain faithful to his religion and yet live a normal life in American society. He could be terribly incisive, but also kind, when he wrote critically of the Reform, which he identified with a rationalistic attitude toward faith. "Rationalism," he claimed "could well appreciate all the virtues of manliness, but it could never value properly those qualities of obedience, submissiveness, meekness and self-denial which constitute a holy life."[32] His argument was that without an interior life lived in the presence of Yahweh, Judaism might well adjust to American culture but it would not produce the people of God demanded by the prophets.

Up to 1880, most of the quarter million Jews in the United States belonged to the Reform persuasion. In the next twenty years another half million came to America, mainly from Eastern Europe, and the scene changed with dramatic suddenness. By 1915 another million and a quarter entered the country, and the Reform was reduced, numerically, to an influential denomination that represented only a fraction of American Jews.

The Jewish Theological Seminary became the source of other organizational moves within the Conservative ranks. In 1913 the United Synagogue of America was established by Schechter to give synagogues in the Conservative tradition the collective strength they lacked, by comparison with the Reform. It was a logical move, since the Reform already had its Union of American Hebrew Congregations, started by Isaac Mayer Wise in 1873, and its Central Conference of American Rabbis, formed in 1889.

While the Conservatives were rallying their forces to offset the liberalism of the Reform, Orthodox Jews were not idle. It took a while for the migrants from Eastern and Central Europe to get their foothold in the United States. Their problem was at once more simple and more difficult than what the Conservative element had to face. It was simple because, in their view, little or no compromise was to be made with traditional Jewish customs. It was harder because the structure of American life, notably in the cities, made it next to impossible to maintain a Jewish way of life with its stringent demands without running counter to prevalent norms.

The impossible was done, however, and Orthodox Judaism in the United States became an organized body as early as 1898, when Rabbi Henry Pereira Mendes (1852-1937) of New York's Shearith Israel founded the Union of Orthodox Jewish Congregations.

Mendes was a Sephardi Jew, born and educated in England. This made him acceptable to the Conservatives, but less pleasing to the Orthodox. His hope had been to coordinate the latter into a national body and thus help to preserve the rich heritage of Torah-true Judaism. The Union still exists as the central agency of the larger Orthodox congregations, but soon after its foundation the East European Jews took over its management and refused to recognize the ordination of rabbis at the Jewish Theological Seminary. Although Mendes had been one of the pioneers of the seminary, the Orthodox could not conceive of a real rabbi who had studied the Talmud in English and not Yiddish. They wanted seminaries patterned on the Yeshivah, the traditional European school devoted mainly to the study of the Talmud and rabbinical literature.

As the Orthodox viewed the situation, they considered rabbinical seminaries as *the* link with the Jewish past. They knew that the Yeshivah was a direct continuation of the Academies which flourished in Palestine and Babylonia in Talmudic times (to the sixth century of the Christian era) and during the Gaonic period (up to the eleventh century). Unless the rabbis were trained in the spirit of these Yeshivot of Asia Minor and Europe, the future of Jewish Orthodoxy was believed insecure.

It is not surprising, therefore, that the East Europeans depended for the most part on private education, often in one room, where they taught their children what they could of Hebrew, the Torah, and the Talmud. Gradually these schools were consolidated and subsidized, even with contributions from broad-minded German Jews. Finally by 1896 the Rabbi Isaac Elchanan Theological Seminary was founded, in New York, as the first Yeshivah in America. In 1915 it merged with an earlier foundation (1887), the Etz-Chaim Talmudical Academy for young people not planning to become rabbis, also in New York. Headed by Bernard Revel (1885-1940), the merger became Yeshivah College in 1928 and a university in 1945. To this day it is the main source of supply for the Orthodox rabbinate.

Typical of the need for getting large-scale cooperation among the Orthodox was the founding in 1902 of a second national organization, the Union of Orthodox Rabbis. Its first members were East

Europeans, and the dominant influence is still in that direction. Membership has since been extended to include the Jewish in Canada, notably in Montreal and Toronto.

Orthodox rabbis in the Anglo-Saxon tradition formed a third national society, the Rabbinical Council of America. Established in 1923, its function was to consolidate ordained rabbis occupying pulpits in North America. Its members came only from recognized Orthodox seminaries.

All of this organization was possible, however, only because Jewish Orthodoxy had a clear historical lineage to which it could appeal, and definite principles to which it subscribed. These principles were closely centered on the Law, as found in the Bible and expanded in the Talmud, but especially as codified by the patriarch of Orthodoxy, the Iberian Jew, Joseph Karo (1488-1575), without whose popular digest, *Shulhan Aruk (Table in Order)*, the very idea of a consistent Orthodox Judaism would have been inconceivable.

Karo's systematic digest of rabbinical ordinances will be seen again, in more detail. Yet something must be said about it here to explain the remarkable cohesiveness of Orthodox Jewry in America, within a short generation of the East European immigration. It also helps to see why, of all traditions, the Orthodox remains the most internally unified, even when external organization is lacking or not so obviously successful.

If Joseph Karo was a legalist, he was also something of a mystic. Indeed, this ambivalence is the usual reason given for his phenomenal ability to attract followers who see in him a rare combination of the best of both worlds, the secular with its demands for structure and law, and the sacred with its eye on God and things of the spirit.

Shortly after he published the *Shulhan Aruk*, Karo was attacked by some of his contemporaries, notably by a Rabbi Moses Isserles (c. 1525-1572), who was then the foremost authority in Poland. Isserles was an Ashkenazi scholar who objected to Karo's so exclusive stress on ancient ordinances, to the neglect of many later customs that were generally considered just as binding on the Jewish faithful. To prove his point, Isserles wrote a series of notes to Karo's codes supplying these omissions. Without intending to, he made the *Table in Order* so complete that no critic could question its abiding value. It became the definitive Jewish code of law throughout the world, and more than anything else, served to consolidate Orthodox Judaism in the United States.

One article out of several hundred in Karo's collection illustrates the balance of law and piety that characterized the *Shulhan Aruk*. It also sheds light on how any group that followed this authority would become bound together by a common code of morality. Isserles' insertion does not undermine the code. It provides a useful counterpoise. The subject of the article is how much alms a poor Israelite should receive.

> How much is to be given to a poor man? Sufficient for his need in that which he lacks (Deut. 15:8). Thus, if he is hungry, he should be fed; if he needs clothing, he should be clothed; if he lacks household utensils, they should be purchased for him; and even if he had been accustomed, before he was impoverished, to ride on horseback with a slave running before him, he should be furnished with a horse and a slave. And so each and every one should be supplied with what he needs. If it is fit to give him (merely) a slice of bread, give him a slice; if it is proper to give him dough, give him dough; if he ought to be provided with lodging, provide a bed for him. If it is fit to give him a warm meal, give him warm food; if cold lunch, then cold lunch. If he has to be fed (like an infant) then he must be fed. If he is unmarried and he comes to take a wife, the community should find him a mate; but first they should rent him a home, prepare him a bed and furnish him with necessary household utensils, and then marry him off.
>
> (*Note by Isserles*: It appears that all this applies to *Gabbaim* over public funds or to many doing charitable work together, but every individual is not bound to satisfy all the needs of a poor man who may chance to come his way. What he ought to do is to arouse public interest in a worthy case; but if he lives far from men, he should give what he can afford.)
>
> A poor woman who has an opportunity of marrying, shall receive not less than fifty Zuz; and if there is enough in the

treasury, she should be maintained as honorably as is befitting her.

A pauper who begs from house to house should be given only a small sum from the *Kuphah*.

A poor man, who goes from place to place, shall receive not less than a loaf of bread . . . If he remains over night, he should be given a couch to sleep upon and a bolster under his head, and oil and a small fruit; and if it is a Sabbath, he shall be provided with food for three meals, and oil, small fruit, fish and herbs; and if he is known (to be worthy), he should be given as much as it is befitting his honor.

If the poor in a city are numerous, and the rich say they should go and beg, and the middle classes say they should not beg but be supported by the members of the community in proportion to their wealth, the law is as the latter say.[33]

Already in Karo's time, Jews feared that the *Shulhan Aruk* would displace the Talmud, or at least reduce the religion of the people to a sterile legalism. Events proved these fears to be wrong. So far from enervating Jewish devotion, it gave a strength that historians believe was nothing short of preternatural. Isidore Epstein, editor of the massive thirty-six volume edition of the *Babylonian Talmud in English* and one of the world's leading Jewish scholars in modern times, testified that Karo's code of laws "proved the greatest single cohesive force in Judaism, and imposed upon the Jews a uniformity of purpose and action which preserved them to the present day, amid all their diverse loyalties and conflicting interests, as one people on earth."[34]

If the Orthodox in America gave special allegiance to this legal system, they gained from it a proportionate reward, namely, a solidarity that other religious bodies have admired even when they did not imitate.

The Orthodox sensed the need for giving daily expression in visible form to the unity of spirit which Judaism professes to have. By Reform and even Conservative standards, they have exalted customs into firmly established principles, of which *Shulhan Aruk* is a classic example and which numerous external practices commonly illustrate.

Thus most Orthodox Jews wear a hat or skullcap at all times, and not only during prayer. Conservatives cover their heads only during acts of worship, whereas the Reform generally pray without hats.

Yet the custom of praying bareheaded or with covered head is not a question of law. It is only a matter of social decorum, which some Jews have raised to the dignity of a sacred tradition. Speculation about its origins comes afterward. In this case, the most favored explanation is that the ancient Jews lifted their prayer shawls over their heads during worship to cover their eyes. This removed distractions from prayer and encouraged the greatest possible concentration. The hat or skullcap, then, is the symbolic descendant of the prayer shawl covering.

When Reform critics of these and similar explanations point out that archaeological remains often portray Jews who wore no headgear, they are answered as might be expected. What matters in Judaism is not the history of a practice but its canonization by adoption.

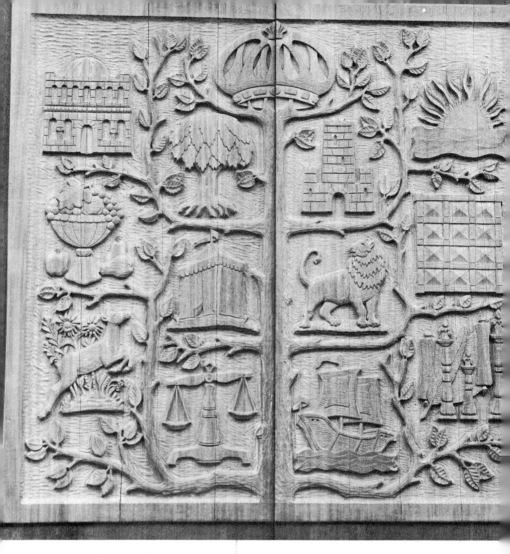

Door of Aron Hakodesh *(Holy Ark).*
Pictorial representation without human
form. Represents the twelve tribes of Israel
based on the blessings of Jacob and Moses.
In Western countries, the Ark occupies
the center of the east side of the synagogue
and houses the Scrolls of the Torah.
The Torah is called a "Tree of Life" whose
branches are the tribes. At the top is a
crown symbolizing the dominant position
of the Torah for a Jew.

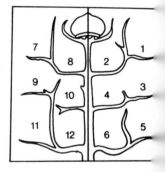

THE TREE OF LIFE

Symbols of the blessings of Jacob and Moses

Tribe	Blessing in Genesis	Symbolism in Deuteronomy
1 Reuben	"Thou art my firstborn, my might and the beginning of my strength"	Rising sun, source of light, warmth and strength (Jacob)
2 Simon	"Weapons of military might or prowess"	Fortified tower, military citadel (Jacob)
3 Levi	"They shall teach Jacob Thine ordinances and Israel Thy law"	Breastplate of the High Priest (Moses and Jacob)
4 Judah	"Thou art likened unto a lion"	Lion—since Judah had the scepter of kingship and emblem of leadership (Jacob)
5 Issachar	"He will take upon himself the burden of the study of the Torah"	Accouterments of the scholar: candle, quill, and scroll (Jacob)
6 Zebulon	"Zebulon shall dwell at the shore of the sea, and he shall be a shore for ships"	Ship in travel, referring to the maritime enterprises of the tribe (Jacob)
7 Dan	"Dan shall judge his people"	Dignified domed structure, expressive of a court of law (Jacob)
8 Gad	"He executeth the righteous-ness of the Lord"	Well-rooted tree, symbol of stability and reliability (Moses)
9 Asher	"As for Asher, his bread shall be fat and he shall yield royal dainties"	Bowl with an abundant measure of fruit; a bountiful supply of produce (Jacob)
10 Joseph	"A prince among his people"	Tent, symbolic of Joseph's loyalty to the study of Jacob's teachings and fidelity in their practice in the privacy of his homelife (Jacob and Moses)
11 Naphtali	"Naphtali is likened to the swiftness of the hind (female of the deer)"	The hind, symbol of swiftness and grace in movement (Jacob)
12 Benjamin	"The beloved of the Lord shall dwell in safety by Him"	Scale of Justice; the Temple of the Lord, with its sacrifices of atonement, would be situated in his territory (Moses)

Jewish children in their classroom. North American Jews, especially the Orthodox, regard children as a responsibility in the fulfillment of the role divinely assigned to Israel. For this reason a religious and moral task devolves on parents to have their children instructed in the practice and knowledge of Judaism from their earliest year.

III

JEWISH ORTHODOXY

Orthodox Judaism goes back to the time of Abraham. If given a choice, it would remove the adjective and call itself simply "Judaism," on the premise that qualifying terms should be applied to define its dissenting branches and not the parent tree.

The term *Orthodox* was first applied to the Jews by Abraham Furtado (1756-1817), French communal leader and merchant of Bordeaux. As president of the Assembly of Notables convened by Napoleon (1806), he represented the cause of French Jewry before the government. At the meeting of the Paris Sanhedrin (1807), he defended a series of recommendations in which he favored civic and cultural assimilation as the price of liberty in continental Europe. He felt the price was worth paying in view of the liberation it promised to bring.

There was more to the Jewish emancipation under Napoleon than is commonly known. The very concept of Judaism, and not only of Orthodoxy, was at stake.

As understood by the leaders of the French Revolution, the new political order was to be founded on the bonds of national fellowship among the French people, to the exclusion of any other, supposedly divisive, forms of union. Faced with this strong nationalism, the Jews had the difficult choice of deciding where they stood. They were being offered political freedom, but on some very severe conditions. Were they essentially a nation within a nation, or were they really patriotic Frenchmen who professed the Jewish faith? Or more practically, would the French people permit a closed blood relationship among the Jews and be satisfied with a Jewish identification of religious interest and a sense of common destiny?

The answer to this dilemma has more than historical meaning and cannot be lightly passed over as we take up the three main forms of Judaism in the United States. It would be easy, but erroneous, to classify the Orthodox, Reform, and Conservative solely on the basis of ritual and faith. The religious differences are still important, as they were in Napoleonic France when the tripartite division really started. But they do not adequately distinguish either these three categories or any individual Jew when he identifies himself in the spectrum of Judaic loyalty. The ethnic factor is also part of the classification.

Napoleon wanted the Jews to be assimilated ethnically, as seen from the orders he gave to the Paris Sanhedrin to favor intermarriage with Gentiles. At one time he insisted that every third Jewish marriage should be with the *Goim*. His sentiments were echoed by "liberators" in other countries, and in general, favored by liberal Jews themselves. They claimed that Judaism was essentially a religious community, that the ethnic or national features of Jewry were by-products of segregation by the Gentiles, and that a return to Jerusalem was a pious dream which had no practical significance for the believing Jew.

The history of Judaism in Europe and later in America shows that many Jews accepted the distinction and settled for a purely—or at least basically—religious principle of identity. A Jew is one who believes and practices the Jewish faith. By the same token, a Jew is more or less orthodox as he is more or less loyal to the spiritual elements of the Judaic religion.

But the principle is incomplete. As the Jews themselves are at pains to point out, the cost of emancipation was more than meets the eye. Not only have Jews been divided among themselves on the degree of their Judaism—giving rise to the Reform and Conservative camps—but the very notion of what constitutes Judaism has been called into question.

In the nearly two centuries since the French Revolution, the threefold division has become fairly well crystallized. At the same time the concept of Judaism itself is now clearer than ever before. Essential to the concept is more than "religion," as understood in Christian terms.

Up to the mid-nineteen hundreds, men as radically different as Moses Mendelssohn and Gabriel Riesser went along with the prevalent notion that the Jewish people are only a religious denomination and should become part of the newly rising nation states.

By the turn of the century, however, the picture was changing. In 1893 the term *Zionism* was coined by Nathan Birnbaum, pseudonym Mathias Acher (1864-1917), who advocated the Jewish return to Palestine as an essential element of Judaism. Before that time, Zionism was mainly a religious aspiration, commonly expressed in the traditional liturgy and in limited readings of the Scroll of the Law, during synagogue worship. In 1897 the First Zionist Congress was held in Basle, where the World Zionist Organization was created and the basic principles of Judaism as religion and nation were formulated.

This Jewish dualism was concisely expressed by Louis Ginzberg (1873-1953), rabbinic scholar and for fifty years professor of Talmud at the Jewish Theological Seminary in New York. A faithful disciple of Theodor Herzl (1860-1904), first president of the World Zionist Organization, Ginzberg insisted that nationalism and religion are the twin components of Judaism. "For us who adhere to historic Judaism," he declared, "Jewish nationalism without religion would be a tree without fruit; Jewish religion without Jewish nationalism would be a tree without roots."[1]

While of great practical importance, it is secondary to our purpose that some Jews would have Judaism tied mainly to national aspirations. Their ideals gave rise to what is called political Zionism. Others would exclude national ambitions entirely, and were opposed to political Zionism—mainly in the Reform rabbinate.

For years, political Zionism split the Jews into the majority who gave it strong support and the rest who opposed it. Critics at one extreme were religious factions who said that divine providence could restore the Jews to their land without political maneuvering, and at the other end were liberals who denied that the Jews were (or should be) a nation since their solidarity was that of a people united exclusively by religious (or religiously cultural) bonds and apart from political ambitions.

The minority opposition to Zionism has notably weakened since the State of Israel was established in 1948. With the restoration of Israel to the Jews, Judaism has become generally recognized by its own followers as a religion and (in some sense) as also a nation. American Judaism is no exception to this dual composition, although the meaning of religion and nation are differently interpreted by different Jews. Orthodoxy as the paradigm of Jewry, therefore, spans both elements, and dissidents from Orthodoxy differ not only on religious matters but also on the delicate question of nationhood.

ORTHODOXY IN CONTRAST

Before we undertake an analysis of Orthodoxy as a compound of faith and culture, we must first clarify what may look like a subtlety, but really is not. Why speak of "Orthodoxy," unless some kind of heterodoxy is implied by way of comparison?

Historically the term *Orthodoxy* has come to distinguish the more inflexible type of Judaism from its less conservative counterparts within the Jewish tradition. The distinction is valid and includes the meaning attached to the name in the present context.

Yet there is another and prior sense in which "Orthodoxy" was understood, long before the modern terminology (occasioned by the emancipation from the ghetto) came into vogue. A Jew was Orthodox because he did not compromise with Christianity or Islam.

Viewed in this light, present-day Orthodoxy has a noble lineage that reaches far back into the first century of the Christian era (*Anno Domini*) and the first century of the Moslem era (*Anno Hagirae*). In both instances, Judaism maintained its identity by developing a distinctive religious culture that was at once definite enough to be truly Jewish and different enough not to be Christian nor Moslem.

Judaism has been undergoing this process of self-understanding, which is unique among the major religions of the world, as a necessary law of its being. At once a people and a religion, it saw two rival religious movements arise from its own past. Having decided to remain itself, it had the difficult task of keeping not only alive but dynamically active, while its believers were living in effective communication with other believers who looked upon Judaism as a precious inheritance, indeed, but no longer as their own main allegiance.

Not a few Christian interpreters tend to see Judaism as something archaic if not anachronistic. They fail to recognize that Jews profess a living faith, whose ancestry is traced, like theirs, to Abraham, Isaac, and Jacob, but whose vitality is perennial. Judaism has not merely survived since the time of Jesus of Nazareth or the age of Mohammed. It continued to grow in depth and self-determination, and its genius is this ability to adapt to changing circumstances without ceasing to be itself.

Fortunately we have the available record of Jewish self-determination on the successive levels, demanded by its history of relationship to three competitive ideologies: Christian since the time of Jesus of Nazareth and Paul of Tarsus, Moslem since the rise of Mohammed in the seventh century of the Christian era, and Secularist since the period of emancipation ushered in by the French Revolution. With notable exceptions, the rabbinical writings— mainly the Babylonian Talmud and the Rabbah Midrashim to the tenth century C.E.—cover the growth of Judaism in contact with Christianity; the writings of Maimonides and his commentators up to modern times reflect Jewish self-consciousness in contrast to Islam (and Christianity); and the work of such Orthodox leaders as Hirsch and Lehmann, Lipkin and Kuk stresses the lasting values of

Judaism as a revelation to the Chosen People confronted with contemporary naturalism.

In order not to get lost in a mass of detail, it seems best to cut through each of these relationships on the basis of certain dominant themes. The resulting picture will hopefully do justice to the spirit of classic Judaism and offer a sound basis for later comparison with Jewish Reform and Conservatism.

CONCEPT OF GOD

The Talmudic conception of God is lucidly clear. Echoing the Torah, the Jewish rabbis saw Yahweh as not only one but unique, as the eternal Almighty whose knowledge encompasses all things past, present, and future. He is seen as infinitely greater than the created world he brought into being, and yet mysteriously dwelling in his creatures. Absolutely just and perfectly holy, he is merciful to those who invoke his name and benevolent to all mankind.

Idolatry in the Talmud and Midrash is a brazen denial of God's unity. For how can a man simultaneously worship another human being or an element of nature, and at the same time pay homage to the invisible God? Jews are encouraged to suffer martyrdom rather than give in to the prevalent idolatry around them.[2]

Every semblance of idol worship is denounced by the Talmudists. In one eloquent passage, the rabbis in Rome were asked why, if an idol does not come within God's will, does he not destroy it?

> They replied: "If men worshipped something which was not necessary for the world, God would destroy it. But behold! they worship the sun and the moon and the stars and the planets—is God to destroy His world because of madmen?"
>
> Others retorted to the elders: "In that case, let God destroy that which is not necessary for the world, and let Him leave alone that which was necessary."
>
> The elders replied: "We would but strengthen the hands of those who worship the latter, for they would say, 'Know that these are gods, for they have not been destroyed.' "[3]

The logic of this dialogue was not lost on the Jewish believer. But more subtle was the danger of falling prey to Persian dualism, which held there was one god for the invisible world of spirit and another for the world of matter. To make sure the Jews would not be led into this error, the Midrash forbade them ever to immediately repeat thanks to God in prayer, lest this might give credence to the heresy.[4] Moreover the whole idea is condemned in the Midrash commentaries.[5]

Another possible tampering with the doctrine of God's unicity was the Christian belief in the Trinity. Where the rabbis reply to the *minim* (heretics, sectaries, and sometimes Christians), they represent the minim as believing in many gods. Concretely, therefore, the Trinity was understood to mean Tritheism and answered accordingly.

The divine omnipotence and omnipresence were so forcefully described in the Bible that rabbinic scholarship was satisfied to repeat the scriptural passages or, more often, merely refer to the inspired text. But God's omniscience was a different matter. Conscious of the problems to which this gave rise when seen in conjunction with human freedom, the Talmudists went out of their way to stress the existence of both realities. Some passages are perfectly orthodox; others are more daring.

On the traditional side, we read that God's infinite knowledge cannot be doubted.[6] Above all he has always known what goes on in the hearts of men: "From the time when the world was first formed, the Holy One, blessed be He, foresaw the actions of the righteous and the wicked alike."[7] A classic passage in the *Ethics of the Fathers* states without qualification that God knows everything, but leaves man with his own liberty intact: "Everything is foreseen, yet freedom of choice is given; and the world is judged by grace, yet all is according to the amount of the work."[8]

The relation of God's decrees to man's freedom is not always plain and the one passage most often quoted on the subject ends in a stalemate. Yet it should be seen to illustrate the struggle in Jewish thought which anticipated the Catholic-Calvinist controversy by at least a thousand years.

We may suppose, says the Gemara, that Israel was particularly unfaithful at New Year's time and so God decided to punish the people by reducing the amount of rains. Suddenly Israel repents and asks forgiveness. What should God do? Presumably he cannot go back on his decrees, which are irrevocable. He therefore keeps to his decision but by a judicious spacing of rainfall to coincide with the time it is most needed, the people do not suffer. So Israel is as well off as if the original decision had not been changed. Then the reverse is considered. God planned a great deal of rain but the people were disloyal. This time he kept to the same absolute quantity but wasted the rainfall by sending it in the wrong seasons and wrong places. He thus vindicated his justice by not changing the decrees, but the question of his omniscience was left untouched.[9]

If there are ambiguous statements in classic Judaism about the reality of man's freedom in the face of omnipotence, the general outlook is never in doubt. God is sovereign but not one who undercuts human liberty. Quite the contrary, through the rightful exercise of freedom, as in prayer, man can literally "influence" the Lord of Hosts: "Just as the pitchfork turns over the grain from one place to another, so does the prayer of the righteous reverse the decisions of the Holy One, blessed be He, from the attribute of anger to the attribute of mercy."[10]

Maimonides carried on the same tradition, and American Jews of the Orthodox persuasion regularly quote his *Guide for the Perplexed* when they explain what they mean by God. He wrote this work, as he said, "to afford a guide for the perplexed," namely, "to thinkers whose studies have brought them into collision with religion."[11] Specifically he was concerned to explain in more erudite terms the Jewish faith to believers who were confused by Islamic interpreters of the Koran, who were also followers of Aristotle. The immediate occasion for writing *The Guide for the Perplexed* was to give one of his disciples a handbook for appraising the system of Kalam, or Moslem theology.

One passage in the book is standard for dealing with the crucial problem of what Jews can say about God that is really positive and yet does not set limits on his absolute being. The context is God's unity, commonly professed by Jews and Moslems.

All attributes, such as "the First," "the Last," occurring in the Scriptures in reference to God, are metaphorical as the expressions "ear" and "eye." They simply signify that God is not subject to any change or innovation whatever; they do not imply that God can be described by time, or that there is any comparison between Him and any other being as regards time, and that He is called on that account "the first" and "the last." In short, all similar expressions are borrowed from the language commonly used among the people. In the same way we use "One" (*ehad*) in reference to God, to express that there is nothing similar to Him, but we do not mean to say that an attribute of unity is added to His essence.[12]

Then follows a closely reasoned analysis of the divine essence as compared with divine existence. Aquinas is known to have used Maimonides in many ways, and certainly in arriving at the now famous real distinction between essence and existence pertaining to God.

Know that the negative attributes of God are the true attributes. God's existence is absolute. It includes no composition. We comprehend only the fact that He exists, not His essence (i.e. we comprehend only that He is, but not what He is). Consequently it is a false assumption to hold that He has any positive attribute; for He does not possess existence in addition to His essence; it therefore cannot be said that the one (either existence or essence) may be described as an attribute of the other; much less has He in addition to His existence a compound essence, consisting of two constituent elements to which the attribute could refer; still less has He accidents, which could be described by an attribute. Hence it is clear that He has no positive attribute whatever. The negative attributes, however, are those which are necessary to direct the mind to the truths which we must believe concerning God; for, on the one hand, they do not imply any plurality, and, on the other, they convey to man the highest possible knowledge of God; e.g., it has been established by proof that some being must exist besides those things which can be perceived by the senses, or apprehended by the mind; when we say of this being, that it exists, we mean that its non-existence is impossible.[13]

Maimonides concluded by defining what the Bible means when it says there is no one like unto God. It means that God is not only One but absolutely Unique. There cannot be another god. That is why failure to give him due praise is so wrong; it is refusal to acknowledge the most necessary of all truths.

The current *High Holiday Prayer Book* used by Orthodox synagogues is a treasure of hymns extolling the greatness of God. It is remarkable how many of them are not invocations or petitions but acts of adoration and worship to honor the majesty of the Most High. A familiar refrain in the morning service for Yom Kippur begins each line, after the first, with a negative—to bring out the greatness of the Lord by comparison with everything else in the world of nature.

There is none like thee among the mighty,
O Lord, nor are there any deeds like thine.
None like thee among the mighty above,
No deeds like thine among the best below.
None like thee among the armies above,
No deeds like thine among the men below.
None like thee among the myriads above,
No deeds like thine among the throngs below.
None like thee among the faultless above,
No deeds like thine among the hordes below.
None like thee among the stainless above,
No deeds like thine among the noble below.
None like thee among the cherubs above,
No deeds like thine among the hosts below.
None like thee among the angels above,
No deeds like thine among the great below.
None like thee among the seraphs above,
No deeds like thine among the chiefs below.
None like thee among the nameless above,
No deeds like thine among the troops below.
None like thee among the holy above,
No deeds like thine among the grand below.
None like thee among the spirits above,
No deeds like thine among the strong below.[14]

Thematic in contemporary Orthodox prayer is this awareness of God's majesty. There is never a shadow of doubt that he is *Kyrios*, Lord, as the ancient Hellenist Jews translated the name *Yahweh*. He is Lord by the twofold title of having brought the universe into being and of surpassing, by the transcendence of divinity, all the works of his hands.

TORAH—WISDOM AND PRECEPT

Judaism was born of the belief that God, for all his transcendence, condescended to reveal himself to his people. Through patriarchs and prophets, he spoke to the Chosen Race, and through them to the rest of mankind, what they are to believe, whom they are to worship, and how they are to conduct themselves in accordance with his will.

It is an axiom of Jewish faith and typical of its Orthodoxy that religion is no mere construct of human reason but an obligating gift of divine revelation.

As already seen, Torah mainly refers to the first five books of the Bible and, by an extension of the word, also pertains to the whole Mosaic law. But its fundamental meaning for a Torah-true Israelite is "divine communication" which binds the receiver to believe and to act on what he believes God tells him to do.

As one reads through Talmudic literature, the first impression is that Torah was mainly if not exclusively concerned with commandments. Did not Rabbi Simlai say, speaking of the Torah, "Six hundred and thirteen commandments were transmitted to Moses on Mount Sinai. Three hundred sixty-five of them are negative prohibitions, corresponding to the number of days in the solar year. The remaining two hundred forty-eight are positive [injunctions], corresponding to the number of limbs in the human body"?[15]

But this is misleading. As preceptive as it is, the Torah is primarily instructive in wisdom from on high. Yet its wisdom is not speculative but practical, and not so much reflective on truth as effective in producing goodness.

The man who reads—and lives—the Torah radiates the heavenly knowledge which imbues him and affects even the passing stranger with whom he comes into contact.

Rabbi Meir said: Whoever occupies himself with the study of the Torah with no ulterior motive merits many things. Furthermore, the entire world is indebted to him. He is called beloved friend [of God]. He loves God and mankind, and he causes God and mankind to rejoice. The Torah clothes him with humility and fear of the Lord, and it prepares him to be just, pious, upright and faithful. It keeps him far from sin and it brings him near to virtue. Through him men enjoy counsel and sound wisdom, insight and strength, as it is written, "I have counsel and sound wisdom, I have insight, I have strength" [Prov. 8:14]. In that chapter of Proverbs, wisdom, or Torah, is speaking. It gives him sovereignty and dominion and discerning judgment. The secrets of the Torah are revealed to him; he becomes like a neverfailing spring and like a river which never halts. He becomes modest, patient and forgiving of insult; it magnifies him and exalts him above all the works of creation.[16]

It would be self-delusion, however, to suppose that all this would come from a cursory reading of the sacred text or to a man who lived a life of indulgence and ease.

This is the way to acquire knowledge of the Torah: Eat bread with salt, drink water by measure [Ezek. 4:11], sleep on the ground, live a life of constraint, and toil in the Torah. If you do this, "You shall be blessed and it shall be well with you" [Ps. 128:2]. You shall be blessed in this world, and it shall be well with you in the world to come. Seek not greatness for yourself, and do not covet honor. Practice more than you learn. Crave not after the table of kings, for your table is greater than theirs and your crown is greater than theirs, and your master is faithful; He will pay you the reward of your labor.[17]

Underlying the rabbinic concept of divine manifestation is the idea of the *Shekinah*, which occurs in the Bible as a verb, *shakhan*, meaning "to dwell."[18] As used in the Talmud and understood by Orthodox Jews today, Shekinah may mean the presence of God in the Temple of old, particularly in the Holy of Holies; or some earthly sign of the hidden celestial glory of Yahweh; or merely the radiance of God's infinite presence among men.

The rabbis had one cardinal principle about the Shekinah, which enters the heart of classic Judaism. They taught that man's sin drives the Shekinah farther away, whereas virtue draws it nearer. In more technical terms, the transcendent God is more immanent to the righteous than to the unrighteous. This holds true of individuals as of societies. Spanning centuries of history, the Shekinah is said to have receded from the earth through the seven heavens, one at a time, because of the successive sins of Adam, Cain, the generations of Enoch, the people at the time of the flood, the nations punished by the confusion of tongues, the Sodomites, and the Egyptians. Conversely it came closer to earth in seven stages because of the good lives, in succession, of Abraham, Isaac, Jacob, Levi, Kohath, Amram, and Moses.

Similar teaching with a more priestly emphasis—in the tradition of the Sadducees as compared with the legalistic Pharisees— holds that the Shekinah departed from the Temple by ten stages, because of the sins of Israel. This may be found in the Talmud and in Midrash.[19] The two authorities differ, however, in their interpretation of where the Shekinah now abides. In the Midrash it hovers at easy recalling distance on Mount Olives, whereas the Talmud sends it back to heaven. Some would hold that the final destruction of the Temple in A.D. 70 drove the Shekinah irrevocably away from Jerusalem; others contend it still remains somewhere near the Wailing Wall.[20]

Maimonides took up the traditional Jewish view of revelation and crystallized it in four of his thirteen articles of faith, the sixth through the ninth. His classification has evoked a library of commentary that, better than almost anything else, serves to distinguish Torah-true Judaism from its various approximations. It is faithful to the Torah as it recognizes supernatural revelation.

His first proposition, in the wording of the Orthodox Prayer Book, states: "I firmly believe that all the words of the Prophets are true."[21] No Jewish authority has improved on his definition of what prophecy means. His use of Aristotelian terms only serves to clarify the meaning.

Prophecy is, in truth and reality, an emanation sent forth by the Divine Being through the medium of the Active Intellect, in the first instance to man's rational faculty, and then to his imaginative faculty. It is the highest degree and greatest perfection man can attain. It consists in the most perfect development of the imaginative faculty.

Prophecy is a faculty that cannot in any way be found in a person, or acquired by man, through a culture of his mental and moral faculties. For even if these latter were as good and perfect as possible, they would be of no avail, unless they were combined with the highest natural excellence of the imaginative faculty.[22]

This "highest natural excellence of the imagination" is the moral predisposition that God requires of a man before He grants him prophetic insight. The "Active Intellect" is partially borrowed from Aristotle and meant for Maimonides as for Jewish theology since—"an absolutely spiritual being, that is neither a corporeal object nor a force residing in a body. It acts intermittently, and yet whatever the cause may be why it does not always act, we do not say that the Active Intellect has passed from a state of potentiality to that of actuality."[23] Essential to this concept is the real distinction between God prophetically inspiring and man being inspired, in Jewish belief. If the language is somewhat ambiguous, the meaning is never in doubt. The Active Intellect is not God but one of his creatures. "The king that cleaves to us and embraces us," the Sage was at pains to explain, "is the Intellect that influences us, and forms the link between us and God. We perceive God by means of that light that He sends down unto us, wherefore the Psalmist says, 'In thy light shall we see light' (Psalm 36:9)."[24]

Prophets like Moses had the same kind of Active Intellect as lesser men. But their exceptional moral dispositions enabled God to inspire them with depth and understanding that no one else received.

Classic Judaism next identifies the Torah and thereby isolates itself from other purported revelations, whether Christian or Moslem. The seventh, eighth, and ninth articles of the Maimonidean creed focus on Moses as the chief of the prophets, as the one whose original Torah is the same now professed by the Israelites and, most pertinent, that "this [Mosaic] Torah will not be changed, and there will be no other Torah given by the Creator."[25] Consequently, the New Testament and the Koran are excluded from prophetic inspiration.

Orthodox Jews have no qualms on the subject and, at this crucial point of faith, they are one with Maimonides and, before him, with all who believed that nothing will ever supersede the Torah of Moses and the lesser prophets of Israel. Speaking for millions of his coreligionists, Rabbi Immanuel Jakobovits is perfectly clear. He is answering the question whether Judaism is *the* one true religion or only one of several true religions.

As a professing Jew, I obviously consider Judaism the only true religion, just as I would expect the adherents of any other faith to defend a similar claim for their religion. I assert this claim on three compelling grounds.

Firstly, it is intrinsic to Judaism, as averred by its teachings and by the unique covenantal bond between God and Israel. The recognition of other faiths as "equally true" is branded as apostasy in Jewish law (*Sanhedrin* 63ᵃ, based on Exodus 22:19). Judaism, to be true to itself, is bound to reject, for instance, the divinity of Jesus or the prophecy of Mohammed as false claims, such as the supremacy of Moses' prophecy and the finality of the Mosaic law (the 7th and 9th of Maimonides's Thirteen Articles of Faith) could not be true.

Secondly the claim is grounded in logic. Two mutually exclusive and conflicting statements of fact can never both be true. The only logical alternative to Judaism's being the only true religion is not that another religion is equally true but that Judaism is equally (or more) untrue.

Thirdly, to me Judaism's claim is an ineluctable personal credo. I could not subscribe to the rigorous demands of Jewish practice and thought if I had the slightest reason to believe that other faiths, far more widely professed and easier to practice, might be equally true. In fact, I feel any such egalitarian view of religion is no religion at all; it lacks the passion and depth of conviction which must inspire any truly religious faith if one is to love it "with all one's heart, and all one's soul, and all one's might," even to the point of dying for it, if necessary, as much as living for it, whatever the cost. A religion which demands nothing is worth nothing; and the least a religion is entitled to demand from its devotees is the kind of exclusive love spouses may expect from each other, parents from their children, and a country from its citizens. For me, in the telling phrase of the Zohar, "God, Israel and the Torah are (equally) one"—each is unique and incomparable.[26]

No one can read these lines without profound admiration for the faith which inspired them, a faith that has the certitude of prophecy come down from God through Moses to Israel, whom Yahweh appointed "as covenant of the people and light of the nations" to the end of time.[27]

MAN'S ORIGIN, NATURE, AND DESTINY

Judaism has always believed that knowledge of the facts of creation comes exclusively from the Torah—which makes Israel the envy of the nations.[28] Its teachers have therefore divided these facts into two categories: those permissible for public teaching and those which are esoteric and not to be communicated to others.[29]

Rabbinic theology holds that God created the world alone, with no one to help him, out of nothing, and without effort or exertion.[30] He created all things for his glory, and his cosmos, unlike that of creatures, does not undergo the ravages of time—as may be seen from the enduring splendor of the heavens.[31]

All living things in the original creation, according to the Talmud, came into being in their full maturity.[32] Consistent with this position is the belief that Adam and Eve were created already in the full mental and physical perfection that others reach in adulthood.

Adam's original nature was extraordinary. He was gifted with a superb intelligence, capable of naming all the animals, of recognizing his own identity, and of addressing God as Lord.[33]

The Talmud pictures Adam as remaining in his original condition for only a short time, perhaps only a few hours before he sinned. Before he offended his Maker, Adam was so gifted he might have been mistaken for a god.[34] He could listen to the voice of the Lord gladly and without fear, because he had not yet turned a deaf ear to Yahweh.[35] God had personally urged him to be faithful, and promised him immortality, even as Elijah was later to earn his.[36] Had he remained faithful, he together with Eve were destined to rule over the rest of creation.[37]

Sustained loyalty to God would have meant unspoiled happiness for him and all his descendants, with continued enjoyment of the delights of Eden.[38] This theme pervades the Talmud, with the wistful reflection on a still innocent Adam, and on the joys that might have been.

The Talmud uniformly teaches that sin began with the disobedience of Adam to the divine precept, and it has continued historically ever since. Equally uniform is the belief that the first transgression took the form of eating the fruit of some proscribed plant, though opinion varies on its precise nature. The fig, the vine, and wheat are mentioned, with perhaps most rabbinic authorities favoring the vine in view of the havoc which the fruit of this plant has since caused in the world.[39]

Outside of Adam and before him was Satan, who led Adam through Eve to disobey God. The idea of a celestial fall of rebellious angels, before Adam, is certainly known in the Talmud. But it belongs more exclusively to the apocalyptic Jewish tradition. What is clear in the Talmud is that Satan has the triple role, since Adam's time, of seducer, accuser, and destroyer of men. He seduces them into sin, then charges them before God, and finally, by divine permission, destroys them in punishment for their sins.[40]

Some Talmudic passages try to excuse Adam's sin, or at least to minimize his guilt. They point out how many crimes his progeny has committed in contrast to only one known sin of Adam. But the general impression is that his sin was grave in the extreme, that he was ungrateful to God, and brought death into the world where only life and happiness might have obtained.[41]

What rabbinic theology does not say, and Orthodox Judaism accordingly, is that *because* of Adam's sin, *therefore* all his posterity are sinners too. The sin of Adam was original, indeed, because it was the first. After him all other men have been sinners, but not because of any direct dependence on his transgression of the divine law.

Man's sinfulness, therefore, is seen rather as the result of his own personal deviation from the moral law, apart from any inherited sin as understood in traditional Christian thought. Yet the ancient rabbis also recognized that man has a strong proneness to evil. A popular theory, still in vogue among the Orthodox, is the idea that every person is born with an inclination to evil. *Yetzer ha-ra* it is called. Some say it enters man's nature as he leaves the womb; others claim it is in man already in the womb.[42] This is balanced, or at least coexistent, with a good impulse, the *yetzer ha-tobh*—but only after a child reaches adolescence, when he undertakes the responsibility of keeping the Torah.

Satan enters the conflict and aggravates the situation by tempting men on the side of their basest inclinations.

Yet in all this struggle, people are considered free and responsive agents. When they sin they are guilty because they need not have done wrong—either against God or against their fellowmen.

Talmudic ethics is sometimes described in such legalistic terms as to seem almost unreal. No doubt many passages to support this view can be quoted. But they should be weighed against an equally impressive series of texts that reflect a different attitude. These texts portray a deep inward, spiritual, contrite conception of sin. In a word, the rabbis were not all legalists.

Corresponding to his sins was man's capacity for atonement, which is a key concept in Orthodox Judaism. Thus if a man had transgressed the moral law, he could also expiate—and the expiation was possible either privately or publicly, whether by oneself or through another. Vicarious atonement was essential to the Jewish theology of sin.

So true is this notion of vicarious merit or satisfaction that without it a whole area of the historic Jewish faith is unintelligible. Thus when the high priest officiated in the Holy of Holies on the Day of Atonement, he was credited with sufficient merit for many people.[43] The whole exodus was supposedly achieved because of the great merits of the tribe of Levi.[44]

Among the holy ones whose virtue was meritorious, none stood higher than the patriarchs, with Abraham, Moses, and Aaron the most powerful before God.[45] Time and again, the combined merits of the fathers of the faithful are said to be effective and all but infinite.[46] On occasion, a counterpoise was recommended, like the role of the patriarchs as intercessors for Israel and not as automatic deliverers of their people from the bondage of sin. But the general attitude was to consider the great men of Israel paragons of loyalty to Yahweh, whose holiness was one reason why God blessed his people.

Two main conceptions of human immortality are traceable in Rabbinic Judaism. One is the essentially Hebrew idea of the resurrection of the body, and the other is the more Hellenistic notion of an immortal spirit. While the former may be more originally Jewish, there is plenty of evidence that the Greek concept has deeply influenced the Talmud and Midrash, although it has been reshaped in the process along more Judaic lines.

Belief in souls or spirits was nothing new in Judaism, as seen in numerous passages of the Old Testament. Daniel, for example, teaches resurrection either to happiness or to punishment, according to one's conduct during his life on earth.[47] So too, portions of the Psalms, together with Job and Ecclesiastes teach the redemption of the soul from Sheol by the Lord.[48] Well before the Christian era, certainly Pharisaic Judaism recognized both aspects of immortality. If the Sadducees remained hostile to the idea of conscious survival after death, this lasted only as long as they had a temple and a voice in the religion of Israel. And all the while they were branded by their rivals as heretics. Talmudists recall how a Sadducee might be forced to avow his belief in the resurrection when reading the Amidah in the synagogue, in which one of the benedictions professed belief in life after death.

By and large, the Talmud offers little assurance of a blissful immortality to anyone but Jews. Israel is the heir of heaven or, at most, those who are Jewish proselytes. All Jews should have this hope, as their birthright; yet they can exclude themselves by certain sins, including the denial of the resurrection as taught in the Pentateuch.[49] Individual Gentiles to whom salvation is conceded are generally described as having practiced extraordinary virtue, or been specially good to the Jews, or abstained from forbidden food as prescribed in the Mosaic law.[50]

In its understanding of immortality, Rabbinic Judaism practically identified the afterlife with a resurrected body rather than in terms of an immortal soul. Certainly the distinction between body and soul is well known in rabbinic literature. The soul of man first meant the breath which gives him life; it was the animating principle he shares with the lower organisms. Then it came to mean his whole personality. Then two aspects of personality were differentiated: such functions as breathing, eating, and reproduction (in common with animals), and operations of a higher order like thought and affection, by which a man becomes aware of God and loves his Creator. This higher activity was attributed to the spirit. Some Talmudists spoke of the spirit as only the noblest part of the soul; others said it was separate. According to the first explanation man's nature is a dichotomy of body and soul; on the second view, it is a trichotomy of body, soul, and spirit. The second view allowed for God's action on the soul beyond its native capacities.

While aware of all these subtleties, the Talmudists preferred to speak of immortal life apart from them—and simply talk about the resurrection of the body. In so doing they left the impression that life after death would include the whole man, and not just a part of him.

Only God can raise the dead. The Midrash explains this by appealing to the opening of the graves in Ezekiel, and adding that no one but he holds the key to human life.[51] Following up the suggestion of Hosea, it is stated that resurrection will take place after three days. A Midrashic commentator says that this period is to be counted "from the beginning of the final judgment."[52] Accordingly death would mean lapsing into unconsciousness until being raised in final judgment. There is, however, another tradition which postulates immediate entrance at death into conscious immortal life; but this view is less common.

Punishment for the wicked in Ge-Hinnam (Greek *Gehenna*) differs according to different writers in the Talmud. Some are annihilated.[53] Others suffer for varying periods and with diminishing intensity.[54] Still others, very few, are consigned to eternal torments.[55]

One of the clearest passages in the Talmud distinguishes three classes of persons at the final judgment: those entering Paradise immediately, those temporarily in hell, and those who suffer eternally.

The School of Shammai say, "On the day of judgment there will be three classes, one consisting of the perfectly righteous, one of the perfectly wicked, and one of the intermediates." The first are straightway inscribed and sealed for perfect life, and the third are likewise straightway sealed for Gehinnom, as it is said, "And many of them that sleep in the dust of the earth shall awake, some to everlasting life and some to shame and everlasting contempt" (Daniel 12:2).

The intermediates descend to Gehinnom, and cry out, as it is said "And I will bring the third part through the fire, and will refine them as silver is refined, and will try them as gold is tried." They shall call on my name, and I will hear them. I will say, "It is my people." And they shall say, "the Lord is my God." And of them Hannah said, "the Lord it is that slays and quickens; though He brings down to Sheol, He raises up" (I Samuel 2:6).[56]

Paradise, as the abode of the just after the resurrection, is an integral part of the Talmudic faith. It clearly distinguishes between the Messianic age and the world to come. In spite of occasional obscurity on the point, the Messianic age is simply a period of special worldly prosperity for Israel under a divinely chosen leader, whereas Paradise belongs to eschatology. It is the promise of unending joy after the sorrows and trials of this life.

Two main views of heaven are found in Rabbinic Judaism. The more spiritual explanation says that whatever people enjoy in the flesh in this life will have no place in the life to come. In that higher life there will be no eating, drinking, or procreation; and all the baser emotions will be done away with.[57]

A more bodily theory teaches just the opposite. Paradise is one long celestial banquet, with food and drink like people enjoy on earth—only in greater abundance and producing greater satiety. A blissful privilege is the absence of any bad side effects, commonly associated with overindulgence.[58]

The two attitudes are not uncommon in other religious traditions. What is perhaps unique is the close correlation between what a man did on earth and what he gets in the life to come. Merit and demerit, sometimes measured almost mathematically, are intrinsic to Talmudic eschatology.

When Maimonides came to codify Jewish belief about man and his destiny, he did very little except to clarify the concepts, and remove some of the legalistic debris that had piled up in the Talmud in a thousand years and then conveniently incorporate the principles into his thirteen articles of faith. Four of these deal directly with man's nature as a contingent being and his destiny in a life after death.

"I believe," according to Maimonides, "that it is right to pray to the Creator and to Him alone, and it is not right to pray to any being besides Him."[59] This injunction places man in immediate dependence on God alone and defines one of the most characteristic features of modern Judaism as distinct, say, from Christianity. No mediation is permissible or conceivable whether of a human being (like a priest), or of spiritual beings (like angels), or of a divinely authorized institution (like the Church).

Needless to say, this is a departure from pre-Christian Judaism which recognized the role of priests who offered sacrifice for the people as their intermediaries with God; who believed in the intercessory powers of angels, described in the rejected book of Tobias: and accepted the mediatorial office of the great men of Israel to atone for the sins of their nation.

Maimonides' position is now practically uniform in the Jewish religion. No one less than God may be the object of prayer. No angel or priest, no saint or sacred institution should "be considered as intermediaries between God and man, whereby mankind may approach closer to God. Only through the Deity Himself can our thoughts and emotions be sanctified."[60]

While some Orthodox Jews are ready to exclude vicarious atonement and priestly mediation on principle, this is rare. Their synagogue prayers regularly address God, "who rememberest the

good deeds of our fathers (Abraham, Isaac and Jacob)." But
the "holy ones" whose merits are invoked are of old; they are not
the consecrated men of God today, nor is the sacrifice now offered
that which the Jews formerly made in the Temple in Jerusalem.

One of the saddest prayers of the Jewish liturgy occurs in the
Morning Service, when the past is recalled with sorrow.

> Lord of the universe, thou hast commanded us to sacrifice
> the daily offering at its proper time with priests officiating,
> Levites [singing] on the platform, and lay representatives of
> Israel attending the Temple service. Now, through our sins the
> Temple is destroyed, the daily offering is abolished, and we
> have neither priest officiating, nor Levite [singing] on the plat-
> form, nor Israelites attending the Temple service.
>
> However, thou hast declared that we may substitute the
> prayer of our lips for the sacrifice of bullocks. Therefore, may
> it be thy will, Lord our God and God of our fathers, that the
> prayer of our lips be favorably regarded and accepted by thee
> as if we offered the daily offering at its proper time and at-
> tended at its service.[61]

In the same Maimonidean tradition, Orthodox Jewry accepts
his belief that "the Creator knows every deed of the children of
men, and all their thoughts," so that God "rewards those who keep
His commandments and punishes those who transgress them."[62] It
is the ancient covenant applied to all mankind.

Nothing could be plainer than the moral responsibility that
each person has for his own conduct, and the corresponding retribution from Yahweh. But where Maimonides placed so much stress
on man's freedom as almost to have made him the master of his
destiny, present-day Jews who strictly follow the Torah favor a less
Pelagian view. For Maimonides, "Every human being may become
righteous like Moses, or wicked like Jeroboam. . . . This means that
the power is in your hands, and whatever a man desires to do
among the things that human beings do, he can do, whether they
are good or evil. . . . We are convinced that our Law agrees with
Greek philosophy, which substantiates with convincing proofs the
contention that man's conduct is entirely in his own hands."[63]

For today's Orthodox Jew, his daily and Sabbath prayers tell a different story. Page after page of the Prayer Book pleads with the Lord to help his people, to deliver them from trial, strengthen them in temptation, and support their native inability to carry out his will as he demands.

Thou favorest man with knowledge, and teachest mortals understanding. O grant us knowledge, understanding and insight. . . .

Restore us, our Father, to thy Torah; draw us near, our King, to thy service; cause us to return to thee in perfect repentance. . . .

Forgive us, our Father, for we have sinned; pardon us, our King, for we have transgressed; for thou dost pardon and forgive. . . .

Heal us O Lord, and we shall be healed; save us and we shall be saved; for thou art our praise. Grant a perfect healing to all our wounds.[64]

On the nature of man's destiny after death, however, Maimonides was more clear than most Jews, at least in America, even among the Orthodox. His article on eschatology is somewhat ambiguous, saying simply that "there will be a resurrection of the dead at the time when it shall please the Creator."[65] But his commentaries leave no doubt.

The resurrection of the dead is a cardinal point of our religion universally acknowledged by our people, incorporated in our prayers, and to which the Talmud frequently reverts—is capable of no other interpretation than the literal. It would therefore be unJewish to disbelieve that the soul will be reunited with the body, for there has been no dissenting voice raised against it among our nation. The resurrection of the dead, or the reunion of the soul with the body, is mentioned in Daniel (12:2), couched in such words that it is impossible to render them otherwise than according to the very letter, "And many of them that sleep in the dust of the earth shall awake, some to everlasting life, and some to reproach and everlasting abhorrance."

When we peruse the Bible, we discover that it abounds in passages that gainsay the resurrection of the dead. For instance, "Shall a man die and live again? (Job 14:14) . . . Shall the dead rise again and praise thee? (Psalm 30:10) . . ."

We maintain that whenever biblical expressions are in opposition to the dogma of the resurrection, they simply describe natural causes and effects and do not by any means subvert a creed universally accepted because the Almighty can, at His will, infuse new life into dead bodies.[66]

There are not many Jewish writers today who subscribe as firmly as did Maimonides to a real, corporeal reunion of man's spirit with his body on the day of resurrection.

The nearest approximation is in the Orthodox liturgy, where God is invoked as the Lord of the living and the dead.

Thou, O Lord, art mighty forever; thou revivest the dead, thou art powerful to save.

Thou art faithful to revive the dead.

Blessed art thou, O Lord, who restorest the souls of the dead.[67]

God, in his great mercy, will revive the dead. Blessed be his glorious name forever.[68]

A safe estimate is that many Jews of the Orthodox persuasion still believe in a bodily resurrection from the dead. But the inroads of the Reform, which denies the resurrection of the body, have made their influence felt across the spectrum of Jewish theological thought. On this critical article of faith, then, "Whoever still sees God's greatness, as they (the Rabbis of old) did, revealed through miracles, that is, through interruptions of the natural order of life, may cling to the traditional belief in resurrection, so comforting in ancient times. On the other hand, he who recognizes the unchangeable will of an all-wise, all-ruling God in the immutable laws of nature must find it impossible to praise God according to the traditional formula as the 'resurrection of the dead.' "[69] He will prefer the less creedal statement found in most books of the liturgy, where "eternal life" is substituted for the "resurrection" or even referring to God, "He who has implanted within us immortal life."

MESSIANIC HOPE

Jews of every theological level look forward to a new era and expect a new age to dawn in which they will somehow be the divine instruments of redemption. Depending on how strong their biblical faith, this expectation is rooted in the predictions of a Messiah made by the ancient prophets.

Among the Orthodox, the Messianic hope is clear: God will one day send his Anointed One to earth. Indeed Judaism differs essentially from Christianity in this fact: that where the followers of Jesus of Nazareth believe he is the Messiah (Greek *Christos*) Jews are still waiting for the Mashijach (Hebrew for *Anointed One*) to come. The very name *Christianity* literally means "Messianity" already fulfilled in the person of Mary's Son.

Rabbinic teaching on the Messiah falls mainly into two classes. One theory places God in complete control while denying any role to man in the Messianic mission; the other takes an opposite stand and says that everything depends on man's conduct.

The predestinarian view says the Messiah will not come until all the full complement of persons destined to be born has been attained.[70] Variously expressed, the general idea is the same: God knows the time and the circumstances and nothing that men do can alter the divine decree.

Also in the Talmud is the contrary opinion, that the time when the Messiah will come is directly influenced by how people believe and behave themselves. Understandably this attitude is more popular and has deeply affected the piety of the faithful. Every precept properly fulfilled hastens the Messiah's coming.[71] A single Sabbath rightly observed—it seems by the whole community of Israel—would bring the Anointed One into the world.[72] One day's universal repentance would do the same.[73]

Opinions also differ on the character of the Messiah. Several passages in the Talmud would seem to make him essentially the same as other men, though even then comparable to Abraham and Job.[74] But a strong theme in the rabbinic literature declares that the Name of the Messiah existed before the world.[75]

Maimonides cut through rabbinic speculation and gave the Jews a realistic picture of the Messianic age. The Messiah will certainly be a king of the house of David who will gather together the scattered people of Israel. But his coming will not radically change the course of human history.

King Messiah will arise and restore the kingdom of David to its former state and original sovereignty. He will rebuild the sanctuary and gather the dispersed of Israel. All the ancient laws will be reinstated in his days: sacrifices will again be offered; the Sabbatical and Jubilee years will again be observed in accordance with the commandments set forth in the Law.

He who does not believe in the restoration or does not look forward to the coming of the Messiah denies not only the teachings of the Prophets but also those of the Law of Moses, our teacher, for Scripture affirms the rehabilitation of Israel, as it is said: "Then the Lord thy God will turn thy captivity, and have compassion upon thee, and will return and gather thee . . . if any of thine that are dispersed be in the uttermost parts of heaven . . . and the Lord thy God will bring thee unto the land which thy fathers possessed" (Deut. 30:3, 4, 5). These words stated in Scripture include all that the Prophets said . . . The prophecy in that section bears upon the two Messiahs: the first, namely, David, who saved Israel from the hand of their enemies; and the later Messiah, a descendant of David, who will achieve the final salvation.[76]

A careful distinction should be made, however, between the age of the Messiah and the final consummation of the world. The first will occur in this life, the second in the life to come.

All Israelites, their Prophets and Sages, longed for the advent of Messianic times, that they might have relief from the wicked tyranny that does not permit them properly to occupy themselves with the study of the Torah and the observance of the commandments; that they might have ease, devote themselves to getting wisdom, and thus attain to life in the World to Come. Because the King who will arise from the seed of David will possess more wisdom than Solomon and will be a great Prophet, approaching Moses, our teacher, he will teach the whole of the Jewish people and instruct them in the way of God; and all nations will come to hear him, as it is said, "and at the end of days it shall come to pass that the mount of the Lord's house shall be established as the top of the mountains" (Micah 4:1, Is. 2:2). The ultimate and perfect reward, the final bliss which will suffer neither interruption nor diminution is the life in the World to Come. The Messianic Era, on the other hand, will be realized in this world; which will continue in its normal course except that independent sovereignty will be restored to Israel. The ancient Sages already said, "The only difference between the present and the Messianic Era is that political oppression will then cease."[77]

The Anointed One to come will be recognized by his conduct. His lineage will be Davidic but only his virtue will give assurance that he is the one of whom David prophesied that of his loins would come the one to deliver Israel.

If there arise a king from the House of David who meditates on the Torah, occupies himself with the commandments, as did his ancestor David, observes the precepts prescribed in the Written and the Oral Law, prevails upon Israel to walk in the way of the Torah and to repair its breaches, and fights the battles of the Lord, it may be assumed that he is the Messiah. If he does things and succeeds, rebuilds the sanctuary on its site, and gathers the dispersed of Israel, he is beyond all doubt the Messiah. He will prepare the whole world to serve the Lord with one accord, as it is written: "For then will I turn to the peoples a pure language, that they may call upon the name of the Lord to serve Him with one consent" (Zeph. 3:9).[78]

Maimonides had no doubt the Messiah would appear one day. His twelfth article of the Jewish creed professed, "I believe with perfect faith in the coming of the Messiah, and though he tarry I will wait daily for him." To forestall the impatience of his people, their greatest theologian warned not to take the prophecies too literally, for example, the prediction that Elijah would precede the Anointed One of the Lord.

Some of our Sages say that the coming of Elijah will precede the advent of the Messiah. But no one is in a position to
know the details of this and similar things until they have come
to pass. They are not publicly stated by the Prophets. Nor have
the Rabbis any tradition with regard to these matters. They
are guided solely by what the Scripture texts seem to imply.
Hence there is a divergence of opinions on the subject. But be
that as it may, neither the exact sequence of these events nor
the details thereof constitute religious dogmas. No one should
ever occupy himself with the legendary themes nor spend
much time on midrashic statements bearing on this and like
subjects. He should not deem them of prime importance, since
they lead neither to the fear of God nor to the love of Him.
Nor should one calculate the end. Said the Rabbis: "Blasted be
those who reckon out the end" (San. 97b). One should wait
[for his coming] and accept in principle this article of faith, as
we have stated before.[79]

Challenged by Christianity, the Jews asked themselves what
kind of person the Messiah was supposed to be, and whether he
would perform such signs and wonders as at least the prophets of
old were known to have done. No, the One to come was not to be
a miracle worker, nor should Israel anticipate such a deliverer. Obedience to the Law, unchanged and unchangeable, is the hallmark
of Messiahship; peace and fidelity to Yahweh is the promise of the
Messianic day.

Do not think that the Anointed King must give signs and
miracles and create new things in this world, or bring the dead
back to life, and the like. It will not be so. For see: Rabbi
Akiva, who was a great sage among the sages of the Mishnah,
it was he who carried arms for ben Koziba, the king, and it was
he who said of him that he was the Anointed King. He and all
the sages of his generation thought that this was the Anointed
King, until he was slain in his guilt. And after he was slain,
they all knew that he was not the Anointed King. But never
had the sages asked him for a sign or for miracles. The root of
these things is the following: This Torah, its statutes and its

laws are for all times. There is nothing one could add to it, and nothing one could take away. . . .

Do not think in your heart that in the days of the Anointed something will be changed in the ways of the world, or that an innovation will appear in the work of creation. No. The world will go its ways as before, and that which is said in Isaiah, "The wolf shall dwell with the lamb, and the leopard shall lie down with the kid" [Isa. 11:6], is but a parable, and its meaning is that Israel will dwell in safety with the wicked among the heathen, and all will turn to the true faith; they will not rob nor destroy, and they will eat only what is permitted, in peace, like Israel, as it is written, "The lion shall eat straw like the ox" [Isa. 11:71]. And everything else like this that is said concerning the Anointed, is also a parable. In the days of the Anointed all will know what the parable signified and what it was meant to imply.[80]

But if there will be no physical portents announcing the Messianic age, there are promised changes in the moral order and in the status of Israel with respect to the Gentile nations.

Said the Rabbis: "The sole difference between the present and the Messianic days is deliverance from servitude to foreign powers" (Sanhedrin 91b).

The sages and the prophets did not yearn for the days of the Anointed in order to seize upon the world, and not in order to rule over the heathen, or to be exalted by the peoples, or to eat and drink and rejoice, but to be free for the Torah and the wisdom within it, free from any goading and intrusion, so that they may be worthy of life in the coming world.

When that time is here, none will go hungry, there will be no war, no jealousy and no conflict, for goodness will flow abundantly, and all delights will be plentiful as the numberless motes of dust, and the whole world will be solely intent on the knowledge of the Lord. Therefore those of Israel will be great sages, who know what is hidden, and they will attain what knowledge of their Creator it is in man's power to attain, as it is written, "For the earth shall be full of the knowledge of the Lord, as the waters cover the sea" [Isa. 11:9].[81]

Always in Maimonides the Messianic hope is balanced with a strong realism, as much as to say: "Yes, he is coming. But be patient, do not expect drastic changes and, above all, do not look for him too soon." The proviso, in the Maimonidean creed, about believing that the Anointed One will come, "though he tarry," was a warning to the anxious not to anticipate the day of the Lord.

Modern Orthodoxy inherited this prudential attitude toward the Messiah and, until recent years, gave it no more prospect of early realization than the Jews in North Africa for whom Maimonides wrote in the twelfth century.

A change took place with the rise of modern Zionism, when the chances of a Jewish resettlement of Palestine began to look more promising.

Among the leaders responsible for the change, Rabbi Tzevi Hirsch Kalischer (1795-1874) is credited with having inspired the *Hibbat Zion* (love of Zion) which made Zionism a function of the Messianic dream.

A strong opponent of the Reform, the Prussian Kalischer proclaimed (1832) that the redemption of the Jews from oppression would come through national agencies. He saw in the return of his people to Palestine their best opportunity for once again offering sacrifice to Yahweh, and to this end he advocated the formation of a Jewish farming community in Palestine. Kalischer strongly influenced the thinking of Moses Hess (1812-1875), the Zionist precursor who broke with Karl Marx over the latter's materialist interpretation of history. Hess' *Rome and Jerusalem* (1862) was the first Zionist classic which explicitly stated or suggested all the main ideas of present-day Zionism and the ideology which created the State of Israel.

Kalischer at first seems to differ from Maimonides in admitting that the Messiah will usher in a miraculous age. He cautions against expecting everything to happen at once.

> The redemption of Israel, for which we long, is not to be imagined as a sudden miracle. The Almighty, praised be His name, will not suddenly descend from on high and command His people to go forth. He will not send His Messiah from heaven in a twinkling of an eye, to sound the great trumpet for

the scattered of Israel and gather them into Jerusalem. He will not surround the Holy City with a wall of fire or cause the Holy Temple to descend from the heavens. The bliss and the miracles that were promised by His servants, the prophets, will certainly come to pass—everything will be fulfilled—but we will not run in terror and flight, for the redemption of Israel will come by slow degrees and the ray of deliverance will shine forth gradually.

Cast aside the conventional view that the Messiah will suddenly sound a blast on the great trumpet and cause all the inhabitants of the earth to tremble. On the contrary, the Redemption will begin by awakening support among the philanthropists and by gaining the consent of the nations to the gathering of some of the scattered of Israel into the Holy Land.[82]

Is there a reason why the Messiah will not come in a sudden burst of phenomena? Kalischer finds the reason in God's centuries-old way of acting with his people. It is always through suffering to glory.

Can we logically explain why the Redemption will begin in a natural manner and why the Lord, in His love for His people, will not immediately send the Messiah in an obvious miracle? Yes we can. We know that all our worship of God is in the form of trials by which He tests us. When God created man and placed him in the Garden of Eden, He also planted the Tree of Knowledge and then commanded man not to eat of it. Why did He put the Tree in the Garden, if not as a trial? . . . When Israel went forth from Egypt, God again tested man's faith with hunger and thirst along the way. . . . Throughout the days of our dispersion we have been dragged from land to land and have borne the yoke of martyrdom for the sanctity of God's name; we have been dragged from land to land and have borne the yoke of exile through the ages, all for the sake of His holy Torah and as a further stage of the testing of our faith.[83]

Consistent with the spirit of Zionism, whose leaders made heroic sacrifices to achieve their goal, Kalischer tells his people to trust and labor and wait. In his own time, God will bring Israel back to Palestine. On their part, the Jews must make a beginning, by slow stages, to resettle in the land given to Moses and the Chosen Race.

If the Almighty would suddenly appear, one day in the future, through undeniable miracles, this would be no trial. What straining of our faith would there be in the face of miracles and wonders attending a clear and heavenly command to go up and inherit the land and enjoy its good fruit? Only a natural beginning of the Redemption is a true test of those who initiate it. To concentrate all one's energy on this holy work and to renounce home and fortune for the sake of living in Zion before "the voice of gladness" and "the voice of joy" are heard—there is no greater merit or trial than this. . . .

For all this to come about there must first be Jewish resettlement in the Land; without such settlement, how can the gathering begin?[84]

Now that the nation of Israel is a reality, how do the Jews of strict observance look upon what has occurred, and how do their Messianic aspirations appear?

The best index seems to be their current forms of liturgy, replete with invocations for the Messiah and—for the first time in two millennia—with prayers for the State of Israel.

It is impossible to read more than a dozen consecutive pages in their *Prayer Book for Sabbath and Festivals* without coming on at least an implicit reference to the Messiah and his kingdom. Certain features in these prayers predominate: the Messiah will be of the family of David, he will inaugurate a new era of peace for Israel, Jerusalem will be rebuilt, the ancient ritual will be reestablished, the expected deliverer is to be the Anointed One, his character will be somehow transcendent, his advent must be prepared for by repentance and fervent petition, and, in many prayers, the coming of the Messiah is connected (if not identified) with a mysterious coming of God himself.

Return in mercy to the city Jerusalem, as thou hast promised; rebuild it soon, in our days, as an everlasting structure, and speedily establish in it the throne of David. Blessed art thou, O Lord, Builder of Jerusalem.

Speedily cause the offspring of thy servant David to flourish, and let his glory be exalted by thy help, for we hope for thy deliverance all day. Blessed art thou, O Lord, who causest salvation to flourish.

Be pleased, Lord our God, with thy people Israel and with their prayer; restore the worship to thy most holy sanctuary; accept Israel's offerings and prayer with gracious love. May the worship of thy people Israel be ever pleasing to thee.

Our God and God of our father, may the remembrance of us, of our fathers, of Messiah the son of David thy servant, of Jerusalem the holy city, and of all thy people of the house of Israel, ascend and come and be accepted before thee for deliverance and happiness, for grace, kindness and mercy, for life and peace, on this day of the New Moon (the Feast of Unleavened Bread, the Feast of Tabernacles).

May our eyes behold thy return in mercy to Zion. Blessed art thou, O Lord, who restorest thy divine presence to Zion.[85]

In a stirring litany for Sabbath Eve, the people recite a sequence of Messianic invocations, which are interrupted with the refrain: "Lord, eternal Master of worlds, Thou art the supreme King of kings. Thy mighty acts and wondrous deeds it is my pleasure to declare."

O God of glory and greatness, Save thy flock from the lions' jaws; Free thy people from captivity, thy people chosen from all nations.

Return to thy most holy shrine, the place where all souls will rejoice and sing melodic hymns of praise—Jerusalem, city of beauty.[86]

This is followed by the pleas: "Our God, have mercy on thy people, on Zion thy shrine and our splendid home: may David's scion come to redeem us, the Lord's anointed, the breath of our life."[87]

So the prayers go on, each differing only slightly from the next, but they permeate Jewish liturgy like the atmosphere. "May it be thy will," God is begged, "that the Temple be speedily rebuilt in our days and grant us a share in thy Torah. There we will serve thee with reverence, as in the days of old and as in former years. Then the offering of Judah and Jerusalem will be pleasing to the Lord."[88]

On occasion the prayers become almost impatient in their urgency, asking that the kingdom be restored "within the lifetime of the entire house of Israel, speedily and soon."[89] At other times they are more restrained as when the Lord is invoked for grace to keep his laws, and thus make Israel "worthy to live to see and share the happiness and blessing in the Messianic days."[90] In any case, the advent of the Anointed One depends on the earnest prayers and holy lives of his chosen ones.

As the State of Israel came into being in 1948, Jewish hopes were at least partially fulfilled. In the words of Emanuel Celler, dean of the United States House of Representatives under President Lyndon Johnson, "Perhaps one day, free men everywhere will share our exhilaration at the realization of a prophetic dream."[91] To Jews everywhere it is already the Messianic prophecy come true.

The chief rabbinate of Israel has composed a prayer "For the Welfare of the State of Israel." It is recited in Orthodox synagogues throughout America.

> Our Father who art in heaven, Protector and Redeemer of Israel, bless thou the State of Israel which marks the dawn of our deliverance. Shield it beneath the wings of thy love; spread over it thy canopy of peace; send thy light and thy truth to its leaders, officers and counselors, and direct them with thy good counsel.
>
> O God, strengthen the defenders of our Holy Land; grant them salvation and crown them with victory. Establish peace in the land, and everlasting joy for its inhabitants.
>
> Remember our brethren, the whole house of Israel, in all the lands of their dispersion. Speedily let them walk upright to Zion thy city, to Jerusalem thy dwelling-place, as it is written in the Torah of thy servant Moses: "Even if you are dispersed

in the uttermost parts of the world, from there the Lord your God will gather and fetch you. The Lord your God will bring you into the land which your fathers possessed, and you shall possess it" (Deuteronomy 30:4-5).

Unite our heart to love and revere thy name, and to observe all the precepts of thy Torah. Shine forth in thy glorious majesty over all the inhabitants of thy world. Let everything that breathes proclaim: "The Lord God of Israel is King; his majesty rules over all." Amen.[92]

Orthodox Jews look upon the State of Israel as the dawn of their Messianic deliverance, and on those outside Palestine as still in the lands of dispersion. But even the least Torah-conscious feel that a new era has opened for Judaism throughout the world.

IV

REFORM JUDAISM

The early history of the Reform movement has already been seen. Its theology is a matter of clear record and dates back to the Pittsburgh Platform of 1885 and the Columbus Platform of 1937. Both documents must be seen together, for the second makes no pretense of supplanting the first. The two combined offer a spectrum of Jewish liberalism that needs to be better known, if only because most Jews in America belong to the Reform persuasion. Their number exceeds the known membership in Reform synagogues.

PITTSBURGH PLATFORM

When the Pittsburgh profession of faith was drawn up, Judaism was struggling for acceptance in America. Kaufmann Kohler, who organized the meeting, told the assembled rabbis that "Mosaic-

Rabbinical Judaism, as based on the Law and Tradition, has actually and irrevocably lost its hold on the modern Jew."[1] The only course open was to reassess the meaning of Judaism and challenge its archaic concept of a once-for-all religion that ignores the passage of time. Judaism, the rabbis were told, is a historical growth. Unless Jews find the focus for all its emanations and manifestations and discover its essence, they cannot hope to survive in the melting pot of American culture.

In a series of eight principles, the Pittsburgh manifesto outlined this essence—always conscious of the pressure under which American Judaism labored to show forth its distinctiveness without appearing to be a nation within a nation.

"Judaism," it was affirmed, "presents the highest conception of the God-idea."[2] Its Bible is, indeed, archaic, as "reflecting the primitive ideas of its own age."[3] Mosaic legislation served its purpose in days gone by, for "training the Jewish people for its mission during its national life in Palestine."[4] Nowadays, Jews should be free to reject all such moral laws and ceremonies "as are not adapted to the views and habits of modern civilization."

Similarly all the laws regulating diet, priestly purity, and dress were useful in ages past but "under the influence of ideas altogether foreign to our present mental and spiritual state."[5] Above all the Messianic hope must no longer be viewed in national or ethnic terms.

> We recognize in the modern era of universal culture of heart and intellect the approach of Israel's great Messianic hope for the establishment of the kingdom of truth, justice and peace among all men. We consider ourselves no longer a nation but a religious community, and therefore expect neither a return to Palestine, nor a sacrificial worship under the administration of the sons of Aaron, nor the restoration of any of the laws concerning the Jewish state.[6]

On a very ecumenical note, and consistent with this definition of Israel as not a nation but a religious community, "Christianity and Islam being daughter religions of Judaism," are welcome as partners in "their mission and aid in the spread of monotheistic and moral truth."[7]

While it is admitted that "the soul of man is immortal," no further explanation of immortal belief is given. Moreover, "we reject as ideas not rooted in Judaism the belief both in bodily resurrection and in Gehenna and Eden (hell and paradise), as abodes for everlasting punishment or reward."[8]

With eschatology removed, Reform Jews agreed to do all they could on a terrestrial plane, "to regulate the relation between rich and poor" and to help solve "the problem presented by the contrasts and evils of the present organization of society."[9]

In the discussion that followed, someone urged that the phrase "divine revelation" be inserted in the second principle, when referring to the Bible. The recommendation was rejected, on the grounds that the Reform rabbinate does not believe "what is generally supposed to have occurred at Sinai," that "revelation leads us into the domain of mysticism," that revelation is "like socialism, a tabooed word," and that "revelation through genius, individual or collective, organically developed, none of us rejects, but the technical term does not convey this meaning."[10] So the original, ambivalent term *consecration* was left unchanged.

In the same spirit, the Pittsburgh Platform went beyond the Philadelphia declaration on the future life. Resurrection had already been dropped at Philadelphia, "but eternal punishment and Paradise pleasure must also be discarded." The motive behind this decision was that "we cannot urge too strongly that righteousness is its own reward, and wrong-doing carries with it its own punishment and that work is the aim of life," not some pretended reward in the life to come.[11]

When publishing the Pittsburgh Platform, its authors threw down the gauntlet to their more orthodox Jewish confreres. In the most incisive language possible, they publicly told the more believing segment of American Jewry that they, the Reform, were now true Judaism, and all the rest were sectarian and heterodox.

That "Declaration of Principles" presents a particular feature which must not be overlooked. It declares, by its tone and position, that we, the much abused reformers, radicals, decried, defamed and debased by the men of the minority who usurped for themselves the titles of conservative and orthodox, or rather the Jews par excellence—we ARE the orthodox Jews in America, and they WERE the orthodoxy of former days and other countries. We can see no good reason why we should ogle you, allow you to act as a brake to the wheel of progress, and confirm you in your pretensions. You do not represent the ideas and sentiments of the American Jews, this phase upon which Judaism entered in this country, you are an anachronism, strangers in this country, and to your own brethren. You represent yourselves, together with a past age and a foreign land. We must proceed without you to perform our duties to God, and our country, and our religion, for WE are the orthodox Jews in America.[12]

As might have been expected this provoked a reaction, not only among rabbis, but from Ethical Culture. The more conservative Jews interpreted the Reform statement as "an insult" to traditional Judaism and proceeded to sever their relations with the Union of American Hebrew Congregations. Those who drafted the statement and their disciples were labeled a "sectarian movement." Hebrew Union College was declared unfit to receive financial support, seeing that its function was to "educate disciples of that new party."[13]

Felix Adler, founder of Ethical Culture, criticized the Platform from a different perspective. He saw in the Jewish Reform an exact parallel with Christian liberalism, which began with an appeal to reason and ended with a denial of religion.

> The leaders of the Reformed Jews were anxious to find a warrant for the changes which they considered necessary; they sought authority for their innovations; they endeavored to harmonize the old with the new, and cutting off what they deemed ephemeral and transitory, they were only the more solicitous to preserve the things which in their estimation were essential and fundamental in Judaism. But have they succeeded in so doing? If we contemplate the history of Reform Judaism during the past fifty years, we perceive a process of disintegration like that in liberal Christian churches. As in liberal Christianity one element of faith after another has been eliminated, so

in liberal Judaism one layer of the law after another has been removed. At first the rabbinical laws were rejected, and the authority of the Talmud was often invoked for so doing. Then the Talmud was put aside, and the cry was raised for a return to the pure, unadulterated religion of the Bible. At last it became evident that the Biblical standard, too, is no longer applicable to modern conditions; the authenticity of the Books of Moses was doubted; it was denied that a Law had ever been revealed on Sinai, and a final appeal was made from the letter to the spirit of the Bible, and this is all that is left of Judaism in the hands of the Reformers—the spirit of the Bible. But the "spirit of the Bible" is an elastic phrase which may mean a great deal or nothing at all.[14]

Adler concluded with the suggestion that Reform Judaism join the Unitarians. Having outlawed Torah and reduced the Bible to a product of mere human genius, "what possible reason is there why this step should not be taken?"[15] The old lines of separation must be wiped out, he insisted—at the risk of no longer being able to recognize an authentic Jew.

COLUMBUS PLATFORM

Fifty years in the history of Judaism is not a long time. But the half-century after the Reform movement in America formulated its position was unlike anything in previous Jewish history.

Jewish migrations to the United States had shifted to the diaspora to America. Zionism had grown in momentum and the rise of National Socialism in Germany posed a threat to Jewish life and freedom such as the Israelites had not experienced since the days of Nebuchadnezzar and the Emperor Titus.

Two events especially changed the course of modern Judaism, the Balfour Declaration of 1917 and the publication of *Mein Kampf* by Adolf Hitler in 1925.

Arthur Balfour, British secretary of state for foreign affairs, sent Lord Rothschild a memorable letter.

I have much pleasure in conveying to you, on behalf of His Majesty's Government, the following declaration of sympathy with Jewish Zionist aspirations which has been submitted to, and approved by, the Cabinet:—

"His Majesty's Government view with favour the establishment in Palestine of a national home for the Jewish people, and will use their best endeavours to facilitate the achievement of this object, it being clearly understood that nothing shall be done which may prejudice the civil and religious rights of existing non-Jewish communities in Palestine, or the rights and political status enjoyed by Jews in any other country."

I should be most grateful if you would bring this declaration to the knowledge of the Zionist Federation.[16]

Walter Rothschild promptly communicated the message to the Zionist Federation. The document was approved by other Allied governments and incorporated into the Palestine Mandate of 1922, which lasted until May 15, 1948, when the British withdrew and the State of Israel came into existence.

Hitler's book was the master plan for Germany and built on a theme that ran through every chapter of its two massive volumes. It breathed hatred of the Jew, just because he is Jewish, and never tired of repeating the slogan: "In the Jew's life as a parasite in the body of other nations and states, his characteristic is established."[17] Insisting that Jews are a nation within a nation, and not only a religious community, Hitler successfully launched the systematic extermination of the Jewish people that fell under his control. His paranoiac hatred was based on the premise that no country is safe as long as it harbors Jews.

Faced with these two developments, of hope for refuge in Palestine and grief over the mounting genocide under Hitler, the Reform rabbinate in America decided to restate its former position and published at Columbus what is today the definitive statement of the liberal wing of American Judaism. Felix A. Levy, an avowed Zionist, presided over the historic conference.

The Columbus Platform is divided into three parts: Judaism and its foundations, Jewish ethics, and Jewish religious practice. On each of these, the new declaration expanded on the previous declaration and clarified what needed clarification in the light of Jewish experiences in other lands.

Judaism and its foundations

Aware of what hostile critics were saying, the new declaration sought to correct the impression left in 1885, that Judaism was essentially a religion and not an ethnic community. It is both. This means kinship between Jews everywhere, no matter how distantly separated or even how divergent in faith. Israelites have a bond between them which nothing can ever dissolve.

Nature of Judaism. Judaism is the historical religious experience of the Jewish people. Though growing out of Jewish life, its message is universal, aiming at the union and perfection of mankind under the sovereignty of God. Reform Judaism recognizes the principle of progressive development in religion and consciously applies this principle to spiritual as well as to cultural and social life.

Judaism welcomes all truth, whether written in the pages of scripture or deciphered from the records of nature. The new discoveries of science, while replacing the older scientific views underlying our sacred literature, do not conflict with the essential spirit of religion as manifested in the consecration of man's will, heart and mind to the service of God and of humanity.

God. The heart of Judaism and its chief contribution to religion is the doctrine of the One, living God, who rules the world through law and love. In Him all existence has its creative source and mankind its ideal of conduct. Though transcending time and space, He is the indwelling Presence of the world. We worship Him as the Lord of the universe and as our merciful Father.

Man. Judaism affirms that man is created in the Divine image. His spirit is immortal. He is an active co-worker with God. As a child of God, he is endowed with moral freedom and is charged with the responsibility of overcoming evil and striving after ideal ends.

Torah. God reveals Himself not only in the majesty, beauty and orderliness of nature, but also in the vision and moral striving of the human spirit. Revelation is a continuous process, confined to no one group and to no one age. Yet the people of Israel, through its prophets and sages, achieved unique insight in the realm of religious truth. The Torah, both written and oral, enshrines Israel's ever-growing consciousness of God and of the moral law. It preserves the historical precedents, sanctions and norms of Jewish life, and seeks to mould it in the patterns of goodness and of holiness. Being products of historical processes, certain of its laws have lost their binding force with the passing of the conditions that called them forth. But as a depository of permanent spiritual ideals, the Torah remains the dynamic source of the life of Israel. Each age has the obligation to adapt the teachings of the Torah to its basic needs in consonance with the genius of Judaism.

Israel. Judaism is the soul of which Israel is the body. Living in all parts of the world, Israel has been held together by the ties of a common history, and above all, by the heritage of faith. Though we recognize in the group loyalty of Jews who have become estranged from our religious tradition, a bond which still unites them with us, we maintain that it is by its religion and for its religion that the Jewish people has lived. The non-Jew who accepts our faith is welcomed as a full member of the Jewish community.

In all lands where our people live, they assume and seek to share loyally the full duties and responsibilities of citizenship and to create seats of Jewish knowledge and religion. In the rehabilitation of Palestine, the land hallowed by memories and hopes, we behold the promise of renewed life for many of our brethren. We affirm the obligation of all Jewry to aid in its upbuilding as a Jewish homeland by endeavoring to make it not only a haven of refuge for the oppressed but also a center of Jewish culture and spiritual life.

Throughout the ages it has been Israel's mission to witness to the Divine in the face of every form of paganism and materialism. We regard it as our historic task to cooperate with all men in the establishment of the kingdom of God, of universal brotherhood, justice, truth and peace on earth. This is our Messianic goal.[18]

Ethics

On a broader base, the revised profession of faith stated the
role of Judaism in world society. Its mission to mankind is mainly a
moral one; to bring justice and peace among men. The Reform
statement fifty years before was almost apologetic on the subject.
Now the issue is placed into a religious context, and the practice of
justice, as the foundation for peace, is seen as a function of the love
of God.

Coming on the eve of the Second World War, the 1937 Platform urged the elimination of tyranny and the promotion of harmony between nations.

Morals and Religion. In Judaism religion and morality
blend into an indissoluble unity. Seeking God means to strive
after holiness, righteousness and goodness. The love of God is
incomplete without the love of one's fellowmen. Judaism emphasizes the kinship of the human race, the sanctity and worth
of human life and personality and the right of the individual to
freedom and to the pursuit of his chosen vocation. Justice to
all, irrespective of race, sect or class is the inalienable right and
the inescapable obligation of all. The state and organized government exist in order to further these ends.

Social Justice. Judaism seeks the attainment of a just society by the application of its teachings to the economic order,
to industry and commerce, and to national and international
affairs. It aims at the elimination of man-made misery and suffering, of poverty and degradation, of tyranny and slavery, of
social inequality and prejudice, of ill-will and strife. It advo-
cates the promotion of harmonious relations between warring
classes on the basis of equity and justice, and the creation of
conditions under which human personality may flourish. It
pleads for the safeguarding of childhood against exploitation.
It champions the cause of all who work and of their right to an
adequate standard of living, as prior to the rights of property.
Judaism emphasizes the duty of charity, and strives for a social

order which will protect men against the material disabilities of old age, sickness and unemployment.

Peace. Judaism, from the days of the prophets, has proclaimed to mankind the ideal of universal peace. The spiritual and physical disarmament of all nations has been one of its essential teachings. It abhors all violence and relies upon moral education, love and sympathy to secure human progress. It regards justice as the foundation of the well-being of nations and the condition of enduring peace. It urges organized international action for disarmament, collective security and world peace.[19]

Religious practices

A critical question still remained. What should be said of the centuries-old Jewish practices that distinguished the Israelites from their contemporaries? Reform Judaism passed them by in a sweeping sentence, asserting that only such customs and ceremonies were to be kept "as possess inspirational value." The focus had, therefore, shifted from a religious concern to meet the heavy demands of the Torah and Talmud, to a subjective interest in the personal needs of the Jewish believer.

Jewish life is marked by consecration to these ideals of Judaism. It calls for faithful participation in the life of the Jewish community as it finds expression in home, synagog and school and in all other agencies that enrich Jewish life and promote its welfare.

The Home has been and must continue to be a stronghold of Jewish life, hallowed by the spirit of love and reverence, by moral discipline and religious observance and worship.

The Synagog is the oldest and most democratic institution in Jewish life. It is the prime communal agency by which Judaism is fostered and preserved. It links the Jews of each community and unites them with all Israel.

The perpetuation of Judaism as a living force depends upon religious knowledge and upon the Education of each new generation in our rich cultural and spiritual heritage.

Prayer is the voice of religion, the language of faith and aspiration. It directs man's heart and mind Godward, voices the needs and hopes of the community, and reaches out after goals which invest life with supreme value. To deepen the spiritual life of our people, we must cultivate the traditional habit of communion with God through prayer in both home and synagog.

Judaism as a way of life requires in addition to its moral and spiritual demands, the preservation of the Sabbath, festivals and Holy Days, the retention and development of such customs, symbols and ceremonies as possess inspirational value, the cultivation of distinctive forms of religious art and music and the use of Hebrew, together with the vernacular, in our worship and instruction.

These timeless aims and ideals of our faith we present anew to a confused and troubled world. We call upon our fellow Jews to rededicate themselves to them, and, in harmony with all men, hopefully and courageously to continue Israel's eternal quest after God and His kingdom.[20]

In the discussion which followed the presentation of the Platform, there were practically no dissenting voices. One exception was Rabbi Samuel Schulman, of Temple Emmanu-El, New York, who felt the document was too weak. He objected to the elimination of the term *chosen* as applied to the Jewish people, and felt that the rise of "brutal racialism" called for a stronger statement than was drafted: "If the Jewish church speaks and it has nothing to say, let it be silent; to speak weakly in a time like this is worse than nothing."[21] His objections were overruled by a vote of one hundred five in favor of the declaration and only five against.

It is not likely that the Columbus manifesto would have seen the light of day, or that a reformulation of Reform principles would have been made except for the founding of the World Union for Progressive Judaism ten years before. The name was adopted as a compromise between "Reform" and "Liberal," both of which carried unsavory connotations in some countries, especially in England. One of the World Union's avowed purposes was "to win the materialists to a living Judaism," by offering them a way of life that rose above institutionalized religion, ritual services, and observances which they considered incompatible with modern life.[22]

Once adopted, the Columbus Platform began to make its influence felt and by 1946 succeeded in completely revamping the Union of American Hebrew Congregations. Founded in 1873, its main practical function had so far been to maintain Hebrew Union College as a seminary for the Reform rabbinate. Now a new spirit of zeal was injected into the society whose objectives were broadened, (1) to encourage and aid the organization and development of Jewish congregations, (2) to promote Jewish education and intensify Jewish life, (3) to foster other activities for the perpetuation and advancement of Judaism.

Parallel with this enterprise, the Union voted in 1946 to outlaw any interference with the mode of worship, the school, the freedom of expression and opinion, or any other activities of the congregations belonging to the U.A.H.C. This was a triumph for Jewish Congregationalism and consistent with the changing stress on a Judaism that was unfettered by community sanctions so common in former days.

CUSTOM AND LAW

It has been said that Judaism differs from Christianity in that the latter is more concerned with creeds, while the former is more concerned with deeds. Christians might well disagree with the comparison, but Jews are likely to admit that the Hallakah, the practice of right actions, is characteristic of their religion.

Reform scholars recognize that no religious practice can be separated from its creedal basis, at least implicitly. And they are willing to concede the same for Christianity, that no doctrinal formulation would be of much worth if it did not show itself in corresponding practice.

But they make a careful distinction between Judaism and Christianity in this context, more so than their more orthodox coreligionists. As they see it, the two religions differ in their concept of the relation between faith and conduct. They paraphrase a passage from the Talmud to say that if a man busies himself with keeping the precepts even though his heart is not in them, eventually the hand will teach the heart. He will mysteriously rise to some semblance of Jewish belief provided he perseveres in the practice of Jewish law.

Contrasting the two approaches, Christianity is said to begin with the doctrinal or theological and hopes to end in right action. Judaism works the other way around. It starts with the concrete and arrives at the philosophical or even creedal. The one is called deductive; the other inductive.

From another viewpoint, Jewish religious life is daily practice on which are gradually built habits of mind. So that instead of beginning with theology, Judaism arrives rather at theology.

This approach to religious practice is considered essential to the reinterpretation of traditional Jewish practices which characterizes the Reform. Given the radical transformation in Jewish life during the past century, how can a Jew expect to remain faithful to his heritage if the customary practices of his religion are no longer —or only minimally—observed? Presumably a Christian has less difficulty adjusting to a different or even alien, environment, since his religion makes fewer demands in practice and more in internal attitude.

Over the centuries of the past history of Judaism, there have been catastrophic changes in the life-pattern of its people—when the Temple at Jerusalem was destroyed by the Romans, when the Jewish community in Palestine was suddenly scattered to the four winds, and the diaspora became normal for all Israelites. How did the Jews make the revolutionary adjustments in these crises in the past? Their method, according to Reform commentators, is the same that has to be made now. Since Jewish law has had no Sanhedrin for almost two thousand years, there was no official legal instrument either to change existing laws, make new ones, or authentically interpret what the faithful were to do under a bewildering variety of circumstances. In the absence of such juridical authority or, rather in its place, arose the creative and original power of the Minhag, the custom of the people.

There is no ambiguity about it. The Minhag which comes from inside the Jewish community, the day-to-day practices of the people, became the raw material which the law took up and sifted, reviewed, and codified, and finally embodied in legal form. Contrary to the popular view that law comes down from the top, from those in authority, and affects the masses—the masses created and law merely organized their creation.

Conscious of the critical nature of this viewpoint, Reform theologians are at pains to justify it from the Talmud.

The doctors of the Jewish law understood very early that they depended upon the creative imagination of the people. In b. Berakot 45a there is a comment upon the fact that the Mishnah gives two forms of the blessing to be recited when drinking water. Which was the proper blessing that the law should determine upon? Rabba bar Rav Chanan said to Abbaye: which is the law? He said to him: "Go forth and see what the people say." That which became customary among the people was the law. In b. *Pesahim* 66a there is a discussion about the procedure with the sacrifices if the fourteenth of Nisan falls on the Sabbath. They asked Hillel what will happen if the people do not prepare their slaughtering knives before the Sabbath came. And he answered: "Just let the people of Israel alone. If they are not prophets, they are the descendants of prophets." In other words, they will know what to do in this emergency, and of course, they did know. They put knives in the wool of the lambs and the lambs carried the knives on the Sabbath.

In j. Yebamot at the beginning of Chapter XII (12c) there is a discussion as to whether the ceremony of Halitsah may be performed only with a shoe or whether it may be performed with a sandal. The Talmud says there as follows: "If Elijah himself came and said (contrary to the present law) that we may not perform the ceremony of Halitsah with a shoe, we would hearken to him, but if he said we may not perform the ceremony of Halitsah with a sandal, we would not hearken to him, for behold many have the custom of performing the ceremony with the sandal and the custom abrogates the law." A similar statement is made in J. Baba Metsia to 7, I (11b). Commenting upon the Mishnah which says: "He who hires workingmen and orders them to work early and late, he cannot compel them to do so in that place where it is not the custom to work early and late," the Talmud says: "This indicates that custom abrogates the law."[23]

This studied appeal to the Talmud to justify its concept of "law" as custom has profound implications not only in Reform Judaism but in other religious traditions which change what had been considered divine mandates, come from above through divinely authorized spokesmen, to human mores rising from below and gradually legalized into morals.

By invoking the Talmud as warrant for allowing custom to grow into law, Reform leaders implicitly recognized their Jewishness and witnessed to the fact that Judaism has a deeper hold on its adherents than most Gentiles recognize.

Not only has the Talmud been restored to an honored place in the Reform but, even while using rabbinic logic to redefine law, the Reformers also find in the Talmud a strong controlling element to protect custom from degenerating into chaos. "Not every custom," they grant, "could be permitted to abrogate any law." Quoting the treatise *Sofrim*, they say that "custom abrogates the law only if it is the custom of respected people (*vatikim*)."[24] These *vatikim* (or *wethikin*) were probably Essenes, or certainly distinguished and conscientious men of old.

Moreover, not only must a custom by Talmudic standards be that of persons outstanding for respect of the Torah, but if a practice "is devoid of proof from the Torah, (it) is to be regarded as an erroneous decision."[25]

Coming from one of the most respected Reform scholars of the century, this twofold reliance on the Torah—in the person of those who create customs and in the principles on which a custom is based—may seem like a return to Orthodoxy. And no doubt for some Jews of the Reform persuasion that is true. But the Torah need not be taken literally as the word of Yahweh. It could be only the work of human genius, apart from any special divine communication, as the classic statements of Reform ideology clearly testify.

The tendency of custom to modify and even to abrogate law was particularly noticeable in the area of Jewish-Gentile relations. It is credited with having helped to "make life possible under a

Gentile government." Writers refer to the adage, "the civil law of the country takes precedence," as an application of this principle of Jewish survival in a non-Jewish land.[26]

If such adjustment of law to custom was not unknown in former times, the drastic changes in recent years make it absolutely necessary—say the proponents of Reform.

They are not so much critical of those who still keep the minutiae of the Jewish laws as skeptical about almost anyone being able to do so. Until about the middle of the eighteenth century, the argument goes, Jews governed themselves by their own code and courts, and they lived almost exclusively in communities of their own people. Contact with the outer world was comparatively rare and incidental.

The Jew lived with Jews and the Jewish law completely governed Jewish life. But when modernity broke the walls of the Jewish community and Jews began to be integrated into the larger European community, the walls of the Jewish legal structure and of Jewish practice began to crack. And now, after a century, they are virtually in ruins. No one has made a realistic, statistical investigation of the present status of Jewish observance. How many Jews are there in the world who really observe the rabbinic laws of the Jewish Sabbath? What percentage of the Jews of the world actually abide by the dietary laws? How many are still guided by the Jewish laws of marriage and divorce? Jewish Orthodoxy is an ideal, an heroic self-discipline, but to what extent is it a living reality among the masses of Jewish people?

Without attempting to deplore the fact as some do sorrowfully, or to rejoice in it as an evidence of emancipation as others might, but looking upon it merely as an actual social-religious fact, there is no doubt that the number of Jews left in Europe and in America who actually observe what all Jews observed one hundred and fifty years ago is pitiably small. Jewish religious life has undergone a cataclysmic change. Certainly even for the small percentage who observe the dietary laws, the Sabbath and Jewish marriage laws, even for them, loyal, self-sacrificing Orthodox Jews in a bewildering modern world, the whole Jewish civil law code, the Choshen Mishpot no longer exists. They no longer, except in rare instances, resort to rabbinical law for the settlement of their business matters such as partnerships, contracts, notes, and loans. They go to the civil law courts. Scholars, of course, still study Jewish civil law. They ask each other abstruse questions about it and give each other ingenious answers, but all this is only the intellectual play of a handful of scholars. It is as the introduction to the Eben Haezer of the Shulhan Aruk puts it: "There are many laws in this book which are not customary in Israel these days . . . but he who studies these matters which are not customary today, nevertheless fulfills the commandment of learning the Law." A few generations ago the law governed life. Now the study of the law is intellectual exercise and pious self-absorption.[27]

There is no way of verifying the harsh judgment that only a "pitiably small" number of Jews are faithful to the precepts that, until modern times, were still observed by most Israelites. Certainly the Orthodox, who form the majority of the world's Jewish population, are Orthodox precisely because they try to remain loyal to the Judaic code. What is significant is that those who, on principle, do not observe these traditions are concerned to prove their case by appealing from nonpractice to practical impossibility. Since an impossible law does not oblige, once the impossibility is assumed, the law becomes nullified.

Having redefined law as custom, Reform leaders are not sure this is objectively valid. "Whether the price paid for this adjustment," they wonder, "is to be considered too great or not," they cannot say. Nevertheless, "it must be acknowledged that it has achieved a great deal. It has kept many generations loyal to Judaism. Many of the American Reform Congregations still have most of the descendants of the founders of the congregations in their membership."[28] This is said to compare favorably with the attendance at worship in other forms of Judaism.

Nowhere else has the principle of religious laicism (to use Christian terms) been more widely applied than among Reform congregations. Without apology, it is admitted that practices and observances in Reform Judaism have varied and developed "in response to the changing feelings and the attitudes of the people." They and not the rabbis have decided the content and spirit of the faith and its expression. Rabbis have, it is true, voiced certain ideological ideals, but "the people themselves by their rejections and their acceptances, by their neglects and by their observances have largely determined their own religious practices."[29] Behind this approach to religion stands a difference between Reform and Orthodoxy that is so radical it provoked the rise of a new kind of Judaism, the Conservative. Where the Reform is built on a personalistic concept of the Torah, trusting to the indwelling spirit among Jews to keep some semblance of fidelity to Israel—their Conservative reactors were less optimistic. They recalled the past of their people and insisted on the need for a prophetic mission to the sons of Abraham.

V

CONSERVATIVE JUDAISM

Historians of their tradition like to point out that among Jews the noun is more important than the adjective. What really matters is that they are Jewish; it is quite secondary what else they do or profess to be.

While this may be correct in describing American Jews in their social relationships, it is not true on the deeper level of religious belief and practice.

HISTORIC ORIGINS

The cleavage began, as we have seen, with the huge immigration from Russia, Poland, and Central Europe, following the influx of German Jews to the United States in the nineteenth century. If the earlier (mainly Sephardim) Jews were Orthodox, the Germans became strongly liberal and, in less than two generations, had transplanted the Enlightenment from Europe to America as the Reform. When the Slavic immigrants came over, the first impulse was to remain Orthodox and isolated in ghettoes, mostly as workmen for the more prosperous Jews who already made their mark in commerce and industry. But the children of these Slavs were uncomfortable, chafing under the double liability of being considered both Jews and foreigners.

Heroic efforts were made to save the Jewish faith and culture of the youth, and the process of Americanization grew apace. Yet a break was bound to come unless some compromise were possible between remaining an authentic Jew and becoming fully integrated into American society.

The option which was offered to the younger generation, and not only among Slavic Jews, was clear once the Reform movement got under way. No one could read the Philadelphia or Pittsburgh Platforms without knowing that the Judaism they professed was not that of Sephardic or Ashkenazic orthodoxy.

Reform Judaism plainly denied the nationhood of Israel and publicly affirmed that Jews are simply members of a religious denomination. They asserted that Jews have no ambitions for a restoration of Palestine as their national home.

On the critical issue of the Jewish law, Reform scholars restated the ancient tradition in very untraditional form. Using the Talmud as guide, they concluded that custom becomes law, provided those who practice a custom are respectable Jews. By means of rabbinic logic, they argued from scattered Talmudic passages dealing with legal interpretation to the legitimacy of legal transformation. A law is abrogated if enough people stop practicing it, and a custom contrary to the law becomes legal in the same way— if enough respected Jews have undertaken a new course of action or decided that a former practice was no longer relevant.

As many rabbis saw it, this was complete surrender of the authority and binding power of traditional Jewish law. Basic observances were dropped and the groundwork was laid for a new prayer book, whose English dress was only symbolic of changes in doctrine and ritual practices held sacred for centuries.

Those who defended the Reform properly explained that no real innovation had been made, that the ideas of the Pittsburgh Conference, already in 1885, were only formulations of existing concessions widely practiced in America.

Too much was at stake, however, to let the official break with Orthodoxy go unchallenged. Hebrew Union College was founded in 1875 to become the nucleus of a new Judaism, truly American and unhampered by its European antecedents. Ten years later came the Pittsburgh consensus. In 1886, in answer to the Pittsburgh meeting, Sabato Morais of the Sephardic synagogue of Philadelphia and H. Pereira Mendes of the Sephardic synagogue of New York organized a group of concerned rabbis to found the Jewish Theological Seminary Association, which started classes in 1887.

In contradistinction to Hebrew Union, the Jewish theological institution would stand firm in its loyalty to traditional Judaism. When Solomon Schechter, reader in rabbinics from Cambridge in England came to head the new seminary in 1902, its future was assured. To this day it is a stronghold of Conservative Judaism and from its inception has graduated about the same number of rabbis as Hebrew Union College of Cincinnati and its sister institution (since 1926) in New York.

For a long time, Conservative Judaism protested that it had no intention of starting a new movement, and even yet has not adopted a formal profession of principles similar to the Reform.

The essentials of the Conservative position are by now fairly definite and traceable historically through the writings of its outstanding thinkers.

Zechariah Frankel (1801-1875), president of the Jewish Theological Seminary in Breslau, is commonly regarded as the patriarch of Conservatism. He coined the term "positive-historical Judaism," by which he meant that Judaism is the product of *historical* development, to be honored by a *positive* acceptance as the substantive element that may not be surrendered no matter what changes or adjustments to the times are called for.

Frankel stressed the absolute need for scholarship and scientific research in Jewish history and religion if Judaism hoped for acceptance by an increasingly sophisticated Western society. He also urged that national factors are necessary for a vital Jewish life, more today than ever before.

Solomon Schechter carried on Frankel's tradition, first in England and then in America. Within a short time, he became enamored of the country of his adoption and vigorously advocated a thoroughly American Judaism. Accepting Frankel's three points—historical substance of Judaism, scholarship, and nationhood—he added two of his own. He spoke of a "Catholic Israel," that is, universal Judaism seeking ever greater organic unity, and "religious nationalism" which meant more than ethnic cohesion and looked to God for its solidarity.

The whole Conservative movement took on new life with the rise of Zionism, and drew heavily on the ideas of Ahad Ha'am (1856-1927), the Russian and Palestinian philosopher. Ha'am was a cultural Zionist who taught that Palestine is the spiritual center of the Jewish people. From Palestine would flow vital energies to all parts of world Jewry, unknown since the fall of Jerusalem under the Romans.

Ha'am was mainly responsible for Zionism becoming an essential element in the Conservative movement as something more than a haven for the oppressed, or a solace to the memory of times past. He instilled in the hearts of his disciples a longing for the spiritual rebirth of Israel, and gave Conservatism its strong ethical stamp.

The American follower of Ha'am, Israel Friedlander (1876-1920), was on the faculty at Jewish Theological and forwarded the movement by associating America with God's providential plans for the future of Judaism. He spoke of Israel as a complete culture, and not a mere religion and much less only a creed.

Another scholar at the seminary, the Talmudist Louis Ginzberg further developed the theology of Conservative Jewry by reinterpreting the ideas and practices of Israel in their historical setting. He showed that the Talmud is to Judaism what the Church is to Christianity—the mainstay of its authentic spirit in spite of apostasies and infidelities and the objective norm for anyone who calls himself a Jew.

One more figure is often identified with Conservative Judaism, although his role was more abrasive than constructive. Mordecai M.

Kaplan had gone through his studies at Jewish Theological but later began a movement of his own called Reconstructionism. This "left-wing" development is so radically different it should be treated separately as a kind of fourth branch of contemporary Judaism.

UNDERLYING PRINCIPLES

Conservative writers describe their position by defining Judaism. They say it is the evolving religious culture and civilization of the Jewish people.

Basic to this concept is the evolutionary outlook. It presumes that all through their history the Jews looked upon themselves as a growing and changing society. Built on the biblical law and never denying it, they amplified and transformed the pattern of their life in a thousand ways. Moses and the prophets, the framers of the Talmud and Maimonides, are all equated as leaders in this transformation. It was not until Joseph Karo and his *Shulhan Aruk* in the sixteenth century that stagnation set in.

Conservatives are highly critical of Karo's compendium of Jewish law, even as modified by Isserles and others. They consider the publication of this work the beginning of a sort of Jewish Dark Ages. There followed in rapid sequence the Thirty Years' War (1618-1648), the Chmelnicki massacres of the Jews (1618-1649), and the collapse of a liberation movement (1666). Jews gave up hope of emancipation in this world and so turned to a rigid Pietism in a desperate effort at deliverance in a world to come—the condition for such liberation was scrupulous observance of the law.

As Conservatives explained it, Judaism has an inner vitality that does not have to freeze itself in formalism and an unchanging obedience to legal prescriptions. Once this inner spirit is discovered and acted upon, all the best elements of the Jewish way of life are released and "adjustment to the times" becomes almost irrelevant. True Judaism is never stifled by the circumstances in which its adherents live. In fact, they are potent factors in transforming the society which surrounds them, rather than become anxious about the adverse influence of their environment on them.

Several pairs of terms are commonplace in studying the bases of Conservatism: the letter and spirit of the law, precedents and traditions, general validity and personal interpretation, content and form, essence and structure. All of these doublets suggest that Conservatism is just as critical of Orthodoxy as of the Reform, but for different reasons.

It disagrees with Orthodoxy for claiming that Judaism has not really developed, at least since Talmudic times and perhaps since the days of the Torah; that whatever changes took place have all been external to the Jewish spirit and that nothing has developed from within.

It also disagrees with Reform and charges it with having so adjusted Jewish laws as to abrogate their divine authority. Here is the heart of the matter—as distinct from what seems to be the same desire for adaptation on both sides. Where the Reform also speaks of evolution, it would credit the development either to forces outside Judaism to which the people conform or, more profoundly, to forces intrinsic to the people themselves and not (ultimately) to a special divine Providence that guides the Chosen Race in its path through history.

As Conservatism sees the Jews, they are a theocratic civilization whose most characteristic biblical name is *Am*, a people; and whose most familiar feature is unity. They are one throughout the world, joined together by a mysterious bond of tradition into the past, of similar observances in the present, and of a common destiny in the future.

Yet underneath all of this is belief in God's selective action in favor of his people. Even as they grow and change, the roots of this development come from him and not, as the Reform would have it, from inside the native capacities of the people themselves.

While the comparison is not fully accurate, it is quite correct to say that, contrasted with Orthodoxy, Conservatism leans toward a concept of Judaism which is more spiritual than ethnic and more doctrinal than moralistic. Compared with Reform, it is more religious than merely cultural, and understands development as more divinely transcendent than humanly immanent, that is, changes in Jewish law are from above, through Yahweh's constant inspiration, rather than from below, through the spiritual consciousness of the people.

When Conservative writers come to define their position they express it in a paradox. They call themselves modern traditional Jews; the "modern" distinguishes them from the Orthodox, and "traditional" sets them apart from Reform.

This would not be very helpful unless both terms were more elaborately explained—as they have been by their ablest commentators on the faith.

While there is no official declaration as in the Reform, Conservatism has a fine synthesis of its beliefs in which religion is the axis around which everything else revolves. Yet religion is conceived quite differently than in Christianity. There are no dogmatic creeds and much is made of the fact that nowhere in the Old Testament does the word *religion* occur. Instead *mitzvah*, or commandment, is the key concept to describe man's relationship with God.

What follows is professedly a summary of Conservative Judaism, assembled by its most representative exponents. If it contains elements that other Jews would also accept, yet the approach is distinctive if not unique and steers a middle course between "rigid Orthodoxy" and "vapid Reform."

FUNDAMENTAL BELIEFS

A familiar Jewish adage says that "God, Israel and the Torah are one." God is the Yahweh of the prophets, Israel is God's chosen people, and the Torah is the response he demands of Israel as a condition for his fatherly care.

God

Although belief in God is not absent from Reform Judaism, his presence is not so central as among the Conservatives. Above all, the Reform does not stress God's role as Creator of the cosmos, as Revealer to mankind, and merciful Provider for all who call on his name.

> God is the great spirit at the heart of the world, who is both the Creator of nature and the Ruler of mankind. While His essence is beyond human comprehension He reveals Himself through His works.

Creation is not a one-time act, but a never-ending process. Long before the theory of evolution was accepted by science, the Jewish Prayerbook declared, "He renews each day continually the work of creation."

God reveals Himself also in history, in the affairs of men. The evidence of His participation in the life of men is the law of consequence, which men call justice or the moral order. It is true that there are far too many instances of evil apparently triumphant and virtue in distress. From Biblical days to the present, sensitive spirits have grappled with the problem of evil, have been compelled to admit that, in part at least, "we do not fully understand either the well-being of the wicked or the suffering of the righteous" (Abot 4:19). Yet all human experience testifies that the law of consequence operates in the lives of individuals, nations and civilizations. "The shop is open and the owner gives credit, the ledger is open and the hand writes. Whoever wishes to borrow may come and borrow, but the collectors go about continually every day, exacting from man, whether he knows it or not and have proof upon which they can rely, and the judgment is a judgment of truth, and everything is prepared for the feast." (Abot 3:16)

God is not a working illusion, a convenient abstraction or a beautiful ideal. He is a reality, a Being concerning whom we may affirm certain basic truths, even in our inadequate human vocabulary. The God of nature and the God of history is one. The unity of God is perhaps the most distinctive Jewish belief through the ages. Under its banner, Judaism fought the polytheism of the pagan world, opposed the dualism of Zoroastrianism and refused to accept or compromise with the trinitarianism of Christianity. For the sake of the unity of God and the Sanctification of the Name, the martyrs of Israel have died in every generation.

This faith is no lifeless theological dogma or theological fetish. Upon the doctrine of the unity of God stands the principle of the solidarity of the human race. All men are God's children and deserve equally to share the blessings of the world called into being by their Father.

Not only our moral system, but our science also rests upon this principle, which scientists call the uniformity of nature. The unity of the Creator means the unity of His creation, so that scientific laws operate throughout the cosmos. Albert Einstein has called attention to the fact that this idea of the uniformity and regularity of nature is an act of faith, which preceded all scientific endeavor. Thus religion, far from being the adversary of science, is when properly comprehended basic to the scientific spirit.

God's justice is the phrase by which religion expresses the law of consequence in the universe. But the world is no machine, mechanical and unchanging in its operation. Rather it is a living organism with processes of growth and regeneration. There is an incurable love of novelty in the universe always cropping out. Biologists speak of the appearance of new types in the evolutionary process called "sports" or "mutations." Not only does genius appear among men, but even ordinary men possess unsuspected reservoirs of spiritual power, which emerge in hours of crisis. While there is life, it is not too late for men to rebuild their lives through repentance and inner reconstruction. In life, there is another chance. We are not completely at the mercy of the iron-clad law of consequence. This opportunity which life affords us all, we call *God's mercy*, "who desireth not the death of the sinner, but that he repent of his way and live." (Ezekiel 33:11).[1]

Man

In Judaism, man's role is different from that of any other religion, outside of Christianity and Islam which are of Judaic origin.

Two aspects of its anthropology are essential to Conservative Jewish belief: that man is an essentially contingent being whose existence depends absolutely on God, and that man's destiny is beyond this world of space and time.

Nowhere else does this form of the Judaic faith reflect its theological heritage more clearly than in considering man's contingency of being, his dual nature of body and spirit, and his character as a free agent responsible for the morality of his actions.

God's activity in the world is for us closely associated with the role of man. Modern science has shown how man is closely linked with all living creatures, it thus incidentally bears additional testimony to the unity of God. Yet evolution recognizes in man, for all his limitations, the most complex and richly developed creature in the world. This unique position of man, Genesis described in the classic phrase "God created man in His image." Similarly the Psalmist praises his Maker, "Thou hast made man little lower than God and crowned him with glory and honor." These richly suggestive phrases enshrine the truth that man possesses, on an infinitely smaller scale to be sure, the basic qualities of wisdom, justice, mercy and truth which are the divine attributes. The Talmud goes further and describes man as "God's partner in the work of creation."

Having been endowed with intelligence, it follows that man is free; he has the capacity to choose between good and evil. Hence man is endowed with free-will, and upon his choice depends his fate. Not only in Moses' day, but in every generation the great call is sounded. "Life and death have I placed before thee this day, the blessing and the curse. Thou shalt choose life, so that thou mayest live, thou and thine offspring" (Deut. 30:19).

In common with all great religions, Judaism has had the conviction that a creature so richly endowed as man cannot be completely destroyed by death and that in some manner, *man's spirit is immortal.* Speculations on the after-life have been frequent in Jewish circles, as everywhere else. But Judaism has very wisely refused to adopt a fixed and obligatory teaching on the character and form of immortality.[2]

Israel

No believing Jew has any doubt that his people have been specially chosen by God. The very name *Israel,* divinely bestowed on Jacob by an angel, means "champion of God." It is not coincidental that this name, rich in religious connotation, was ultimately to replace the prosaic "Hebrew" by which the descendants of the family of Abraham came to be known.

An Israelite, in biblical language, is an object of God's predilection. The story of Jacob and Esau, and Jacob's (Israel's) divine election over his older brother perfectly symbolizes the status of his descendants in the plan of God.

By the same token, Israelites are messengers of Yahweh to the Gentiles. As they see their prophetic role, God has first enlightened them that through them he might reveal himself to the rest of the human race.

While God reveals himself both in nature and in history it requires a seeing eye and a sensitive heart to recognize His presence. Herein lies the distinctive role of Israel as the instrument of Revelation. The Jewish people has never possessed great military power or unique artistic or scientific gifts. Its distinction has lain in its genius for religion. By virtue of this endowment a tiny, impotent people was able to develop a faith of universal scope, and a vision of the one living God of humanity. Palestine is a small land but it was roofed over by the vault of a heaven that embraced the furthest ends of the earth.

The special role of Israel as the people of Revelation is no idle boast. No other people has produced a group of men comparable in spiritual insight and moral character to the Hebrew prophets. Their work was carried to fulfillment and translated into concrete institutions by the legislators and sages of Israel. The pages of history testify to the unique role of Judaism, which has inspired the two mightiest religions of the modern world, Christianity and Mohammedanism. Both creeds have taken over important sections of their religious outlook and ethical code from Judaism. It is surely no mere coincidence that precisely where they have neglected or misunderstood Jewish teaching, as in the areas of family morality, social justice and international relations, the world finds itself confronting catastrophe today.[3]

Torah

Among the main contributions of Conservative Judaism is its comprehensive idea of law in Jewish religious culture. Where the Orthodox might want to limit Torah to the Bible and to the Talmud insofar as it reflected the biblical tradition; and where the Reform would reduce it to ethical ideals—the Conservative stress is at once deeper than the Reform and broader than what Orthodoxy commonly affirms.

Equally significant is the Conservative recognition that laws binding in conscience not only refer to moral conduct, but they also include ritual.

As Israel is the instrument of Revelation through the ages, so Torah is its substance. In its broadest sense, Torah includes everything significant that the Jewish genius has produced from the days of Moses to the present. In a more specialized sense, Torah is the term for the authoritative Jewish religious tradition embodied in the Bible and the Talmud, the medieval Responsa and Codes, down to the interpretations of accredited religious and scholarly authorities in our own age. As was noted above, Conservatism emphasizes that the Torah is not a narrow rivulet but a broad river with many currents, following the contours of the shore and the changing depths of the riverbed along its course of nearly four thousand years. It seeks to heed the wise words of President Lowell of Harvard, "The art of life lies largely in distinguishing the eddy from the stream."

In common with orthodoxy and in contradistinction to Reform, Conservative Judaism recognizes that the Torah is binding and the Jewish law may not be set aside for the sake of caprice, convenience or fashion. Unlike orthodoxy, however, it has learned that like every other living manifestation of human culture, Jewish law must necessarily grow if it is to remain alive. These two principles are not contradictory. Exactly as American law is binding upon all Americans, though the law is perpetually being modified by legislative enactment and judicial interpretation, so Jewish law is binding upon us though it is subject to change and development.

Torah or Jewish law contains two aspects, already formulated by Sardia in the tenth century: a) the *ethical* and hence the universal, binding upon all men, and b) the *ceremonial*, and hence the particular, which bears a specific Jewish character. The first element being broadly human, can be and in large measure has been taken over by all civilized men. The second, which is rooted in the historic experience of Israel is naturally binding upon Jews alone. To cite an analogy, freedom is cherished by Frenchmen and Americans alike. The American expresses his loyalty to this in terms of his own group experience by a celebration on July 4th, while Frenchmen link their love of liberty with Bastille Day on July 14th. Freedom is neither French nor American—it is human. Independence Day, however, is specifically American; Bastille Day is uniquely French. It would be no gain for the world and quite conceivably prove a loss, if Frenchmen and Americans were both to observe the same holiday. What is important is that both peoples cherish the same ideal of freedom.

Largely because Judaism recognizes the right and need for varying expressions of the human aspiration for God, it does not engage in missionary activity. Unlike its daughter religions, which failed to comprehend or accept its profound principle of religious toleration, Judaism does not condemn all non-adherents to damnation. Talmudic teachers fifteen hundred years ago declared that there were basic religious and moral duties incumbent upon the non-Jew as a human being, the fulfillment of which makes him worthy of salvation as the Jew who observes the entire Torah. These "Laws of the Sons of Noah" include abstaining from idolatry and blasphemy, from murder, theft, sexual immorality, and eating of the limb of a live animal, beside the positive obligation to establish a government of law and order. These laws are universally binding; all else will reflect varying historical experiences and consequently will differ with each people.[4]

The invidious comparison with Christianity and Islam is not characteristic of Judaism as a whole. By its own definition of the Messianic hope, Israel is committed to share what it has received from Yahweh with the rest of mankind. Addressing the Jews in the name of God, Isaiah told them, "I have made you a witness to the peoples, a leader and a master of the nations. See you will summon a nation you never knew, those unknown will come hurrying to you, for the sake of Yahweh your God."[5]

JEWISH ETHICS

At the risk of oversimplifying the differences, it may be said that Orthodox Judaism is mainly concerned with ritual, Reform with theology, and Conservatism with ethics. Certainly Conservative writers give more than ordinary attention to the ethical dimension of their religion, to the point that Jewish principles of morality are presented as normative—on scriptural grounds—for the human race and not only for Israelites.

Maimonides is quoted to the effect that, except for Judaism, Christianity and Islam would have no ethical center. On the other hand, "Thanks to these new religions," declared the Egyptian Moses, "the world has been filled with the words of the Law and the Commandments." Through the Gospel and the Koran, mankind has received the Torah.

As Jewish apologists describe it, their ethics is the crowning glory of Judaism. Its moral code is basically realistic. Rather than glorify the instincts as did paganism, or suppress them as did "ascetic Christianity," it looks on human drives as morally neutral. They can be used to benefit man or destroy him. But there is nothing within man whether as inherited tendency or inborn defect to militate against him. "Traditional Judaism," according to Conservative theologians, "never accepted the doctrine of 'original sin,' insisting that man can attain to holiness."[6] Significantly this notion of original sin as a condition of total depravity (taught by the classic Protestant Reformers) is regularly offered as the Christian teaching on man's inherited guilt.

One aspect of Jewish ethics that stands out luminously is its practicality. The prescriptions of the Torah are detailed in the extreme. Every phase of daily life is touched by them, family relations and education, health and hygiene, business dealings and table manners, conduct at public worship and the duties of public office.

Nothing more surely reveals Judaism as a civilization than these minutiae of conduct covering every aspect of private and public behavior.

At the heart of Jewish ethics, however, is a principle that boldly confronts the morals of Christianity. Depending on the viewpoint, the Judaic code may be called juridical or rational, as contrasted with the Christian which claims to be charismatic and creedal.

While the Old Testament first gave the world its Golden Rule, "Thou shalt love thy neighbor as thyself" (Leviticus 19:18), Judaism (it is said) wisely made justice and not love the cornerstone of moral conduct. Where love is so subjective, fleeting, and unpredictable, justice is definite and unmistakable.

In other words, the only real norm of morality is the Sinaitic Decalogue, which forbids men to deprive others of what they already own—life, property, a wife, or good name. It does not presume to dictate beyond the call of duty, to give where no claim of justice exists or to deprive self in order to enrich someone else. Less still does it contemplate self-immolation as anything but an ideal in the practice of charity. If altruism above justice occurs among Jews, this should be seen as desirable, indeed, and terminal; it is not a moral imperative and primary responsibility, as demanded by Christ of those who profess to believe in his name.

Hence the extreme demands for loving one's enemy and turning the other cheek are not characteristic of Judaism. Instead, Judaism demands dealing justly with one's foe, as, for example, returning his lost property (Exodus 23:4, 5), or refusing to nurse a grudge or seek vengeance (Leviticus 19:17, 18). It is hardly necessary to point out which approach is truer to human nature and which has been more largely successful in the moral education of men. The long history of the saints and martyrs of Israel proves how often the rational code of Judaism led to holy living and holy dying. Jewish survival is an eternal monument to countless men and women whose souls were moulded by the Torah and who went beyond the demands of the law to heroic self-sacrifice and noble self-denial.[7]

Finally Jewish ethics is unembarrassingly earthbound. It allows for happiness in a life to come, but stakes its claims strongly on the here and now. The Bible is quoted to show that God promises to reward his faithful servants in this life. Francis Bacon's observation that "Prosperity is the blessing of the Old Testament, adversity is the blessing of the New," is taken at its face value.

This is so true that, without it, no proper estimate can be made of the Jewish outlook on life. Man's welfare on earth, physically, psychologically, and culturally, is the focus of motivation for serving God. And no apologies are given for what others might consider an earthy morality.

RECONSTRUCTIONISM

Ironically the Conservative movement in American Judaism has given birth to an offspring that, in many ways, is less traditional than the Reform. Labeled Reconstructionism, it is mainly the creation of one man, Mordecai Kaplan, but its future is assured through the many rabbis and community leaders whom he taught at the Jewish Theological Seminary.

In June 1961 several hundred disciples of Rabbi Kaplan, then professor emeritus of philosophies of religion at Jewish Theological, gathered to celebrate his eightieth birthday. The birthday tribute to Kaplan, as rabbi, teacher, and dean of the Teachers Institute, was reflected by the Jewish press throughout the world.

> Emotional attachment made him value the Jewish practices which Reform wanted to discard, but philosophical training made him unable to accept Divine Revelation, which was the sanction for those practices on which Orthodoxy insisted.
>
> Other organizations have put into operation such of his ideas that appealed to them. They obtain the credit; he is left with a dated theology. His organized followers are devoted, but few.
>
> It is a tribute to the intellectually hospitable climate of New York that by his eightieth birthday, recently this individualist had become an institution in American Jewry.[8]

When the London *Jewish Chronicle* said that Kaplan's organized followers are few, this could not mean those professedly belonging to the Federation of Reconstructionist Congregations and Fellowships, founded in 1954. Their membership is large. It could also not mean readers of the *Reconstructionist*, the twice-monthly publication of the Jewish Reconstructionist Foundation, started in 1935.

So seriously did other Jews take Kaplan's movement, ostensibly within the Conservative ranks, that in 1945 the Union of Orthodox Rabbis excommunicated him when his Foundation issued a new, revised prayer book. Some said it was less radical than the standard Reform manual, and the excommunication was attacked by the Reform and Conservative rabbinate. But the censure brought into sharp focus the significance of this "fourth power" in North American Judaism.

Friendly critics describe Reconstructionism as pragmatic in philosophy, liberal in theology, and rationalistic in emphasis. Kaplan and his followers chose the unusual name because it symbolizes their central thesis: to reconstruct the bewildering variety of American Jewish belief, practice, and social consciousness.

Faced with this conglomeration, Kaplan argued that a new principle of unity had to be found, which would transcend the countless differences and needless overlappings in Jewish organizational structure. The principle should be a return to the *Kehillah* pattern of Central and Eastern Europe. Instead of imitating the waning congregational format on the American scene, so popular among Protestants, Jews should develop what he called an organic community.

Synagogue and school would occupy a "nuclear" position in this Jewish community, yet catering to different interpretations of Judaism according to the choice of people in a given locality. Moreover, the community organization would be equipped with working committees to handle such diversified activities as Zionism, public relations, philanthropic and recreational facilities—all coordinated to avoid independent or supplementary agencies.

Local communities would be federated on a national scale, and finally into a world community that could take its place alongside the great nations of the world. In his own words, "World Jewry should unite as a people, and apply to the United Nations for recognition of its claims to peoplehood."

Basic ideology

Reconstructionism is built on two main principles: that the great contribution of Judaism in history was its ethical teaching, and that, given the secular tempo of the age, the future of Judaism depends on a reappraisal of God and the supernatural in this-worldly terms.

Beginning with the premise that morality is essentially man's relation to man, Kaplan divided this relationship into two categories —the natural and the ethical. A natural relationship rests on the expectation I have that the person with whom I am dealing will act toward me according to the power I have to help or to harm him, that is, either to give him what he wants or deprive him of what he already enjoys.

Thus, if he owes me some money, I naturally expect him to repay me because he knows I can enforce my demands—by invoking the courts and, if necessary, having him put in jail.

But, if he knows I have no power of coercion or will not use it, and yet I expect the debt to be paid, then my expectation is not a natural but an ethical one.

No human society could long endure if obedience to its laws depended entirely on coercion. It is impossible to devise a social machinery that could apply force always and wherever needed to have the laws obeyed. There are too many ways for people to evade law enforcement. Even if it were possible, such a society would be unlivable, where we could not rely on people to act ethically. The uncertainty about their actions would bring chaos into our most personal relationships and reduce society to an anarchy of fear.

It was precisely here that the world received so much from Judaism: "The service that the Jewish people rendered to human civilization may be said to consist in having restored confidence in the original and underived character of the ethical values and in their independence of the considerations of expediency and self-interest."[9]

If the objection is raised that other people, before the Jews and beyond them, also held to the ethical (and not merely natural) norms of conduct, Kaplan replied that the Jews were unique in making the ethical an essential part of their national ethos; that the prophets made ethical behavior a condition for the nation's corporate existence; and the teaching of ethical values to others was the great mission of Israel to the Gentiles.

Historically, it is true, the Jews were accustomed to identify the motives for ethical conduct with belief in God and his revelation. They literally thought that Yahweh had communicated the Ten Commandments to Moses and the Israelites and, through them, to the rest of mankind. Their faith in Sinai was uncritical in the elementary sense of unquestioning.

As long as Jews believed this, all was well, and no problems were raised—except the perennial one of having them remain faithful to their own principles. In fact, there was no other effective way of teaching men to act ethically than telling them they were responsible for their actions to One who stood above them, who could read the human heart and inexorably apply divine sanctions to human behavior.

The worth of a civilization depends not only upon the ideals and values it professes, but upon its ability to energize them. Judaism formerly possessed that ability to an eminent degree. The concept of divine revelation reinforced the moral standards of Judaism so that they acquired the potency of physical causes. At a time when the disintegration of the ancient religions and loyalties shook men's faith in the values and standards essential to the stability of the social order, Judaism performed a much-needed service to mankind. The nations were far less prepared than they are even today to be governed by an ethical code which is based on man's recognition of his spiritual nature. Men were still accustomed to look to extraneous authority for the sanction of the right. They were too heteronomously minded to be spiritually self-reliant. The philosophers and their schools were not able to inspire sufficient certitudes, because they had no way of proving the objectivity and imperativeness of the moral law. It was at that juncture that Judaism saved civilization by supplying a transcendent sanction not only to the moral law as such, but even to some of the specific laws for the regulation of human conduct.[10]

So much for the glorious past. In the Torah of Moses and the prophets, the "transcendent sanction" was perfectly clear. "Not by might nor by power but by my Spirit, saith the Lord of Hosts," was the message.[11] Or still more concisely, "For not by strength shall man prevail."[12]

The present age, however, no longer believes in the supernatural. It is agnostic about God and too intellectually mature to subscribe to the simple and once effective notions of transcendence described in the Bible.

Yet man must practice morality. He must behave ethically or society is doomed.

Faced with the dilemma of remaining mentally infantile but ethical by accepting the biblical ideas of God, or growing mentally yet degenerating ethically by denying transcendent sanctions of law —modern thinkers have discovered in man himself the full meaning of a moral life independently of any consequences said to have been imposed by a revealing God.

What individual thinkers like Immanuel Kant have worked out in elaborate theory, Judaism should now begin to practice and teach others through all the media at its disposal in modern times.

The fact that supernatural revelation is now questioned might mean that the human race will once more be plunged into the hopeless skepticism characteristic of the Roman world at the beginning of the common era, unless the human mind learns to free itself from dependence upon supernatural authority to validate moral law. It is imperative that men break away from the habit of identifying the spiritual with the supernatural.

The reality of the spiritual should be conceived in terms of the supersensible which interacts with and functions through the sensible and perceptible world. The human mind, in sensing that reality, has with some already attained a mature form of spiritual grasp, the product of a first-hand realization that the world is not characterless, that it acts with a uniformity which gives meaning to existence, and that the salvation for which man strives is to live in rapport with that meaning. But this spiritual maturity is far from being general. The majority of mankind are still in the stage of spiritual adolescence. They have outgrown the traditional ideology, but they have not yet acquired an ideology which, taking into account the new knowledge, might help them achieve an affirmative and spiritual adjustment to life.

The Jews ought to realize the seriousness and extent of the spiritual maladjustment in their own lives and in those of the rest of mankind, and take a leading part in effecting the new orientation which is the only means of preventing the eruption of a new barbarism.[13]

Concretely this means the Jews must see themselves as ethical reconstructionists. Their role in society today is no different than it was in the days of Isaiah and Jeremiah. Only their approach will be different.

Judaism and economic justice

Philosophers have found a speculative way of explaining ethics in terms of man's intrinsic dignity apart from revelation and the supernatural. Jews are called upon to do the same in a world that is going anarchical but is also too mature any longer to believe in a personal God.

Once traditional theism is redefined in subjective terms, the rest follows. According to Kaplan, God is what the world means to the man who believes in the possibility of maximum life and strives for it.

This is not to deny that religion served a useful purpose in the past, nor that for some belief in God and divine rewards or punishments is still effective as moral motivation. It does mean that modern man must learn, and Jews should help teach him, that for people to live together they must know how to tame their will-to-power.

How is this to be done? First by having Jews realize that their civilization had always affirmed in the most vigorous fashion the imperative character of the moral law, apart from all considerations of expediency, aesthetic interest, or any other source of validation. Secondly, Jews must understand and so convince others that "the problem of the good life cannot be *why* we should live the good life, but *how* we should live it. For, it is no more possible to prove why we should live the good life than why we should live at all, especially when life bears down hard on us."[14]

This skepticism about the reasons for moral behavior and the practice of virtue follows on the loss of faith in a divinely promulgated Torah.

If there are Jews who still believe in God and the supernatural, they can profitably speak to others who share this now largely abandoned creed. But neither the Jew for himself, nor as a prophet to his fellowman, should feel constrained by such doctrinal limitations.

The assumption of traditional Judaism, that the specific laws and social arrangements which incarnate justice, loving kindness and walking humbly with God were supernaturally revealed to ancient Israel, is for many no longer tenable. But interpreted functionally, that assumption implies that *all* human laws and social arrangements must be subjected to the moral test of being effective as a means of taming man's will-to-power. Otherwise they are only pretentious disguises for selfish exploitation of power and its antisocial use.[15]

Judaism, even minus Yahweh, or at least without supernatural faith in his sanctions, can yet effectively show the way to moral behavior by insisting that an ethical life is, earthly speaking, a happy and prosperous life; and demonstrating in practice how this is to be done.

Without analyzing too closely why morality insures prosperity, Reconstructionism teaches that they are inextricably related. No doubt, "in former days men interpreted earthquakes and tidal waves as afflictions sent by God for the sins they had committed. The knowledge since acquired of the working of the natural law has negated any connection between human sin and the tremors of the earth."[16]

Unfortunately the healthy tendency to deny any connection between human misery and sin went too far. It also divorced men's relations with one another from the consequence of these relations—as though behavior had nothing to do with peace and earthly prosperity.

Jews of all people ought to know from experience the harm done to society by its misdeeds. Collectively and individually they have been among the worst sufferers in the calamities that befell humanity since the First World War. "To no people has the world depression which mankind has brought upon itself through its sins of avarice, exploitation and cruelty been so disastrous as to the Jews." This should be enough to realize that "the only kind of world which can be safe for them is one built upon economic justice."[17] Having been convinced themselves, they are in a strong position to convince others that no one, Jew or Gentile, can hope to enjoy life except in a moral society.

Kaplan's vision of Judaism as a civilizing society drew on his more fundamental insight, that Jews have an instinctive—almost charismatic—sense of justice and social equity. Their role in the modern world is to share this inherited wisdom with others and reconstruct society according to these norms.

LIAISON IN AMERICAN JUDAISM

Among the less well-known features of Conservative Judaism is its role of liaison between the two extremes of Reform and Orthodoxy. The function is perhaps less obvious in theory. But in practice Conservative congregations often serve as a haven for the Orthodox who find it hard to accept all the Jewish regulations and yet have no intention of compromising with what they consider the historic faith. At the same time, they offer Reform Jews an opportunity for more traditional religion without having to accept a demanding Orthodox code.

This role of serving as a balance wheel in American Judaism is graphically brought out in the "Standards for Synagogue Practice" adopted by the United Synagogue of America, which federates the Conservative communities in the United States and Canada.

Sensitive to the traditional concern for preserving the ancient religious heritage, the United Synagogue insists on the faithful keeping of the Sabbath.

The observance of the Sabbath being one of the basic tenets of Judaism, congregations shall require and enforce ap-

propriate observance of the day on the premises owned or controlled by them, and at functions away from their premises
which are sponsored by them.[18]

In the same way the Jewish dietary laws are reinforced, at least
in all situations connected with the synagogue.

Recognizing *kashrut* as another basic tenet of Judaism,
congregations shall take all steps necessary to ensure proper
observance of *kashrut* at all functions on the premises of the
synagogue and at functions away from the synagogue which
are held under their auspices.[19]

This is a familiar distinction, warranted by rabbinical authorities, that allows exceptions to the general law when a Jew is not
acting formally as a member of the Jewish community.

The United Synagogue was also instrumental in getting provisions written into the constitution of the World Council of Synagogues that are favorable to Orthodoxy on such crucial issues as
the synagogue, the Hebrew language, and the State of Israel.

We, the representatives of like-minded congregations from
different climes and continents, do hereby establish the World
Council of Synagogues for the following purposes.

To foster the Jewish tradition in its historic continuity.

To promote the study of Torah and the observance of
mitzvot.

To advocate the centrality and preeminence of the synagogue in the life of the Jewish people.

To further the study of the Hebrew language as the repository of our sacred literature and our accumulated spiritual
and cultural heritage, and as the most potent cultural bond
among Jews throughout the world.

To deepen our dedication to the prophetic ideal of creating in the land of our fathers a Jewish community which shall
pattern its life by the ideals and teachings of the Torah, and
which shall seek to be "a light unto the nations."[20]

At the same time, organized Conservatism seeks to mitigate
the abrasive elements that divide Judaism and urges Jews to tran-

scend these differences in practice—no matter how they may think ideologically.

> Where two or more congregations exist in one community, their relationship should be cooperative and not competitive. Each congregation should regard every other congregation, whether Conservative, Orthodox or Reform, as equally sacred. The differences in doctrine or observance, which may exist between congregations should not diminish the respect due to a congregation dedicated to the service of God.
>
> Where there is more than one affiliated congregation in a community, each should regard itself as complementing the work of the other. Wherever possible, joint advisory committees shall be appointed to minimize areas of competition and to extend and further areas of cooperation.[21]

This kind of Jewish ecumenism is stronger and deeper than anything comparable among Christian denominations. It is only dimly recognized by those who are not Jews.

The effect of such cooperative spirit is a matter of record. Conscious of their midway position in modern Judaism, Conservatives have done yeoman service for the Jewish people to make them aware of their common origin and common destiny.

They have succeeded remarkably on two fronts. The Orthodox in the nineteenth century warned against the inevitable disintegration of the Jewish religion because of adjustment to a Gentile culture. The Reform feared the collapse of Jewish culture unless it adjusted to the American way of life. Neither prediction has come to pass, due in large measure to the Conservative understanding of Judaism.

Above the Ark
are the tablets of
the Decalogue.
In front of the Ark
is the Ner Tamid
(Eternal Light)
recalling the
perpetual flame
on the Altar of
the ancient
Sanctuary.
Within the Ark
are the Scrolls of
the Torah.

Scrolls of the Torah in the Ark

Wearing the phylactery after Bar Mitzvah

Dipping bread into honey before New Year

*Torah Scroll removed from the Ark and then
carried in procession to the Reader's table*

Ritual of lifting up the Scroll after the reading of the Torah

HOLY DAYS—
ORIGIN AND MEANING

Historians of religion write extensively about what they call "sacred time." By this they mean periodic intervals in the cultural life of a people when they commemorate certain past events which are believed to have religious significance. Contrasted with sacred time is profane time, the ordinary sequence of daily activity with no special relevance for man as a religious being. All religions recognize the difference.

Sacred time, as distinct from the profane, is reversible. It always looks back to what occurred before, when God is thought to have entered human history to reveal his mind or manifest his will. In rhythmic chronology these interventions of the divine are recalled by those in whose favor God showed himself. They become the feast days or holy days of that people, to be repeated every year, or every month, or every week—depending on the calculation and conditioned by the importance of the event commemorated.

If the concept of sacred time is common to all religions, it is of the essence of Judaism and has since become part of Christianity and Islam which derive from the Jewish religion.

So closely identified is Judaism with sacred time that the two are almost indistinguishable. Without regular successive holy days there would be no Jewish religion, but at most a Jewish way of life; and without a proper understanding of what these holy days signify, a person may know something about Judaism but he does not enter into its spirit.

People in the Western world are little aware of the fact that, except for the Jews, the periodic celebrations to which they are so accustomed would not even exist. The very idea of a weekly "day of rest" is part of the Jewish heritage.

Only two of the three principal divisions of time, the week and the year, are significant in the Jewish calendar. There are sacred months, of course, but within the month only minor ritual feasts are still commemorated. One reason may be that the ancient Hebrews often consciously avoided duplicating what the pagan nations around them were doing. It is certain that the phases of the moon had attained highly religious meaning among the contemporary cultures of the Old Testament Jews, notably among the Egyptians.

THE SABBATH

Among the prominent festivals of the Jewish calendar, the weekly Sabbath is most important. It is the ritual thread that runs through the entire year and the constantly recurring feast that typifies Judaism as a theistic religion. Even after the precise day was changed by Christianity (to Sunday) and by Islam (to Friday) it remains in both religions the one historic heritage that also characterizes these cultures as monotheistic, as distinct from Oriental religions like Hinduism and Buddhism which do not have the Judaeo-Christian-Moslem equivalent of a weekly Sabbath.

Equally important in Jewish belief is that the Sabbath was divinely ordained. It is therefore closely bound up with the Torah as God's communication to the Chosen People and to this day remains the focus of ritual attention among the Jews. Their weeks of seven days may be described as starting from level ground as each Sabbath ends at sundown and rising to a crescendo until they reach a peak when the next Sabbath begins six days later. The Sabbath unifies Judaism and symbolizes its distinctive features among the living religions of the world.

Origins and development

Some Assyriologists maintain that the Jewish Sabbath originated in Babylonia. They refer to certain Babylonian inscriptions which specify the seventh, fourteenth, nineteenth, twenty-first, and twenty-eighth days of each month as sacred. These days were connected either with the phases of the moon or the number seven. The nineteenth day was included because, when added to the thirty days of the preceding month, it totaled forty-nine, which was seven times seven. According to the same hieroglyphs, the king was not to eat meat roasted on coals, nor any food touched by fire, nor change his clothes, ride in his chariot, nor discuss matters of state on five sacred days of each month.

But this monthly quintet was not a periodic day of rest, nor did it apply to all the people but only to the king, nor did the sequence run through the whole year but occurred only on a given month each year.

Other scholars trace the Sabbath to the Babylonian *Shabattum*, the day of the full moon, considered an unlucky day on which the gods were to be appeased by special sacrifices. Except for the similarity in sound, there are no valid reasons for correlating the two ritual observances. There is no proof that the Jewish Sabbath had anything to do with the full moon, and besides, from the beginning the Sabbath among the Jews meant a weekly festival and not a monthly occurrence, as known in Babylonia.

A common objection against a Babylonian origin is the frequent coupling of Sabbath and the New Moon in the Old Testament. But the two naturally come together throughout the year and they could, therefore, be mentioned in one phrase even though the Sabbath referred to a weekly and the New Moon to a monthly commemoration. Moreover the two feasts are still combined in biblical writings that are known to be from postexilic times, when the Sabbath was beyond doubt the seventh day of each week and could not possibly have been identified ritually with a monthly celebration.

It seems that the Sabbath was observed long before the time of Moses, since there are references to six days of work and one day of rest (*shabbath*) in the earliest Pentateuch writings. In its first stage, the Sabbath was literally a day of repose, as expressed in Exodus, "For six days you shall do your work, but stop on the seventh day, so that your ox and your donkey may rest and the son of your slave girl have a breathing space, and the stranger too."[1]

Moses received the Decalogue on Mount Sinai, including the precept to keep holy the Sabbath Day.[2] Thus an ancient custom became part of God's revelation to his people, although it may be presumed that the Sabbath had already been revealed in patriarchal times.

What the Mosaic code did, however, was to associate the Sabbath with a basic tenet of the Jewish faith, that Yahweh created the world and mankind. His symbolic labor of creation which lasted six days was to be ritually recalled by the people working six days, and then, like God, abstaining from their labors every seventh day.

Given the circumstances of the times, the Sabbath thus became the first religious festival of Israel. It was the only ritual law prescribed on Sinai and the one precept which, if faithfully kept, would forever distinguish the Jews from their polytheistic neighbors.

During the Babylonian Exile the Sabbath acquired a new spiritual meaning, when the exiled Israelites had almost nothing else to reassure them of their faith and keep them in religious solidarity during the long years of oppression in a strange land. They remained loyal to Yahweh by keeping faithful to this commandment, when every other ritual observance (with the possible exception of circumcision) was denied them. From the exile on, the Sabbath became an expression of sacrifice and a symbol of fidelity in the midst of an alien people.

Ezekiel, who lived among the exiled Jews, ascribed to the Sabbath a highly religious meaning that would have been quite impossible except for the Babylonian captivity. "I gave them my

Sabbaths," he quoted the Lord as telling his people, "to be a sign between me and them, so that they might learn that I, Yahweh, am the one who sanctifies them."[3] Observance of the Sabbath became the mark of identification of a Jew—revealed through Moses the lawgiver, as circumcision had earlier become the sign of distinction for a Jew—revealed through Abraham the patriarch.

In the days of the Second Temple, the Sabbath developed in two directions: as a humanitarian institution to give rest for men and women, and even the beasts of the field; and as a religious festival on which the pious Jew could refrain from work in order to give himself more entirely to prayer and communal worship in the synagogue. Some writers believe that the synagogue came into prominence (if not existence) at the time of the Babylonian captivity, when Sabbath and synagogue complemented one another. With Temple destroyed and sacrifice made impossible, the Jews combined time and place by worshiping together on the day of rest. Later on the synagogue would become the mainstay of the Jews outside of Palestine; and always this would be associated with the Sabbath as the time when the followers of Moses professed their belief in the Yahweh of Sinai.

It was also during the time of the Second Temple that the Sabbath became the symbol of Jewish rigorism. From the days of Ezra and Nehemiah in the fifth century before the Christian era, complete abstention from work came to be identified with "keeping holy the Sabbath day." The Scribes and Pharisees must be credited for this change of attitude, from looking upon the Sabbath as a joyous blessing to having it imposed as an onerous legalism.

Until the nineteenth century the Jewish Sabbath could be observed with as much strictness as the believer wished, even in the most distant reaches of the diaspora. But with the new economic life introduced by the industrial revolution, Jews entered more freely into commercial and business activity which carried on through the week, and therefore included Saturdays. Coupled with this was the *Haskalah* or "Enlightenment" among the Jews, which shook to the foundations their most sacred traditions. As Sunday observances spread among their contemporaries, they found the Sabbath more and more difficult to keep.

We have already seen how this affected the faith and practice of Jews in Europe and America, and was one of the main reasons for dividing them into three groups. To this day the best single index of Orthodoxy (contrasted with Conservatism and the Reform) is fidelity to the Sabbath as interpreted by the Talmud and the *Shulhan Aruk*.

Present-day practices

Aware of the historic value of Sabbath observance, American Jews are making every effort to reinstate this basic ritual festival among their people.

Some of the Reform urged the transfer of the Sabbath to Sunday, but this met with little favor. Even where Sunday services are held, they do not replace the Sabbath. They are at most for the convenience of those who cannot attend the synagogue on Saturday.

More common are late Friday night services, after the evening meal, around eight or eight-thirty. Women and children are invited along with the men to participate. Huge candles are lighted on the altar, the Chazan recites *Kiddush*, and a choir sings such well-known hymns as *L'choh Dodi* together with other traditional melodies. The rabbi delivers a sermon and, at least among the Reform, the *Bar Mitzvah* service is often combined with the Friday night synagogue celebration.

The weekly Sabbath has always been a domestic feast even where the synagogue service is omitted or unavailable. It begins in the home when the Jewish mother at sunset on Friday lights the Sabbath candles. If lighting the candles goes back to the beginning of the Christian era, the recitation of a blessing during the process of lighting began only in post-Talmudic times. Both customs are now commonplace in Jewish homes.

While lighting the tapers one after the other, the mother recites a prayer that has not substantially changed in centuries.

Lord of the Universe,
I am about to perform the sacred duty
Of kindling the lights in honour of the Sabbath,
Even as it is written:

And thou shalt call the Sabbath a delight,
And the holy day of the Lord honourable.

And may the effect of my fulfilling this commandment be
That the stream of abundant life and heavenly blessing
Flow in upon me and mine;
That thou be gracious unto us,
And cause thy presence to dwell among us.

Father of Mercy
O continue thy lovingkindness
Unto me and unto my dear ones
Make me worthy
To (rear my children so that they)
Walk in the way of the righteous before thee,
Loyal to thy Law and clinging to good deeds.

Keep thou far from us
All manner of shame, grief, and care;
And grant that peace, light and joy
Ever abide in our home.
For with thee is the fountain of life;
In thy light do we see light. Amen.[4]

This form of the prayer is originally British Orthodox, and American versions differ in their emphasis, but they express the same sentiments.

After the candles are lighted the family sits down to a special Sabbath Eve meal, part of whose ritual goes back to Mosaic times. There are loaves of white bread (*challos*) baked on Friday. Two loaves are commonly served, one each for the traditional two servings of cooked food on the Sabbath. Fish is the usual staple of the Sabbath diet, customary since the Talmudic era.

The evening meal on Friday night opens with the blessing over the wine, performed by the father of the family. *Kiddush* (sanctification or blessing) is still meant to be done at home, even where the ritual is duplicated (or repeated) in the synagogue. The father says over the *Kiddush* cup, "Praised art Thou, O Lord our God, King of the world, who created the fruit of the vine." The cup is then passed around to each person at table to take a sip of wine. Next the father breaks a loaf of bread and recites another blessing: "Blessed art Thou, O Lord our God, King of the world, who brings forth bread from the earth." Pieces of the blessed bread (also called *challah*) are passed around the table in commemoration of olden days. It is believed that two loaves are placed on the table on Sabbath Eve to recall the double portion of manna given to the Israelites in the desert on Friday, to give them enough for the Sabbath on which they were forbidden to gather a portion for that day.

After the meal many Jewish households sing the Sabbath hymn, *L'choh Dodi* (Come, my beloved), even if the song is repeated at the synagogue. The hymn was composed by Solomon Alkabetz (1505-1584), Cabalist friend of Joseph Karo. This song is considered "one of the finest pieces of religious poetry in existence," and has been set to countless melodies. Practically every phrase in the poem is taken from some part of the Bible, mainly from the Messianic passages of Isaiah, Jeremiah, and the Psalms. The Sabbath is personified and compared to a bride, in the same sense as Israel is likened to a bride in Jeremiah. The stanzas are recited alternately by the father and the family; or in the synagogue, by the congregation and the reader.

> "Observe" and "Remember," in a single command, the One God announced to us. The Lord is One, and his name is One, for fame, for glory and for praise.
> Come, my friend, to meet the bride; let us welcome the Sabbath.
> Come, let us go to meet the Sabbath, for it is a source of blessing. From the very beginning it was ordained; last in creation, first in God's plan.
> Come, my friend, to meet the bride; let us welcome the Sabbath.
> Shrine of the King, royal city, arise! Come forth from thy ruins. Long enough have you dwelt in the vale of tears! He will show you abundant mercy.
> Come, my friend, to meet the bride; let us welcome the Sabbath.

Shake off your dust, arise! Put on your glorious garments, my people, and pray: "Be near to my soul, and redeem it through the son of Jesse, the Bethlehemite."
Come, my friend, to meet the bride; let us welcome the Sabbath.

Bestir yourself, bestir yourself, for your light has come; arise and shine! Awake, awake, utter a song; the Lord's glory is revealed upon you.
Come, my friend, to meet the bride; let us welcome the Sabbath.

Be not ashamed nor confounded. Why are you downcast? Why do you moan? The afflicted of my people will be sheltered within you; the city shall be rebuilt on its ancient site.
Come, my friend, to meet the bride; let us welcome the Sabbath.

Those who despoiled you shall become a spoil, and all who would devour you shall be far away. Your God will rejoice over you as a bridegroom rejoices over his bride.
Come, my friend, to meet the bride; let us welcome the Sabbath.

You shall extend to the right and to the left, and you shall revere the Lord. Through the advent of a descendant of Perez we shall rejoice and exult.
Come, my friend, to meet the bride; let us welcome the Sabbath.

Come in peace, crown of God, come with joy and cheerfulness; amidst the faithful of the chosen people come, O bride; come, O bride.
Come, my friend, to meet the bride; let us welcome the Sabbath.[5]

The hymn begins with a refrain from the Talmud, in which the author refers to a rabbinic explanation of the discrepancy between the two versions of the fourth commandment. In Exodus 20:8 the text reads, "Remember the Sabbath Day," and in Deuteronomy 5:12, "Observe the Sabbath Day." The Talmud says that God pronounced both words, "Remember" and "Observe," simultaneously.

The last verse, "Come in peace," is sung as the family (or congregation) turns toward the door, as if to welcome a guest. This recalls the times when Israelites in a strange city were invited to
Jewish homes on Friday night. In the Sephardic, Italian, and Yemenite rituals, the hymn ends with the phrase, "Come O bride, Sabbath Queen," which is repeated in some places three times.

Observant Jews abstain from any kind of work on the Sabbath.
They will not even kindle a fire, although others who are not Jews
may perform such services for them. They do not engage in manual
labor or business; they do not buy or sell, cook or straighten up the
house. Their warrant for this strictness is the meticulous preoccupation of the Talmud with keeping the Sabbath as a day of complete
rest. Since the time of the Pharisees, those who did not compromise
with the precept would be blessed (even miraculously) by God. A
classic passage occurs in a Talmudic commentary on Leviticus.

It is written, "If thou turn away thy foot from doing thy
business on my holy day" (Isaiah 53:13). Hence, a man is forbidden to walk out to his field upon the Sabbath in order to see
what it may need. It happened that a certain pious man walked
out to his vineyard upon the Sabbath to see what it needed,
and he found a break in its fence, and he thought about repair-
ing it, and it was the Sabbath. "Now I will not do it at all,
because I thought about it on the Sabbath day." What did God
do? God prepared a caper bush, and it made a fence for his
vineyard, and the man sustained himself from it all the days of
his life.[6]

The difficulty of keeping the Sabbath as a complete day of rest
is insurmountable in a country like the United States. Many Jews
do not believe that the minutiae of Sabbath observances are binding in conscience. They are surrounded by people whose day of rest
is Sunday, with Saturday the best day for buying and selling. Moreover, there are so many divergent views among authorities in interpreting what "work" and "rest" mean that the average Jew is
satisfied to follow some of the ritual at home and perhaps attend
synagogue. One feature in Conservative and Reform practice that
may attract him is a late evening service followed by a social hour.

Depending on his orthodoxy, he will close the Sabbath with a solemnity comparable to the one that opened it, including special food and drink and formulated prayers.

The ritual of saying farewell to the Sabbath is called *Havdalah* (separation), because it marks the separation of the holy day from the rest of the week that follows. Ideally the ceremony is performed just after dark on Saturday evening. Blessings are recited over the wine, and a box of spices is shaken as "Princess Sabbath" leaves.

> Sovereign of the Universe,
> Father of mercy and forgiveness,
> Grant that we begin the working days
> Which are drawing nigh unto us, in peace;
> Freed from all sin and transgression;
> Cleansed from all iniquity, trespass and wickedness;
> And clinging to the study of thy Teaching,
> And to the performance of good deeds.
>
> Cause us to hear in the coming week
> Tidings of joy and gladness.
> May there not arise in the heart of any man envy of us,
> Nor in us envy of any man.
> O, our King, our God, Father of mercy,
> Bless and prosper the work of our hands.
>
> And all who cherish towards us and thy people Israel
> Thoughts of good, strengthen and prosper them,
> And fulfil their purpose;
> But all who devise against us and thy people Israel,
> Plans which are not for good, O frustrate them
> And make their designs of none effect;
> As it is said,
> Take counsel together, and it shall be brought to nought;
> Speak the word, and it shall not stand;
> For God is with us.[7]

The reference to God, bidding him "Speak the word," recalls the opening verses of Genesis in which the Lord is reported to have spoken, and the different days of creation came into being.

PASSOVER

The Pasch or Passover bears the same relation to the year that the Sabbath has to the week. It is the greatest feast of the Jewish calendar and may properly be called "Passover Week" because it lasts a full seven days.

Its influence on Christianity is seen in the celebration of Easter, which is the crowning point of the Christian liturgical year.

Jewish commentators on the Pasch differ immensely. As a rule, the more Orthodox bring the origin of the feast closer to the time of Moses; the more liberal tend to find its beginnings in religious cultures that preceded the Jewish.

What follows is the Reform interpretation of how the Passover developed through stages until it reached maturity in the last century of the Second Temple.

Four periods are commonly traced in the history of the Passover, two before the time of Moses and two since, corresponding to four kinds of celebration with which the feast has been associated—namely shepherds and agriculture, deliverance and hope. Each has left its mark on the Jewish understanding of religion.

Historical development

Reform historians agree that the Passover was originally connected with the ritual celebration of the ancient Jews as a tribal people who wandered from place to place tending their flocks. Every spring they would have a family festival when they sacrificed a sheep or goat to God and performed a variety of rituals that later on acquired deeper and more exalted meanings. The sacrifice was offered just before nightfall, after which the animal was roasted whole and all the members of the family were to make a hasty meal in the middle of the night. No bones of the animal were to be broken, nor was any part to be left uneaten by the time of dawn. The daubing of tents with the blood of the slain animal was also practiced, for reasons that are obscure in those early days.

As the Jews became a more settled and agricultural people, the spring celebration took on other connotations and practices. The basic theme now became associated with the cutting of grain and was called the Festival of Matzoth (Unleavened Bread). It seems the grain harvest began with the cutting of the barley and ended with the reaping of the wheat, all told lasting about seven weeks.

Basic to the festival was the ceremony of *Omer*, when the first sheaf of the freshly cut barley was offered by the priest on the first day of the harvest as a sacrifice to God. In the meantime the barley harvest was started by getting rid of all the sour dough (fermented dough was used to leaven bread) along with all the old bread.

Besides the Matzoth festival, the early Jewish farmers also observed the Feast of Harvest (*Shovuos*) and the Feast of the Ingathering (*Sukkos*), which has since become Pentecost and Tabernacles and, together with Passover, are still the three great festivals of joy in the Jewish tradition. It is important to bear in mind that originally the Passover and the Feast of the Unleavened Bread were distinct feasts, though observed at the same time. Passover was more ancient, going back to the time when the Jews were desert nomads; the Feast of the Unleavened Bread came later, when they settled down and became farmers. Also it appears that where the Passover was at first a home celebration for the whole family, the ritual connected with unleavened bread pertained to the whole Jewish community.

With the coming of Moses and the liberation of the Jews from the bondage of Egypt the Passover entered a new phase. Their miraculous escape from Pharaoh and his taskmasters became central to the faith and affected every aspect of Jewish culture. The meaning of *Pesach* was determined for all time as "the passing by or over," recalling the fact that the angel of the Lord passed over the homes of the Jews and slew the firstborn of the Egyptians. They baked their matzoth and ate them in a hurry because the Jews were in a rush to get out of Egypt and had no time to leaven their bread or bake it properly. The bitter herbs they had formerly eaten at the Pasch became symbolic of the bitterness of their life among the pagans in Africa. The fruit salad they prepared, the *charoses*, was meant to signify the mortar they mixed while the Jews were enslaved by the Egyptians.

As the Jews became more centralized and their religion nationalized in Palestine, the Passover became a national holy day to an extent never known before. What had been the family part of the

Pasch, with sacrifice offered by the head of the household, took on national proportions. By the time of the Second Temple, Jerusalem was the only place where sacrifices could be offered.

During this period, Messianic hopes rose to an unprecedented height. The Jews came to associate their forthcoming deliverance with the memory of a deliverance long since passed, but rekindled to a meaning it never had before. In ages gone-by, it was liberation from Egypt; now it became the hope of freedom from Rome. Jews came to believe that the Messiah would be a kind of second Moses and, in fact, that he would deliver his people on the selfsame eve, the eve of the Pasch.[8]

Pesach thus became the festival par excellence of both the first and second redemption. Wherever Jews lived, it came to symbolize the confidence of Israel in Yahweh as Savior, that he would deliver his people from Rome (or its later equivalent) as he had freed Israel's ancestors from the slavery of Egypt.

Many changes have taken place since Roman times, but the basic structure of the Sabbath has not substantially changed. Orthodox and Conservative Jews observe the feast for eight days; the Reform for seven days. There are major public ceremonies at the beginning and end of the Passover, with private celebrations in between.

Ritual observances

Passover regularly falls on the tenth day of the first month of the Jewish calendar, called Nisan, which corresponds to the English equivalent of March-April. In popular language, the term *Passover* suggests how the Jewish people escaped from Egyptian bondage by passing through the Red Sea "from darkness into light, from slavery into freedom." The name is also made to refer to the Angel of Death, who killed the firstborn among the Egyptians but passed over the firstborn of the Israelites who marked their homes with the blood of the Paschal Lamb they had newly sacrificed.

The spiritual tempo of the Passover is determined by this memory of the past. The Israelites were told by Moses to sacrifice the Paschal Lamb and make ready for their journey into the desert. Moreover, they were told that in their haste to leave the land of slavery, where they had tasted such hardships, they were to set out with dough still in their kneading troughs; this would later be baked in the hot sun, forming thin cakes.

Commemorating the flight from Egypt and the birth of Israel as a free people, the descendants of the desert wanderers were ordered to keep the Feast of the Unleavened Bread. To this day believing Jews eat matzoth for a whole week during the Paschal season, which is ushered in by the Search after Leaven.

Since it is the leaven in bread and other foods that causes fermentation, none of it is to be allowed in the house during the eight days of the Passover. The father of the family is authorized to go from room to room in search of *Hometz* (leaven). After he gathers up the last crumb, he thanks God for having made the commandment to remove the leaven, and prays that any piece he may have overlooked be "destroyed and become like the dust of the earth."

Then begins the Seder, which literally means "Order" (of the feast), that is, the prescribed sequence in which the rite is to be carried out. In an Orthodox household, the ritual waits until the father returns from the synagogue. He takes his place at the head of the table and seats himself in a chair that was piled up with cushions to recall the couches once used (since Roman days) at the festive meal. Part of the symbolism is that formerly only free men were allowed to recline at meals while their slaves stood and served them. For the Jew, the Passover marked the beginning of their national existence as a free people, no matter how enslaved they may find themselves in whatever country they live.

In addition to the father's place is an empty chair for the prophet Elijah, whom folklore identifies as visiting every Seder table. As Jewish liturgists explain it, the chair is for Elijah the Friend who will introduce the Messiah to a finally free Israel. The Passover is a good time to be reminded of this divine promise. A large goblet of wine on the table also awaits the symbolic return of Elijah.

A large platter is set before the father and bears the symbols of the feast. There is a folded napkin with three matzoth placed in between each fold. The three pieces of unleavened bread stand for each of the three divisions of the Jewish nation—Cohen, Levi, and

Israel. There is a lamb bone, which signifies the sacrificial lamb of the Exodus; a roasted egg typifies the hope of the people and their expectation of final resurrection from the dead. Just as from an apparently dead egg comes forth life, and from winter comes spring, so the Israelites look forward to freedom and to restoration to life on the last day.

The parsley and horseradish root are the greens that symbolize the advent of spring. When the parsley is dipped into salt water, the action is said to recall the many tears shed in slavery; and when the bitter horseradish is eaten with sweet *Haroseth* (apples and nuts mixed with wine), the red color suggests the bricks made during Egyptian slavery. The mixture of bitter and sweet is a reminder of the history of Judaism over the centuries, that is, of a people persecuted by their enemies and yet never losing hope.

Among the prominent features of the Seder are the four questions asked by the youngest child in the family about the meaning of the feast. They begin with the query: "Wherefore is this night distinguished from all other nights." According to the original Talmudic text, the questions should be: (1) Why do we eat only unleavened bread? (2) Why do we eat bitter herbs? (3) Why do we eat roasted meat only? (4) Why do we twice dip the herbs? But when the Paschal Lamb was abolished, the question about the roasted meat was omitted and replaced by the question: Why do we have to eat in a reclining position?

The questions were formulated according to the biblical statements found in Exodus (13 and 14), and intended to stimulate wonder in the children's minds and thus take the opportunity of teaching the young about the history of Israel.

Various answers are given to the questions, depending on the tradition followed. One recommendation, based on the Talmud, is that the narrative should begin with reproach and end with praise. At this point, the father may read at length from the book of Exodus, or he may summarize the story and point up the specific meaning of each Passover rite, as in the following extract from a contemporary manual.

This Unleavened Bread which we eat—because of what is it? It is because there was no time for the dough of our fathers to become leavened before the supreme King of kings, the Holy One, Blessed be He, revealed himself unto them and redeemed them, as it is said: "And they baked unleavened cakes of the dough which they brought forth out of Egypt, for it was not leavened: because they were thrust out of Egypt, and could not tarry, neither had they prepared for themselves any victual."

This Bitter Herb which we eat—because of what is it? It is because the Egyptians embittered the lives of our fathers in Egypt, as it is written: "And they made their lives bitter with hard bondage, in mortar and in brick, and in all manner of service in the field: all their service wherein they made them serve, was with rigour."[9]

Another feature of the service directed to children is the hiding of the *matzo*. Part of the middle matzo is kept for the dessert (*Afikomen*); part is hidden and the child who finds it is given a special present. Again directed to the young is the *Chad Gadyah*, the story first written in Aramaic and sung to an old melody. It tells about the Kid that the Father (Yahweh) bought for two pieces of money. Moreover, a child is normally asked to open the door during the Passover ceremony, to invite any stranger who may then be passing by.

The full Paschal liturgy as celebrated in many Orthodox households since the eleventh century consists of fourteen parts. Each has a technical name and a definite action to perform.

Kaddesh. Recitation of the *Kiddush*, which literally means "sanctification" and stands for the ceremonial blessing which consists of two parts: a benediction over the food and a benediction proclaiming the holiness of the occasion.

Urehatz. Washing of the hands. Going back to ancient times, the symbolic washing of one's hands meant, in this case, the symbolic separation between the profane and the sacred. Leaving behind one's secular occupations (shown by the washing), a person began the religious celebration of the Passover.

Carpas. Partake of the parsley which has been dipped in salt water. Some rituals prescribe a recitation at this point of a blessing, which begins: "Blessed . . . Who createst the fruit of the earth." Other liturgies require only the dipping of the parsley.

Yahatz. The middle matzo is broken and one part is hidden, which is to be eaten at the end of the meal as the Afikomen. One variant adds that a second cup of wine is filled and the recitation of the Haggada begins.

Maggid. Tell the story of Israel's deliverance from Egyptian slavery. Different versions follow different customs. An elaborate form begins with an expression of hope for freedom.

> Behold! This is the bread of affliction which our fathers ate in the land of Egypt. Let all those who are hungry enter and eat thereof; and all who require, come and celebrate the Passover. At present, we celebrate it here; may we celebrate it next year in the land of Israel. This year we are subdued here, but next year we hope to be free men.[10]

Here follows the recitation of the four questions which the child asks the father, and his answers.

Rahatza. Once more the hands are washed. The meaning is again symbolic separation, but this time not from the secular to the sacred, but from one level of the sacred to a higher level of sacred action which immediately follows. The action is the ritual eating of the Paschal meal.

Matzi, matza. A blessing is recited over the unleavened bread. One rubric requires that the upper matzo is taken and the benediction over bread is pronounced. Then the benediction: "Blessed . . . Who commanded us to eat unleavened bread."

Maror. Partake of the bitter herbs and recite the appropriate benediction: "Blessed . . . Who commanded us to eat bitter herbs."

Corech. Combine matzo, Maror, and *Haroseth* and eat all three together. A familiar custom is to break the third matza, take two pieces of it, and put between them some herbs with *Haroseth* while saying: "This is to commemorate the practice of Hillel in the time of the Temple who thus used to eat in fulfillment of the biblical statement, 'Together with unleavened bread and bitter herbs they shall eat it'—the Paschal Lamb."[11]

Shulhan orech. Partake of the Passover meal. A standard American Jewish cookbook lists twenty-four different recipes for the Passover, including dairy products, fish, poultry, and beef or lamb.

Tzafun. Finish the meal by eating the previously hidden Afikomen (Greek *aphikomion*=dessert). The reason for eating matza instead of a regular delicacy is to retain a taste of the matza after
the meal.

Barech. Grace is recited. According to one ritual, a third cup of
wine is filled just before grace. In the third benediction of grace,
the mystical passage *Yaale Ve-yavo* is inserted with the particular
mention of the Passover.

Our God and God of our fathers, may the remembrance of
us, of our fathers, of Messiah the son of David thy servant, of
Jerusalem thy holy city, and of all thy people of the house
of Israel, ascend and come (*yaale ve-yavo*) and be accepted before thee for deliverance and happiness, for grace, kindness
and mercy, for life and peace, on this day of the Feast of Unleavened Bread.[12]

This paragraph is perhaps the most sacred Messianic invocation in the Jewish liturgy.

Hallel. At this point the remainder of the Hallel is recited. Literally *Hallel* is the Hebrew for "praise." Technically it refers to the
cluster of six Psalms (113-18) which the Talmud regards as a single
composition. Another theory holds that they were first brought
together for the rededication of the Temple after the wars of the
Maccabees and then accepted as a divinely prescribed part of the
liturgy for the three pilgrim festivals.

In some rites, the Great Hallel is added. This is Psalm 136,
which begins with the word *Halelujah*=Praise ye the Lord. It is
instructive to note that the Hebrew translation of the response in
the Psalm is "His mercy endures forever." The tone of the Great
Hallel (*Hallel Ha-Gadol*) may be seen from its first three (thanksgiving) verses.

Give thanks to the Lord, for he is good,
    His mercy endures forever;
Give thanks to the supreme God,
    His mercy endures forever;
Give thanks to the Lord of lords,
    His mercy endures forever.[13]

The term "Great Hallel" is used to distinguish it from the "Egyptian Hallel," which is another name for Hallel (Psalms 113-18). It differs from all the other Psalms in having each verse close with the same refrain, probably designed to be sung in full chorus by the people.

After this recitation, the fourth cup of wine is taken with its appropriate benediction, and after the wine is consumed another benediction is recited. Everybody, the Talmud prescribes, "even the poorest who subsist on charity shall drink four cups of wine." Since Jewish tradition considers wine as symbolic of the climax of joy, it should be taken in greater abundance on the Passover. Talmudists further explain that the four cups of wine typify the four promises of redemption made to Israel.

> Say this, then, to the sons of Israel, I am Yahweh. I will free you of the burdens which the Egyptians lay upon you.
> I will release you from slavery to them, and with my arm outstretched and my strokes of power I will deliver you.
> I will adopt you as my own people, and I will be your God.
> Then you shall know that it is I Yahweh your God, who have freed you from the Egyptians' burdens.[14]

Throughout the centuries of Jewish history, these four freedoms have become enshrined in the hearts of the people. Their alliterative spelling in Hebrew adds to their dignity: *Wehotzhethi* =bringing out of bondage, *Wehitzalti*=deliverance from servitude, *Wegaalti*=redemption from all dependence on Egypt, and *Welakahti*=election as the Chosen People of God.

Worth noting is that "Egypt" is a deeply symbolic concept in Jewish thought. It stands for all those who in any way have opposed or oppressed Israel from the days of the Pharaohs to the present time.

A fifth cup of wine (honoring Elijah), set in the middle of the table at the beginning of Seder, is sometimes prescribed for drinking at the time of the Great Hallel. Not only is Elijah expected to announce the redemption of Israel, but he is commissioned to decide its legality, since he is supposed to settle all doubts in religious matters.

Nirtza. There is a closing prayer for acceptance of the service. In the ritual practices of the Ashkenazim and Sephardim, the folk song about the Kid and the two Zuzim (pieces of money) is an essential part of the Passover ceremony. A common rabbinical interpretation identifies the Kid with the Temple. It was bought by the father for two Zuzim, symbolizing the fact that David paid twenty-four Zuzim for the Temple place, collecting from each of the twelve tribes two Zuzim.

"Then came the cat." This is Nebuchadnezzar, king of Babylon, who destroyed the Temple.

"Then came the dog." This is Cyrus, king of Persia, who conquered Babylon.

"Then came the stick." This is Alexander the Great who subdued Persia.

"Then came the fire." This refers to the Maccabees who burnt the stick, and won a victory over the Greeks.

"Then came the water." This is Rome; and quenched the fire—destroyed the power of the Maccabees.

"Then came the ox." This is Ishmael, or the Islam, and drank the water—and conquered (eastern) Rome.

"Then came the slaughterer and killed the ox." This is Messiah, son of Joseph, who will destroy the mighty ox.

"Then came the angel of death and killed the slaughterer." According to Rabbinic tradition, this Messiah will fall a victim in his fight.

"Then came the Holy One, blessed is He, and killed the angel of death." In the future God will abolish death and destruction, and humanity will enjoy eternal life and peace.[15]

In allegorical form, this *Chad Gadyah* synthesizes the whole meaning of the Passover for the Jews. It is at once a memory of deliverance in the past and a promise of delivery from suffering and death into the eternal future.

PENTECOST

The second of the three great feasts of joyous solemnity in the Jewish year is Shavuot. Also called Shabuot or Shovuos, which is the Hebrew for "weeks," it was originally a wheat harvest festival.

In Temple times, the custom was to bring two loaves to the priests and to offer the first fruits (*bikkurim*). Later on, the Mishnah and Talmud called it *Atzeret* (termination), to indicate the end of the Paschal season at fifty days after the Pasch. Since Greek was commonly spoken by the Jews of the diaspora, the feast came to be known as Pentecost (*pentecostes*=fiftieth) to designate that the required number of days had been counted.

This countdown from the Pasch to Pentecost is called the Days of Omer. An *Omer* literally meant a measure about the size of a half gallon, and contained some of the wheat of the first harvest brought to be sacrificed at Jerusalem. The prescription in Leviticus is specific.

> From the day after the sabbath (Pasch), the day on which you bring the sheaf of offering, you are to count seven full weeks. You are to count fifty days, to the day after the seventh sabbath, and then you are to offer Yahweh a new oblation.[16]

After further specifying what the oblation was to be, Yahweh told Moses that, "This same day you are to hold an assembly. This shall be a sacred assembly for you. You will do no heavy work. This is a perpetual law for your descendants, wherever you live."[17]

Synonymous with Days of Omer is the Period of Sephirah (counting), during which special mourning customs prevail and marriages are not solemnized. One exception is the thirty-third day in the counting of *Omer*, the *Lag Bo-Omer*. According to legend an outbreak of plague among the pupils of Rabbi Akiba in the second century of the Christian era ended on this date. So the day is considered a "scholars' feast," when the normal prohibitions (including the cutting of hair) are suspended. In present-day Israel the day is celebrated by the lighting of bonfires and a mass pilgrimage at Meron to the tomb of Rabbi Simeon ben Yohai, pupil of Akiba, who is said to have died on this day.

Rabbinic commentators explain the role of Pentecost in connection with the Passover. Where the Pasch commemorates the deliverance of the Jews, Pentecost annually reminds them of the purpose of this deliverance. The purpose is twofold: gratefully to remember that God's revelation was first given to Israel and prayerfully to recall that they are his Chosen People because he wants them to transmit his revelation to the rest of mankind. Pentecost, therefore, symbolizes the gift of the Torah to Israel and the duty to communicate the Torah to the Gentiles.

In the United States this double aspect is associated with the Confirmation services held for the graduates of the synagogue school. Reform synagogues have commonly adopted the practice as a reaction to the Bar Mitzvah service which the Orthodox limit to boys at the age of thirteen. Confirmation programs among the Reform are in addition to the *Bar Mitzvah*, and designed to take care of groups of boys and girls. After much experimentation, the Reform custom now is to confirm the young people on Pentecost "so that each new generation of Israel accepts its responsibility in Judaism on the same day that Israel received God's law on Mount Sinai."[18] Tradition has it that Moses received the Decalogue on what later became the Feast of Shavuot.

TABERNACLES

The third major feast of gladness in the Jewish year has a variety of names. Most frequently called the Feast of Tabernacles, it is also known as *Sukkos* (alternate spellings, *Succoth* and *Sukkoth*), which is the Hebrew for "tabernacles" or "tents." Its most familiar feature is the building of a temporary hut or tent, within the home (or synagogue) to commemorate the wandering of the Israelites in the desert and their living in tents, on their way to the Promised Land.

Reform writers generally disagree with this interpretation as too literal and prefer to associate the practice with the temporary shacks erected in the fields and orchards during the harvest season or with the booths built by the pilgrims who came to Jerusalem to observe the autumn festivals. Other interpretations are also given. But the prevalent explanation identifies the feast with Israel's promised destiny—originally in Palestine and eventually throughout the world.

Tabernacles is celebrated for eight days by the Orthodox and Conservatives. The first and last two days have special ceremonies in the home and synagogue. Devout Jews build a small structure in which they can eat their meals throughout the holy day to remind them of the hardships of their ancestors experienced by living in frail huts en route to Palestine.

As usually built, the Sukkah has improvised walls and a covering of leafy branches and twigs instead of a roof. It should not be lower than five feet nor higher than thirty; and it must be exposed to a view of the heavens. A permanent Sukkah is forbidden, on the premise that the whole mood should be relived each year.

On its harvest side, the feast is celebrated by the ritual of the *Lulav* (rabbinic Hebrew for "sprout"). This consists in waving a cluster of six sprouts, that is, a palm branch, three myrtle twigs, and two willow sprigs. In the right hand is held the Lulav, while a citron is placed in the left hand. At appropriate times during the service, the ensemble is moved to and fro in the four directions of the compass, and up and down. This is to symbolize that God should be thanked by all people for his generous granting of the harvest everywhere.

While the cluster is taken in hand, litanies of praise are sung, with interjections of "Hosanna," meaning "O save us."

Immediately at the close of the Feast of Tabernacles, a one-day holiday is celebrated under the name of "Eighth Day of Solemn Assembly." On this day special prayers for rain are offered to God. The ritual, as observed among the Orthodox, is among the most elaborate in Jewish liturgy. One after another of the great men of Israel's past are associated with water as a symbol of divine blessings. Abraham "sowed by all streams of water," Isaac dug wells and "did discover water," Jacob "crossed the Jordan's water," Moses "struck the rock and there gushed out water," and the Temple priest "bathed five times in water." After each reference to water in the history of the Chosen People comes the refrain, "For his sake, do not refuse water."[19]

PURIM AND HANUKKAH

Besides the three major feasts of gladness which trace their origin to the Bible are two others that have been observed since biblical times, actually since the writing of the Jewish canon. Purim and Hanukkah typify the development of Judaism as a religious culture and, in some cases, are celebrated with as much solemnity (or at least popular appeal) as even the Passover.

Purim

The Feast of Lots (Hebrew *Purim*) commemorates the deliverance of the Jews in ancient Persia through the mediation of Esther, after their annihilation had been decreed by Haman, vizier of King Ahasuerus. According to the book of Esther, Haman had ordered all the Jews of Persia to be slain on the fourteenth day of the month of Adar. He was angry with the Hebrews because one of their number, Mordecai, refused to pay him homage. Queen Esther was a Jewess and the niece of Mordecai, who had raised her as his own daughter. She risked her life to appeal for her people with the king. Through her intercession, Haman was foiled and was hung from the very gallows he had prepared for Mordecai. What was to have been a day of great mourning became the day of deliverance.

Purim is called the Feast of Lots because Haman had selected the extermination date by casting lots.

Some Jewish critics regard the book of Esther as a romance written to explain a festival already adopted. But most Jews, certainly all the Orthodox, regard the feast as truly historical and confirmed in Persian sources.

The book of Esther (*Megillat Ester*) is read in the synagogue on the eve and morning of Purim. The custom arose of making an uproar by sounding rattles, stamping the feet, and so forth, whenever the name of Haman was mentioned in the course of the reading. Fancy dress and masks came to be worn on that day and, at least since the Middle Ages, the practice of giving Purim plays started in Spain, France, and Portugal.

Characteristic of the spirit of the feast is the closing prayer for Purim morning, in which blessings and curses are mixed in memory of what Yahweh had done centuries ago.

The Jews of Shashan (capital of Persia) shouted for joy
When they all saw Mordecai robed in purple.
Thou hast ever been their salvation,
Their hope in every generation,
To show that all who hope in thee

Shall never be ashamed nor confounded.
Cursed be Haman who sought to slay me;
Blessed be Mordecai the Judaean!
Cursed be Zeresh, my menacer's wife;
Blessed be Esther, my protectress![20]

This is the simplest form of ritual for Purim, found in the Sephardic and Italian liturgies. The most elaborate form is the Ashkenazic, which has a long alphabet acrostic that runs poetically through the whole story of Esther and closes with a eulogy called *Lily of Jacob*. It compares the liberation in Persia with the miraculous deliverance from Egypt.

Over the centuries Purim has become symbolic for Jewish deliverance. Whenever a Jewish colony or even single family was saved from some terrible fate, for example, from pogrom or exile at the hands of a latter-day Haman, the day of liberation became a special, local Purim patterned after the universal feast of the same name.

Families might have their own Purims that were to be commemorated annually by the children and grandchildren, down the generations, in perpetual gratitude to God for his mercy to persons of this particular name.

Among other Purims that have somehow entered Hebrew history, three are commonly mentioned in Jewish liturgies. The first recalls the tragic dilemma in which the Jews of Egypt found themselves in 1524, when they stood firm by the Moslem Sultan Suleiman II, against the rebellious governor of Cairo. In retaliation the governor imprisoned many Jews and ordered their general massacre on the twenty-eighth of Adar. Unexpectedly the governor was overthrown on that very day, and ever since the Jews of Egypt celebrate the occasion as a second Purim.

A similar feast is kept sacred in Germany, in remembrance of a sudden liberation of the Jews threatened with a pogrom in 1614; and a Purim in Lithuania recalls what the Jews consider a miraculous preservation of their people from an explosion at Vilna in 1804.

As might be expected, Purim has a special meaning for the inhabitants of modern Israel, where a Purim carnival (*Adloyada*) is celebrated with extraordinary ceremony.

Some Jewish commentators associate the universal feast of Purim not only with Queen Esther but also with the story of Judith and Holofernes. Although the book of Judith is not in the canon of the present Hebrew Bible, the courage of this valiant widow is joined with that of Esther, and the two together typify the prominent role of women in the history of Israel.

Hanukkah

If Purim symbolizes the deliverance of the Jewish people at various periods in their struggle for corporate existence, Hanukkah is the main feast which signifies the saving of the Jewish religion. Both holy days are commemorative of salvation; the first of the Jews and the second of Judaism.

The word is variously spelled *Chanukkoh* or *Hanukkah*, which in Hebrew means "dedication," and commemorates the victory of Judah the Maccabee over Antiochus Epiphanes and the subsequent rededication of the Temple and altar in Jerusalem. Judah and his brothers assigned a period of eight days to praise the Lord in thanksgiving.

After the destruction of the Temple in A.D. 70, the feast was linked with the miracle of the cruse of oil which burned for eight days and the duty of kindling lights was thereby instituted. One light is kindled on the first night and an extra one is added each succeeding night. The eight-branched lamp (*Menorah*) built to hold these lights has often been the object of rare artistic design and, since the first celebration of Hanukkah, has become a symbol of Jewish ritual, much as a chalice and host typify the central rite of Christianity.

Scholars consider Hanukkah the clearest dated festival of the Jewish calendar, that is, 165 B.C.E. Along with definite historical beginnings, however, Hanukkah shows much the same kind of development as we find in Purim. Where Purim has come to stand for Jewish deliverance from religious persecution, Hanukkah is the anniversary of Jewish faith and communal liturgy.

Features of the Hanukkah celebration are the kindling of the lights, eating of cheese dishes, having games and plays, and reading the scroll of Antiochus.

In the olden days, lights were kindled only in the home. Later on they were also kindled in the synagogue. Formerly they were lighted at the left side of the door leading to the street, opposite the *Mezuzah*. If a person lived in an upper story and had no door leading to the street, the lights were to be placed in the window. The blessing recited over the Hanukkah lights dates from the time of Amoraim, in the third to the sixth centuries of the Christian era. During the Middle Ages the song, "Rock of Ages," appeared among the Ashkenazim. It has since become a classic in world Judaism. Composed by Mordecai, an unknown liturgical poet of the thirteenth century, the *Maoz Tzur* (Fortress Rock) is a powerful profession of trust in God. The second through the fifth stanzas recount the deeds of Yahweh in favor of his people in Egypt and Babylon, in Persia, and under the Greeks. The first verse sets the main theme.

O God, my saving Stronghold,
To praise thee is a delight!
Restore my house of prayer,
Where I will offer thee thanks;
When thou wilt prepare havoc
For the foe who maligns us,
I will gratify myself
With a song at the altar.[21]

The custom of eating cheese delicacies on Hanukkah is an old one. Some trace the origin of pancakes to this custom among the ancient Jews of baking pancakes made with cheese on the Feast of Lights. Ritual commentators explain the practice by referring to the legend that Judith fed cheese to Holofernes, the leader of the Jewish foes. As a result he became very thirsty and drank much wine. In his drunken stupor she beheaded him.

Among the games played on Hanukkah, spinning *dreidel* tops is one of the most popular. The tops are made with four wings, each of which has a letter of the Hebrew alphabet: N (nun), G (gimmel), H (he), and SH (shin). Taken together the four letters are supposed to represent an acrostic of the sentence, *Nes Godol Hoyoh Shom* (A great miracle happened there), referring to the marvelous victory over their enemies by the Maccabees.

Theatricals have also been part of Hanukkah celebrations since at least the Middle Ages. Men would put on women's clothing and parade through the streets. Plays were shown to the people, and the custom still prevails in places where the Jews form a community.

The Feast of Hanukkah is also one of the few occasions in the year, along with the Passover, when the Hallel is recited and a description of what happened under Judah Maccabaeus is inserted in each Amidah or benediction of the liturgy.

Purim normally occurs in later February and through the month of March. But Hanukkah comes toward the end of November and up to December 25. It is therefore popularly associated with the Christian celebration of Christmas.

ROSH HA-SHANAH

The Jewish New Year (*Rosh Ha-Shanah*) is celebrated by Orthodox Jews on the first two days of the Jewish month Tishri, ranging from early September through early October. Reform Jews keep the festival only on the first day of Tishri.

Like Yom Kippur, which comes ten days later, Rosh Ha-Shanah is a Day of Awe. Unlike the Passover, Purim, or Hanukkah, Rosh Ha-Shanah has no trace of joy. Its theme is serious consideration and a feeling of moral responsibility. Also unlike other feasts of the Jewish year, Rosh Ha-Shanah is not a communal celebration but directed to a person's own individual welfare.

A word about the Hebrew calendar will help to bring out the meaning of the Jewish New Year. The calendar in most common use throughout the world is based on the sun. Moslems calculate both the year and the month according to the phases of the moon. The Moslem year is therefore shorter than the general year by some eleven days. Jews follow a calendar that partakes of both the other two. Their months are figured according to the moon, with twelve months of twenty-nine and a half days each; but their year is determined by the sun. To take up the extra eleven days, lost in the Moslem calendar, they add a whole month in leap years. Thus every second or third year there is a thirteenth month, a second Adar.

The contemporaries of the ancient Jews followed different kinds of calendars and, as a result, also had different beginnings of the year. The Babylonians and Persians began their year in the spring. Egyptians started in the summer, to correspond with the rise of the Nile on which their life depended. Romans celebrated each new year in the winter, and the inhabitants of Palestine had theirs in the fall.

Whatever custom the Jews may have borrowed from the nations around them, their Torah prescribed a "feast of ingathering, at the end of the year."[22] On religious grounds, then, they started the year in autumn, when all the work of harvesting was done and the earth was ready once again to receive the rains needed to bring forth new growth for the year to come.

A problem arises from the fact that elsewhere in the Bible the first month of the year is said to be Nisan, so that the months were numbered beginning with the spring and making the Passover the opening feast of the new year. Jewish historians explain the apparent discrepancy by saying that the original practice was to start the year in the fall, and this has never been lost. But for a time, the Jews were influenced by the Babylonians, who observed the New Year in the spring. In time they reverted to their pristine custom and also invested the celebration with deeper religious significance.

As described in the Pentateuch, in a context filled with references to the number seven, the Israelites are told by Moses: "The first day of the seventh month shall be a day of rest for you, a sacred assembly proclaimed with a trumpet call. You must not do any heavy work and you must offer a burnt offering to Yahweh."[23]

Actually the first day of every month was an occasion for blowing the horns at the New Moons of other months. But long blasts were to be sounded on the New Moon of the seventh month.

All the evidence indicates that the first of Tishri, the seventh month of the year, was to be the Jewish New Year, for the same reason that the seventh day of each week was a Jewish Sabbath. In one case weekly and in the other annually, the Jews were to solemnize their faith in God's creation of the world by abstaining from servile work as he is said to have rested from his labors on the seventh day.

As early as the destruction of the Second Temple, Rosh Ha-Shanah already had most of the features with which it is connected

today. The Shofar was blown in the synagogue and numerous interpretations were read into the practice. Like today, the feast was
mainly a synagogue celebration. Long services were introduced and
the custom of using different leaders of prayer for the Morning and
Musaf (added) Services came into vogue. Still more prayers and the
religious poetry (Piyut) of the Middle Ages became customary, until
now the liturgy of Rosh Ha-Shanah is perhaps the richest in contemporary Jewish worship. The standard edition of the *High Holiday Prayer Book* runs to five hundred pages, and deals exclusively
with the services for Rosh Ha-Shanah and its complementary feast
of Yom Kippur.

One Piyut, out of more than a score, illustrates the dominant
theme of the Jewish New Year: the remembrance of God's creative
power, begun at the dawn of creation and still going on in his providence over angels and mankind. Each of eight verses is introduced
with the refrain, sung by the people: "The Lord is King, the Lord
was King, the Lord shall be King for ever and ever." The first and
last verses typify a characteristic Jewish hymnology, correlating
heaven and earth in singing the praise of Yahweh.

The heroic sons of a mighty race
Shout in thunder the Lord is King;
The angels whose figure the lightnings trace
Flame to the world that the Lord was King;
And seraphs whose stature is one with space,
Proclaim that the Lord shall be King forever.

The universe throbs with Thy pauseless praise,
Chorus eternal, the Lord is King.
Thy glory is cried from the dawn of days,
Worshippers calling the Lord was King.
And ever the saints who shall witness Thy ways
Shall cry that the Lord shall be King forever.[24]

Rosh Ha-Shanah stands midway between the Sabbath and the
Sabbatical Year as an annual witness to man's complete dependence
on God. It is logically followed, ten days later, by Yom Kippur as
the great day on which the Jewish nation makes a public confession
of its sins.

YOM KIPPUR

It is symbolic of the true spirit of Judaism that its greatest holy day is not the Passover nor even Purim or Hanukkah but Yom Kippur, which is the Day of Atonement. The implication is that somewhere near the center of the Jewish faith is a realization of God's sovereignty and of man's need for reconciliation.

As far back as the period of the Second Temple, Yom Kippur was already the holiest day of the year. They called it "The Great Day" or, simply, "The Day." Whether in Palestine or dispersed throughout the world, they fasted and prayed on that day as on no other. According to the Jewish philosopher Philo, who lived in Egypt in the first century of the Christian era, even the most unbelieving Jew became pious on Yom Kippur.

That was the one day in the year when all eyes were turned to Jerusalem. It was the only day on which the High Priest was allowed to enter the Holy of Holies. The High Priest normally performed the Temple rites. On Sabbath days and festivals, he showed himself to the people dressed in golden robes. But on Yom Kippur he became another man, a sinner like the rest of Israel. His prayers on that day were directed to the God of mercy, begging forgiveness for himself and the Chosen Race. For seven days before Yom Kippur, he left his home to live in the Temple. During that week he conducted the service alone, offered daily sacrifices, sprinkled the blood of the animals, burned the fragrant incense, and supervised the lighting of the Menorah. All of this was a prelude to the liturgy of The Great Day, to make sure that no mistake in word or gesture would be made in solemn acts of atonement to Yahweh.

In the centuries since the destruction of the Second Temple, the Jews have not substantially changed the meaning of the Day of Atonement. With the Temple gone and bloody sacrifice no longer offered, there is no High Priest to preside and the Holy of Holies is only a fond memory. But the spirit of the feast remains the same.

The first ten days of the month of Tishri, which begins with Rosh Ha-Shanah and ends with Yom Kippur, are called the Ten Days of Penitence. In anticipation, the days are colored by the solemnity of Yom Kippur. Orthodox Jews fast till noon every day, with the exception of the Sabbath and the eve of Yom Kippur, when fasting is forbidden. The Saturday before Yom Kippur is called Sabbath Shuvoh, named from the opening words of the Bible read on that day. It is observed with great strictness and the sermon in the synagogue on Sabbath Shuvoh is an exhortation to repentance for sin.

The second day before Yom Kippur is called the day of Kaporos. This is the day on which the modern equivalent of the ancient scapegoat is offered and sacrificed in place of sinners.

In former times a goat was used. After ceremonial prayers, the animal was led to a spot about ten miles beyond Jerusalem, where a precipice overhangs a ravine. The goat was taken in solemn ritual to the cliff and then suddenly pushed over the precipice, its life departing as it fell into the ravine. The symbolism was unmistakable. What sinful men deserved for their offenses, God was pleased to visit on the animal; its death was a means of expiation for their sins.

Nowadays instead of a goat, fowl are used, a rooster by the men and a hen by the women. Customs differ, but the main features include reading from the Psalms, circling the fowl about the head nine times and slaughtering the animal by the Shohet according to prescribed ritual.

The ritual of Atonement consists of three parts: the spiritual confession of one's sins, the physical offering of the fowl or its equivalent in money, and the verbal affirmation of sorrow and a plea for forgiveness.

The order of Kaporos allows different formulas. A common one used by the Orthodox in the United States offers at least seven versions. First comes a long recitation, based on the Bible, recalling God's mercy and the need for offering ransom for one's sins.

> Children of men, such as sit in darkness and in the shadow of death, being bound in affliction and iron, he brought them out of darkness and the shadow of death, and break their bands in sunder. Fools because of their transgression, and because of their iniquities, are affected. Their soul abhorreth all manner of food; and they draw near unto the gates of death. Then they cry unto the Lord in their troubles, and he saveth them out of their distress. He sent his word, and healed them, and deliv-

ered them from their destructions. Oh that men would praise
the Lord for his goodness, and for his wonderful works to the
children of men! If there be a messenger with him and inter-
preter, one among a thousand, to shew unto man his upright-
ness: Then he is gracious unto him, and saith, Deliver him
from going down to the pit: I have found a ransom.[25]

Then follow various prayers of atonement, depending on who
is praying for whom.

If a person atones for himself, he recites three times: "This is
my change, this is my redemption. This rooster is going to be killed,
and I shall be admitted and allowed to a long, happy and peaceful life."[26]

If anyone atones for another person, he says the same thing except to change "my" to "your." If a man atones for a woman, he
substitutes "chicken" for "rooster," and vice versa when the one for
whom expiation is offered is a man. Following the rite of Kaporos
is a series of benedictions, all somehow centered on the memory of
God's forgiving kindness to his people in the past, and a promise of
like mercy even now.

Running through the Yom Kippur liturgy is a strong Messianic
theme. Time and again, in prayer after prayer, the penitent looks
forward to the hope of deliverance through the Anointed One.

Blessed art thou, O Lord our God and God of our fathers.
. . . who rememberst the pious deeds of the patriarchs, and in
love wilt bring a redeemer to their children's children for thy
name's sake.[27]

Give them glory, O Lord, unto thy people, praise to them
that fear thee, hope to them that seek thee, and free speech to
them that wait for thee, joy to thy land, gladness to thy city, a
flourishing horn unto David thy servant, and a clear shining
light unto the son of Jesse, thine anointed, speedily in our
days.[28]

One of the most inspiring features of the Yom Kippur liturgy
is a long list of sins from which the Jew asks to be delivered. Fifty-
three kinds of transgression are enumerated, each specific and each

to be confessed in unison with other believers. Typical admissions of guilt illustrate the whole confessional litany.

> For the sin which we have committed before thee under compulsion, or of our own will; For all these, O God of forgiveness, forgive us, pardon us, grant us remission.
> And for the sin which we have committed before thee with utterance of the lips . . .
> For the sin which we have committed before thee by unchastity . . .
> For the sins which we have committed before thee in business . . .
> And for the sin which we have committed before thee with wanton looks . . .
> For the sin which we have committed before thee by ensnaring our neighbor . . .
> And for the sins for which we are liable to the penalty of forty stripes . . .
> And for the sins for which we are liable to the penalty of death by the hand of heaven . . .
> And for the sins for which we are liable to the penalty of excision and childlessness; for all these, O God of forgiveness, forgive us, pardon us, grant us remission.[29]

Jewish commentators speak of three exalted moments in the Yom Kippur celebration. The first comes on the eve of the feast, when the synagogue cantor sings *Kol Nidre*. There is no more significant prayer in Jewish liturgy than this remission of guilt. It has been called the great covenant prayer of Israel. Its intent is twofold: absolution from all vows from that day to the next Day of Atonement, and a petition for mercy over the sins of the past year.

Whereas the Hebrew text does not state what precise vows are meant, it is commonly understood that the *Kol Nidre* does not release a person from obligations made to his fellowmen. Only hostile critics of the Jewish people still claim the opposite.

The *Kol Nidre* comes in three parts. First the rabbi invokes the heavenly court and the memory of the ancient Sanhedrin to pronounce absolution; then rabbi and people together pray for mercy;

and finally, the famous *Kol Nidre* chant sung in a variety of melodies. The following ritual is widely practiced in Conservative American congregations.

> *Reader*: By Authority of the heavenly Tribunal, and of the Court below, with divine sanction and with the sanction of this holy congregation, we declare it lawful to pray together with those who have transgressed.

> All vows, bonds, promises, obligations, and oaths to God wherewith we have vowed, sworn and bound ourselves from this Day of Atonement unto the next Day of Atonement, may it come unto us for good; lo, of all these, we repent us in them. They shall be absolved, released, annulled, made void, and of none effect; they shall not be binding nor shall they have any power. Our vows to God shall not be vows, our bonds shall not be bonds; and our oaths shall not be oaths.

> *Reader and Congregations*: And the congregation of Israel shall be forgiven, as well as the stranger that dwells among them, since the people have transgressed unwittingly.

> O pardon the iniquities of this people according to Thy great mercy, as Thou hast forgiven this people from the days of Egypt until now.

> The Lord said: "I have forgiven according to thy word."

> Blessed art Thou, O Lord our God, King of the universe, who has kept us in life, and hast sustained us, and enabled us to reach this season.

> *Meditation*
> Kol Nidre—chant of ages,
> Chant of Israel, chant of sorrow,
> Measuring off the throbbing heartbeats
> Of a people bowed in anguish,
> Crushed by tyrants, thwarted, broken,
> Wand'ring ever—homeless, weary.
> Generations set your motif
> Out of trials, hopes and yearnings,
> Added each its variations
> To your theme and to your cadence.
> Diverse lands and diverse periods

Poured their soul into your music.
When we hearken with our hearts tuned,
We can hear the lamentations
Through time's corridor resounding;
We can see revealed before us
Heroes, martyrs, saints and scholars,
Loyal, steadfast sons of Israel
Sanctifying God, their Father.[30]

A second tense moment in the Yom Kippur service comes in
the ritual on the next day. Poetic descriptions and beautiful songs,
sung by the cantor and congregation, relive the Temple service of
ancient Israel. When the cantor mentions the prostration in the
court of the Temple, the whole congregation throw themselves to
the ground and bury their faces in supplication. This recalls what
their ancestors did when, on the Day of Atonement, they heard the
High Priest call out the thrice-holy name of God.

The third moment of exaltation occurs at the *N'iloh*, which are
the concluding prayers of Yom Kippur. Literally the word means
"to close," and referred to the closing of the Temple gates of
heaven, after a sinner has done a wholehearted penance and promised amendment during the next year.

In Orthodox congregations the emotional experience is inde-
scribable. The sun is just setting and the great Yom Kippur candles
are almost burned down. The congregation is standing after hours
of fasting and prayer. The whole atmosphere is charged with a
sense of awe, at the past that is ending and the future still to come.
Just before the sounding of the Shofar the people cry out: "Hear,
O Israel: the Lord our God, the Lord is One. Blessed be the name
of His glorious kingdom for ever and ever. The Eternal, He
is God."[31]

For centuries *Kol Nidre* dominated the Yom Kippur ceremonies. Only with the rise of Reformed Judaism in Europe and the
United States was this focus changed. Many Reformed synagogues
have replaced the *Kol Nidre* with a new prayer. Others have
substituted the recitation of Psalm 130 with its plea for divine
mercy on a sinful people. Orthodox congregations, along with the
Conservative, still keep remission of vows on The Great Day.

MINOR FESTIVALS

The Jewish calendar centers around its principal festivals. They illuminate the faith of the people and express their sense of community with the historic past.

Along with the great holy days is a bevy of minor feasts which round out the life of a pious Jew in the United States. Among others, *Rosh Chodesh, Chamishoh Osor B'Ov, Chamishoh Osor Bi-Sh'vot,* and *Sh'mitoh* deserve some attention.

Rosh Chodesh

Rosh Chodesh is the Hebrew for "New Moon." In pre-Christian times, it was celebrated as a special monthly holiday, with its own sacrifices.[32] The Talmud still provides for elaborate observances of the feast. Best known was the proclamation of the New Moon in Jerusalem, which was then communicated throughout Palestine and beyond its borders by a system of beacons. A survival of the old custom is the "Blessing of the New Moon." This is a solemn formula read in the synagogue on the Sabbath preceding the New Moon.

Depending on the calendar, the New Moon is sometimes observed for two days. Formal celebration, however, is often confined to the recitation of the Half Hallel.

Some historians associate the feast of the New Moon with the pagan custom of worshiping the moon-god. The current practice among the Orthodox centers on the ritual of "sanctifying the moon," which is done as soon as the first phase of the moon appears in the sky. Not unlike the celebration of the new year, Rosh Chodesh is a monthly reminder that Yahweh is the God of the heavens, that he made the sun and the stars and the moon.

In ancient times, no work was done on the feast of the New Moon. Later it developed into a woman's holiday. Once a month, the housewife was to be completely freed from her regular duties. As the Reform explain it, according to legend this was to reward the women for refusing to join their menfolk in worship of the Golden Calf while Moses was on Mount Sinai receiving the tables of the Law from the Lord.

Today this custom has disappeared, although some have suggested its revival as a symbol of women's loyalty to the faith.

Chamishoh Osor

Chamishoh Osor comes in two forms. The first is the fifteenth of the month of Ov (Chamishoh Osor B'Ov), the second is the fifteenth of the month of Sh'vot (Chamishoh Osor Bi-Sh'vot). Both were originally animistic holidays observed by the primitives among whom the Jews arose as a religious people.

The fifteenth of Ov is a midsummer day and would have remained related to the offering of wood to the Lord, had it not been for the tradition which now links it with Yom Kippur. According to the Mishnah, the happiest days of the year were those on which maidens danced in the vineyards. This reference in the Talmud gave rise to the many interpretations, all directed to explain why the fifteenth of Ov was an occasion for joy. Some commentators say it was on that day that the last survivor died of those who had crossed the desert with Moses. Others again held that on that day Benjamin was readmitted into the tribes of Israel. To this day Chamishoh Osor B'Ov begins with grape harvest season and Yom Kippur closes the same.

Closely related to the preceding is the midwinter feast of the fifteenth of Sh'vot. It seems to have also been a nature festival, as a kind of new year of the trees. A common practice in Orthodox circles is to eat fruit of certain trees as a form of religious piety. The most common is the so-called St. John's bread which grows in Palestine.

Like the fifteenth so the seventh days are sacred in Jewish piety. The seventh of the month of Adar is remembered as the anniversary of the death of Moses.

Sh'mitoh

Related to the weekly Sabbath is the celebration of the seventh year, called the year of Sh'mitoh. Another name for this practice is the Year of Jubilee.

There are two laws connected with the Sh'mitoh; one refers to land and the other to money. According to a law described in the Pentateuch, Jews were not to till the soil every seventh year. Whatever grew wild during that year was to be harvested by the poor. All debts were to be remitted without demanding compensation.

Gradually this idea was enlarged to become the law of the Year of Jubilee. Seven times seven Sh'mitohs plus one became the Great Year of deliverance in Israel. Every slave was to be given freedom, and every peasant who lost his land was to regain the inheritance he had been forced to sell.[33]

It is not clear how faithfully these years of liberation were practiced by the Jews of old. Today they retain only the symbolism of freedom, reflected in certain Jewish prayers. More familiar is the notion of gratitude to God in celebrating the Jubilee of married life or of service in some enterprise, commonly practiced in the Western world.

VII

DIETARY LAWS
AND CUSTOMS

Among all their religious laws and observances, the dietary precepts of the Jews are outstanding. Some would say that these precepts have been the main factor in shaping and maintaining the distinctive character of the Jewish community.

From childhood on, the Jewish believer is told how important is the food he eats in making him a true Israelite. Whether at home or away from home he is taught always to be careful about what he eats and drinks and how he should take his meals.

RELIGIOUS MOTIVATION

A great deal has been said about the background and purpose of the Jewish dietary laws. They have been traced back to taboos existing before the emergence of Israel, and apologists are fond of referring to them as health regulations that have little to do with man's spirit.

To a believing Jew, however, these laws have a deeply religious significance, even when they are considered good for the body as well as the soul.

Before everything else they are the laws of God. He knows their purpose even when mortal men may not be able to grasp it. They are to be kept in obedience to his will and in recognition of his sovereignty. He has prescribed them and it is man's duty to obey.

If this seems like attributing arbitrariness to God, it actually represents a profound insight into man's relationship with his Creator. Many of the laws that men are expected to follow arise from the sheer needs of human nature, whether conceived as individuals or as living in a community. Thus sobriety is prescribed because overindulgence is injurious to health and deprives a man of the full use of his faculties. Stealing and lying are forbidden because they tend to undermine the basic confidence and justice necessary for a peaceful society.

But where God prescribes regulations which are not demanded by the necessities of personal and social living, he enters man's life as Lord of creation. He tells people to do something or avoid something else, not because it is obviously useful or rationally beneficial but because, as God, he wants his creatures to recognize their dependence on him and his divine mastery over them.

It is no coincidence that the opening chapters of Genesis describe, in symbolic form, how God put mankind to the test from the beginning of its history by forbidding a certain kind of food. If Jewish and Christian scholarship has sometimes reduced the story of the Fall to mere allegory, this is not the attitude of Orthodox Judaism. It finds nothing strange in the prohibition of food as a condition for proving one's loyalty to God, since eating is a profound symbol of God's creative providence.

The laws of Kashrut, moreover, are considered a most effective way of preserving the uniqueness of the Jewish people. Unable to share the table of their gentile neighbors, they become joined to one another in a communion that only the Jews could realize. Their identity is thereby retained and their heritage perpetuated in a way and to a degree unparalleled in any other religious culture.

Finally, the dietary laws are regarded as symbolic acts which express belonging to a group. Fraternal orders have their symbols, such as the handshake, by which the members recognize and are drawn to one another. Religious bodies have similar provisions to help bind their members in fellowship and give them a sense of solidarity. But no religious system, even the monastic societies of the Orient, have anything which approximates the binding power of Kashrut when it is faithfully observed.

It is true that Jewish leaders have, at various times, argued beyond religious motives for the dietary laws. The most prominent was Maimonides, whose explanation formed part of his classic treatise, *The Guide for the Perplexed.*

Maimonides divided all the Jewish precepts into fourteen categories and placed the rules about food in the thirteenth class. His main premise was that "the food which is forbidden by the Law is unwholesome." In other words, whatever a Jew is forbidden to eat or drink is also unhealthy. Sometimes the meat comes from an animal whose "habits and food are very dirty and loathsome." Or again it may be something which "interrupts the digestion, and produces cold and thick blood; it is more fit for fuel."[1]

Yet even Maimonides never lost sight of the fact that these prohibitions were first of all divine precepts. His commentary on them is under the heading of "Commandments of God." If he supported the laws of revelation with arguments from reason, it was only to make it easier for the Jews in his day and ever since to accept what they have always found it hard to understand.

PROHIBITIONS AND REGULATIONS

There is no prohibition or restriction regarding vegetable food. All the regulations have to do with foods of animal origin, whether as part of the animal itself or as one of its products.

While the Talmud has extensive prescriptions on the diet and the preparation of food, the basic laws are traceable to the Bible, especially to the eleventh chapter of Leviticus and the fourteenth of Deuteronomy.

Prohibited foods

The largest area of legislation concerns foods that may not be eaten under any circumstances.

Cattle are the main prohibition. In the words of Leviticus, the sons of Israel are told to distinguish among the "beasts of the earth." Some are lawful and others are forbidden.

> You may eat any animal that has a cloven hoof, divided into two parts, and that is ruminant. The following, which either chew the cud or have a cloven hoof, are the ones that you may not eat: the camel must be held unclean, because though it is ruminant, it has not a cloven hoof; the hyrax must be held unclean, because though it is ruminant, it has not a cloven hoof; the hare must be held unclean, because though it is ruminant, it has not a cloven hoof; the pig must be held unclean, because though it has a cloven hoof, divided into two parts, it is not ruminant. You must not eat the meat of such animals nor touch their dead bodies, you must hold them unclean.[2]

Essential to the above provisions is that an animal must have both characteristics, parted hoofs and chewing the cud, to make it permissible. This excludes animals which have only one of these qualities: the camel and hare, which have no parted hoofs; the pig which does not chew its cud. They are therefore unclean.

Less detailed but also definite are the rules about "all that lives in water."

> Anything that has fins and scales, and lives in the water, whether in sea or river, you may eat. But anything in sea or river that has not fins or scales, of all the small water-creatures and all the living things found there, must be held detestable. You must hold them detestable; you are not to eat their flesh and you must avoid their carcasses. Anything that lives in water, but has no fins or scales, is to be held detestable.[3]

Accordingly fish may be eaten if they have met two conditions: they must have fins and also scales. All shellfish are therefore eliminated, and also eel and sturgeon, which have no scales.

The Bible gives a list of "unclean" birds, mostly birds of prey; all others may be eaten. Since the exact meaning of the Hebrew terms for these birds has become obscured, only those birds are permitted which have always been regarded as "clean." This includes chickens, geese, ducks, pigeons, and turkeys.

Swarming things with wings are prohibited, with the exception of locusts and grasshoppers, which may be eaten.[4] Yet they are not commonly available and thus considered forbidden by custom if not by law. In the same category are all the things that swarm on the earth, from mice to crocodiles. They may not be eaten.[5] In general, all animals that live by the destruction of other lives, whether wild beasts or birds are forbidden as food for man. Jewish writers look upon this as a divine injunction against violence and a call to peace.

Restrictions on permitted food

Even permitted foods may be consumed only under certain conditions. Three proscriptions are universal: animals that have died on their own,[6] animals that have been torn by others,[7] and all blood.[8]

The prohibition on blood has had numerous interpretations. Its provisions are simple enough, although the penalty seems extreme: "Wherever you live, you must not eat blood, whether it be of bird or of beast. Anyone who eats blood, whoever he may be shall be outlawed from his people."[9]

According to Maimonides, the Jews were forbidden to partake of blood because some of their pagan contemporaries ate blood as an act of worship. They considered it a food of the spirits which animated living things. By taking blood, a person was supposed to receive something of the spirit which dwelt in the animal. Eating blood, therefore, was a form of animism.[10]

Certain animal fats, including those of permitted animals, are forbidden. The biblical precept reads: "All the fat belongs to Yahweh. This is a perpetual law for all your descendants, wherever you may live: never eat either fat or blood."[11] In practice, vegetable shortening is used in the frying of meats and fish; and butter for vegetables and dairy products. In the cooking of meat, all excess fat is cut off beforehand or poured off before eating.

In the same way certain sinews are forbidden. The prohibition goes back to Genesis, where Jacob is described as having struggled with the Lord. As he left the place, called Peniel, the Bible says he was "limping because of his hip. That is the reason why to this day the Israelites do not eat the sciatic nerve which is in the socket of the hip; because he had struck Jacob in the socket of the hip on the sciatic nerve."[12]

Shehitah. Meat may not be eaten except from animals that were killed. If they died of natural causes, they may not be used. The slaughter of animals is carefully supervised. Legislation on the subject is already found in the Deuteronomic code.

> When Yahweh your God enlarges your territory as he has promised you, and you say, "I should like to eat meat," if you want to eat meat you may eat as much as you like. If the place in which Yahweh your God chooses to set his name is too far away, you may slaughter any of your herd or flock that Yahweh has given you in the way that I have laid down for you; you may eat in your towns as much as you will.[13]

An animal must be slain according to the laws of Shehitah (slaughtering). Any other meat is considered unclean (Trefah), whereas the Jewish religion permits the eating only of Kosher (clean) food.

Among the provisions in the laws of Shehitah is the rule that only a certain individual, the Shohet, is allowed to slaughter animals intended for food. His qualifications are carefully determined by Talmudic law and interpretation. He must be not only devout, but has to be specially trained and properly certified. The only authority qualified to grant a Shehitah is the Bet Din, or rabbi, who must put the candidate through a comprehensive examination before giving him certification.

Few institutions of the Jewish religion are more easily misunderstood than Shehitah. Yet, as the Jews explain it, the commandment, "Thou shalt not kill," applies not only to homicide but also to indiscriminate killing of animals. Not everyone should be permitted to slaughter animals, even for human use. The rabbis who wrote the Talmud taught that a person who kills an animal wantonly is likely to be careless about human life. Once the importance of meat in the sustenance of man is assumed, the act of slaughtering as a religious rite becomes more intelligible.

The Shohet has definite rules laid down by the law. Perhaps the most fundamental was expressed by Maimonides: "since the need of procuring food necessitates the slaying of animals, the law enjoins that the death of the animal should be the easiest."[14]

What this means in practice is that animals and birds must be killed by cutting through the artery and veins and the windpipe at the neck. Only a very sharp knife may be used; even the smallest nick in the blade disqualifies it. The Shohet must sever the body in one stroke; he may not pause and must exert downward pressure without meeting any obstacles in the animal's throat. Any one of these conditions, if absent, renders the animal unclean and the Shohet may not allow the meat to be eaten.

The provision about animals dying a natural death means more than the prohibition to eat meat from animals that have not been slaughtered. Part of the Shohet's duty is to examine the cattle or fowl before he kills it. It must be sufficiently healthy to survive for at least another year. Signs of disease, either before or after slaughtering, render the meat unfit for Jewish consumption. Such things as damage in the lung, an ulcerated stomach, or a discolored brain, are common signs of sickness which the Shohet must be able to recognize. The faithful Jew trusts implicitly in the conscience of the man who slaughters whatever animals may be eaten.

Comparable to the role of the Shohet is the importance of the Jewish butcher who handles the meat that he sells. He, too, must be a responsible person. The sinews in the hind quarter of the animal, which are prohibited, are also very difficult to remove. In order to be on the safe side, therefore, many Orthodox Jews will not eat that part of the animal, unless they know the butcher has the knowledge and skill to cut out the forbidden portion and has been certified to that effect by the rabbi.

The prohibition of blood has its own restrictions. In this case, the housewife has to be conscientious and competent. She will normally soak whatever meat she buys in water for about half an hour. Then she covers it with salt on all sides and leaves it stand for an hour longer. Only after the salt has been washed off is the meat ready for cooking. Another method that some cooks prefer is to broil the meat and allow the blood to flow out freely in the process. Some foods, like liver, cannot legally be prepared in any other way.

Only fresh meat may be used. Rabbinical authorities differ among the Orthodox. But a good general rule states that if meat has been stored for three or more days before all the blood has been taken out, or at least has been softened by washing, it becomes Trefah and may not be eaten without committing sin.

Only when the entire foregoing process is completed does a Jew consider the meat fully Kosher, which may be translated as "all right."

Not only must the food be Kosher, but the kitchen utensils used in the preparation must also be legally clean. These include knives, pots and pans, bowls and plates. Since animal fats are Trefah, Kosher dishes may not be washed with soap made from fats, although detergents may be used. For some years now, such items as detergents and vegetable foods, for example, beans in cans, often carry the seal of the Union [of] Orthodox [Jewish] Congregations. This testifies that their production was supervised and their ingredients are usable in Jewish households. The ordinary seal is the letter *U* inside a circle, and may be found on many products sold in general food stores.

A number of meat-packing houses in the United States have special Kosher departments, directed by a certified inspector called a Mashgiach. His duty is to inspect every carcass that has been properly slaughtered and stamp it with an official seal. Jewish writers on the subject explain to children that paying the Shohet and the Mashgiach increases the cost of the meat-packing. But the extra cost is part of the sacrifice that a follower of Moses is expected to make.

Large communities in cities like New York also have a Kashrut Council (*Vaas Hakashrut*). Its function is to supervise the whole process of handling meat from the stockyard to the kitchen table. Formal certificates of Kashrut are issued every year to packing plants and stores that are sensitive to Jewish religious needs. In view of its large Jewish population, the State of New York (among others) has passed special statutes which prohibit the misrepresentation of Trefah foods as Kosher. The laws are supported by severe penalties.

Meat and Milk. There is one more religious prescription affecting Jewish food. Meat and milk may not be mixed and to do so is considered against the divine law.

The Talmud points to three different places in the scripture where such mixture is prohibited. The exact words are somewhat cryptic: "You shall not seethe the kid in the milk of its mother."[15] This triple prohibition has been understood to convey three separate messages: you may not eat meat and milk products at the same meal, you may not cook these products together even though for different meals, you may never use any mixture of the two combined. For centuries fowl was not included in the prohibition because, it was argued, this animal has no "mother." But the present custom is to include fowl among meats that may not be mixed with milk.

This means that meat and milk products may never be served together, so that no butter may be eaten at a meat dinner nor may ice cream follow a meal where meat was served. A waiting period must be allowed between the consumption of meat and milk dishes.

For the same reason the two may not be cooked together, which seems obvious, except that the law goes further. While meat is cooked, its juices are believed to penetrate the pores of the pots and pans; when it is cut, they enter the knife; when it is served, they seep into the chinaware. Conversely the same applies to milk.

A Kosher home, therefore, must have two complete sets of dishes, from skillets to spoons, and no utensil from the one set may ever be used or washed together with a utensil of the other set. If they are ever mixed up by mistake, they can no longer be used unless the dish or the pan has been cleansed by boiling or burning out the food as the utensil is brought to red heat. One exception is allowed; glass is said to have no pores and may be used either way.

A Jewish home that wants to be Kosher always has two sets of dishes. But it may also have a third set, for food in neither the meat nor milk category, such as vegetables and fruit. In addition an

Orthodox household has complete double sets of dishes for the Passover. The reason is that utensils from the rest of the year are unclean for use during the Paschal season; they have been permeated by grain products.

TABLE AS ALTAR

One feature of Judaism that goes back to its earliest history is the association of the table on which food is served with an altar on which sacrifice is offered. Jewish prayers from Mosaic times were provided for beginning and ending every meal with a prayer. The meal was a sacred rite and the prayer was to hallow this meaning.

Different prayers are provided for meals on weekdays and those on the Sabbath or holy days.

During the week, two short prayers are customary: one for the washing of hands and another before eating.

> Blessed art thou, O Lord our God, King of the universe, who hast sanctified us by thy commandments, and hast given us command concerning the washing of the hands.

> Blessed art thou, O Lord our God, King of the universe, who bringest forth bread from the earth.[16]

The grace after meals takes on such a variety of forms that a standard Orthodox manual offers no less than seven types, each to be modified according to the different seasons of the year. A familiar prayer for new moons and festivals is typically Messianic. It runs through six paragraphs, including responses from those at table. The first paragraph illustrates the whole formula.

> Our God and God of our Fathers! May our remembrance rise and come and be accepted before thee, with the remembrance of our fathers, of Messiah the son of David thy servant, of Jerusalem thy holy city, and of all thy people the house of Israel, bringing deliverance and well-being, grace, loving kindness and mercy, life and peace on this day of the New Moon.[17]

An Orthodox Jew will not place any food in his mouth without reciting the appropriate blessing. Different blessings are available for bread and fruit, vegetables and pastry, for wine and even for water.

A custom that goes back to pre-Christian times includes the singing of short melodies or *Zemirot* at table. Sabbath meals had special hymns and these were memorized from childhood. A verse or two were chanted before the meal began and, on such holidays as the Passover or Shavuot, other verses would be sung in unison between the courses of the feast-day meal.

Consistent with this concept of the table as an altar, Jews wash their hands before they sit down to eat. As one rabbi expressed it, in a passage of the Talmud that can be traced to the ancient Pharisees, "He who eats without cleaning his hands is like one who partakes of impure food." In an Orthodox home, the table ritual also includes washing one's fingers after the meal. Women are not obliged to this second custom, but men are required to do so when at least three are present to recite grace as a Mezuman. The Mezuman is the quorum of three persons necessary for the public recitation of thanksgiving after a Jewish meal.

In keeping with the religious atmosphere that should pervade the eating of food, meals are not to be hurried. Rabbinic prescriptions simultaneously warn against eating either too fast or too much. In the words of a famous Talmudist, "He who lingers at table prolongs his life." Conversation at meals is encouraged and partly explains what may surprise Christian readers of the Gospel. Some of the most important episodes in the life of Jesus of Nazareth took place at table, like the Last Supper and the conversation with the disciples at Emmaus after the Resurrection.

The symbolism of religious belief is carried into the smallest details, beyond the ordinary dietary laws. Terms like Gefilte fish, Chulent, Tzimmes, Kreplach, Kneidlach, Blintzes, Latkes, and Hamantaschen are all associated with certain occasions and special holidays. Their preparation is as minute as the most elaborate liturgical ceremony, since family meals in a fervent Jewish household are actually forms of liturgy.

PRACTICE IN TRANSITION

One of the paradoxes of Judaism involves the dietary laws. Superficially it would seem that the Reform came into existence mainly as a reaction against the extreme prescriptions of Orthodoxy, especially regarding food. Certainly there is enough in liberal Jewish literature to suggest that this was a large issue.

As we read the history of the Reform, however, a different picture emerges. A typical instance is the directive on Kashrut given to the Canadian Reform congregations.

> It would be irresponsible and reprehensible to advocate the total disregard of the dietary laws. It would prove Reform to be very superficial indeed. There laws not only have hygienic but also a deeper ethical significance, because they keep us apart from all that is bestial and crude. They teach us the lovely virtue of self-discipline and may thereby assist us to become a holy people, a demand which the Torah relates to these laws.[18]

Reform writings on the subject may be misleading. What looks like the studied absence of any reference to dietary laws does not mean that liberal Judaism ignores these prescriptions. To say, as some do, that only "a residue of Reformers practice Kashrut on some level" is gratuitous. No doubt the majority of American Jews do not observe all or even most of the prescriptions on what they should eat and how the food should be prepared. Yet, those who know the Jews well know that they are never oblivious of what the Mosaic code tells them about food. It is a safe estimate that even the most unorthodox Jewish household keeps some form of dietary regulations and, in some cases, at great sacrifice to taste and personal convenience.

VIII

RITUAL AND PRACTICES

As might be expected, the whole life of a believing Jew is surrounded with customs and practices that reflect his loyalty to the faith of Israel.

We have already seen how the sequence of days, months, and years takes on religious meaning in the Jewish way of life. We have also seen how deeply this way of life is affected in such areas of human conduct as food and drink.

But this is not all. From birth until death the Jewish religion provides a religious concern for those who profess it, beyond anything comparable either in Christianity or in the religious cultures of the Orient. The reader is reminded that we are here speaking mainly of Orthodox Judaism and of other forms only as they approximate the paradigm of historic Israel.

It is impossible to do full justice to these traditional customs. The ones here treated will be the most important, allowing for such variations as even the strict Talmud provides. Where certain customs are differently followed by the Conservative and Reform, this will be indicated.

CIRCUMCISION

The rite of circumcision dates back to the time of Abraham. Some historians trace the custom to Semitic religions before the Jews came on the scene. What is distinctive, however, about the Jewish practice is the meaning it acquired when the Jews were first called out of the land of Canaan. In a few terse sentences, Yahweh commanded Abraham to circumcise and called this rite the covenant between himself and his people.

When Abraham was ninety-nine years old Yahweh appeared to him and said, "I am El Shaddai. Bear yourself blameless in my presence, and I will make a Covenant between myself and you, and increase your numbers greatly."

"Now this is my Covenant which you are to maintain between myself and you, and your descendants after you: all your males must be circumcised. You shall circumcise your foreskin, and this shall be the sign of the Covenant between myself and you. When they are eight days old all your male children must be circumcised, generation after generation of them, no matter whether they are born within the household or bought from a foreigner not one of your descendants."

Then Abraham took his son Ishmael, all those born in his household and all those he had bought, in short all the males among the people of Abraham's household, and circumcised their foreskins that same day, in accordance with God's commands to him.[1]

The ceremony of circumcision is called *Milah* or sometimes *Brit Milah* which means "covenant of circumcision." The physical part of the ritual consists in cutting away the foreskin of the male child on the eighth day after birth. Circumcision is also called "the covenant of Abraham," to signify it was this way that Abraham showed his acceptance of God's covenant with him and his seed forever. Men converts to Judaism must also undergo circumcision. In biblical times and into the early Christian era, male slaves in Jewish families were circumcised.

The Talmud forbids an uncircumcised person to participate in many Jewish rites such as eating the Paschal Lamb.

In the history of Judaism, circumcision has always been a sign of fidelity to the religion of Abraham and Moses. At various times, for example under Antiochus Epiphanes and the Romans, faithful Jews underwent martyrdom rather than give up the practice. It has also been a symbol to distinguish the Jew from the unbeliever.

On the other hand, as Jews became more lax in their observance of the Mosaic law they also tended to neglect the rite of *Brit Milah*. More than once in the Bible the prophets had to rebuke the people for neglecting this divine precept. The Jews of the diaspora in Greek times are known to have undergone operations to remove the sign of their circumcision. Consequently rabbinic teachers came to insist on the act of *periah* (pushing back the skin to expose the *glans*) as a necessary feature of circumcision.

A boy must be circumcised on the eighth day even if it happens to be the Sabbath or on the solemn feast of Atonement. The only exception is when the child is too weak or his health would be seriously endangered.

The service is held in the presence of at least a quorum of three men either at the home or in the synagogue or often today in the hospital.

When the child is brought in, all the people present rise and say: "Blessed is he that cometh." The father then pronounces his acceptance of the covenant made to Abraham.

> I am here ready to perform the affirmative precept to circumcise my son, even as the Creator, blessed be he, hath commanded us, as it is written in the Law, And he that is eight days old shall be circumcised among you, every male throughout your generation.[2]

At this point the circumciser (*Mohel*) begins the liturgy proper. He should be an expert surgeon and, as the manuals say, "a learned

and forthright man." He places the child on a special chair, called
the chair of Elijah, which is reserved for this ceremony. The reason
for having a chair of Elijah is given in the Talmud. The prophet
complained to God that Israel was neglecting the covenant.[3] The
Lord thereupon ordered him to be present at every circumcision
until the end of time, as a witness of Israel's loyalty to the agreement between God and Abraham.[4]

As he lifts the child and places him on the chair, he first ex-
claims: "This is the throne of Elijah. May he be remembered for
good!" Then he invokes the Lord.

> For thy salvation I have waited, O Lord. I have hoped,
> O Lord, for thy salvation; and have done thy commandments.
> I have hoped for thy salvation, O Lord. I rejoice at thy word,
> as one that findeth great spoil. Great peace have they who love
> the Law; and there is no stumbling for them. Happy is he
> whom thou choosest, and causest to approach that he may
> dwell in thy courts.[5]

All present respond: "O let us be satisfied with the goodness of
thy house, thy holy temple." The Mohel then places the child on
the knee of the godfather (*Sandek*), and just before circumcising invokes this blessing: "Blessed art thou, O Lord, King of the universe,
who hast sanctified us by thy commandments, and hast given us
command concerning the circumcision."[6]

During the circumcision, the child enters into the covenant of
Abraham. His father thanks the Lord for this privilege: "Blessed
art thou, O Lord our God, King of the universe, who hast sanctified
us by thy commandments, and hast commanded us to make our
sons enter into the covenant of Abraham our father."[7] To which
the bystanders answer: "Even as he has entered into the covenant,
so may he live to study the law, to be wedded, and to perform
good deeds."[8]

The Mohel next recites the blessing over wine and another over
the entrance of a new son into the nation of Israel.

> Blessed art thou, O Lord our God, King of the universe,
> who from the womb didst sanctify Isaac the well-beloved,
> didst set thy statute in his flesh, and seal his offspring with the

sign of the holy covenant. On this account, O living God, our Portion and our Rock, give command to deliver from destruction the dearly beloved of our flesh, for the sake of the covenant thou hast set in our bodies. Blessed art thou, O Lord, who makes the covenant.[9]

Part of the ceremony is naming the Jewish boy. It follows right after the circumcision. Normally the name is that of some near relative who is deceased. The custom is intended to keep the family memory alive. Sometimes the Hebrew names of famous Jews are chosen. Since 1948 zealous Zionists have been giving their children modern Palestinian names. Children are often given a second name, common to the country of their birth.

The actual conferring of the name begins with the invocation: "Our God and God of our fathers, preserve this child to his father and to his mother, and let his name be called in Israel .... son of ...." It ends with a hope: "The little child ...., may he become great," and again a prayer that the new Israelite will study the law, be happily married, and perform good works.

Rituals differ on what follows. The Sephardic, Oriental, and Yemenite liturgies have several songs after the circumcision. One final prayer is common among Orthodox Jews in America. Its main invocation is a plea: "May his heart be wide open for Thy holy Land, like the opening of a hall, that he may learn and teach, keep and fulfill Thy laws."[10]

A meal is served as part of the ceremony. Sharing in this meal is considered so pleasing to God that Jews are allowed even to break a fast to eat it, with the exception of the great fast for the Day of Atonement. Before the meal, during, and after, appropriate prayers are said to express the joy that once more the principal commandment given to Abraham has been fulfilled.

At the closing grace, a poem by Abraham ben Isaac HaCohen is inserted. Dating from the eleventh century this poem begins each stanza with, "May the All Merciful (*harahaman*) . . . ," and a petition for the child and his parents. The final prayer is an act of hope that the Messiah may soon come to redeem his people.

While there is no comparable ritual for Jewish girls, they are brought to the synagogue shortly after birth, preferably on the following Sabbath. The girl's father is called up to the Torah where he recites a special prayer in the child's honor. The main invocation recalls the great women of the past: "He who blessed Sarah, Rebecca, Leah and Rachel, Miriam the prophetess and Esther the queen, may He bless this dear girl. Let her be called (the girl's name and her father's name are pronounced) in a lucky hour. May she grow up in health and peace, and may her parents live to celebrate her wedding."[11]

As in the case of circumcision, the services for naming the girl include a special meal at the synagogue and the home.

REDEMPTION OF THE FIRSTBORN

If the child is a boy and the first in the family, another ceremony follows at the end of the month. It is called *Pidyon Haben* or *Pidyon Havechor* which literally means "to redeem the firstborn male."

According to biblical injunction, every firstborn of the womb whether of man or animal is considered as belonging especially to the Lord.[12] Human beings were to be redeemed and clean animals sacrificed.[13] In olden times the redemption consisted in the payment of five shekels, or their equivalent, to be made to a priest thirty days after the first son was born.

Redemption was always considered the release from Temple service. This could mean acting as priests, musicians, or servants in Jerusalem. The practice proved a hardship on many families and naturally the parents did not want to part with their older children.

Eventually the tribe of Levi was set aside to serve in the Temple in place of the firstborn. A passage in the book of Numbers reads: "And I behold have taken the Levites instead of every firstborn; and the Levites shall be mine."[14]

In accordance with this relaxation of the original laws every firstborn male child has to be redeemed. This means he is freed from service at the Temple by the payment of five shekels to a Levite who serves in his stead. Since the descendants of the ancient Levites are Kohens, Jewish children now born as Cohens are technically not to be redeemed. They are waiting for the restoration of the Temple at which they are to serve.

Redemption does not apply to children born in a cesarean operation or subsequent to a miscarriage. This is Talmudic custom.

There are numerous rituals for *Pidyon Haben*. A popular version followed in the United States is a dialogue between the boy's father and the Cohen.

Father, (presenting his child to the Cohen): "This is my first-born of his mother, and the Holy One, blessed be he, hath given command to redeem him, as it is said, And those that are to be redeemed of them from a month old shalt thou redeem, according to thine estimation, for the money of five shekels, after the shekel of the sanctuary, the shekel being twenty gerahs; and it is said, Sanctify unto me all the first-born, whatsoever openeth the womb among the children of Israel, both of man and beast: it is mine."

Cohen, (receiving the father's money): "Which wouldst thou rather give me, thy first-born son, the first-born of his mother, or redeem him for five selaim, which thou art bound to give according to the Law?"

Father: "I desire rather to redeem my son, and here thou hast the value of his redemption, which I am bound to give according to the Law."

Cohen returns the child to his father.

Father: "Blessed art thou, O Lord our God, King of the universe, who hast sanctified us by thy commandments, and given us command concerning the redemption of the son."

"Blessed art thou, O Lord our God, King of the universe, who hast kept us in life, and hast preserved us, and enabled us to reach this season."[15]

The boy's redemption after birth is only the beginning of a life-long liturgy associated with the practice. As he grows up, he is expected to fast on Erev Pesach because it was on that day that the firstborn among the Egyptians were slain while the Hebrews were spared. As a substitute for fasting, he may attend a special ceremony in the synagogue. Called the *Siyum Hatorah* the service includes a treatise from the Talmud which releases the firstborn of the duty of fasting on the day before the Pasch.

BAR MITZVAH

Where circumcision symbolizes a child's entrance into the Jewish community, Bar Mitzvah is the rite of initiation into Jewish religious responsibility. Boys are the only ones who are thus formally initiated, although Reform synagogues have for some years allowed girls to go through a ritual similar to the Bar Mitzvah.

Anticipating the Bar Mitzvah at the age of thirteen, Jewish boys in former days used to start Hebrew school with a simple ceremony called Ben Torah or Son of the Torah. Whenever possible the ceremony would take place on Shavuot, which is the traditional Torah feast. The young boy was wrapped in a *Tallit* or prayer shawl, and escorted by relatives and friends to the synagogue. There he was blessed before an open scroll of the Bible, and the Ten Commandments were read to him. From the synagogue he went to the Heder or school for his first class, to learn one easy lesson, a quotation from the Torah: "Moses commands as a law, an inheritance for the assembly of Jacob," smeared with honey on a slate. As the new pupil repeated each word of the lesson, gifts of fruit and sweets were dropped in front of him. The modern version is known as the Consecration Ceremony, with variations in the custom and adjustment to local circumstances.

Bar Mitzvah comes years later, and should be distinguished from the celebrations that are now common when a boy or girl finishes studies in Hebrew school. The graduation ceremonies are more nearly like commencement exercises from school and are not the same as Bar Mitzvah, which is essentially a religious rite that marks the attainment of manhood, since Bar Mitzvah literally means "one who is obliged to fulfill the commandment."

While Bar Mitzvah is not specifically mentioned in the Bible, allusions to it in the Talmud suggest that the practice goes back to very ancient times. The first definite reference to the ritual dates from the thirteenth century. As in so many other areas of Jewish custom, the *Shulhan Aruk* is the classic source for the Bar Mitzvah ceremonial.

The theory is that, up to the age of thirteen, a father bears the sins of his son. After that the boy is personally responsible for what he does. Accordingly the father recites the following prayer:

"Blessed be thou our God, King of the Universe, who hast relieved me from punishment for this one (the son)." The implication was not that the father abdicated further care for his son, but that from then on the boy was on his own as never before.

If Bar Mitzvah means that the father is freed from certain duties, it also means that the son assumes new obligations that cover the gamut of Jewish faith and practice.

Different Jewish traditions follow different Bar Mitzvah patterns. In some communities the climax of the celebration is the first wearing of the phylacteries or *Tefillin*. These are two black leather boxes fastened to leather straps, containing four portions of the Pentateuch written on parchment. The passages are from Exodus (13:1-16) and Deuteronomy (6:4-9, 11:13-21). They are bound on the person's arm and head, as prescribed in the Bible.[16] From the time of his Bar Mitzvah, according to Orthodox teaching, the Jewish boy is to wear the phylacteries on weekdays, but not on Sabbath, and on certain festivals. Originally they were worn all day, but now the men use them only during morning prayer, with one exception, on the ninth of Av the Tefillin are worn during the afternoon prayer.

In most communities, however, the Bar Mitzvah ritual includes a reading and chant by the boy, along with a special sermon that he gives the congregation. He is then blessed by the rabbi after being duly instructed in the duties he will have as an adult member of the House of Israel.

While some Reform congregations provide a Bar Mitzvah only for boys, all Reform groups have Confirmation for boys and girls. This practice is consistent with the basic Reform principle that men and women are to be treated as equals in the Jewish religion. In fact, Confirmation was the first distinctive liturgical ceremony introduced by the Reform when it separated from Orthodoxy.

Another change introduced by the Reform was to consider Confirmation a communal service and not, as the traditional Bar Mitzvah, directed to the individual. Where Bar Mitzvah normally takes place on a Sabbath nearest to a boy's birthday, the Confirmation rite is commonly reserved for one day a year, the feast of Pentecost. Commentators explain that this is the most appropriate date in the liturgical calendar, since it is on Shabuot that Judaism commemorates the giving of God's law to Moses on Mount Sinai. Confirmation rites ask for grace to keep the law faithfully.

Both the Bar Mitzvah and Confirmation are associated with the gathering of relatives and friends and giving a feast either at home or at the synagogue. The occasion is a high point in Jewish homes, comparable in religious importance to a family wedding.

One of the problems that parents face in a country like the United States is that many boys look upon Bar Mitzvah as the beginning and end of their Jewish education. Some fathers and mothers postpone enrolling their sons in a Jewish school until a year or less before the date of the ceremony, and withdraw them immediately after. Rabbis complain that a growing number of Jewish young people learn little more than a few chants and how to recite a couple of Psalms.

To counterbalance this tendency, a variety of Jewish high-school classes and youth organizations have been established. The best known is connected with the Jewish Community Center, formerly the Young Men's (Women's) Hebrew Association. The purpose of the Center, found in some twenty countries, is to perpetuate Judaism through a program of recreation, health training, and education in Jewish culture.

MARRIAGE AND DIVORCE

The prospect of marriage and rearing a family looms large in the thinking of Jews. Their reading of the passage in Genesis, to "increase and multiply," is taken as a divine mandate. Private prayers and the public liturgy are filled with references to a happy marriage and the offspring they ask for from a kind Providence.

Unequivocally Jewish writers say that Judaism makes obligatory the requirement to reproduce and continue the human race. They speak of this as "the first commandment in the Bible," and believe that men are specially bound by the mandate to marry and procreate the human species. Rabbinic commentators specify what this means: to beget at least one male and one female each. The same duty does not apply to women, who may remain unmarried, if they so desire.

Betrothal

According to ancient custom there are two stages to matrimony in Jewish tradition. First comes betrothal and then marriage. Betrothal, called *Erusin* or *Kiddushin*, is the ceremony by which a woman becomes engaged to the man who betrothes her in a union that (from her side) is as binding as marriage. She is forbidden to marry anyone else, unless her betrothed dies or divorces her.

Three ways of betrothal are recognized as legal Jewish practice, which is founded on the Talmud. The man may give the woman a sum of money as a symbolic token of his intention to marry her; he may sign a formal deed by which he confirms his betrothal in writing; or he may have intercourse with her, after he has informed witnesses that the act is a sign of his marital intentions.

The Babylonian Talmud (like the Palestinian) has a long treatise exclusively on Kiddushin. The Mishnah of its opening chapter states explicitly that "A woman is acquired in three ways and acquires her freedom in two. She is acquired by money, or deed, or by intercourse." She acquires her freedom by divorce or by the death of her betrothed.[17]

In view of the grave difficulties surrounding a betrothal by intercourse, the Talmud first defends the practice on biblical grounds, and then severely qualifies it. Modern rabbinical scholars admit that "a woman may be acquired by intercourse" and that "intercourse only effects *Erusin* (betrothal)" but not actual marriage.[18] Strong reaction has outlawed this custom, and also the second type of betrothal is rare nowadays.

Current practice favors betrothal by the giving of money. The man actually makes the offer but the woman must give her consent to make the engagement valid. The second step in the ceremony is *Nessuin*, which literally means "home-taking," and allows cohabitation with intercourse.

Traditional practice includes special blessings for both Erusin and Nessuin, to be recited by the rabbis over the engaged couple. In former days, a long interval was to elapse between Erusin and Nessuin. This was gradually decreased to thirty and less days, always favoring the man. Finally it became customary to follow the betrothal ceremony by the rite of "home-taking," and immediately after the marriage. This is the present situation in the United States, though by no means universal elsewhere.

Marriage rite

It is universal Jewish belief that marriage is a divine institution, prescribed for Adam and Noah, when they were told to be fruitful and fill the earth.[19] Since marriage was instituted by God and blessed by him in Paradise, it does not depend on human whim but is "a covenant with God," at which "Yahweh is witness."[20] Moreover, because marriage is God's covenant, the prophets frequently pictured the relationship between God and his people as a marriage contract that was binding on both parties, on the side of God to never fail in his love and on the part of Israel to remain loyal to its Lord.[21]

The Talmud is no less insistent on the divine origins and ordination of marriage. In a dramatic passage commenting on Leviticus, the rabbis explain that since the sixth day of creation God has been especially concerned with directing the institution of marriage. Since he made the first pair and bade them procreate, the divine providence has been mainly spent in guiding the destinies of men and women through the tortuous ways of marital and family life.[22]

Not all Jewish marriage ceremonies are the same. As might be expected, the Orthodox is generally the most elaborate and precise.

As a rule, the marriage ritual begins with a short passage usually sung by the cantor. "He who is mighty" is invoked that "He may bless the bridegroom and the bride."

The couple is then placed under a decorated canopy (*Huppa*) which is symbolic of the marriage chamber. Immediately the rabbi takes a cup of wine and blesses it.

Then follows the Betrothal Blessing (*Bircath Erusin*) which is taken directly from the Talmud.[23] It was this benediction that formerly was recited at the previous engagement ritual. It praises God for the laws of chastity and for instituting marriage.

The groom is next given a ring which has no stone, and he places it on the bride's forefinger of the right hand while saying, in Hebrew, "Behold, thou art consecrated unto me by this ring, according to the Law of Moses and of Israel."

It appears that rings were unknown in early Talmudic times. Coins were used instead. The medieval *Shulhan Aruk* speaks of a ring but allows a coin. To this day, the Yemenite ritual has the formula: "Behold, thou art consecrated unto me with this coin."

At this point the *Kethuva* (*Ketubbah*), literally "writing," is read as the formal marriage contract. Orthodox congregations read the document in Aramaic. Essentially the Kethuva contains the duties of the bridegroom toward his wife. By rabbinic law, no marriage is valid without such a prior declaration in writing. Witnessed by two people, it is carefully preserved by the bride.

In olden days (and still in some countries) the financial clauses of the document varied with each marriage. They now generally follow a set formula. Also additional clauses (*Tenaim*=conditions) used to be inserted in the Kethuva. Some traditions in Europe add a synopsis in the vernacular, stressing the moral obligations which the husband assumes when he marries.

In the United States, Conservative synagogues have introduced significant modifications in the traditional document; Reform Jews have abrogated its use entirely.

Seven benedictions follow, beginning with the blessing of the wine and ending with the canticle of praise which identifies happiness with the state of wedlock.

> Blessed art thou, O Lord our God, King of the universe, who created the fruit of the vine.
>
> Blessed art thou, O Lord our God, King of the universe, who hast created all things in thy glory.
>
> Blessed art thou, O Lord our God, King of the universe, Creator of man.
>
> Blessed art thou, O Lord our God, King of the universe, who hast made man in thine image, after thy likeness, and hast prepared unto him, out of his very self, a perpetual fabric. Blessed art thou, O Lord, Creator of man.
>
> May she who was barren (Zion) be exceedingly glad and exult, when her children are gathered unto her in joy. Blessed art thou, O Lord, who makest Zion joyful through her children.
>
> O make these loved companions greatly to rejoice, even as of old thou didst gladden thy creature in the Garden of Eden.

Blessed art thou, O Lord, who makest bridegroom and bride to rejoice.

Blessed art thou, O Lord our God, King of the universe, who hast created joy and gladness, bridegroom and bride, mirth and exultation, pleasure and delight, love, brotherhood, peace and fellowship. Soon may there be heard in the cities of Judah, and in the streets of Jerusalem, the voice of joy and gladness, the voice of the bridegroom and the voice of the bride, the jubilant voice of bridegrooms from their canopies, and of youths from their feasts of song. Blessed art thou, O Lord, who makest the bridegroom to rejoice with the bride.[24]

This panegyric on the joys of marriage is intrinsic to the faith of Judaism. So much that among the best-known tributes to *Women in Israel* is the responsive reading, used in Orthodox congregations, in which it is said: "A man without a wife is without joy, without blessedness and without happiness. One should love his wife as himself, and honor her more than himself. One should genuinely respect his wife, for his house is blessed only for her sake."[25] The idea of genuine happiness without a woman's love in marriage is foreign to the spirit of Jewish culture.

Besides the seven classic benedictions, the Yemenite ritual has other biblical selections and psalmodies which are said (or sung) in unison. It also has a wide range of wedding songs in Hebrew and Arabic. The Persian, Babylonian, and Oriental-Sephardic rites also include a rich repertoire of wedding melodies. American Jews borrow heavily from these traditions, depending on their religious ancestry. With rare exception, the songs at weddings are also set to a traditional mode. Melodies in some cases have not varied for centuries.

In some communities the custom still prevails of having the bride walk around her husband seven times before the marriage actually begins. Also customary is to have the blessings of Erusin and Nessuin over a cup of wine from which both groom and bride take a drink. Then the groom breaks a glass as a sign of mourning over the destruction of the Temple and symbolic of the trials of the Jewish nation.

213 Marriage and Divorce

The Orthodox liturgy calls for fasting on the part of groom and bride until after the ceremony, right after which they are to go into a separate room where they eat together. According to the same ritual, a marriage feast is served on each day of the following week, called the "Seven Days of Feasting." At these meals, the seven benedictions from the marriage rites are repeated every day. In some synagogues, special features are added to the service when the bridegroom attends on the Sabbath after his marriage.

Law of Niddah

Among the distinctive features of Jewish marriage customs is the Law of Niddah, which is the Hebrew for "separation." Some would classify this as an aspect of morals, but it is more accurately a ritual prescription which has obvious moral implications.

The term *Niddah* is used to describe a woman during the time of her menses, and states that conjugal relations during the whole of this time are forbidden by the Scriptures. The book of Leviticus is detailed in its prohibition of intercourse during this period. All through the wife's menstruation, she is held to be ritually unclean, that is, may not be touched at the risk of making anyone who touches her morally stained before the Lord. Finally, "If a man sleeps with her, he will be affected by the uncleanness of her monthly periods. He shall be unclean for seven days. Any bed he lies on shall be unclean." The same precept holds good if her periods are irregular.[26]

Superficially it may seem that the Law of Niddah is a reflection on womanhood and the term *uncleanness* only reinforces the conclusion. But actually, as Jewish commentators explain it, the custom is the very opposite of derogatory of women. It is also close to the heart of marital morality as conceived in the Jewish religion. Fertility and reproduction are inseparable from Judaism.

The whole seventh treatise in the Mishnah order of *Tohorot* contains ten chapters on the subject of Niddah. It has Gemara commentaries in the Babylonian and Palestinian Talmuds, though the latter covers only the first three of the ten chapters of the Mishnah. Two kinds of Niddah are considered: that connected with a woman's monthly periods, and the one associated with childbirth.

A standard manual for Orthodox Jewish women places the matter into proper religious perspective.

> The indications, duration of the menses and interval between one monthly period and the next, vary in different persons. There is generally (in healthy persons) a certain amount of regularity, and therefore the time for anticipatory separation can, more or less easily, be determined. It is the irregular interval and casual occurrences which give rise to complicated questions in respect to the law of "separation."
>
> Holy Writ sets out the laws of regular and irregular conditions (Leviticus 15:19-28). The questions involved in these few verses are rather complicated, and our sages have discussed them with reverence, care, and consideration. It is with pride, however, that they declare that "the daughters of Israel have of themselves adopted a practical, strict and uniform standard."[27]

In setting down the norms which underlie the practice, current manuals in Europe and America reduce these principles mainly to three: the first visible sign of menstruation should be taken as the beginning of the time of Niddah; as a rule the "time of separation" consists of twelve days, five to account for the menses and seven extra days of purification; during this time the wife is not to have intercourse with her husband.

Nothing could be clearer than the injunctions placed on those who would follow the biblical precept faithfully.

> The Bible forbids conjugal association during the whole time of Niddah separation, as an iniquitous, abominable contamination; a heinous and immoral offence almost on a par with idolatry (Leviticus 18:19-30, 20:18; and Ezekiel 18:5-6 ff).
>
> Holy Writ demands that Israel shall avoid all unholy practices which are an "abomination unto the Lord," and it exhorts the Jewish people to make every endeavour to uphold their personal and national sanctity.
>
> Traditional teaching emphatically demands a temporary separation between husband and wife at the time of her "menses." A certain distance has to be maintained.

Their mutual affection will not suffer thereby. . . . They stand to gain much more by the observance of this demand made by modesty and religion than by the relaxation of their requirements.[28]

In the history of Israel, the Law of Niddah has received extensive commentary and always the concern has been to defend a practice which, naturally speaking, makes considerable demands on the faith and generosity of married people. Maimonides deals with the subject in his *Guide for the Perplexed*, under the general heading of "The Divine Commandments." He assigns two main purposes for the sacrifice which Niddah requires of those who follow the Torah. By it the sexual appetite is better held under control; which is also one reason he gives for the rite of circumcision. The biblical limitations on the time of intercourse are intended to protect married persons from indulging in it "only for the sake of pleasure."[29] Conversely, the spiritual motivation necessary to observe the precept of separation is conducive to promoting between husband and wife, and between parents and children a deep bond of friendship. Maimonides speaks of "perfect love" and "mutual assistance" as benefits to be expected from keeping the Levitical code. "To effect this is one of the chief purposes of the Law," in this case of Niddah prescriptions.[30]

Divorce

In Jewish tradition, the act of dissolving the marriage tie between husband and wife is effected by a bill of divorcement called *sepher keritut* in the Pentateuch (Deuteronomy 24:3) and *Get* in the Talmud.

The husband takes the initiative, either personally or through an intermediary, by handing over to the wife the appropriate document in the presence of witnesses.

Following the biblical rule, a husband may divorce his spouse if he finds in her an "unseemly thing." Cryptic to begin with, this phrase has given rise to numerous interpretations by Talmudic authorities. According to the school of Shammai it means "a thing of indecency." Consequently marriage could be dissolved only on proved grounds of unchastity on the part of the wife. The school of

Hillel, on the other hand, explained the phrase "anything unseemly" to mean anything that might involve the disruption of domestic harmony or mutual affection.

One of the best-known episodes in the Talmud which reveals the more lenient attitude toward divorce occurs in a Midrash on the book of Leviticus.

> Rabbi Jose, the Galilean, had a bad wife who despised him in the presence of his disciples. They said to him, "Divorce her."
>
> One day Rabbi Jose and Rabbi Elazar ben Azarya were sitting and expounding the Law. When they had finished, the disciples said to Rabbi Jose, "Let the master pay heed to us, and now we will go to your house." He said to them, "Yes."
>
> When they got there, his wife lowered her face (in shame) and went out. He looked into the pot upon the stove, and called to her and said, "Is there anything in the pot?" She said, "There are bread and vegetables in it." He went and opened the lid, and found in it chickens. So Elazar knew that she did not behave well to her husband. When they sat down to eat, Rabbi Jose said to her, "Did you not say that there were vegetables in the pot, and we have found chickens in it?" She said, "It is a miracle."
>
> When they had eaten, Rabbi Elazar said, "Divorce your wife; she does not act to your honor." He said, "Her dowry is too great for me; I cannot divorce her." They said to him, "We will provide the dowry; and then do you divorce her." They did so. They provided the dowry, and he divorced her; and they made him marry another wife, who was better than the former one.[31]

In the sequel to this Talmudic narrative, the divorced wife is later shown mercy by her former husband, when the man she remarried was cruel to her. Both aspects of the story are in the spirit of Hillel: permission to divorce and remarry for reasons much less than infidelity, and commendation for being kind to an estranged wife (or husband) after the marriage bond is broken.

Sterility on the part of the wife is generally recognized as sufficient grounds for divorce. From a strictly rabbinic standpoint, only the husband has the right to institute divorce proceedings. Yet, in practice the wife has considerable freedom to do the same. Even the Talmud allows such things as apostasy, misbehavior, or even an uncontrolled temper as reasons why a husband may be forced to sue for a Get.[32]

As early as the beginning of the eleventh century of the Christian era, rabbinic authorities decided that a man may not divorce his wife without her agreeing to the dissolution of marriage. Maimonides went further. His code decreed that "if the husband debars his wife from participating in certain joyous functions, she may sue for and obtain a divorce." Or again, if she complains that he is repulsive to her and that she finds life miserable with him, she can demand that he divorce her. The reason is that "she is not like a captive woman who is compelled to consort with a man against her will."[33]

Evidently Jewish tradition has sided with Hillel, and divorce with the right to remarry is granted for many other reasons than adultery. Nevertheless, Orthodox Jews still regard a religious dissolution by appropriate rabbinic authorities as necessary for remarriage.

Unexpectedly, Reform Jews are also unwilling to recognize a merely civil divorce and permit the partners to remarry. They point out that even the Orthodox rabbis understand that in America at least their rabbinic courts have no power to dissolve a marriage. Only the civil courts, which give a license to marry, have the corresponding authority to "unmarry" a couple. So, instead of granting an official Get, they offer the interested parties a document which reads like a compromise with the State.

> *To the Woman*: The woman (Name) has received a Get from her husband (Name) according to the law of our holy Torah; but this divorce is only according to our holy Torah. But she is not permitted to marry another man until she obtain permission from the law of the state, since, according to the law of the state, this Get has no validity.
>
> *To the Man*: The man (Name) has divorced his wife (Name), but the divorce is only according to our holy Torah. He is not permitted to marry another woman until he obtain

permission from the law of the state, since, according to the law of the state, this Get has no validity.[34]

Then the Get document is torn up and discarded. In practice, certainly among the Orthodox, the rabbi does not give the parties a formal Get until after they have obtained a civil divorce. Even then, the custom for a long time has been to draw up the Get, tear it into pieces, and give the woman only a brief résumé (*P'tur*) telling her she is free to marry on religious grounds.

Reform rabbis object to the Orthodox practice of allowing a husband to divorce his wife according to the traditional Get; but their objection is not based on the idea of dissolving a marriage. They maintain that the biblical Get discriminates in favor of the man, whereas the Reform believes that men and women should be equal before the law—Jewish as well as civil. They recall the incredible laxity of Hillel in giving a husband the right to put away his wife for any whim or fancy. "The school of Hillel says (he may divorce her) even if she scorches the soup. . . . Rabbi Akiba, in order to make it absolutely clear, says, even if he found another prettier than her."[35] Rebelling against this complete dominance of man over woman, the Reform synagogues finally declared that when a marriage is dissolved, the action is purely civil.

> The dissolution of marriage is, on Mosaic and rabbinical grounds, a civil act only which never received religious consecration. It is to be recognized, therefore, as an act emanating altogether from the judicial authorities of the state. The so-called Get is in all cases declared null and void.[36]

Though written in 1869, this statement has never received full acceptance in the Reform. To this day the whole subject of divorce is unsettled. Yet, out of consideration for the religious scruples of Orthodox and Conservative Jews, Reform rabbis generally refuse to officiate at marriages that are turned down by the Orthodox and Conservative. Where a couple wants to be remarried after a civil divorce (and without a Get), Reform leaders are told to decide according to their own judgment. While they all approve remarriage, they differ as to who should perform the ceremony.

Sexual morality

One aspect of the Jewish view of marriage has particular significance for Christians. It is impossible to generalize, here as anywhere, in describing the typical position of Judaism on marital morality. Yet, if a comparison can be made, it would be something like a contrast between sex under the Mosaic law and sex as found in the New Testament. The two viewpoints are not the same. They differ as radically as the person of Jesus differs in the Jewish and Christian philosophies of life.

To Christians, Jesus of Nazareth was not only the Messiah. He was the great teacher of mankind, whose example and precepts are considered normative in the moral order.

Among the things he taught and preached, his attitude toward marriage and sexual morality is crucial. Christian tradition believes that he was born of the Virgin Mary, that he never married, that he forbade remarriage after divorce and counseled those who received the grace to follow his own pattern of celibacy.

All of this is strange to Jews, since they do not consider Jesus the one who was sent to teach the nations. They find it specially difficult to understand an ethic which, presumably, demands the subordination of physical pleasure to supernatural ends.

> Judaism maintains that if one denies himself the physical enjoyments of love, he also denies the spiritual potential within him. The sexual love relationship is a high adventure of the human spirit; an opportunity for a man and woman to make a oneness of their separateness. One does not thwart his body, but rather sanctifies it through love. Voluntary abstinence from sexual relations in marriage is a sin—against the health of the body, the fulfillment of soul, and the welfare of society.[37]

St. Paul is further held responsible for insisting on even more than his Master in preaching sexual restraint. So that "Judaism is not burdened as is Christianity with Paulinian derogations of sex."[38]

True to its own spirit, Judaism stresses the duty of obedience to the Decalogue which forbids indulgence and self-gratification. Christianity, in the spirit of its Founder, accepts the Decalogue but goes beyond it to teach the sublimation and sacrifice of noble pleasures for the sake of higher goals, in the words of Jesus, "For the Kingdom of Heaven."

Two areas of sexual morality where this dialectic is most pronounced, especially between Judaism and Catholicism, is in contraception and abortion. Modern Judaism favors both practices; Roman Catholicism prohibits both. Behind the respective difference is a corresponding concept of sex, in one case admitting the dignity of sexual activity but not insisting on its necessary connection with pregnancy and childbirth, and in the other case relating such activity to that fullness of love-giving which never deliberately excludes conception or directly terminates pregnancy.

The Jewish position on contraception is well known. Except for the extreme Orthodox, religious leaders endorse the practice and Jewish spokesmen have been in the vanguard of the national and international agencies advocating planned parenthood by scientific means.

The position of the Reform group was stated succinctly by the Central Conference of American Rabbis. Two sentences in the statement summarize their attitude.

We hold that apart from its procreation function, the sex relation in marriage serves positive spiritual values.

Parents have the right to determine the number and to space the births of their children in accordance with what they believe to be the best interests of their families. Contraceptive information and devices should be legally and inexpensively available to married persons.[39]

Unexpectedly, the Conservative branch came out early in favor of contraception; this was partly due to the fact that the practice was assumed to be acceptable among the Reformed and at that date the Orthodox seemed to frown on intercepting the procreative process. The Conservatives were urged to state their mind, and did so through their national body, the Rabbinical Assembly of America.

Jewish tradition explicitly recognizes the desirability of the use of contraceptives when the health of the mother or the children is involved. We regard it as legitimate, and completely in consonance with the spirit of Jewish tradition, to permit the use of contraceptives on economic grounds as well, when the earning capacity of the family makes the postponement of childbearing or the limitation of the number of children so-cially wise and necessary. Proper education in contraception and birth control will not destroy, but rather enhance, the spir-itual values inherent in the family and will make for the ad-vancement of human happiness and welfare.[40]

An examination of the published approvals of contraception by the major religious bodies in North America would show that the foregoing statement by the Conservative branch of Judaism goes furthest in advocating the practice—on economic and social grounds.

Contrary to popular opinion, that Orthodox Judaism forbids contraception, its highest authorized assembly, the Rabbinical Alli-ance of America, formally gave its sanction—yet with unusual qual-ification. Devices are not to be used by the husband, declared the Alliance. It concluded, however, that "in cases where the health of the female is jeopardized certain birth control measures are allowed, and then only through direct consultation between the medical and rabbinic authorities."[41] Practically speaking, Orthodox wives con-sult a physician who decides that contraceptive drugs or devices are medically indicated. He reports his recommendation to the rabbi who then approves what the doctor recommended.

An outstanding rabbinic scholar synthesized the Jewish tradi-tion on contraception, covering fifteen hundred years of practice. "The Talmudic-Rabbinic Law," he wrote, "does not consider the use of contraceptives, as such, immoral or against the law. The Talmudic-Rabbinic Law requires that every Jew have at least two children in fulfillment of the biblical command to propagate the race, which is incumbent on every man."[42] The reference to two children is based on the Talmud and has recently been voiced in America as a suitable norm for national legislation.

The Jewish attitude toward abortion follows the same general pattern. Talmudic grounds in favor of abortion are cited by all writers on the subject. The classic passage occurs in a context where the pregnant mother is not personally ill, but delivery would be dangerous: "When a woman giving birth to a child is in danger, the unborn child may be cut to pieces and removed, for her life takes precedence over the life of the unborn child."[43]

Implicit in this judgment is the centuries-old teaching of the Pharisees and rabbis that since the fetus is essentially part of the mother a human person is not directly killed when pregnancy is terminated for any good reason which favors the mother.

One of the ways in which Judaism has ritualized the view that intrauterine life is part of the mother until birth, and not an independent person, is the custom of burying an aborted or miscarried child outside the cemetery. No funeral services and no memorial prayers are offered. In some cases this restriction of personhood applies even to an infant which dies within the first thirty days.

The prevalent stance today was expressed by the world pioneer in population control, Alan Guttmacher, to the effect that "Jewish thought . . . approves of abortion when it is required for a woman's life or health."[44] At stake may be her physical health or emotional welfare. These take precedence over the life of the unborn child, as the Jewish proponents of legalized abortion successfully argued their case in New York State.

BURIAL AND MOURNING

Jews trace their traditional care for the dead to the story in Genesis in which Abraham is described as purchasing the Cave of Pachpelah in which to place his beloved wife Sarah. No price was too high for the burial plot, and, when asked to pay four hundred shekels of silver, Abraham paid the cost gladly that he might have a cemetery where "I will bury my dead."

The Talmud prescribes that as death approaches and, while the person is still conscious, a confession of one's misdeeds should be made. The reason given is a quotation from Ecclesiastes: that "there is not a righteous man upon earth that doeth good and sinneth not."[45] It is moreover believed that "all who die expiate their offences by death." Yet, to make sure of this expiation, a deathbed confession is made.

With minor changes, the confessional formula has not changed since ancient times.

I acknowledge unto thee, O Lord my God and God of my fathers, that both my cure and my death are in thy hands. May it be thy will to send me a perfect healing.

Yet if my death be fully determined by thee, I will in love accept it at thy hand. O may my death be an atonement for all my sins, iniquities and transgressions of which I have been guilty against thee.

Bestow upon me the abounding happiness that is treasured up for the righteous. Make known to me the path of life; in thy presence is fulness of joy; at thy right hand, bliss for evermore.

Thou who art the father of the fatherless and judge of the widow, protect my beloved kindred with whose soul my own is knit.

Into thy hand I commend my spirit; thou hast redeemed me, O Lord of truth. Amen, and Amen.

As the end approaches, the dying person either says by himself or others say it for him: "The Lord reigneth; the Lord hath reigned; the Lord shall reign for ever and ever"—repeated three times. Followed by another invocation, repeated three times: "Blessed be His Name whose glorious kingdom is for ever and ever." And finally, seven times: "The Lord is God," concluding with the great Shema, "Hear O Israel, the Lord our God, the Lord is One."[46]

The moment the person dies, those nearby utter the words of resignation: "*Baruch Dayan Emet*=Blessed be the true Judge." Then they perform the *Keriah* custom by slightly tearing one or another piece of their clothing as a sign of sorrow. Another form of grief is to cover or to put away such objects as mirrors or articles of decoration in the house. In the meantime a large candle is lighted and kept burning (with renewals) for thirty days, except on the Sabbath, in memory of the person who died.

Burial has always been regarded by Jews as a sacred duty to be performed for all without discrimination, including criminals, suicides, and enemies slain in battle. From antiquity the burial practice has been to place the body in an earthen grave or in a rock-hewn cave. Behind the practice was partly the biblical injunction that man was dust, and into dust he would return, but more important was the firm belief in the resurrection of the body and therefore its sacredness during life and after death.

In ancient times the body was often first buried in the ground. After disintegration, the bones were gathered up and placed in stone ossuaries in the family burial cave. Later on the practice of having burial galleries underground gave rise to the catacomb system in Rome, which the Christians adopted as their own.

To this day it is customary, whenever possible, to bury the person on the day he dies. Neither cremation nor embalming are traditional Jewish customs. Where practiced, this is a concession to the non-Jewish culture in which the people live. As a rule, burials are hastened on Fridays and on the eve of holidays, so as not to interfere with the festive character of these days.

The family spares no trouble in paying tribute to the dead. Formerly the wealthy buried their relatives in costly garments and jewelry, but this led to a great deal of abuse. Rabbi Gamaliel reacted against the practice because it humiliated the poor. So that now, following the Talmud, the corpse is to be carefully bathed and cleansed and clothed in a plain white linen or cotton shroud (*Tachrichin*) regardless of the person's wealth or fame. Coffins are used in America, but the custom is not universal. In the Orient many Jews are buried without coffins; and when used, they are to be made of simple wood.

Watch is kept over the deceased until he is buried. Two large candles, placed at the head of the coffin, burn continuously until the body is taken from the room. Meantime the Psalms and other appropriate hymns are sung.

The funeral procession (*Halvayah*) is a simple ceremony but considered by the Orthodox to be a sacred duty (*mitzvah*). Jews are extraordinarily faithful in paying the last honors to their dead.

Whenever possible, the procession stops at the synagogue to perform *Hesped* or eulogy for the deceased. The synagogue service is not essential, however, and prominent Jews are often eulogized at the institution in which they have been most active.

The Hebrew name for cemetery is symbolic. It is *Bet Almin*, the Eternal Home. As the history of American Judaism testifies,

Jews are so concerned to have their own burial grounds that this is usually their first acquisition when they settle in a new locality. Basic to their tradition is to be buried among Israelites. It is a personal tragedy and a community disgrace for a person not to be brought to *Kever Yisrael* (a Jewish grave). Even otherwise nominal Jews try to make sure they will be buried "among their own." Not infrequently American Jews (as others too) will direct that a small sack of soil from Palestine be placed in the grave with their bodies. Denied the chance of living and dying in Eretz Yisrael, they want at least to have some of the soil from the Holy Land near them after death. The same sentiment explains why Jews are customarily buried with the head toward the East, that is, toward Zion or the Promised Land.

Unlike Christian burial services, which concentrate on the ritual in church, Jewish funeral rites are mainly at the grave. The prayers and hymns led by the rabbi or Hazen before the body is lowered into the ground witness to the deep faith of Israel in man's undying spirit and his final resurrection from the dead. One expressive prayer typifies the rest.

> The gates of heaven mayest thou find opened,
> And the town of peace mayest thou see,
> And the dwellings of confidence.
> And angels of peace to meet thee with joy;
> And may the High Priest stand to receive thee;
> And thou, go thou to the end,
> For thou shalt rest, and rise up again. . . .
> The gates of the sanctuary may Michael open,
> And bring thy soul as an offering before God;
> And may the redeeming angel accompany thee
> Unto the gates of the Heavens, where Israel dwell;
> May it be vouchsafed to thee to stand in this beautiful place;
> And thou, go thou to the end,
> For thou shalt rest, and rise up again.[47]

Along with expressions of hope in the life to come are prayers of faith in the justice of God. In the spirit of Job, the rabbi asks: "Who dare say, 'What doest thou?' to him who ruleth above and below, who taketh away life and giveth it. The Lord hath given and the Lord hath taken. Praised be the name of the Lord."[48]

After the grave is filled in, the famous *El Maley Rahamin* ("God, full of compassion") is recited. Originally in the Ashkenazim tradition, this prayer expresses sentiments that are paralleled in Christianity. It is a synthesis of Jewish eschatology.

> O Lord and King, who art full of compassion, God of the spirits of all flesh, in whose hands are the souls of the living and the dead.
>
> Receive, we beseech thee, in thy great lovingkindness the soul of ...., who hath been gathered unto his people.
>
> Have mercy upon him, pardon all his transgressions, for there is none righteous upon earth, who doeth only good, and sinneth not.
>
> Remember unto him the righteousness which he wrought, and let his reward be with him and his recompense before him.
>
> O shelter his soul in the shadow of thy wings. Make known to him the path of life: In thy presence is fulness of joy; at thy right hand, bliss for evermore.[49]

The *El Maley* is followed by two Psalms, chosen to bring out the fact that what is important in life is not wealth or fame but the virtues of a man who fears God. As the relatives and friends leave the cemetery, they hear the consoling words: "May the Omnipotent comfort you together with all the mourners of Zion and Jerusalem."

An ancient custom prescribes that the mourners begin seven days of Shivah, introduced by having hard-boiled egg and ashes placed before them when they return from the burial. The egg symbolizes life and reminds the bereaved not to lose hope; the ashes are a sign of sorrow. Strictly Orthodox Jews observe Shivah by not leaving the house, except to go to the synagogue on a Sabbath or holiday. They extend the mourning up to one month after death, during what is known as Sheloshim, or thirty days of abstention from entertainment and festivities. On rare occasions, the Sheloshim lasts a whole year. It obliges only the nearest relatives: parents and children, brothers and sisters, husband and wife. Others may observe the Sheloshim if they so desire.

To keep alive the memory of the dead, the tombstone is not generally unveiled until, on, or before the first anniversary of death. Again the *El Maley* is sung and the Kaddish (consecration), the most famous Jewish doxology, whose central formula is: "May His great Name be blessed for ever and for all time." Every year the anniversary is observed at home or in the synagogue. Among other customs, a memorial lamp or candle within a glass is lit at sunset and kept burning until the end of the next day.

Jews have a deep sense of kinship with those who have died, and of faith in praying for their speedy entrance into Paradise. The prayer for one's mother is characteristic.

> May God remember the soul of my respected mother ...., who has passed to her eternal rest. I pledge charity in her behalf and pray that her soul be kept among the immortal souls of Abraham, Isaac, Jacob, Sarah, Rebekah, Rachel, Leah, and all the righteous men and women in paradise. Amen.[50]

Implicit throughout the Jewish liturgy for the dead is the belief in some kind of expiation after death, for those who have not been fully cleansed when they entered eternity.

PERSONAL PRAYER AND DEVOTION

One of the characterisics of Jewish piety is its strong sense of community. There is nothing quite like it in Christian spirituality.

From earliest times, the Jews have been remarkably conscious of their status as a people. This was reflected in their prayers which, with few exceptions, are worded in the plural rather than the singular. It was natural to them, when they prayed, to say, "Our God," instead of "My God." They would ask, "Grant us peace," rather than "Grant me peace."

The Talmud almost prescribed this collective form of prayer. Since every person is able to ask God to help others, not to do so would be wrong, for "all Jews are responsible for one another."

This tendency toward collective piety is still present in Judaism, and finds expression everywhere. The synagogue symbolizes in brick and stone the group consciousness of believers in a certain locality. The weekly Sabbath and recurring holy days show the same spirit of unity as measured in sacred time. Dietary laws with their minute regulations further strengthen togetherness; while customs like circumcision and Yahrzeit (annual commemoration of the dead) bind the Jewish people to one another beyond anything comparable in Christianity or Islam.

Less well known, but equally important as a binding force in Judaism, is the use of common prayer books. The earliest such book still extant is from the ninth century of the Christian era; the best known is called *Mahzor Vitri* and was written by a disciple of the French rabbinical scholar Rashi (1040-1105).

Each of the three main forms of American Judaism has its own editions of prayer books, with the amount of Hebrew diminishing as the book is intended for less Orthodox users. Yet among these is a certain consistency. The intention is to provide (as far as possible) a complete manual for different occasions. The daily manual, called *Siddur*, contains the full Sabbath and festival services and prayers for special occasions. For the High Holy Days, there is a *Mahzor* which concentrates on Rosh Ha-Shanah and Yom Kippur, and for the days of atonement in between. A *Kinot* or book of lamentations is needed for the Fast of Av; a Psalter (*Tehillim*) contains the full text of all the Psalms traditionally ascribed to David; and the *Selihot* features the prayers of forgiveness for the days before Rosh Ha-Shanah.

Jewish writers feel strongly about this matter of communal and, in fact, scheduled prayer. Apart from the intrinsic value of praying together and at prescribed times, is the matter of personal frailty.

> The individual, when he is his own standard, will pray when he feels he needs to. Prayer then finds its occasion and its value in response to his private moods and feelings. What happens under those circumstances to regular prayer with respect to frequency, intensity, and unselfish content is a commonplace of modern versions of religiosity. The man who objects that he cannot pray on schedule often does not pray at all. And when, in this hectic world, he finally allows a conscious desire to pray to take priority over all the important things he should be doing now, he finds he does not have the knack.

Obviously prayer in response to the inspiration of a moment has a unique significance, one well worthy of cherishing.
But it is a supplement to, not a substitute for, regular public
worship—and the acquired habit of turning to God in prayer
is readily transferred from the congregational to the private
situation.[51]

In the light of the foregoing, it is somewhat inaccurate to speak
of private prayers or devotions among the Jews, because strictly
personal or individual piety is not stressed in Judaism.

Yet an important distinction should be made. If the form and
content of prayer are consciously collective, the soul of Jewish devotion is still deeply personal. The whole history of Israel urges the
faithful to maintain close internal communion with the Lord.

Prayer has always been considered a grave duty, and essential
to prayer is the idea of awareness of God's presence. "Remember
that you stand before God when you pray" is the Talmudic injunction. Maimonides went on to explain what this means. His commentary on living in God's presence and keeping a spirit of recollection
is among the most incisive in religious literature.

> The intellect which emanates from God unto us is the link
> that joins us to God. You have it in your power to strengthen
> that bond, if you choose to do so; or to weaken it gradually till
> it breaks, if you prefer this.
>
> It will only become strong when you employ it in the love
> of God and seek that love; it will become weakened when you
> direct your thoughts to other things. You must know that even
> if you were the wisest man in respect to the knowledge of God
> —whenever you turn your thoughts entirely to necessary food
> or business, you are then not with God and He is not with you.
> For that relation between Him and you is actually interrupted
> in those moments.
>
> The pious were therefore particular to restrict the time on
> which they could not meditate on the name of God, and cau-
> tioned others about it saying, "Let not your minds be vacant
> from reflections upon God." In the same sense did David say,
> "I have set the Lord always before me; because he is at my

right hand, I shall not be moved." i. e., I do not turn my thoughts away from God. He is like my right hand, which I do not forget even for a moment on account of the ease of its motions, and therefore I shall not be moved, I shall not fail.

When we have acquired a true knowledge of God, and rejoice in that knowledge in such a manner that, while speaking with others or attending to our bodily wants, our mind is all the time with God; when we are with our heart constantly near God, even while our body is in the society of men; when we are in that state which the Song on the relation between God and man poetically describes in the following words, "I sleep but my heart is awake; it is the voice of my beloved that knocks"—then we have attained not only the height of ordinary prophets, but of Moses our teacher.[52]

This ideal of personal intimacy with God is part of the spirit of Judaism and remains as valid and vital among believing Jews today as in the time of Maimonides.

Symbolic articles

The use of symbolic articles around the home or on one's person is intended to foster awareness of the divine presence. Some of the articles date from Mosaic times; others were introduced more recently. A sure mark of Orthodoxy in a Jewish family is the extent to which such external features of devotion are visible. In Brooklyn, New York, for example, which has an extraordinary number of Orthodox synagogues, many of these customs are faithfully practiced.

On entering a Jewish home, the first thing to be seen is a sign beside the door called a *Mezuzah*, which means "doorpost," and usually hangs in a slanting position. Some homes have a Mezuzah fastened at the door of every room.

Ideally the case for the Mezuzah is made of olive wood from Palestine, but it may be of glass or metal. Inside the case is a sheet of parchment with writing on both sides. On one side is the single word, *Shaddai* (Almighty), on the other side are two texts from Deuteronomy where the precept of having the Mezuzah occurs. The first passage is repeated five chapters later.

Listen, Israel, Yahweh our God is the one Yahweh. You shall love Yahweh your God with all your heart, with all your soul, with all your strength. Let these words I urge on you today be written on your heart. You shall repeat them to your children and say them over them or at your rising. You shall fasten them on your hand as a sign and on your forehead as a circlet. You shall write them on the doorposts of your house and on your gates.[53]

The Mezuzah is also found on the right side of the entrance of Jewish buildings. Observant Jews never enter or leave the house without reverently placing their fingers to their lips and then touching the sacred receptacle.

Inside the house, the most prominent object is the *Mizrach* (East), which can be of paper or embroidered velvet. It is a picture hung on the eastern wall toward which the Orthodox Jew turns when he prays. This is an old custom, to pray in the direction of the City of David. The Mizrach sometimes represents scenes from the Bible, like the sacrifice of Isaac; it may be inscribed with some biblical verse or contain just the single word *Mizrach*.

Though generally limited to synagogues, some homes still have the *Zedakah* (justice) box in the living room. During the days of the First Temple, a chest with a hole in the top was placed near the entrance where worshipers dropped their money for the maintenance of the sanctuary. A replica of this chest is used in the home for receiving coins to be given to the poor or (in former times) to be sent to the refugees in Palestine.

The Tallit or prayer shawl is in the style of the upper garment worn by Jews before the Christian era. As a ritual vestment, it is put on by adult men, according to specifications. Among the Orthodox it is often only the married men who wear the Tallit during the morning (and additional) prayers (on the ninth of Av in the afternoon, and on the Day of Atonement at all services). Made of wool, it is a four-cornered piece of cloth whose corners have the knotted Tzitzit (fringes) as prescribed by the Bible: "Speak to the sons of Israel and tell them to put tassels on the hems of their garments. . . . They will remind you of all my commandments."[54]

Centuries ago, the fringes were worn on the outer garments in daily use. Later on, however, due perhaps to fear of criticism, a small undergarment with fringes was substituted. Commonly known as the Small (*Katan*) Tallit, or the *Arba Kanfot* (four corners), it is the form now in vogue.

Strictly speaking, the Arba Kanfot is part of the Orthodox Jew's daily clothing, whereas the Tallit is worn only during prayer. The stripes of the Tallit are usually blue. Sometimes black bands are added as a sign of mourning over the destruction of the Temple.

So typical is the Tallit of Jewish tradition, that the flag of the State of Israel is based on this ritual garment. The flag is of blue and white stripes, where the sky blue stands for heaven (to which the Jew aspires after death) and the white for peace (which he hopes to enjoy on earth). Between the blue stripes is the *Magen David* (Shield of David). This is a mystical symbol consisting of two superimposed triangles forming a star or hexagram. Traceable to a synagogue at Caphernaum in the third century of the Christian era, its meaning is disputed, but most likely it recalls the six-pointed star shape of King David's shield.

The *Kittel* is another ritual garment made of white cloth and reaching to the ground. Originally put on every Saturday, it is now worn only at the Passover and on the High Holy Days in the synagogue. Some Orthodox require the groom to wear the Kittel at his wedding, and many Jews use it on Rosh Ha-Shanah and Yom Kippur. When a person dies, the Kittel becomes the shroud in which he is buried.

At the age of thirteen, boys put on the Tefillin for their morning prayers during the week. The term itself in Aramaic means "attachment," and is popularly connected with the Hebrew for "prayer" (*Tephillah*). The more common name is phylacteries, which are two leather boxes connected with leather straps for attachment to the arms and forehead at times of prayer. Implicit in the practice is the same idea which inspired the Mezuzah, to literally touch the biblical texts that speak of Yahweh and his promises to Israel. Some rabbis teach that two sets of Tefillin should be worn, corresponding to the two traditions represented in the chosen passages.

In order to impress the one who prays still further, it is recommended that he tie the head phylactery into a knot having the
form of the Hebrew letter daleth (D); the one on the arm in the
form of yod (Y), which then is combined with the letter shin (SH)
painted on two sides of the box to form the most sacred name of
the Lord, *Shaddai*.

Hasidism in America

There is one aspect of American Judaism that can be easily
overlooked, if for no other reason than that Jews themselves seldom
advert to it and their writers (with minor exception) practically ignore its existence. This is the presence of a mystical element among
the people, usually the less cultured and literate, that has been
deeply influential not only on Jewish but American culture.

Its roots go back to the same reaction that, in the Middle Ages,
produced the phenomenon of Cabalism. Uncomfortable with the
towering load of precepts and devotional detail, and hungry for a
more immediate union with God, Hasidism came into existence in
the eighteenth century mainly through the preaching and writing
of Israel Baal Shem Tov (1699-1761), rabbi in the Ukraine.

Baal Shem Tov's message was simple. He taught that all are
equal before the Lord, the ignorant as well as the learned; that purity of the heart is better than study; and that devotion to prayer
and the great commandments of the Decalogue are more pleasing
to God than ascetical practices.

If Baal Shem Tov borrowed anything from the Cabalists, it
was mainly their discomfort with the literal interpretation of the
Law. His plea was for a more personal religion that centered on
what a man is rather than on what he does; or that considers a
man's actions before it asks what he doctrinally believes.

There was a strong emotional element in Hasidism which instinctively appealed to those who were looking for something more
fruitful than the legalism of the Talmudists or the rationalism of the
German Enlightenment.

Essential to Hasidism was the idea that a man's character, not
his teaching, is primary. Personality thus took the place of doctrine,
and the Hasidic saint emerged as the center of religious fervor and

loyalty. The story is told of a Hasidim who said, "I did not go to the *Maggid* (preacher) of Meseritz to learn Torah from him but to watch him tie his boot-laces."[55] This extravagant statement points to a new focus in Judaism. What really counts is not a man's ideas, no matter how exalted, or his knowledge of the Law, but his holiness and nearness to God.

Most people are familiar with Hasidism only through the writings of the Jewish philosopher Martin Buber. His influence on American Judaism has been profound. Buber conceived religious faith as essentially a dialogue between God and man. This conception he synthesized in the idea of "I and Thou," which was thoroughly Judaic in its belief that religion is a personal relationship between Yahweh and his people, but was also typically Hasidic in its stress on the individual's intimacy with the Divine.

The influence of Buber, however, has been oblique and more speculative than practical. Where it entered the Jewish community, its impact scarcely went beyond the academic. Besides the ideas of Buber are often couched in such eclectic terms that they can hardly be called Jewish at all. They are catholic, as being relevant to all religious traditions, and therefore Hasidic only in their inspiration but not in their application to the Jewish people.

Hasidism in the strict sense has found expression in America in two ways: in the growing amount of literature available even to the common people, and in the rise of new forms of Jewish piety due to the preaching and example of living Hasidim.

The literature is drawn from sources that reach back to Baal Shem Tov and may be as recent as the sayings of his disciples recorded from the concentration camps of Auschwitz and Buchenwald. Thousands of parables and stories have been recorded, and many are still oral traditions.

It is impossible to recapture the depth of spirit which must have animated those who left a written memorial of this Hasidic wisdom. Nor does it matter, because, on its own premise, this form of Judaism is less concerned with what a man says than the kind of man he is. Sometimes the sayings are identified, at other times anonymous, but always they are aphoristic, expressing in a few words the inner spirit rather than some form of doctrine.

In the hour of his death the Baal Shem said: "Now I know the purpose for which I was created."

The Talmud declares that wine taken in moderation unfolds the brain of a man. He who is a total abstainer is rarely possessed of wisdom.

Who is a true believer in God? The man who believes that the Shekinah is within him always and guards him; that he is in the Creator and the Creator within him; that he looks upon the Creator, and Creator looks upon him; that the Creator may accomplish His will—He may create worlds and destroy them in a moment; that in Him is the source of all good, and of all misfortune; that His influence and His Living Power are present in everything; that only God is to be feared and trusted.

Remember that man is born unto affliction. Every man on earth must encounter tribulations and pain. If he takes refuge from them in the Lord, he will be comforted.

Rabbi Sullivan of Karlin said: "The greatest of all miracles is to bring into the heart of a Jew the living influence whereby he may be enabled to pray properly unto his Creator."

Said the Medzibozer to his grandson, Israel, who was accustomed to gesticulate in his prayers: "A wick of linen burns quietly and gives a better light than a cotton wick which burns noisily. Believe me when I say that a sincere movement of your smallest toe is sufficient to show your enthusiasm."

Let your heart hear what your mouth speaks if you wish to offer proper prayer.

The main weapons of a Jew are his prayers. All his battles against evil impulses and obstacles he wins through prayers. The holiness of Israel comes through prayers.[56]

Clearly we are in a different atmosphere when we hear the Hasidim talk about the meaning of religion. The stress on a man's intention rather than his deeds is not normally associated with the externals and prescriptions of traditional Judaism.

Nevertheless Hasidism is authentically Jewish and not the least of its values is to reveal what Judaism, at its best, really is and not what its critics make it out to be.

The Hasidic influence in America has also found expression in the lives of thousands of Jews. Orthodox communities on the East Coast have been among those most deeply affected. A good example is the colony at Williamsburg, in the Brooklyn area of New York. Several generations of Hasidic *rebbes* (rabbis) have succeeded in creating there a seedbed of Orthodoxy that can only be described as phenomenal. Kindergartens and all-day schools for boys and girls, residences for Jewish leaders and new synagogues came into existence as if by magic. Yet Williamsburg is by no means unique. Some of the most influential rebbes settled elsewhere, in communities that soon began to feel their spiritual influence. One result is common knowledge: the establishment of Jewish parochial schools whose main purpose is to instill the faith of the prophets in the hearts of the young.

*The synagogue ready for a wedding service. In front
of the Ark is the Chuppah (canopy) under which
bride and groom and clergy stand. Also seen are
two cups of wine over which blessings are recited
in the course of the service and from which the
groom and bride partake. Inside the right aisle is
a partition which, in Orthodox synagogues, separates
men and women during worship.*

Louis Brandeis–Brandeis University, 1956

*Menorah with its illuminated branches. Originally
seven branches, since the destruction of the Temple it has six.*

JEWISH LAW AND
RABBINIC MORALITY

Most people assume that Judaism is, above all, an ethical religion. Everything about it confirms this fact. The dominant theme of the Jewish Bible is the covenant between Yahweh and his people. He called them from the land of the Gentiles to say how gracious he would be if they were obedient to his will. The Torah, which may be simply rendered "Law," summarizes in a single word what this will of God is understood to be. Those who praise (*barak*) the Lord by their obedience are blessed (*barak*) by him in return.

Since the rise of Rabbinic Judaism, the ethical emphasis has not changed; if anything, it has deepened with the years. What those who are not Jews are tempted to regard as superficial, or at least secondary, Jews understand is at the heart of their religion. Definite prescriptions and elaborate ritual are not an overlayer to

the Jewish way of life; they practically constitute it and the constitution has profound meaning for all believers and not only for
the Jews.

MEANING OF LAW IN JUDAISM

In order to appreciate the inner meaning of Jewish morality, it
is useful to see it in contrast with the ethical systems that exist outside the Jewish tradition. These would include the moral philosophies of ancient Greece and Rome and their counterparts today. As
Jewish commentators explain it, the genius of Judaism has been to
add the religious dimension to morality. Philosophy since the time
of Aristotle has made some high demands on human conduct, not
excluding great sacrifice for the sake of another. It was Cicero who
wrote that whatever leads a man to do his duty does not offer pleasure as its reward.

Biblical Judaism accepts all of this, as the whole sequence of
its Decalogue confirms. Only it says something more.

It is no coincidence that the first third of the Ten Commandments given to Moses on Sinai are concerned not with man's relation to man but with his relationship toward God. Jewish morality,
therefore, begins with the thundering affirmation which Yahweh
communicated to the first lawgiver of his people.

I am Yahweh your God who brought you out of the land
of Egypt, out of the house of slavery.

You shall have no gods except me.

You shall not make yourself a carved image or any like-
ness of anything in a heaven above or on earth beneath or in
the waters under the earth; you shall not bow down to them
or serve them. For I, Yahweh your God, am a jealous God.

You shall not utter the name of Yahweh your God to misuse it, for Yahweh will not leave unpunished the man who
utters his name to misuse it.

Observe the sabbath day and keep it holy, as Yahweh your
God has commanded you. For six days you shall labour and do
all your work, but the seventh day is a sabbath for Yahweh
your God.[1]

Only then follow the other precepts of the moral law, of man's obligations to his fellowmen.

The great contribution of the Jewish prophets to the concept of morality was this third partner to the relationship. The Judaic moral system is three-dimensional. First comes God and only then the rights of men to one another and to human society.

As we look more closely into what this means, we see it implies practically all the elements that the Western world has come to identify with the practice of virtue and the observance of law. It proclaims the idea that law begins with the rights of God, which he has as man's Creator, and that religion is fundamentally the acknowledgment of these rights on the part of creatures. It also says that the laws between man and man derive from an objective norm of morality, which is the mind and will of God. It declares man's inability of himself either to know all that he should do or, more seriously, to be able to do it without the assistance of divine help. It states that the moral law is not coercion by a blind force like the laws of physics or chemistry, but the loving (though demanding) invitation of a Father who bids his children to freely obey him that he might finally satisfy all their wants.

The priority of the divine is intrinsic to the spirit of Judaism and has since become the heritage of Christianity and Islam. This is more than merely saying that God comes first and man a very distant second. For the Jew who believes in God, his first obligation is not to himself nor even to others but to the eternal Other from whom everything derives and toward whom everything tends. Obedience to this Other is the basis of all human altruism.

The idea of God's primacy in the moral order was taken for granted in the canonical books of the Jewish Bible; it became thematic in what the Jews now consider the Apocrypha but which reflect their most ancient tradition. The youngest of the Maccabean brothers boldly asserted that Yahweh "alone is God."[2] According to Ecclesiasticus, "there is but one eternity," and from the author of the book of Wisdom it is "a silly delusion" to equate anyone with God.[3] Always the Jews were reminded that if man's purpose on earth is to serve, it is God who must be served before anyone else and even before man himself.

This preoccupation with serving the Lord underlies the elaborate ritual of the Jewish religion, where the highest service is acknowledging one's creaturehood before God.

If God is the first object of moral obligation in the Judaic code, he is also the first premise in applying this code to the thousands of duties that men have to one another in human society. Whatever else may be said of the Torah, it is not relativistic. Its prohibition of lying and adultery or avarice and stealing presumes that these sins are always wrong because the God who proscribes them is always, by his very nature, the same.

The Jewish faith told its followers there are certain limitations which the author of human nature placed upon man. In respect to these limits by obedience to divine law, man shows his dependence on God by an implicit prayer of adoration that is no less real because it is not formal or ritualistic. That is why sin is not only a mistaken judgment deliberately acted upon but it has a relationship to God which Judaism has always defended.

Not only God's will but his mind is the standard of man's conduct. What he prescribes is good and what he forbids is bad because the precept and prohibition derive from his eternal wisdom that will never change.

Circumstances may differ and the applications of the Decalogue may vary, as the later Talmud spent a million words to show; but never for a moment is there any doubt that the principles underlying these variations are unchanged.

The Jewish faith also believes that man's nature is not the same as it was originally before the tragedy described in Genesis. Consequently the Jewish attitude toward law is unlike anything in the jurisprudence of Athens or ancient Rome, or even in the religious culture of the Orient. Judaism never developed a complete theology of original sin comparable to what is found in Christianity. But the basic concept is there. Having deliberately estranged himself from the Lord at the beginning of history, man is now laboring under a disability which only a primordial sin could explain.

Man finds himself in constant collision from within and conflict from without. He is often called upon to fight against his own impulses and against urgings from those around him. This means sacrifice of what he would like to do but desists from doing for reasons of conscience, and acceptance of what he would like to avoid but does not because he is convinced that this would be wrong.

Given the inherent difficulties in so many decisions to be made, a Jew believes that God does not let him swim on his own. He is helped constantly by divine assistance with light for the mind and strength of the will. Moreover, such help is to be asked for, and the asking—which is prayer—occurs as often as a contingent being consciously recognizes his contingency before God.

One aspect of law is so characteristic of Judaism that without it the very concept of moral obligation is unthinkable. Jewish scholars explain what this means by comparing law and law: the law prescribed on every page of the Bible and the law familiar in political science and the speculations of philosophy.

They find an apt summary of the meaning of law outside the Jewish tradition in the moral philosophy of Immanuel Kant and quote him as saying that there are two irreconcilable concepts of law: one based on revelation and the other on the autonomous reason. The first he calls revealed morality, the second rational morality; the first is typically Jewish, the second stands for everything that Judaism denies.

Where Maimonides had taught there is no genuine conflict between the law of reason and the law of Sinai, Kant thought otherwise. In a lucid passage from his *Fundamental Principles of the Metaphysics of Morals*, Kant is quoted by Jewish moralists to illustrate the difference. If the will is moral, Kant says, "It is not merely subject to law, but subject in such a way that it must also be regarded as imposing the law on itself, and subject to it for that reason only." This is no mincing of words. By this standard, the Sinaitic Code is not a statement of laws but the imposition of another's will.

All past efforts to identify the principle of morality have failed without exception. For while it was seen that man is bound by his duty to laws, it was seen that he is subject only to his own, albeit at the same time universal legislation, and obligated to act only according to his own, albeit universally legislating will. So long as one thought of man as merely subject to a law, whatever its content, without this law originating in his own will, one had to think of him as impelled to action by something other than himself.[4]

But this is impure morality. Any law which imposes obligation from outside the person who is expected to obey is, by Kantian standards, heteronomous and therefore impure. To be pure, law must be autonomous or self-imposed.

This has a familiar ring because so many people now live by these norms. It is not, however, Jewish morality. As a Jew sees the dilemma, a chasm separates the idea of self-obligation and of duty coming from God. The first is idolatry of the Ego; only the second can truly be called Law.

Hebrew commentators on the Torah explain the difference in different ways. At one extreme, the Orthodox insist that the revealed morality of Judaism is not autonomous because it stands in essential relationship to a commanding God. At the other extreme, Reform Jews protest that morality is not completely heteronomous either. Men are told to obey for their own sake and not only in submission to God. Yet both interpretations agree that morality is tridimensional. Man's duty to others rests on his prior duty as a man responsible to God.

When Jews enter the further question of how a law can be anything but an imposition from the outside, if the Lord commands it, they appeal to that most distinctive feature of their religion—its sense of awareness of the constant presence of God.

In one sense the Law given to Moses came from outside the prophet and outside the people to whom he communicated the Decalogue. But the term *outside* is misleading and may be untrue.

Yahweh is not really outside any of his creatures; he dwells in them and within them in a way that no philosophy but only a believing heart can understand. The effect of this Presence in man is to make him share in the divine prerogative of liberty. Man becomes free, and his freedom is a gift. In this sense man is not autonomous, since the very power to choose between obeying God or rejecting him has been given from above.

Without the Other, man might have the self-sufficient power for all kinds of choice, but the power of choice to accept or reject the divine commanding Presence he would not have. How could he accept God, unless God had become present to him, for him to accept? How could he reject Him, unless He had become present to him, for him to reject? The divine commanding Presence, then, may be said to give man choosing power. It may even be said to force the actual choice upon him. For in being present, It singles out; and in singling out It rules out every escape from the choice into some spurious third alternative.[5]

This is the vision of Israel. It never doubts that what God commands is not man making his own laws but God telling man to do the will of his Master. At the same time a Jew realizes that God is not only the transcendent Creator of the universe but also the immanent Lover who dwells in the closest intimacy with the beings he has made. They are free to do his will but only with the freedom that is also his. If this is a mystery, as the prophets were ready to admit, it is also the glory of man's obedience and a sign of God's love. Except for human liberty, law would be a misnomer because there would be no option to obey. But there would be no liberty in man unless God abided in him and together with man made it possible for him to choose.

This divine Presence in man freely responding to law is complemented by God's presence in the law itself. What he commands is not the arbitrary dictum of a capricious will but the expression of a wise providence directing man to his final end. Once again the Hebrew notion of law has revolutionized the moral judgment of mankind. Some would exclude God from the moral order and call the Torah a tissue of legalism that inhibits personality. They miss what the Jew knows: that God is present in every law, no matter who the human legislator may be. He is there because the law is nothing but his way of leading creatures to the destiny—which is himself—prepared for them.

RABBINIC MORALITY

Already in pre-Talmudic times the Jewish concept of the law was challenged from within its own ranks. Among others the Sadducees propounded a religion that was primarily the Temple cult without a basis in divine faith. According to them, individuals and groups should aspire to well-being in this world without expecting recompense in the world to come.

Sadduceeism and Pharisaism

The Sadducees did not believe in a future life, resurrection, or the immortality of the soul. They rejected the existence of angels and spirits as inconsistent with a thoroughgoing secularism. Yet they were slavishly devoted to the written law. The death penalty, they taught, should be inflicted for a host of "crimes," so that Sadducean morality became a byword for extreme severity.

Some historians dismiss the Sadducees as irrelevant to a proper understanding of Judaism today. It is said that their whole power and existence were bound up with the Temple worship. On the destruction of the Second Temple, they disappeared from Jewish life and history.

This view is too simple and fails to take into account what Judaism has always been: a prophetic religion against which there have always been strong reactions among the Jews themselves. The Sadducees typify the reaction of rationalism, which is uncomfortable with the concept of religion, notably as delineated in the Mosaic law. The inner tension in modern Judaism, especially in the United States, is unintelligible without taking this tendency into account. No one can read a dozen pages by a Reform critic of Jewish Orthodoxy without sensing that it is the Sadducees come back to life again.

Parallel with the Sadducees of ancient times were the Pharisees, whose Hebrew name *Perushim* probably meant "set apart." A Pharisee avoided needless contact with others for reasons of ritual purity. Like the Sadducees their exact origin is unknown; also like them, they were a relatively narrow body that was closed to the masses. Though small in number they exercised great influence on the people whom they sought to inspire with their concept of holiness by propagating traditional religious teaching.

An impassable gulf separated the Pharisees from those ignorant of the Law or from those who did not observe the Law. The Pharisees would eat in groups among themselves, observing all the rules of purity that were binding on priests when they ate consecrated food in the Temple. They tried to extend their influence over the Temple at the expense of the Sadducees, whom they regarded as unbelievers. Not satisfied with the six hundred prescriptions of the Bible, they added numerous customs of their own—all to the dismay of the Sadducees. Between the two parties was an antagonism that extended to every sphere of human conduct. As a rule, the Pharisees admitted the principle of evolution in their legal decisions, whereas the Sadducees seldom allowed the least adjustment to changing times.

In the popular mind, therefore, the Pharisees were considered more lenient in their interpretation of the Law, while the Sadducees were rigorists who clung to the exact wording of the written text. Moreover, the Pharisees placed the life of Israel within a framework of tradition (Oral Law) which they said was equally as vital as the Written Law (Bible). The Pharisaic doctrine of morality sought to embrace the whole life of the Jewish community, affecting the deepest question of human existence: the problem of good and evil, the perdurance of the human spirit, and the eschatology of man's destiny. What the Sadducees denied, the Pharisees affirmed: man did not die at death, his body would rise from the grave, the liberation of Israel would come under a personal Messiah, and the Day of Judgment would close this world of space and time only to begin the Kingdom of God that would never end.

This was the picture of Pharisaism as an ideal, since not all Pharisees lived up to these principles. The Talmud lists seven kinds of hypocrites, all Pharisees. If the vocabulary of Western culture still retains this image, picturing a deceitful man as a Pharisee, this should be put down to an accident of history. There were Pharisees who lived a double life. But Pharisaism itself was mainly responsible for strengthening the morality of post-Christian Judaism. It introduced a flexibility which allowed Jewish ethics to remain basically unchanged to this day. As such it is an integral part of historic Judaism.

Rabbinic morality cannot be understood without reference to its ancestry in the moral outlook of the Sadducees and Pharisees. It would be over-simplifying the case to say that present-day rabbinic ethics is a convergence of these two streams. But without them it would not exist.

To place the matter into focus, two facts of history must be borne in mind. For sometime before the Christian era, Israel no longer enjoyed the guidance of the prophets as a whole. Isaiah and Jeremiah were long since dead, even if their writings were treasured as the word of God. But if the Jews could live without prophets, they could not do without teachers. This explains the rise and influence of such groups as the Sadducees and Pharisees.

By the end of the first century of the Christian era, the Jews were, in effect, no longer a nation having a home within the geographic limits of Palestine. If they were to remain together, they had to find, or develop, another base of unity than the obvious one of cohabitation in a certain locality. They found this principle in their common loyalty to Yahweh and obedience to the Torah. Centuries of persecution and the experience of the Jewish diaspora had prepared the way.

It was out of this twofold necessity—the silence of the voice of prophecy and the loss of their national identity—that rabbinic morality came into being. It built on the traditions of the past, including the spirit of the Sadducees and Pharisees, while adding a new dimension of its own.

What was this new dimension? It was the implicit assumption that the Jewish code of morals could remain essentially constant if the Jewish people, as a people, could be invoked to speak authentically to every contingent need as it arose. What the prophets used to proclaim in the name of Yahweh, the Jewish people could also say, since they were now instruments of his voice.

In more prosaic terms, the whole people of Israel was repository of the Law, in every sense in which that community was conceived.

It was the Jewish community which decided a generation after the destruction of the Second Temple what writings belonged to revelation. If the Pentateuch and the Prophets were prescriptive on the Jews now as they had been before, it was because the people of Israel through its appointed leaders had determined the Pentateuch and who the Prophets were.

Seeing that the Bible was inadequate to cope with the changing scene, the Jewish community gathered together the wisdom of its sages and produced the Talmud. Six hundred years of tradition became normative, along with the Bible, for the believing Jew.

In the early Middle Ages, the Talmud needed updating and the Torah had to be reexamined to meet Jewish exigencies that had not existed before. Moses Maimonides supplied the deficiencies and once again it was the people of Israel whose approval of Maimonides made his writings accepted in Israel. His thirteen articles of faith would have remained so many declarative sentences without the approbation of the Jews.

As the Jews became more stabilized in communities that were large enough to organize, they began to practice their customs and ritual to a degree unknown for more than a thousand years. These customs were eventually codified and their meaning explained. The *Shulhan Aruk* of Joseph Karo supplied this need. Its elaborate provisions and sometimes difficult prescriptions became part of modern Judaism because, once more, the people canonized the work of Karo and made it their own.

Much has happened in Judaism since the time of Karo. A modern editor of a Jewish anthology placed quotations from the *Shulhan Aruk* under the subtitle of "The Medieval Night." It was his way of showing the embarrassment that many Jews in America feel today about the classic work of Orthodox legalism. At the same time, Karo is venerated as the greatest teacher since Maimonides by those who still believe in the full observance of Jewish law.

What is rabbinic morality today? Basically it is founded on the same principle which guided the Talmud and Maimonides: Israel as a people has been chosen by God to teach the nations. Its collective wisdom, enshrined by its laws, is in the line of the great prophets. What they received personally, Israel now has collectively. What Israel believes as a body, Israelites are to follow as its members.

As we approach the three main divisions of modern Judaism, rabbinic morality takes on three different forms; but these forms are still radically one. Always the community is primary; only its manner of teaching or prescribing varies.

Among the Orthodox the Jewish community speaks through the historical continuum that reaches back to the Torah and extends throughout the centuries of distillated wisdom of the rabbis. When a member of this type of Judaism wants to know what to do in a given situation or how to meet a current problem, he asks the community of history for the answer. It means nothing to him that the case he examines is a thousand years removed from his own. No matter, what the Jews believed should be done a millennium ago is also to be done today. The Law, they believe, is independent of such human limitations as time.

The best example of this type of Rabbinism is the volumes of *Responsa* that are still being published and added to, as collections of replies given by the rabbis to questions they were asked. A current edition of the *Responsa* raises such questions as Jews and hunting, relying on Gentile chemists, polygamy in Turkey, books printed on the Sabbath, artificial insemination. Such questions (in the hundreds) are treated with characteristic subtlety and in every case the answer depends on what has been the interpretation in a similar situation over the years of rabbinic scholarship.

The case involving a mixed marriage between a Jewish woman and a Gentile man is a good example of how the *Responsa* are made. In this instance, Rabbi David Hoffman (died in Berlin in 1921) was asked about a Christian who was already married to a Jewess by civil law. The *responsum* is technically called "*Yoreh Deah*, no. 83."

It is made clear in the Shulhan Aruk, "Yoreh Deah," No. 268.12, that we do not receive any proselyte who comes to be converted because he desires a certain Jewish woman. However, the *tosafot* in Yebamot 24b (Talmud) already raises an objection against this point of view. The objection is based on the fact reported in the Talmud, Shabbat 31a, that a Gentile came to Hillel to be converted, and said, "I want to become a high priest;" nevertheless, Hillel did convert him. So in Manahot 44a we are told that a woman came to Rabbi Hiyyah and said that she wanted to be converted in order to marry a young scholar. The *tosafot* answers its own objection by saying that

they, Hillel and Rabbi Hiyyah, were confident that these candidates would ultimately become sincerely selfless in their
motivations.

Thus when it is clear to the eyes of the court that the candidate really has a spiritual motive then, even though he has
in mind a certain Jewess, it is permitted to accept him as a
proselyte.

Now, consider, in this case before us that he has already
married the Jewish woman and she has given herself to him
and is pregnant by him. So it is clear that she is willing to be
married to him even if he does not convert. That being the
case, there is some justification in our holding the point of view
that he is converting for a spiritual motive.

Furthermore, if we do not accept him, she will be married
to him in sin, because it is forbidden by the Torah for a Jewess
to be married to a Gentile. If so, it is better that we accept
him as a proselyte than that she should be married in sin.

Furthermore, if she remains married to this man, then her
children, which by Jewish Law are full Jews, will follow their
father into Gentile life and will thus be sinners. And what have
these innocent sheep committed? Since this is the case, it is
better that the court should commit the minor sin of accepting
the proselyte, so as to accustom him to Jewish life in order that
there may be worthy Jewish children from this couple. But, at
all events, the court must warn the Gentile to be very careful
to fulfill Jewish religious Law, especially with regard to the
Sabbath and forbidden food. And it would be well to receive
an affirmation from him in lieu of a formal oath.[6]

What appears from this sample of Jewish casuistry is the twofold respect for the community of Israel: it is from the people who
profess the faith of Abraham that the principles of moral judgment
are to be drawn, and it is in the interests of these same people that
moral judgments are to be made.

This is not the whole picture of rabbinic ethics among the
Orthodox. The Jewish community is considered the carrier of moral
wisdom through the ages. But its authorized spokesmen are certain

charismatic individuals whom the same community believes have been endowed with insight that compares with the prophets Amos or Osee.

From the Orthodox standpoint, Israel as a religion is miraculously gifted to receive and retain God's message to the world. Its teachers are rabbis, but rabbis specially, even supernaturally, enlightened by the Lord.

At the other extreme, the Reform also hold that the Jewish community is bearer of extraordinary knowledge about man's duties toward society. Unlike the Orthodox, however, the Reform do not look upon the community as a religion—at least not mainly—but rather as a people. This concept allows a broad spectrum of definitions of Judaism. It may be a group of individuals in whom the Spirit of God somehow dwells, without subscribing to the Orthodox notion that the indwelling is miraculous and beyond the ordinary laws of nature. Or it may be simply a cluster of highly intelligent persons who have pooled their knowledge in a way unknown outside the Jewish nation.

In any case, when it comes to enunciating the law, those who do so are not charismatics but gifted scholars. The rabbis, then, speak with authority only because they have learned to synthesize the gathered genius of the Chosen People.

The problem is to insure that this community is responsive to the mind of the great Lawgiver. Those who invest the rabbis with spiritual insight more or less directly from God have no difficulty. No matter how undemocratic rabbinic teaching may be, as in matters of ritual and diet, it is still binding. In that event the rabbi speaks as one of the *Nabim* enlightened from above. His directives may be uncomfortable, even annoying, but so were the prescriptions of Isaiah and Jeremiah.

When the community, however, is itself the source of rabbinic understanding, the implication is that wisdom rises from below. The people are the ones who instruct their teachers, and the teachers, in a sense, are only mirrors of the popular demand. This kind of democracy was perhaps inevitable in a country like America. It has also produced a tension in American Judaism that is quite unique in the history of Israel.

Illustrative of the different approach taken by the Reform, is the handling of intermarriage problems similar to the example cited from the Orthodox *Responsa*. The question was presented to the Central Conference of American Rabbis: what should be the practice, "If, after a Jew and a Christian have been married by civil ceremony or by Christian ceremony, they come to the Rabbi to be remarried in a Jewish ceremony"? The Conference replied in terms that seem to be more strict than those of the Orthodox.

Since it is the point of view of the Conference that all sincere applicants for conversion be accepted whether marriage is involved or not, and since too we recognize the validity of civil marriage, but urge that they be sanctified by religious marriage ceremony, we surely would accept such a proselyte and officiate at the religious marriage.

However, it should be clear that the fact that the couple is already married by civil law does not obviate the necessity of conversion of the Gentile party before the Jewish services can take place.[7]

The concluding proviso, that the Christian must first become a Jew before his marriage can be blessed by a Jewish ceremony, goes beyond the requirements set by the Orthodox. The latter were willing to sanctify the marriage without first demanding conversion to Judaism.

This is significant. Reform Judaism, no less than the Orthodox, looks upon the gathering of its people as a standard of moral practice. In fact, the Reform have an organization to deal with these questions, the Central Conference, in a way that the less structured American Orthodox do not possess. It may be considered symbolic of the greater weight given to group decisions among the Reform than among the Orthodox who are more willing to trust the charisms of an individual rabbi.

But when it comes to the actual content of what is decided, the Reform will often be more solicitous to safeguard the interests of the Jewish community than the Orthodox. One reason may be that they are more conscious of the need for human prudence and effort in maintaining cultural solidarity besides reliance on the divine promise made to the patriarchs and prophets. Certainly requiring conversion to Judaism before blessing a marriage indicates great solicitude about "the one problem of mixed marriage," which poses "a greater threat to Jewish survival than any of the other,"⁸ in the Western world.

The same attitude was revealed in another decision of the Central Conference, but this time favoring the well-being of the Jewish people rather than their solidarity.

In response to a number of queries, the Conference's committee on *Responsa*, chaired by Rabbi Solomon B. Freehof, chose to research the problem of a young mother who had contracted rubella (German measles) in the third month of pregnancy. After rehearsing and comparing the earlier responsorial literature, the committee confirmed and extended the opinion of the Sephardic Chief Rabbi of Jerusalem, Ben Zion Uziel (died 1953).

He [Uziel in *Mishpetei Uziel* 3 (Jerusalem, 1947) 46f.] concludes . . . that an unborn foetus is actually not a *nephesh* [soul-person] at all and has no independent life. It is part of its mother, and just as a person may sacrifice a limb to be cured of a worse sickness, so may this foetus [in the case before Rabbi Freehof] be destroyed for the [rubella-afflicted] mother's benefit. . . . One may not destroy anything without purpose. But if there is a worthwhile purpose, it may be done. The specific case before him [Uziel] concerned a woman who was threatened with permanent deafness. . . . Uziel decides that since the foetus is not an independent *nephesh* but is only part of the mother, there is no sin in destroying it for her sake.⁹

Then, passing from probably permanent deafness in the case before Rabbi Uziel to possible mental anguish in the case before the Reform committee, Rabbi Freehof decided that abortion was justified.

In the case which you are discussing, I would, therefore, say that since there is strong preponderance of medical opinion that the child will be born imperfect physically or even mentally, then for the mother's sake (i.e., her mental anguish now and in the future) she may sacrifice part of herself. This decision thus follows the opinion of Jacob Emden and Ben Zion Uziel against the earlier opinion of Gair Chaim Bachrach.[10]

The basic consistency in these and similar responses is the Jewish concern for the welfare of their people. No matter how complex the issue or how deep its moral implications, one norm of rabbinic ethics that underlies the solution of human problems is this reference to the community of Israel. Decisions are handed down by recognized community leaders, and their judgment is strongly determined by what benefits (or injures) those who belong to the community.

While pertaining to the State of Israel and not directly concerning America, one aspect of law among the Israelis finely illustrates this concept of rabbinic morality—that the Jewish community is somehow normative in world (and also American) Judaism.

The modern State of Israel is not a theocracy, where the governing power would be vested in religious leaders, say the rabbinate of Jerusalem. Its government is a democracy, whose officials are elected by all the citizens, including Moslems and Christians, and represents the political will of the population. Faced with different political options, the new state did not want persons having priestly powers to become the civil rulers of the country.

Yet, though the laws of Israel are essentially civil and not religious, the juridical structure of the new nation reflects a strongly rabbinic—and not merely political—ideology. Not unlike the Established Church in England, Israel gives Judaism a quasi-established status. Similar to the Archbishop of Canterbury, the Chief Rabbi has a legal position in Jewish religious matters, although many would say that his influence on the conduct of the government is minimal.

The matter becomes crucial when such institutions as the Sabbath and the festivals are integrated into community life, and the observance of dietary laws is sanctioned by national regulation.

An American Jewish observer of the scene saw here the unresolved tension between political democracy and rabbinic morality.

The one serious source of friction between the civil and religious leaders has been the matter of religion in public life.

The rabbis insisted—and the government unwillingly agreed—
that on the Sabbath, the nation's official day of rest, public con-
veyances would be restricted, dietary laws would be observed
in all state institutions including the armed forces.

Those who support these state-buttressed religious observances believe that the system preserves the rights of religious
conscience. An Orthodox youth who is drafted into the Army,
they argue, has the right to follow his religious principles in the
matter of diet. Therefore the kosher laws must apply to army
food. Similarly, the strict Sabbath enforcement, it is claimed,
will not interfere with the non-observant, but will insure full
freedom of conscience to the Orthodox.[11]

Behind these and similar provisions is a matter of principle:
that the Jewish community, as defined by rabbinic leadership, enjoys a certain primacy in the moral order.

257

THE JEW
IN AMERICAN SOCIETY

A vast literature has been created on the Jew in American society. Apologists and antagonists have contributed to the writing. In between we find sociological studies that attempt to steer a middle ground between extravagant praise of what the Jews have contributed to the upbuilding of America and the hostile criticism that reminds one of Hitler's *Mein Kampf.*

Not the least problem that faces anyone who writes on the subject is to define Judaism in American life. If the Jews have always been hard to define, American Jews defy classification as an entity. Their own commentators ask if they are a religious fellowship, a historical continuum, a cultural group with peculiar racial traits, or a people. They seem to be all of these and more. They are therefore different from all other ethnic groups in the United States and their position as a subcommunity of the larger American society is exceptional.

To estimate their position accurately, we should address ourselves not only to what Jews have in common with the rest of the American people but also what sets them apart from those who are not Jews. We should avoid the common mistake of comparing the Jews as a group with the total non-Jewish population. The latter is divided into geographic regions, ethnic minorities, economic blocs, religious denominations, and national origins. Not so the Jews. They are at once a people and a religion, a culture and a faith. Any comparison between them and other Americans must find other categories than those familiar to the social sciences.

All that has been said so far about Jewish history, about the belief and practice of Judaism, is here brought to bear on the final question we want to ask: What is the past and may be the future of Judaism in the one country where Jews have found the greatest freedom and have made their greatest impact in modern times?

CONTRIBUTIONS TO AMERICAN CULTURE

It is a commonplace in writing about the Jews to say that their influence on the society in which they live is always greater than their numbers would indicate. All the evidence from the history of ancient Rome or of medieval France and Spain supports this view, and the situation in America confirms the fact.

Every aspect of national life has been touched by the presence of Jews in American society. But certain areas stand out. Business and industry, education and politics, organizational structure and communications have been the most affected.

Jewish contributions in these fields have been extraordinary. Men like Bernard Baruch, financial adviser to American presidents; Henry Morgenthau, Secretary of the Treasury; Louis Brandeis, Justice of the Supreme Court; David Dubinsky and Samuel Gompers, pioneers in the organization of labor unions; Edna Ferber and Fannie Hurst, novelists; the four Warner brothers (originally Eichelbaum) in the motion-picture industry; Oscar Hammerstein and Irving Berlin, composers; the Nobel Prize winners, Albert Michelson, Albert Einstein, and Karl Landsteiner; Morris Cohen and Walter Lippmann, philosophers; and Herbert Lehman, states-man—are household names in American history.

Less familiar but equally influential have been such newspapers as the *New York Times* and periodicals like the *New York Times Magazine*. Publishing houses under Jewish auspices are also among the most respected in the country.

The phenomenon of Jewish influence in America is more than a recital of what individual Jews may have done in the interest of the national society. The impact has been that of a whole people whose ideals and distinctive spirit have been partly responsible for what America is today.

It seems almost trivial to mention the names of outstanding Jews. What really matters is not even the fact of their influence, but the character of the influence they exercised. The first we might call its body, the second its soul. The body is a chronicle of leading Jewish biographies and the data which these life stories include. The soul is the variety of elements by which Judaism has helped to shape American culture.

At this point anyone who writes on the subject reveals himself. It is not that objectivity is impossible, nor that different writers fail to give a full account of what happened. But the contributions of the sons of Abraham are too bound up with the American way of life for anyone to talk about them without passing judgment on what he describes.

With this apology, the present writer feels justified in saying what he does and is satisfied that the reader will take him at his word. There is no end of books published by Jews in which they deal, in some form or another, with the Jewish American scene. Each one is different and each gives a different estimate of the same basic facts. When Nathan Glazer writes about *American Judaism* he gives a different picture from what Bezalel Sherman says about *The Jew Within American Society*. Yet both are Jews and both have the same data before them.

These different (and divergent) views are valuable, as coming from Jews. Perhaps something can be said for still another view, coming from a Christian and a Catholic who loves the Jewish people without being blind to their limitations.

RELIGIOUS PLURALISM

It has become fashionable to talk about America as a pluralistic society. The term is misleading. It does not mean simply that Americans reflect a variety of racial strains and religious affiliations. In that sense our country is not much different than other nations in the Western world, say Canada or England, or even modern France and Holland.

Our pluralism is more than mere plurality. We believe it is also a unity, and some have coined the word *pluriunity* to describe a unity in plurality and plurality in unity. We like to think that the motto *E Pluribus Unum* is not a historical relic to commemorate the unification of the thirteen colonies but still serves as a formula for American pluralism today.

The real problem is for different people to form a nation without ceasing to be themselves. It was easy enough for the conquered races and religions of ancient Egypt, Spain, and Gaul to be assimilated into the Roman Empire. They conveniently lost their identity under the aegis of imperial Rome.

This is not what happened in America, or at least we hope it never will. We pride ourselves on being one nation but of different peoples. Among the differences we most cherish and profess to maintain, religion is paramount. The vision of religious pluralism is part of our Constitution and is fixed forever, we believe, in the First Amendment which provided that no one will suffer discrimination because of his creed or because his faith is not the same as that of other Americans.

Much has happened since the Constitution was written and by now the First Amendment might have become an interesting but irrelevant piece of legislation. It might have, except for the presence in American society of a people whose very existence is built on resistance to absorption by the culture in which they live.

It is customary to speak of the three major faiths of America: Protestantism, Catholicism, and Judaism. But the division is hardly accurate because it fails to take into account the more than fifty million who profess none of these religions and, for all practical purposes, belong to no organized religion at all. Yet most Americans are either Protestants or Catholics or Jews. I believe that

among these the Jews have been mainly responsible for the continuing existence of such pluralism as we still enjoy. If ever the day
comes when most Americans will have lost their distinctive religious belief, it will be because the vital influence of historic Judaism in our society has disappeared.

We have seen enough about the spirit of Judaism over the centuries to say that part of its ethos is the desire for self-identity; that
a Jew believes his mission in the world is to remain true to himself
and resist every effort of his environment to make him anything
else. His faith may become dim and his fidelity to the Mosaic code
weak, but he never forgets he is a Jew even when everything
around him conspires to make him change.

A Jew wants to remain such in answer to two powerful drives
in his being: one that comes from his sense of belonging to a
Chosen People and the other from the covenant that his ancestors
made with the Lord.

The two instincts are inseparable and support one another. For
our purpose it is enough to know that Judaism in America has done
more than perhaps anything else to keep us from becoming a national religion. As far back as our Founding Fathers, men like
Jefferson and Madison looked forward to a nation that would not
be divided by religious differences. With shrewd political wisdom
they hoped that America would be spared the conflict that other
nations had experienced over differences in religion. If some of
those who framed our Constitution had had their way, this conflict
would have been nipped in the bud by reducing the faith of Americans to a common—and least—denominator.

It was here that Jews played such an important role. Their
contribution from the beginning was more than either the Protestants or Catholics had made. It was certainly greater than anything
which their relatively small numbers gave reason to expect.

Protestantism had begun its assimilation to the national culture
already in colonial times. Coming from Europe as separate denominations, Protestants soon discovered that their separation as Christians made it difficult to cooperate as Americans. Whatever else
disestablishment meant, it revealed a distaste for belonging to a
church which favored one religion over another. In less than forty

years after the Republic was founded, not only had the churches been separated from political power, but thousands of their adherents became separated from the churches. American democracy took on more and more the forms of allegiance that had formerly belonged to the churches.

There was something in the nature of Protestantism that encouraged what critics have called secularization. More accurately it was the fusion of the Protestant spirit (essentially invisible) with the visible structure and institutions of civil society. Students of American church history generally agree on the following judgment: "During the second half of the nineteenth century, there occurred a virtual identification of the outlook of denominational Protestantism with 'Americanism' or 'the American way of life.' "[1]

The situation has not substantially changed. The only difference is that, in the past hundred years, the process has been accelerated. Conservative estimates place the number of completely assimilated Protestants whose "religion" is loyalty to America at fifty million. Protestant churchmen see the same process going on in the churches. Preaching the gospel and reconciling men with God is replaced in many cases with making good Americans and teaching them how to become better citizens.

Catholicism in the United States had long resisted the same process. First- and second-generation immigrants from Central and Southern Europe lived together in enclaves and rather successfully remained faithful to the principles of their faith. The establishment of the parochial school system in the 1880s was a powerful force that helped to maintain a vital Catholicism in the American melting pot of nations.

The long and dreary opposition to everything Catholic was painful and often frustrating to its victims. But it served to protect them from the neutralizing elements that were hostile only because Catholics were supposed to be divided in their allegiance to the country. Organizations like the American Protective Association actually helped to make more Catholics more faithful to their religion and more conscious of their identity. As late as 1928, a Catholic candidate for the presidency lost the election, it is believed, mainly because of his faith.

Immigration from Catholic countries practically stopped after the First World War. Gradually American Catholics became better known and with knowledge prejudice was reduced. In increasing numbers the children of immigrants entered public life and were soon accepted on a par with those whose ancestors were of colonial stock. It became less and less fashionable to ask if a man was Catholic when asking for a job or seeking election to a public trust.

All the while something was happening inside the Catholics of America. The society to which their forebears had come was nominally free and they were legally exempt from discrimination. Actually they suffered for their religion as only those who understand that period of American history can testify.

As the pressure from an alien culture diminished so did the sense of identity which characterizes Catholics wherever their Church is stigmatized.

There is too much evidence in contemporary America to question the fact that Catholics are paying the price for acceptance. Such distinctive signs of Catholicism as parochial schools and Catholic colleges, the religious garb of men and women in the service of the Church, and periodicals that only recently prided themselves on being Catholic—all these are secularizing at a revolutionary pace. Such terms as adaption to society and involvement in the world have become mottoes of acculturation, and the end is not in sight.

Catholics are being warned by some of their own leaders that, "In our pluralistic society, we are not called to continue or foster any kind of 'vertical pluralism' "[2] symbolized in the parochial school system. They are told to stop acting as though their faith was still threatened by American forms of thought: "When we consider the present size of the Catholic community and the progress we have shown in many spheres of life in America in the recent past, such defensiveness is fast becoming an unworthy sectarianism."[3]

It would be naïve to suggest that the Jews have not been subject to the same pressures or that they, too, have not become part of the American landscape. Enough Jews have changed their names and stopped their practice of Jewish customs to prove that Judaism was not exempt from the common law of assimilation.

Yet the Jews are different. For one thing their Judaism is not only religious, it is also ethnic. A Jew knows that no matter what he believes in the religion of Abraham and Moses, he never ceases being a Jew. Sigmund Freud had become so unreligious that he wrote the classic treatise on *The Future of an Illusion*. The illusion was any religion based on the belief in an objectively real God. But Freud never thought of himself as anything but a Jew.

This fact alone would explain many things that cannot be said of others than Jews. When a Christian becomes immersed in the non-Christian society in which he lives, he runs the risk of dividing loyalty between the faith he professes and the culture to which he belongs. There is conflict, and in many cases faith suffers at the expense of the culture to which he is drawn. Ideally a Christian can remain a citizen of two societies, of his church as a religious man and of the world as a man of his times. Not a few Christians, Catholics and Protestants, have approximated the ideal, and their contribution to American pluralism has been significant. They remained truly Catholic or Protestant without ceasing to be truly American. But the dialectic is not easy to maintain, especially when the world offers a man advantages that his religion cannot give.

Jews cannot make the distinction between their faith and culture. Their faith is their culture, and their ethnic solidarity is part of the Jewish faith.

We do not have to speculate on what this means. The history of American Judaism is the story of a people for whom, in the best sense of the word, the ghetto was not a passing phenomenon; it became a permanent institution.

The other groups created ghettos for the first time only in America: the Jews brought the ghetto here with them. During the course of long centuries, the ghetto was the closest thing to a national territory that the Jews possessed. There were times and places where the ghetto walls were solidly built and carefully guarded from the outside; and there were times and places where the walls were invisible and unsupported. America belongs to the latter category. Here the ghetto boundaries were purely symbolic, and theoretically the Jews could readily cross them. Formally, their departure from the ghetto would have had the law on its side, especially where the law was informed with the spirit of the Declaration of Independence. But the Jews had to reckon with unwritten, and therefore more potent, laws, the law of their own ethnic requirements and the law of unfriendly majority social attitudes.

The totality of religious customs, communal needs and cultural requirements, which the Jews have always had to conserve in order to maintain their collective existence, they were able to carry on only within their own environment. This was the source of the psychic impetus which supported the ghetto walls from within. On the other hand, those Jews in whom this impetus had greatly diminished, if not altogether disappeared, quickly sensed that the ghetto walls were also shored up by the pressures from the outside. It is clear that the ghetto was not simply imposed upon Jews from the outside; it was also held together by an inward Jewish force.[4]

The word *ghetto* has taken on pejorative connotations. In some Christian writers it has become synonymous with segregation from society for reasons of self-interest, and has anti-Semitic overtones. Yet, as applied to Judaism, in other countries or in America, it is the expression of a deep faith which knows—from four thousand years of experience—that to remain true to Judaism is to maintain a Jewish society. If this demands separation from the "Gentiles," that may be unpleasant but it is also inevitable. Almost the first words of Yahweh to Abraham were to bid him "leave the land of his people," and the pattern has not changed.

There is one more feature of Jewish exclusiveness, based on faith, which has helped to shape religious pluralism in the United States. From the Jewish viewpoint, the main rival to Judaism in the Western world is Christianity. Whatever the differences among Christians, they are as nothing compared with the dichotomy between the disciples of Moses and the followers of Jesus of Nazareth. A better word might be dualism, to emphasize what is paramount in the Jewish mind: that Judaism, to remain itself, must not compromise with Christianity.

The Jews consider themselves the Chosen People. Since the dawn of their history, they have considered themselves a people whom the Lord called out of the nations to become specially his own.

In a country like America, however, where they live so close to Christians, they have learned that Christians also consider themselves chosen by God. They claim to have a mission not unlike that of the Jews and founded, like theirs, on God's selective communication to man. Out of the dialogue with Christians, Jewish theologians have come to speak of the two facets of the Jewish soul, which they identify as first the immediate relationship to the Existent One, and second, the power of atonement in an unatoned world. On these two elements rests the ultimate division between Judaism and Christianity.

To understand something of this basic division is to appreciate what Jews have done to maintain religious pluralism in America. It was no accident of history but the result of a distinctive concept of religion and of human society.

As regards the first element, the Jews believe in the nonincarnation of God, who yet reveals himself to the "flesh" and is present to man in a mutual relationship. In contrast with Christians who also profess the unity of God, Jews insist that "we do not unite ourselves with Him." The God in whom they believe and to whom they are pledged does not unite himself with human substance on earth. But this very fact urges them the more to demand that the world should be perfected under the kingship of the Mighty One.

Similarly, the Jews look upon the world as yet unredeemed and therefore that salvation is still to be accomplished. They look back at no Savior with whom a new redeemed history began or who appeared at any definite point of time. Since they have not been stilled by anything which has happened, they are wholly directed toward the advent of that which is still to come.

Thus on both counts Christians and Jews are divided, and no one understands this division better than the Jews. What divides the two religions is their attitude toward the Messiah. To the Christian, the Jew is the incomprehensibly obstinate man who refuses to admit what has happened. To the Jew, the Christian is the incomprehensibly arrogant man who affirms that the redemption has been accomplished in a world that seems so obviously unredeemed.

Those who know Judaism best speak of this gulf which no human power can bridge.

So much for the division. It is real and profound and inevitable. To ignore it or try to hide it behind rhetoric or false piety is to do an injustice to both religions. Christianity is literally Messianity because it believes that the *Christos*, which is the Greek for the Hebrew *Mashijach*, has already come. By the same token Judaism is non-Christian because it still looks forward to the Christ foretold by the prophets, and its Messianic age has not yet dawned.

If this were the whole story, we could hardly speak of the Jewish contribution to American pluralism. Pluralism implies differences, indeed, but also unity. In spite of the deep cleavage between the two cultures, the Jews have discovered a real kinship with the Christians among whom they live. What divides them from Christians is a fact of history. They do not believe that Jesus of Nazareth was the Messiah of the Lord. They are still waiting for him to come. But, then, Christians are waiting for his coming too. They look forward to it as his second advent, when the Son of Man foretold by Daniel will come to establish the Kingdom that will never end.

On this basis, the common expectation of Christ is also the focal point of a common hope. This hope, shared by Christians and Jews, is the reason why American Jews are not only tolerated by believing Christians but accepted by them as fellow pilgrims awaiting the One who is to come.

CONCEPT OF LIBERTY

Freedom is built into our national consciousness. It is symbolized in the Declaration of Independence, legalized in the First Amendment, and is so typical of our way of life that nothing better describes our nation than to call it "the land of Liberty."

Yet liberty is ambiguous. Rich in connotation, it can mean almost anything a man wants it to mean.

On the Statue of Liberty in New York harbor is the inscription written by a Jewish poetess, "Give me your tired, your poor, Your huddled masses yearning to breathe free." This inscription is also a token of the contribution of Judaism to the concept and practice of liberty in America.

The Jewish legacy to American culture on the side of liberty is so fundamental that on its proper understanding rests everything else. Only in the degree that Christians understand the Hebrew concept of freedom, can they appreciate the value of Judaism (along with Christianity) for sustaining American society or be willing to defend Judaeo-Christian principles in the interest of the common good.

The Jewish religion begins with an article of faith that Christians inherited, but which they take for granted like the air they breathe. This is not surprising since it permeates the atmosphere of Western civilization; and nothing quite like it exists in the Hindu and Buddhist culture of the whole Orient. It says that man was created by God as an individual, a person whose purpose on earth is to serve the Creator as a means and condition for attaining heaven.

Implicit in this simple creed are some momentous assertions: that man's origin and destiny are not of this world but that he comes from infinite power and is made for infinite love; that his first duty and privilege are to live in harmony with God; that he is an individual before he voluntarily enters society, and therefore his rights as a person take priority over the rights of any group to which he belongs; and consequently his freedom is a divine right to choose what is conducive to fulfillment (here and hereafter) according to God's plan for him, and to reject what faith and reason tell him are a hindrance to the purpose of his existence—which is to receive happiness in return for serving God.

From this primary concept of freedom, postulated by the Jewish faith and adopted by Christianity, follow certain consequences that have deeply affected American society.

Since the freedom in question stems from an intellectual option, it assumes that the mind is duly enlightened on the alternatives from which the autonomous will is to choose. Enlightenment of mind may come either from native insight and reflection or from revelation. Judaism claims that liberty is based on both sources of knowledge, that is, human reason and a faith that responds to the revealed word of God.

This liberty is more than freedom from coercion or restraint, as though men were only free because (or when) they are not forced to act by outside pressures or not forbidden by external threats. Their liberty is internal in the sense of their enjoying complete self-determination (under God) to make their own decisions. They cannot be forced to consent to anything they do not want—even though under duress they may have to perform external actions, or desist from performance, against their internal judgment.

The history of Judaism is a witness to this meaning of liberty. No people in the annals of man has paid more dearly for a longer time to remain faithful to their internal convictions against the most extreme forms of duress and compulsion. No one can read the accounts of the Jewish prisoners at Dachau without sensing he is in contact with this mystical power of the human will.

One aspect of liberty, inherited from Judaism and influential in American culture, is also the source of most misunderstanding. As Jews see it, freedom would be inhuman if it were not also social in nature. If the only freedom men possessed was to determine their own individual lives, Judaism, or for that matter, Judaeo-Christian civilization, would be impossible.

The social dimension of Jewish liberty is manifold. Freedom is social because Yahweh is believed to have formed a new people, Israel, to which he promised his special providence and care. As a Jew conceives freedom, he sees it as not only a personal prerogative but a privilege for his people.

Centuries of tradition have confirmed this idea of "freedom for the community." When Moses pleaded with Pharaoh to allow his people to leave Egypt, he urged the deliverance of the Jews as a nation; when later on the prophets castigated the sins of Israel, they threatened the enslavement of the Jews as a people, and when they repented, Yahweh freed them not as individuals but as the body of Israel; during their long subjection to the Romans, Jewish leaders always spoke of liberation for the People of God from the yoke of the Gentiles.

In the nineteen centuries since the destruction of the Second Temple, the same theme has prevailed. Freedom from their enemies and the right to serve God according to the law of Moses is the constant subject of Jewish prayer, but not for the Jew as a person so much as for all the elect of Israel.

If this vision of liberty is characteristic of Judaism and made its impact on American culture, it has also created problems. With their strong sense of solidarity, Jews have insisted on privileges for themselves as a group which others, who are less organized or community-conscious, would not demand. One effect has been an uneven competition between those who were satisfied with liberty for the individual but no match for others who wanted (and got) freedom for the group.

Needless to say, this could also be beneficial to society. People who were annoyed with the Jewish understanding of liberty as freedom not only for a man but for a people had to ask themselves why they did not profit from both aspects of liberty. In most cases they had to admit the reason was their own lack of community. Fragmentation into hundreds of religious sects and division into scores of ethnic cliques highlighted the lack of cohesion among most Americans.

Unlike anyone else in America, the Jews understood what it means to be free as a people. The ambiguities which this has created for them, as for their fellow Americans, stem from the understanding of the term *people*. Are "people" a religion or a nation? If a religion, then the "freedom for community" sought by the Jews was not basically different from the demand made by other religious groups. In this sense, Judaism has been a powerful catalyst to clarify the meaning of religious freedom beyond the rights of a single individual.

But if the Jewish people are a nation, then we enter the maze of political philosophy and raise the most embarrassing questions that can be asked of the Jews. Certainly institutional liberty affects other groups than organized religious bodies. Business corporations and social agencies have rights and, therefore, liberties that the rest of society must respect. But a nation is not a corporation like General Motors nor an agency like the Better Business Bureau. It is, by common consent, a self-sustaining entity whose interests are autonomous and whose welfare must be served at any cost. In the nineteenth century, Napoleon raised this question when he granted the Jews of France freedom from restrictive legislation. He did so, he said, only in the hope that the Jews could assure him that they were indeed a religion and not a nation within a nation, that is, Israel within the bosom of France.

The issue which faced French Judaism in the early nineteenth century is the same that faces American Judaism today. This is one reason why the establishment of the State of Israel in 1948 has caused such tension in the minds of American Jews. The problem was stated pointedly in some reflections on the twentieth anniversary of the founding of Israel.

So far as the government is concerned, Israel is officially a secular state, governed by democratic processes. But there is constant and powerful pressure from Orthodox Jews to make it a religious state, governed by the laws of Moses.

The conflict reflects a dilemma that has divided Jews for countless centuries. That is the question of what is a Jew. Does the term Jew apply only to someone born into a Jewish family, or is a person who voluntarily embraces the religion of Judaism also a Jew? Are Jews a nation, a religion, or both? Does someone who does not practice Judaism cease being a Jew?

The Supreme Court of Israel was faced with the necessity of ruling on these questions in an immigration case a few years ago. (Israeli law allows all Jews from anywhere in the world to settle in Israel and become citizens.) The high court ruled, in a split 3-to-2 decision, that Jewishness is a matter of both nationality and of religion. Specifically, it held that a person born a Jew forfeits his rights to automatic Israeli citizenship if he formally adopts another religion.[5]

Those who are critical of American Jews for their clannishness and their demands for liberty as a people should remember that the question this raises for others is also a fundamental problem for the Jews.

CHURCH AND STATE

Closely related to the Jewish concept of freedom as something institutional and not only individual is the idea of Church and State separation which is so typical of the United States. Human freedom in Jewish thought is social by its very nature. Not only persons but communities have rights, given them by God, and consequently they, too, claim immunity from coercion and from immoral restraint.

The social character of freedom in Judaism has another dimension that has entered the stream of our national culture. As Jews see themselves, they are simultaneously members of two societies. Faith tells them to be loyal to both, and in this, Jesus of Nazareth was speaking also for the Jews. They are to give to the state what belongs to Caesar and to God what belongs to God.

Yet history shows that these two societies, which ideally should cooperate with one another, are often in conflict, and the unwilling victim is the citizen-believer faced with deciding, not whether to be loyal to one or the other, but where their respective rights collide. He is often asked to steer a middle course between statism that denies the claims of God and religionism that ignores the just claims of the state.

Until modern times this dilemma was more theoretical than practical. With the origin of the modern state, however, it rose to the surface with brutal clarity. If in former times the Jews had difficulties with organized religion, and at times suffered at the hands of misguided and overzealous Christians, they were now to experience a new and immeasurably more terrible conflict.

State after state oppressed them. The climax was reached under National Socialism in Germany and in the gas chambers of concentration camps.

When they were first granted rights and privileges after the French Revolution, a new era of freedom seemed to have dawned. Such limitations as they had experienced from a church to which they did not belong were gradually removed and the prayers of deliverance appeared finally to be heard.

Out of this emancipation from "Christian bondage" there soon developed a philosophy that is still dominant in Jewish thought. It says quite plainly that Jews are better off the less Christian the society in which they live. In the degree in which a nation or a culture is not under domination by the Christian Church, Jews are assured immunity from harm and liberty to be themselves. There seems to be too much evidence from continental Europe to suggest anything else.

Understandably the Catholic Church and its leaders are the focus of complaint. It was the church and its rulers who caused the Jews so much anguish in the past. It is still the church which, at least by its silence, is charged with sharing in the guilt of those who persecute the Jews.

Symptomatic of this attitude is the reaction of a respected Jewish leader commenting on the responsibility of the Roman pontiff in the Nazi genocide of his people.

When we needed the voice of the Catholic Church in behalf of the Jewish people, Pius XII kept his mouth stubbornly shut. No matter how many apologies are offered, they are unconvincing to a man who, like myself, has made Jewish history the major interest of his life outside the rabbinate itself. The overwhelming evidence is such as to leave no room for doubt that the act was criminal in the full sense of the word. We cannot determine scientifically just how many Jews were burned because of the silence of Pius XII, but that a good many, perhaps hundreds of thousands, would be living today had he not kept silent, is beyond any serious historian's doubt. And the fact that in Rome today, *The Deputy* is kept off the boards, is an indication that the story that *The Deputy* has to tell is substantially well founded. And to this day not a single valid argument against, or refutation of, the *facts* presented by Hochhuth has been offered. Pius XII kept silent at a time when articulateness in behalf of bedevilled European Jewry would have been a true Godsend.[6]

Jewish writers and agencies are fairly agreed that Church and State should be kept as separate as possible. Their premise is that otherwise the state will reflect the church's teaching which is Christian and to that extent alien to Judaism.

Consistent with this outlook, one area of American life on which the Jews have expressed themselves most clearly is the teaching of religion in public schools. Aware of the risk to their religious identity, they have spoken in defense of excluding religion in any shape or form from the classrooms of tax-supported institutions.

They begin with the principle that "Religion has always been and continues to be the central core of Jewish life."[7]

To this they add the conviction that "Religious liberty is an indispensable aspect of democratic freedom; indeed, it is the very foundation of American democracy." But democracy in America is built, they feel, on "our basic law that puts religion outside the jurisdiction of the state."[8] Any infringement on that principle of complete separation of Church and State threatens religious liberty and brings all other freedoms into jeopardy.

Accordingly the state should not under any pretext allow or encourage the teaching of religious values.

The maintenance and furtherance of religion are the responsibility of the synagogue, the church and the home, and not of the public school system; the utilization in any manner of the time, facilities, personnel, or funds of the public school system for purposes of religious instruction should not be permitted.

The public schools must recognize the realities of religious differences in the community and among their pupils. They should continue as they have done throughout their history to teach pupils that acceptance of and respect for such differences are basic to American democracy and contribute toward harmonious living in a free society. This implies no need, however, on the part of the public schools to teach religious doctrines or to teach about religious doctrines.[9]

Much the same attitude prevails on the delicate subject of financial support of religion-centered education. Every time the question of federal or state aid to parochial schools comes up, Jewish groups express their strong opposition.

According to the Synagogue Council of America, "We are opposed to governmental aid to schools under the supervision or control of any religious denomination or sect whether Jewish, Protestant, or Catholic including outright subsidies, transportation, textbooks and other supplies."[10]

Similar statements have been issued by the Union of Orthodox Jewish Congregations, the Rabbinical Assembly of America, and the American Jewish Congress. Notwithstanding the needs of Jewish all-day schools, the American Jewish Committee reaffirmed the characteristic position that "Public funds should be used for public education," adding that it would be "unfair and discriminatory to ask the general taxpayer to foot the bill in whole or in part for . . . private-school education."[11]

Implicit in this stance is the feeling that to subsidize church-related schools would increase the division between Judaism and a dominant Christian culture.

While still typical, this attitude is slowly changing. A growing number of Jews in the United States sees a greater threat to Jewish values in the rampant secularism of the country than was ever posed by the Christian churches.

More and more the question is being asked whether a secular state is really as friendly to Jewish interests as the doctrinaire liberalism of the Reform would lead one to believe. Books and monographs are being published on the challenge to Judaism from its accommodation to what claims to be a religiously neutral society.

Perceptive rabbis are visibly worried that "American Jews, who have so many achievements, have thus far failed in one important respect. They have not yet learned how to transmit to those who will follow the Judaism which made their own achievements possible." There is too much evidence that the price of accommodation has been assimilation to religious neutralism.

> There are many indications that as Jews abandon the ideals, practices and standards of their Jewish tradition they risk betraying not only themselves, but also the essential spirit of America.

> Many sensitive and thoughtful young American Jews are aware of the power and life-giving worth of the tradition they have inherited. They are conscious of the growing spiritual problems which the complex modern world presents.[12]

Some Jewish observers are more specific. The most respected figure in American Jewish Conservatism dared to say that, "The modern Synagogues are graves, where prayers receive their decent burial."[13] To which another commentator added, "They have dignity, decorum, and elegance, but one item is lacking—the religious turmoil."[14] Referring to the preoccupation with Church and State separation, he put his finger on the real danger, the prospect of isolation from God.

> Our rabbis are concerned with the problem of church and state. Actually there is much greater separation between our synagogue and God than there is between the synagogue and the state. The synagogue has become the house of speeches, not the house of prayer.[15]

Awareness of the problem has made Jewish leaders more than ever zealous to face up to its demands. After all Judaism is essentially a religion that says "No" to an irreligious society. This offers the prospect of unprecedented cooperation with other believers in the interests of Judaeo-Christianity.

THE CHOSEN PEOPLE

Any estimate of Judaism would be incomplete that did not take into account the belief in its own destiny as the Chosen People. What was only obliquely mentioned before (in speaking of liberty) should be examined at closer range. It has considerable bearing on the Jew in American society.

God's election of the Jews is bound up with the original covenant that he made with their father, Abraham. The patriarch was made the head of a new family, whose selection was an act of divine providence and to whom were promised the most extravagant blessings from the Lord. They had only to remain faithful to Yahweh, and he would be faithful in his promises to them. In one sentence, this was the covenant between the Lord and the children of his predilection.

Ever since, the Jewish people have seen themselves as "a nation apart," thanks to the undeserved graces that the Lord would bestow on his own. To this day, when a convert to Judaism is received into the fold, the ritual prescribes that he be adopted into the family of Abraham; and all the liturgical prayers of the people emphasize their participation in the gifts reserved for the *gens electa*. Almost every page of the Jewish Prayer Book reflects this basic theme.

Blessed art thou, O Lord, Builder of Jerusalem. Speedily cause the offspring of David to flourish.

Be pleased, Lord our God, with thy people Israel and with their prayer.

It is our duty to praise the Master of all, to exalt the Creator of the universe, who has not made us like the nations of the world and has not placed us like the families of the earth; who has not designed our destiny to be like theirs, nor our lot of all their multitude.[16]

Their election by God binds the Jews to their part of the covenant. He led them out of slavery in Egypt and worked marvelous signs in their favor; they are to hear his voice and remain faithful to his commandments. Time and again they failed in obedience and were punished for their infidelity, and, though God will judge them by stricter standards than any other nation, they will never be utterly rejected or abandoned. They will always be his people and he will be their God.

Until modern times the nature of God's election and of Judaism as his "chosen one" was closely akin to the biblical notion that appears in the Torah and that centuries of reflection had crystallized in the Talmud. But as Judaism developed under its newly emancipated condition since the early eighteen hundreds, the concept of its status as a Chosen People was variously interpreted, depending on the religious philosophy which the interpreters professed and determined by their nearness to or distance from Maimonides in the twelfth century. Exhorting the Yemenite Jewry to withstand persecution, he told them, "Know, you are born in this covenant and raised in this belief, that the stupendous occurrence, the truth of which is testified by the most trusty of witnesses, stands in very deed alone in the annals of mankind. For a whole people heard the word of God and saw the glory of the Divinity. From this lasting memory we must draw our power to strengthen our faith even in a period of persecution and affliction such as the present one."[17]

There are now two main approaches in Jewish thought to the idea of a covenant and to Israel's role as a Chosen Race among nations. One approach is naturalistic, where the idea of religion without miraculous revelation is dominant and God himself is represented as the sum of man's highest ideals; the other is frankly revelational, admitting to a divine intervention in favor of his people and through them to the rest of the world.

Jewish writers are conscious of the difference between these approaches, which they summarize in the comparison between *The Natural and the Supernatural Jew*.[18] It is not only the title of a book but the expression of two concepts of an elected Israel.

Spokesmen in the Reform tradition typify the first concept. They complain that apologists for the doctrine of Israel's election do not think through the role of religion in human civilization. They too easily assume that "religion is supernaturally revealed truth," and then argue that when such truths were communicated only by one's own people, these people had been chosen by God. "But when one abandons the idea of supernatural revelation, what becomes of religion?" It is found to be the organized trust of a people for deliverance from the evils that befell mankind. On the part of the Jews it is a composite of their saints and heroes, customs and folkways, sacred literature and common symbols which have been hallowed by their relation to the Judaic search for the goal of human destiny. Yet, while the Jews are not a Chosen People in the traditional sense, they have a duty to help others find a conception of God that imposes on its adherents loyalty to a universally valid code of ethics. "It is only in that sense that the Jewish religion is universal."[19]

Within this naturalistic notion of the Chosen People there is room for the whole spectrum of Jewish hopes and aspirations—but always on this earth and in terms of this-worldly ideals. A man like Einstein could see the purpose of his Judaism fulfilled in the marvelous advancement of science to which he dedicated his life, and a Zionist like Weizmann could look upon the State of Israel as a partial fulfillment of God's plan for his people.

For the supernatural Jew Israel's covenant began with the premise that God communicated a special revelation to his people. They are predestined custodians, to whom Yahweh entrusted the prophetic wisdom that he wants finally to be shared by all nations. It was a clear vision of this fact which inaugurated the neoorthodox

movement in modern Judaism. Jews who believe not only in God
but in God's special election of the Hebrews are uncompromising
on what this means. Just as they received from Yahweh the revelation of his covenant, so they are destined to pass it on to the rest of
mankind. Except for Abraham and Moses, there would not have
been an Israel; except for Israel the world would never have
learned about the God who spoke to the patriarchs and prophets.
This is still the mission of the Jews, as those among them who believe in their prophetic role in history are ready to testify.

Israel is not a "natural" nation: indeed, it is not a nation at
all like the "nations of the world." It is a *supernatural* community, called into being by God to serve his eternal purposes in
history. It is a community created by God's special act of covenant, first with Abraham, whom he "called" out of the heathen
world and then, supremely, with Israel corporately at Sinai.
Jewish tradition emphasizes the unimportant and heterogeneous character of the People Israel apart from God's gracious
act of election, which gives it the significance it possesses in
the scheme of world destiny. The covenant of election is what
brought Israel into existence and keeps it in being; apart from
that covenant, Israel is as nothing and Jewish existence a mere
delusion. The covenant is at the very heart of the Jewish self-
understanding of its own reality.[20]

What this has meant to America is impossible to define. But its
presence in the national life is one of the great imponderables of
our history. We gather something of what this means from the fact
that, in less than a century, the beleaguered Jewish immigrants from
the slums of Russia and Poland have become leaders in every phase
of American society. Their phenomenal development is unique in
modern civilization.

THE MISSION OF ISRAEL

If Jews look upon themselves as the Chosen People, they also
believe in their special mission. Depending on whether their Judaism is of the "natural" or "supernatural" kind, their sense of purpose
is correspondingly qualified.

It is here, finally, that the place of the Jew in American life is at once very easy and very difficult to describe. What makes it easy is the fact that Jews have been so obviously successful, and their achievements are a living witness to strong motivation. It has gained them the admiration and envy of lesser people who are unwilling or unable to exert themselves in the same way.

What makes it also difficult is that success is not a neutral commodity. It has character and is subject to moral evaluation. No one knows this better than the Jews themselves, and the best appraisers of Israel's mission to America are their own spiritual leaders. They follow in the best tradition of the prophets when they remind the people, much as Isaiah did, of their purpose in God's plan.

> You, Israel, my servant, Jacob whom I have chosen, descendant of Abraham my friend.
> You whom I brought from the confines of the earth and called from the ends of the world; you to whom I said, "You are my servant, I have chosen you, not rejected you."
> I, Yahweh, have called you to serve the cause of right; I have taken you by the hand and formed you; I have appointed you as covenant of the people and light of the nations, to open the eyes of the blind, to free captives from prison, and those who live in darkness from the dungeon.[21]

This, then, is the mission of Israel in times past as today: to enlighten the world and set it free. To teach others and deliver them from all kinds of bondage has been the Jewish role in the family of nations—and America has been no exception.

Different Jews have understood this role differently, always conditioned by their degree of supernaturality. The more firmly they believed in the transcendence of Yahweh and the prophetic character of their mission, the more religious has been their influence on other peoples and the more spiritual their communication. Conversely, though, as their self-identity has been more secular and earthbound, their sense of mission has been more humanistic and concerned with the things of this world.

But in either case the goal has been functionally the same. The Jew thinks of himself, almost instinctively, as destined to impart to others something of the wisdom which he has received, and to emancipate them from something of the frequent oppression to which others have subjected him.

Those who are not Jews are tempted to mistake the function for the mission, and to judge Israel by such Israelites as have, in the words of Jeremiah, "rejected the word of Yahweh,"[22] and apply to all the descendants of Abraham what is only the conduct of some.

Much the same judgment could be made of Christians who are Christian only in name, and whose values are not determined by the things of heaven nor their hearts set on the Kingdom of God.

The future of Judaeo-Christianity in America is in the hands of those, Jews and Christians, who both see themselves as the Chosen People and who understand what this means: that God has blessed them beyond their fellowmen, but only that they might teach the world about the greatness of Yahweh and help free it from the slavery of sin.

EPILOGUE

The literature on Jewish-Christian relations in America is growing into a library. Literally scores of books and monographs are being published on every phase of this relationship, most of it directed to reducing tensions between the two religions and encouraging mutual cooperation for the common good.

Less obvious is the only valid basis on which this cooperation is truly promising and toward which Jews and Christians should be striving as they face the testing hour of American democracy.

When Yahweh answered Job from the heart of the tempest, "Who is this obscuring my designs with his empty-headed words," he was speaking for the ages. It is so easy to cover with semantic varnish the radical differences that divide Jews from Jews and Christians from Christians, often more than ever separates believing Jews from believing Christians. On the other hand, as Jews and Christians come to recognize their common faith in God's revelation and the providential role he intends for both of them—the prospects that lie ahead are filled with hope for a suffering humanity.

Few men in modern times have written more eloquently about these prospects than the Yiddish author, Sholem Asch, who spent forty-five years in America and whose books are a living symbol of faith in Judaeo-Christianity.

No Christian with a spark of faith can read what this spokesman for his people has to say without being moved to anguished sorrow over the sins committed by nominal Christians against the Jews in our day. After describing the tragedies of the Nazi persecution, he poses two questions that can be answered in only one way.

> With whom was he to be found, who had said, "Blessed are they who are persecuted for righteousness' sake"? On which side, do you think, is "the son of God" and on which the son of Satan—the Anti-Christ?[23]

But Sholem Asch knows Christians too well not to know that authentic Christianity is as far removed from hatred as Christ is from Satan, and that on this level Judaism and Christianity have a great destiny in store for them. In this sense, both have suffered immensely for their faith and at the hands of the same enemy, no matter what his name. If only Christians and Jews would penetrate behind the veil of terms and recognize each other as brothers in the spirit, united by their allegiance to the coming Messiah.

He is quick to point out, however, that the Messiah is no empty moniker for the believing Jew, no more than Jesus Christ is for the believing Christian.

Then, with disarming honesty, Asch admits that the Messiah has been quite irrelevant to those of his people who settled through compromise for comfort in this life with no need for concern about the life to come.

> The wealthy, educated Jew, perhaps, did not have to look forward to the messianic order of the world; he was able to find comforts enough in the existing order and made it, naturally, the point of departure for the messianic world; he could easily subtract a vast amount from the messianic ideal and make it fit into the rationalistic, liberal age.[24]

Not so the Jew who was brought up in a faith which made the Messiah the answer to all his expectations. He looks forward not only to a new and better life on earth, but to a whole new order of the world, "an order of the world where the visions of the prophets, of Isaiah and Ezekiel, become living realities." This kind of Jew "could not have survived a day, with the deprivations and worries which chased after him like wolves, except for his belief in the Messiah as a means of escape, a reward for all his sufferings, all the wrongs and persecutions loaded upon him by an unjust world. The Messiah for him is the one who will answer every question and will straighten out everything which is now awry."[25]

It is here and here only that faith meets faith, the Jewish and the Christian, when both persons are truly religious in looking beyond this world to the Messianic kingdom which is to come.

> The religious Jew in his spiritual outlook is the same believer in his Messiah as the religious Christian. The mystery of the Messiah acted on both of them and created in them a single spiritual character. The religious Jew waits every minute of the day for the coming of the Messiah, as the religious Christian awaits the Second Coming—not for a righteous ruler who will install a just order in the world, or a "liberal" order, but for a mysterious personage, half-God, half-man, who was with God before he created the world.
>
> Only for such a Messiah was it worth while to have passed through all sorrows and to spin out the thread of Israel's existence, which began to be woven in the hands of Abraham and has extended down to our own time. Only with the strength that emerges out of messianism could Jewry survive in the lime kiln which the world has lighted for it. Rob the Jews of the messianic mystery and they must fall apart, as have so many other faiths which were built upon the sandy foundations of rationalism.[26]

Much the same could be said of Christians whose loyalty to Christ has to be paid in carrying the cross. Never before in history have faithful Christians been more brutally persecuted for their religion—by a godless Marxism that tortures their bodies and by an equally cruel (though more subtle) Secularism that tears apart their souls. Christians, no less than Jews, look upon the twentieth century as the Age of Martyrs.

What has sustained the courage of suffering Jews in times past, and especially today, sustains the courage of suffering Christians, too. It is their Messianic hope—foretold by Ezekiel and repeated by John—of that final deliverance when the Lord "will make His home among them; they shall be His people, and He will be their God. He will wipe away all tears from their eyes; there will be no more death, and no more mourning or sadness. The world of the past has gone."[27]

Put the two hopes side by side, says Sholem Asch, and you see how unique is Judaeo-Christianity. Alone among the faiths of mankind, it has the strength, born of this vision, to press forward in a hostile world. The strength thus received is not only for survival, but for salvation; and not for Jews and Christians only, but for all who become inspired by the same Messianic ideal.

It is my profound belief that only the Jewish-Christian idea contains in itself the possibility of salvation for our tortured world. The Jewish-Christian idea makes us equal partners in your Christian ideal, just as it makes you equal partners in our Jewish one, in spite of the fact that we belong to separate faiths.

The substantial fact that you and we believe in the same God of Israel, that both of us have taken upon ourselves the yoke of heaven, that we believe in salvation, in redemption, in the promise, that we await the redeemer, the Messiah, each day, each hour, and each minute; that we expect him to come upon the clouds of the sky, that we believe the world cannot become perfect without the redeemer—all this has given us, it might be said, a common faith, a common psychology, and common character traits.[28]

The real essence of the matter is that both religions have the same prophetic destiny. "Our hope for a life after death has made us partners in a moral possession which is the sole consolation of our life; the expectation of the Messiah is our only reward. All of this together has created our civilization, which is founded upon the common element of the Jewish-Christian idea. We are equal partners in our common heritage."[29] Only the future will tell how wisely Jews and Christians have learned from the past.

ACKNOWLEDGMENTS AND REFERENCES

SELECT BIBLIOGRAPHY

CALENDAR OF FEAST DAYS

WORLD JEWISH POPULATION

JEWISH POPULATION IN THE UNITED STATES

NATIONAL JEWISH ORGANIZATIONS

JEWISH EDUCATION IN AMERICA

287

ACKNOWLEDGMENTS
AND
REFERENCES

The author and publisher are gratefully indebted to about thirty copyright holders for permission to use quotations from their books, monographs, and periodicals. Special gratitude is due to the American Jewish Committee and the Jewish Publication Society of America for their generous cooperation in furnishing the statistical data on American Judaism. This includes all the information on Jewish population, organizations, and education.

References follow the numerical sequence in the text. Where publishers requested a certain wording in the acknowledgment, this has been followed in each case.

A full complement of titles on American Judaism would fill another sizable volume. Yet if the works cited as references are combined with the select bibliography which follows, a representative library on Jewish faith and culture in America is offered to the reader.

I Sacred Writings

1 Baba Bathra, Tractate in Fourth Order of the Talmud, 12ᵃ.
2 Treatise *Betzah* (Yom Tob), chap. I, Mishnah I.
3 Treatise *Abuda Zara*, chap. I, Mishnah II.
4 Treatise *Sanhedrin*, chap. X, Mishnah IV.
5 *Babylonian Talmud*. New York: 1916, Vol. 8, p. 256.
6 Treatise *Aboth*, chap. II, Mishnah XVI.
7 *Ibid.*, chap. III, Mishnah XIII.
8 *Ibid.*, chap. IV, Mishnah XVII.
9 *Ibid.*, Mishnah XIX-XX.
10 *Ibid.*, chap. V, Mishnah XV.
11 Treatise *Pesachim*, chap. II, Gemara VII.
12 *Ibid.*, chap. X, Gemara III.
13 *Ibid.*, *Tosephtha—Aboth of Rabbi Nathan.*
14 *Ibid.*

15 Treatise *Derech Eretz-Zuta*, chap. I.
16 Treatise *Sabbath*, chap. XXII.
17 Jacob S. Minkin, *The World of Moses Maimonides*. New York: Thomas Yoseloff, 1957, p. 27.
18 Moses Maimonides, Commentary of Mishnah *Sanhedrin* X. 1.

II Origins and Development in America

1 *Rerum Halicarum Scriptores*. Citta di Castello: S. Lapi, 1900, pars 1, Vol. 2, p. 224.
2 Lee J. Levinger, *A History of the Jews in the United States*. New York: Union of American Hebrew Congregations, 1954, p. 41.
3 *Documents Relating to the Colonial History of New York*, Vol. XIV, p. 315.
4 *Ibid.*, p. 341.
5 *Ibid.*, p. 351.
6 Henry Wadsworth Longfellow, "The Jewish Cemetery in Newport," *Complete Poetical Works*. Boston: Houghton Mifflin Company, 1899, p. 192.
7 Abram Vossen Goodman, *American Overture: Jewish Rights in Colonial Times*. Philadelphia: 1943, p. 123.
8 Edward Davis, *The History of Rodeph Shalom Congregation, Philadelphia 1802-1926*. Philadelphia: 1926, pp. 27-28.
9 *Publications of the American Jewish Historical Society*, No. 21, p. 74.
10 *Ibid.*, pp. 2-3.
11 Peter Wiernik, *History of the Jews in America*. New York: 1931, p. 99.
12 *Ibid.*, pp. 100-01.
13 William Addison Blakely, *American State Papers Bearing on Sunday Legislation*. Washington: Religious Liberty Association, 1911, p. 195.
14 Anita L. Lebeson, *Jewish Pioneers in America*. New York: 1931, p. 286.
15 Moses Mendelssohn, in W. Gunther Plaut, *The Rise of Reform Judaism*. Vol. 1, *A Sourcebook of Its European Origins*. New York: World Union for Progressive Judaism, 1963, p. 6.
16 *Ibid.*
17 *Ibid.*, pp. 6-7.
18 Cecil Roth, "The European Age in Jewish History," in Louis Finkelstein, editor, *The Jews: Their History, Culture, and Religion*. New York: Harper and Brothers, 1949, Vol. I, p. 270.
19 Ludwig Börne, *Gesammelte Schriften*. Milwaukee: 1958, pp. 31-32.
20 Quoted by Koppel S. Pinson, *Modern Germany*. New York: The Macmillan Company, 1957, p. 70.

21 Lewis Browne, editor, *The Wisdom of Israel*. New York: Random House, 1945, pp. 638-40.
22 Benno M. Wallach, "Dr. David Einhorn's Sinai," Unpublished thesis, Hebrew Union College, 1950, p. 197.
23 W. Gunther Plaut, *The Growth of Reform Judaism*. New York: World Union for Progressive Judaism, 1966, p. 30.
24 *Ibid.*
25 *Ibid.*
26 *Ibid.*, p. 31.
27 David Philipson, *The Reform Movement in Modern Judaism*. New York: 1931, p. 349.
28 *Jewish Theological Seminary Students Annual*. New York: 1914, p. 17.
29 Leopold H. Haimson, *The Russian Marxists* (Harvard University Russian Research Center Studies, 19). Cambridge: Harvard University Press, 1955, p. 60.
30 Emma Lazarus' preference was for Jewish themes. Her essays in *The Century* and the *American Hebrew* establish her as a pioneer of American Zionism.
31 Nathan Glazer, *American Judaism*. Chicago: University of Chicago Press, 1957, p. 66.
32 Solomon Schechter, *Studies in Judaism*. Philadelphia: Jewish Publication Society of America, 1908-1924, Vol. I, p. 72.
33 Joseph Karo, *Shulhan Aruk*, article 250:1-5.
34 Isidore Epstein, *Judaism*. Baltimore: Penguin Books, 1963, p. 265.

III   Jewish Orthodoxy

1 Louis Ginzberg, *The United Synagogue of America* (Sixth Annual Report). New York: 1919, p. 21.
2 Midrash Rabbah on the Book of Lamentations, I. 16, 50.
3 Abodah Zarah, Tractate in Fourth Order of the Talmud, IV. 7.
4 Berakhoth, Tractate in First Order of the Talmud, V. 3.
5 Midrash Rabbah on the Book of Deuteronomy, II. 33.
6 Berakhoth, 3[a], passim.
7 Midrash Rabbah on the Book of Genesis, III. 8.
8 Pirque Aboth, Tractate in Fourth Order of the Talmud, II. 16.
9 Rosh ha-Shanah, Tractate in Second Order of the Talmud, 17[b]-18[a].
10 Yebamoth, Tractate in Third Order of the Talmud, 64[a].
11 Moses Maimonides, *The Guide for the Perplexed*. New York: E. P. Dutton and Company, 1936, pp. 3, 9.
12 *Ibid.*, I. 57, pp. 80-81.
13 *Ibid.*, 58, p. 82.

14 *High Holiday Prayer Book,* translated and annotated by Philip Birnbaum. New York: Hebrew Publishing Company, 1951, p. 658.
15 Makkoth, Tractate in Fourth Order of the Talmud, 23ᵇ.
16 Mishnah *Avot* 6.
17 *Ibid.*
18 In Exodus 33:22-23, and elsewhere.
19 Rosh ha-Shanah, 31ᵃ; Midrash Rabbah on the Book of Lamentations, Proemium XXV.
20 Midrash Rabbah on the Book of Exodus, II. 2.
21 *Prayer Book for Sabbath and Festivals,* translated and annotated by Philip Birnbaum. New York: Hebrew Publishing Company, 1950, p. 448.
22 Maimonides, *Guide for the Perplexed,* II. 36, p. 225.
23 *Ibid.,* II. 18, p. 182.
24 *Ibid.,* III. 52, p. 391.
25 Birnbaum, *Prayer Book for Sabbath,* p. 448.
26 Immanuel Jakobovits, "The State of Jewish Belief," *Commentary,* Vol. 42, No. 2, August 1966, p. 106.
27 Isaiah 42:6.
28 Midrash Rabbah on the Book of Exodus, XXX. 12.
29 Hagigah, II. 1.
30 Midrash Rabbah on the Book of Genesis, I. 3: I. 5-9; XII. 10; XXVII. 1.
31 *Ibid.,* XII. 13.
32 Rosh ha-Shanah, 11ᵃ.
33 Midrash Rabbah on the Book of Genesis, XVII. 4.
34 *Ibid.,* XIV. 1.
35 Midrash Rabbah on the Book of Numbers, XI. 3.
36 Midrash Rabbah on the Book of Ecclesiastes, III. 15, 1.
37 Midrash Rabbah on the Book of Numbers, XII. 4.
38 Midrash Rabbah on the Book of Genesis, XV. 5.
39 Midrash Rabbah on the Book of Leviticus, XII. 1.
40 Baba Bathra, 16ᵃ.
41 Midrash Rabbah on the Book of Numbers, XIX. 8; XIII. 3; XXIII. 13.
42 Midrash Rabbah on the Book of Genesis, XXXIV. 10.
43 Midrash Rabbah on the Book of Leviticus, XXI. 6.
44 Midrash Rabbah on the Book of Numbers, III. 6.
45 Midrash Rabbah on the Book of Genesis, XLIV. 16.
46 Midrash Rabbah on the Book of Leviticus, XXXVI. 6.
47 Daniel 12:1-4.
48 Psalms 49 and 73; Job 34:14; Ecclesiastes 12:7.
49 Sanhedrin, XI. 1.

50 Abodah Zarah, 10[b], 18[a]; Midrash Rabbah on the Book of Ecclesiastes, I. 9, 1.
51 Midrash Rabbah on the Book of Leviticus, XVIII. 1.
52 Midrash Rabbah on the Book of Esther, IX. 2.
53 Midrash Rabbah on the Book of Genesis, VI. 6.
54 Midrash Rabbah on the Book of Exodus, VII. 4.
55 Midrash Rabbah on the Book of Ecclesiastes, V. 8, 4.
56 Sanhedrin, XI. 1, 2.
57 Berakhoth, 17[a].
58 Midrash Rabbah on the Book of Leviticus, XII. 5.
59 Article 5.
60 Carol Klein, *The Credo of Maimonides*. New York: Philosophical Library, 1958, pp. 120-21.
61 Birnbaum, *Prayer Book for Sabbath*, p. 104.
62 Articles 10, 11.
63 Moses Maimonides, "Repentance," 5, "Eight Chapters," 8, in Minkin, *World of Maimonides*, pp. 244-45.
64 Birnbaum, *Prayer Book for Sabbath*, pp. 8-10.
65 Article 13.
66 Maimonides, "Ma'amar Tehijat ha-metim," in Minkin, *World of Maimonides*, pp. 402-05.
67 Birnbaum, *Prayer Book for Sabbath*, pp. 52, 84.
68 Birnbaum, *High Holiday Prayer Book*, p. 56.
69 K. Kohler, *Jewish Theology*. New York: The Macmillan Company, 1923, p. 297.
70 Yebamoth, 63[b].
71 Midrash Rabbah on the Book of Deuteronomy, VI. 7.
72 Midrash Rabbah on the Book of Exodus, XXV. 12.
73 Midrash Rabbah on the Song of Solomon, V. 2, 2.
74 Midrash Rabbah on the Book of Numbers, XIV. 2.
75 Midrash Rabbah on the Book of Genesis, I. 4.
76 Maimonides, "Kings," 11, in Minkin, *World of Maimonides*, pp. 398-99.
77 Maimonides, "Repentance," 9, in *ibid.*, p. 399.
78 Maimonides, "Kings," 11, in *ibid.*, p. 400.
79 *Ibid.*
80 *Ibid.*, pp. 400-01; also in Arthur Hertzberg, editor, *Judaism*. New York: George Braziller, 1961, p. 219.
81 Maimonides, "Kings," 11, in Minkin, *World of Maimonides*, p. 401; Hertzberg, *Judaism*, p. 220.
82 Zvi Hirsch Kalischer, *Derishot Tsiyyon* (1862), in Arthur Hertzberg, *The Zionist Idea*. Garden City, New York: Doubleday and Company, 1959, pp. 111-12.

83 *Ibid.*
84 *Ibid.*, p. 113.
85 Birnbaum, *Prayer Book for Sabbath*, pp. 12-14.
86 *Ibid.*, p. 72.
87 *Ibid.*, p. 74.
88 *Ibid.*, p. 372.
89 *Ibid.*, p. 278.
90 *Ibid.*, p. 256.
91 *Jewish Chronicle*, London, November 3, 1967, Balfour Declaration Supplement, p. iv.
92 Birnbaum, *Prayer Book for Sabbath*, p. 436.

I V Reform Judaism

1 Kaufmann Kohler, in Plaut, *Growth of Reform Judaism*, p. 33.
2 *Ibid.*, Pittsburgh Platform, Principle I.
3 *Ibid.*, Principle II.
4 *Ibid.*, p. 34, Principle III.
5 *Ibid.*, Principle IV.
6 *Ibid.*, Principle V.
7 *Ibid.*, Principle VI.
8 *Ibid.*, Principle VII.
9 *Ibid.*, Principle VIII.
10 *Ibid.*, p. 35.
11 Rabbi Hirsch, in *ibid.*, p. 36.
12 *American Israelite*, quoted in *ibid.*, p. 37.
13 Editorial in *American Hebrew*, in *ibid.*, p. 38.
14 Felix Adler, in *ibid.*, p. 39.
15 *Ibid.*, p. 40.
16 *Jewish Chronicle*, London, November 9, 1917, p. 10.
17 Adolf Hitler, *Mein Kampf*. New York: Reynal and Hitchcock, 1939, p. 420.
18 Plaut, *Growth of Reform Judaism*, pp. 96-98.
19 *Ibid.*, p. 98.
20 *Ibid.*, pp. 98-99.
21 *Ibid.*, p. 100.
22 Lilian H. Montagu, in *ibid.*, p. 91.
23 Solomon B. Freehof, *Reform Jewish Practice and Its Rabbinic Background*. New York: Union of Hebrew Congregations, 1963, Vol. I, pp. 7-8.
24 *Ibid.*, p. 8.

25 C. G. Montefiore and H. Loewe, editors and translators, *A Rabbinic Anthology*. Philadelphia: Jewish Publication Society of America, 1963, p. 669.
26 *Ibid.*
27 *Ibid.*, pp. 10-11.
28 *Ibid.*, p. 12.
29 *Ibid.*, p. 13.

V Conservative Judaism

1 Robert Gordis, "Conservative Judaism," in Ahron Opher, editor, *Judaism, Orthodox-Reform-Conservative*. New York: 1944, pp. 55-56.
2 *Ibid.*, pp. 56-57.
3 *Ibid.*, pp. 57-58.
4 *Ibid.*, pp. 58-59.
5 Isaiah 55:3-5.
6 Gordis, "Conservative Judaism," p. 60.
7 *Ibid.*
8 "Jewish Chronicle," London, in Morris Fine and Milton Himmelfarb, editors, *American Jewish Year Book, 1962*. New York: American Jewish Committee, 1962, p. 213.
9 Mordecai Kaplan, *The Future of the American Jew*. New York: The Macmillan Company, 1948, p. 80.
10 Mordecai Kaplan, *Judaism as a Civilization*. New York: The Macmillan Company, 1934, p. 460.
11 Zechariah 4:6.
12 I Samuel 2:9.
13 Kaplan, *Judaism as a Civilization*, p. 461.
14 Mordecai Kaplan, "The Contribution of Judaism to World Ethics," in Finkelstein, *The Jews: Their History, Culture, and Religion*, Vol. I, p. 710.
15 *Ibid.*
16 Kaplan, *Judaism as a Civilization*, p. 472.
17 *Ibid.*, p. 471.
18 Abraham J. Karp, *A History of the United Synagogue of America, 1913-1963*. New York: United Synagogue of America, 1964, p. 102.
19 *Ibid.*, p. 103.
20 *Ibid.*, p. 98.
21 *Ibid.*, p. 104.

VI Holy Days—Origin and Meaning

1 Exodus 22:12.
2 Exodus 20:8.
3 Ezekiel 20:12.
4 *Authorized Daily Prayer Book*. London: Eyre and Spottiswoode, n.d., p. 108.
5 Birnbaum, *Prayer Book for Sabbath*, pp. 32-34.
6 Leviticus Rabbah, Behar, XXIV, 16.
7 D. A. de Sola, *Sephardi Prayer Book*. New York: Oxford University Press, n.d.
8 Midrash Rabbah on the Book of Exodus, Mekhiltah and Yalkur, XII. 42.
9 William W. Simpson, *Jewish Prayer and Worship*. London: Student Christian Movement Press, 1967, p. 48.
10 A. Z. Idelsohn, *Jewish Liturgy and Its Development*. New York: Schocken Books, 1967, p. 179.
11 *Ibid.*, p. 183.
12 Birnbaum, *Prayer Book for Sabbath*, p. 334.
13 *Ibid.*, p. 132.
14 Exodus 6:6-7.
15 Idelsohn, *Jewish Liturgy*, pp. 186-87.
16 Leviticus 23:15-16.
17 Leviticus 23:21.
18 Freehof, *Reform Jewish Practice*, Vol. I, p. 26.
19 Birnbaum, *Prayer Book for Sabbath*, pp. 416-20.
20 *Ibid.*, pp. 434-36.
21 *Ibid.*, p. 428.
22 Exodus 23:16, 34:22.
23 Leviticus 23:24.
24 Morris Silverman, editor, *High Holiday Prayer Book*. Hartford: Prayer Book Press, 1951, pp. 83-84.
25 A. T. Philips, *Daily Prayers*. New York: Hebrew Publishing Company, n.d., p. 639.
26 *Ibid.*, pp. 639-41.
27 *Ibid.*, p. 645.
28 *Ibid.*, p. 647.
29 *Ibid.*, pp. 663-67.
30 Silverman, *High Holiday Prayer Book*, pp. 207-08.
31 *Ibid.*, p. 481.
32 II Kings 4:23; Isaiah 1:14.
33 Exodus 23:11-12; Leviticus 25; Deuteronomy 15:1-3.

VII Dietary Laws and Customs

1 Maimonides, *Guide for the Perplexed*, III. 48, pp. 370-72.
2 Leviticus 11:3-8.
3 Leviticus 11:10-12.
4 Leviticus 11:13-19.
5 Leviticus 11:29-30.
6 Leviticus 11:39.
7 Exodus 22:30.
8 Leviticus 7:26.
9 Leviticus 7:26.
10 Maimonides, *Guide for the Perplexed*, III. 46.
11 Leviticus 3:17.
12 Genesis 32:33.
13 Deuteronomy 12:20-21.
14 Maimonides, *Guide for the Perplexed*, III. 43.
15 Exodus 23:19, 34:25; Deuteronomy 14:21.
16 Philips, *Daily Prayers*, p. 191.
17 *Ibid.*, p. 201.
18 Plaut, *Growth of Reform Judaism*, pp. 265-66.

VIII Ritual and Practices

1 Genesis 17:1-2, 10-13, 23.
2 Philips, *Daily Prayers*, p. 171.
3 I Kings 19:10-14.
4 *Pirke de Rabbi Elieper*, chap. 29.
5 Philips, *Daily Prayers*, p. 171.
6 *Ibid.*, p. 173.
7 *Ibid.*
8 *Ibid.*
9 *Ibid.*
10 *Ibid.*, p. 177.
11 Ben M. Edidin, *Jewish Customs and Ceremonies*. New York: Hebrew Publishing Company, 1941, p. 51.
12 Exodus 8:11-16.
13 Leviticus 27:26.
14 Numbers 3:12-13, 45-51.
15 Philips, *Daily Prayers*, pp. 179-81.
16 Deuteronomy 6:8.
17 H. Freedman and I. Epstein, editors, *Hebrew-English Edition of the Babylonian Talmud*, "Kiddushin," I. London: Soncino Press, 1966, p. 1a.

18 *Ibid.*, pp. 9b-10a.
19 Genesis 1:28, 9:1.
20 Proverbs 2:17; Malachi 2:14.
21 Osee 1:2; Isaiah 50:1; Jeremiah 2:2.
22 Midrash Rabbah on the Book of Leviticus, VIII. 1.
23 Kethuvoth, 7ᵇ.
24 Philips, *Daily Prayers*, pp. 167-69.
25 Birnbaum, *Prayer Book for Sabbath*, p. 466.
26 Leviticus 15:24.
27 Harris M. Lazarus, *The Ways of Her Household: A Practical Handbook for Jewish Women on Traditional Customs and Observances.* London: Myers, 1923, pp. 12-13.
28 *Ibid.*, pp. 6-7.
29 Maimonides, *Guide for the Perplexed*, chap. 49, p. 376.
30 *Ibid.*, p. 373.
31 Midrash Rabbah on the Book of Leviticus, Behar, XXIV. 14.
32 Ketubbot, 76ᵃ.
33 Ishut 13:3.
34 Freehof, *Reform Jewish Practice*, Vol. I, p. 100.
35 *Ibid.*, p. 103.
36 *Ibid.*, p. 107.
37 Earl G. Grollman, *Judaism in Sigmund Freud's World.* New York: Bloch Publishing Company, 1965, p. 43.
38 *Ibid.*
39 Alan Guttmacher and others, *Birth Control and Love.* New York: The Macmillan Company, 1969, pp. 150-51.
40 *Ibid.*, p. 151.
41 *Ibid.*
42 Jacob Z. Lauterbach, in Norman E. Himes, *Medical History of Contraception.* New York: Gamut Press, 1963, p. 77.
43 Mishnah *Oholoth*, VII, 6.
44 Guttmacher, *Birth Control and Love*, p. 222.
45 Ecclesiastes 7:20.
46 Idelsohn, *Jewish Liturgy*, p. 171.
47 De Sola, *Sephardi Prayer Book*, p. 198.
48 Edidin, *Jewish Customs and Ceremonies*, p. 80.
49 *Authorized Daily Prayer Book*, p. 123.
50 Birnbaum, *Prayer Book for Sabbath*, p. 352.
51 Eugene B. Borowitz, "The Individual and the Community in Jewish Prayer," in Arnold J. Wolf, editor, *Rediscovering Judaism.* Chicago: Quadrangle Books, 1965, p. 119.
52 Maimonides, *Guide for the Perplexed*, pp. 386-87.
53 Exodus 13:1-16; Deuteronomy 6:4-9, 11:13-21.

54 Numbers 15:37-40.
55 Gershom G. Scholem, *Major Trends in Jewish Mysticism.* New York: Schocken Books, 1961, p. 344.
56 Lewis I. Newman and Samuel Spitz, editors, *The Hasidic Anthology: Tales and Teachings of the Hasidim.* New York: Schocken Books, 1963, pp. 68, 85, 105, 262, 328, 337, 338.

IX Jewish Law and Rabbinic Morality

1 Deuteronomy 5:6-14.
2 II Maccabees 7:37.
3 Ecclesiasticus 42:21; Wisdom 14:14, 27, 29.
4 Quoted by Emil L. Fackenheim, "The Revealed Morality of Judaism and Modern Thought," in Wolf, *Rediscovering Judaism*, p. 58.
5 *Ibid.*, p. 67.
6 Solomon B. Freehof, *A Treasury of Responsa.* Philadelphia: Jewish Publication Society of America, 1963, pp. 297-98.
7 Freehof, *Reform Jewish Practice*, p. 85.
8 David Kirshenbaum, *Mixed Marriage and the Jewish Future.* New York: Bloch Publishing Company, 1958, p. viii.
9 *Yearbook 68.* New York: Central Conference of American Rabbis, 1958, p. 122.
10 *Ibid.*
11 Morris N. Kertzer, *What Is a Jew?* New York: World Publishing Company, 1967, p. 159.

X The Jew in American Society

1 Sidney E. Mead, "American Protestantism Since the Civil War," *Journal of Religion*, January 1956, p. 2.
2 Mary Perkins Ryan, *Are Parochial Schools the Answer?* New York: Holt, Rinehart and Winston, 1963, p. 175.
3 Thomas F. O'Dea, *American Catholic Dilemma.* New York: New American Library, 1962, p. 132.
4 C. Bezalel Sherman, *The Jew Within American Society: A Study in Ethnic Individuality.* Detroit: Wayne State University Press, 1965, pp. 148-49.
5 Michael Kraft, "A Peoples' Conflict, Israel the State vs. Judaism the Religion," *Israel.* New York: Cowles Education Corporation, 1968, p. 52.
6 Morris Margolies, "Survey of Jewish-Christian Relations," *Jewish Christian Relations.* St. Marys, Kansas: St. Mary's College, 1966, p. 34.

7 Synagogue Council of America and the National Community Relations Advisory Council, "Declaration of Principle," in Joseph L. Blau, editor, *Cornerstones of Religious Freedom in America, Selected Basic Documents.* New York: Harper and Row, 1964, p. 304.
8 *Ibid.*
9 *Ibid.*, pp. 304-05.
10 *American Jewish Year Book, 1962*, p. 177.
11 *Ibid.*, pp. 177-78.
12 Leon A. Jaick, "Being a Jew in America," in Benjamin Efron, editor, *Currents and Trends in Contemporary Jewish Thought.* New York: Ktav Publishing House, 1965, pp. 291-92.
13 Abraham Joshua Heschel, quoted in Kirshenbaum, *Mixed Marriage and the Jewish Future*, p. 138.
14 Kirshenbaum, *Mixed Marriage and the Jewish Future*, p. 138.
15 *Ibid.*
16 Birnbaum, *Prayer Book for Sabbath*, pp. 12, 20.
17 Moses Maimonides, "Letter to the Jews of Yemen," in F. Kobler, editor, *A Treasury of Jewish Letters.* Philadelphia: 1954, Vol. I, p. 185.
18 Arthur A. Cohen, *The Natural and the Supernatural Jew.* New York: Pantheon Books, 1963.
19 Kaplan, *Future of the American Jew*, pp. 219-20.
20 Will Herberg, *Judaism and Modern Man.* New York: Meridian Books, 1959, p. 271.
21 Isaiah 42:1-7.
22 Jeremiah 8:9.
23 Sholem Asch, *One Destiny: An Epistle to the Christians.* New York: G. P. Putnam's Sons, 1945, p. 65.
24 *Ibid.*, p. 72.
25 *Ibid.*, pp. 72-73.
26 *Ibid.*, pp. 73-74.
27 Ezekiel 37:37; Revelation 21:3-4.
28 Asch, *One Destiny*, p. 83.
29 *Ibid.*, p. 84.

SELECT BIBLIOGRAPHY

Baeck, Leo. *The Essence of Judaism*. New York: Schocken Books, 1948.

Berger, Elmer. *A Partisan History of Judaism*. New York: Devin-Adair Company, 1951.

Birnbaum, Philip. *A Book of Jewish Concepts*. New York: Hebrew Publishing Company, 1964.

———— translator. *High Holiday Prayer Book*. New York: Hebrew Publishing Company, 1951.

———— translator. *Prayer Book for Sabbath and Festivals*. New York: Hebrew Publishing Company, 1950.

Cohen, Arthur A. *The Natural and the Supernatural Jew*. New York: Pantheon Books, 1963.

Edidin, Ben M. *Jewish Customs and Ceremonies*. New York: Hebrew Publishing Company, 1941.

Efron, Benjamin, editor. *Currents and Trends in Contemporary Jewish Thought*. New York: Ktav Publishing House, 1965.

Epstein, Isidore. *Judaism*. Baltimore: Penguin Books, 1963.

———— editor. *Babylonian Talmud*, 2 volumes. New York: Bloch Publishing Company, 1948.

Fine, Morris, and Milton Himmelfarb, editors. *American Jewish Year Book, 1968*. Philadelphia: Jewish Publication Society of America, 1968. Published annually.

Finkelstein, Louis, editor. *The Jews: Their History, Culture, and Religion*, 2 volumes. New York: Harper and Brothers, 1949.

Freedman, H. F., and M. Simon, editors. *Midrash Rabbah*. New York: Bloch Publishing Company, 1939.

Freehof, Solomon B. *Current Reform Responsa*. New York: Ktav Publishing House, 1969.

———— *A Treasury of Responsa*. Philadelphia: Jewish Publication Society of America, 1963.

Glazer, Nathan. *American Judaism*. Chicago: University of Chicago Press, 1957.

Goell, Yohai, compiler. *Bibliography of Modern Hebrew Literature in English Translation*. New York: Ktav Publishing House, 1969.

Gottman, J. *The Philosophy of Judaism.* New York: Meridian Books, 1960.

Grollman, Earl. *Judaism in Sigmund Freud's World.* New York: Appleton-Century-Crofts, 1966.

Herberg, Will. *Judaism and Modern Man.* New York: Meridian Books, 1959.

Hertzberg, Arthur, editor. *Judaism.* New York: George Braziller, 1961.

Heschel, A. J. *Man Is Not Alone: A Philosophy of Religion.* New York: Farrar, Straus and Young, 1951.

Karp, Abraham J., editor. *The Jewish Experience in America,* 5 volumes. New York: Ktav Publishing House, 1969.

Kertzer, Morris N. *What Is a Jew?* New York: World Publishing Company, 1967.

Kravitz, Nathaniel. *3000 Years of Hebrew Literature.* Chicago: The Swallow Press, 1971.

Landman, Isaac, editor. *The Universal Jewish Encyclopedia,* 10 volumes. Brooklyn: Universal Jewish Encyclopedia, 1939-1943.

Leviant, Curt, editor. *Masterpieces of Hebrew Literature.* New York: Ktav Publishing House, 1969.

Marcus, Jacob Rader. *Studies in American Jewish History.* New York: Ktav Publishing House, 1969.

Margolis, Max L., and Alexander Marx. *A History of the Jewish People.* New York: Harper and Row, 1965.

Minkin, Jacob S. *The World of Moses Maimonides.* New York: Thomas Yoseloff, 1957.

Montefiore, C. G., and H. Loewe, editors. *A Rabbinic Anthology.* Philadelphia: Jewish Publication Society of America, 1963.

Newman, Louis I., and Samuel Spitz, editors. *The Hasidic Anthology: Tales and Teachings of the Hasidim.* New York: Schocken Books, 1963.

Plaut, W. Gunther. *The Growth of Reform Judaism.* New York: World Union for Progressive Judaism, 1966.

—————— *The Rise of Reform Judaism,* 2 volumes. New York: World Union for Progressive Judaism, 1963.

Roth, Cecil, editor. *The Standard Jewish Encyclopedia.* New York: Doubleday and Company, 1959.

Schauss, Hayyim. *Guide to Jewish Holy Days.* Translated by Samuel Jaffe. New York: Schocken Books, 1962.

Schoeps, Hans Joachim. *The Jewish-Christian Argument.* Translated by David E. Green. New York: Holt, Rinehart and Winston, 1963.

Scholem, Gershom G. *Major Trends in Jewish Mysticism.* New York: Schocken Books, 1961.

Sherman, C. Bezalel. *The Jew Within American Society: A Study in Ethnic Individuality.* Detroit: Wayne State University Press, 1965.

Silverman, Morris, editor. *High Holiday Prayer Book.* Hartford: Prayer Book Press, 1951.

Sokolow, Nahum. *History of Zionism 1600-1918.* New York: Ktav Publishing House, 1969.

Sperling, H., and M. Simon, translators. *Zohar,* 5 volumes. London: Soncino Press, 1931-1934.

Stitskin, Leon D., editor. *Studies in Torah Judaism.* New York: Ktav Publishing House, 1969.

The Union Prayerbook for Jewish Worship, revised edition. New York: Central Conference of American Rabbis, 1951.

Wolf, Arnold Jacob, editor. *Rediscovering Judaism.* Chicago: Quadrangle Books, 1965.

Year	Purim	Passover	Pentecost	Rosh Ha-Shanah
1971	Mar 11	Apr 10	May 30	Sep 20
1972	Feb 29	Mar 30	May 19	Sep 9
1973	Mar 18	Apr 17	Jun 6	Sep 27
1974	Mar 8	Apr 7	May 27	Sep 17
1975	Feb 25	Mar 27	May 16	Sep 6
1976	Mar 16	Apr 15	Jun 4	Sep 25
1977	Mar 4	Apr 3	May 23	Sep 13
1978	Mar 23	Apr 22	Jun 11	Oct 2
1979	Mar 13	Apr 12	Jun 1	Sep 22
1980	Mar 2	Apr 1	May 21	Sep 11
1981	Mar 20	Apr 19	Jun 8	Sep 29
1982	Mar 9	Apr 8	May 28	Sep 18
1983	Feb 27	Mar 29	May 18	Sep 8
1984	Mar 18	Apr 17	Jun 6	Sep 27
1985	Mar 7	Apr 6	May 26	Sep 16
1986	Mar 25	Apr 24	Jun 13	Oct 4
1987	Mar 15	Apr 14	Jun 3	Sep 24
1988	Mar 3	Apr 2	May 22	Sep 12
1989	Mar 21	Apr 20	Jun 9	Sep 30
1990	Mar 11	Apr 10	May 30	Sep 20
1991	Feb 28	Mar 30	May 19	Sep 9
1992	Mar 19	Apr 18	Jun 7	Sep 28

Yom Kippur	Tabernacles	Hanukkah	Year
Sep 29	Oct 4	Dec 13	1971
Sep 18	Sep 23	Dec 1	1972
Oct 6	Oct 11	Dec 20	1973
Sep 26	Oct 1	Dec 9	1974
Sep 15	Sep 20	Nov 29	1975
Oct 4	Oct 9	Dec 17	1976
Sep 22	Sep 27	Dec 5	1977
Oct 11	Oct 16	Dec 25	1978
Oct 1	Oct 6	Dec 15	1979
Sep 20	Sep 25	Dec 3	1980
Oct 8	Oct 13	Dec 21	1981
Sep 27	Oct 2	Dec 11	1982
Sep 17	Sep 22	Dec 1	1983
Oct 6	Oct 11	Dec 19	1984
Sep 25	Sep 30	Dec 8	1985
Oct 13	Oct 18	Dec 27	1986
Oct 3	Oct 8	Dec 16	1987
Sep 21	Sep 26	Dec 4	1988
Oct 9	Oct 14	Dec 23	1989
Sep 29	Oct 4	Dec 12	1990
Sep 18	Sep 23	Dec 2	1991
Oct 7	Oct 12	Dec 20	1992

CALENDAR
OF
FEAST DAYS

WORLD JEWISH POPULATION

It is not possible to ascertain the exact number of Jews in the various countries of the world. The figures below were based on local censuses, communal registrations, and estimates of varying degrees of accuracy. Changes due to natural increase have been taken into consideration only to the degree that they were reflected in data obtained from local sources.

DISTRIBUTION BY CONTINENTS

The estimated world Jewish population is 13,628,000: about 6,822,000 (over 50 percent) in the Americas; 4,054,000 (30 percent) in Europe (including the Asian parts of Turkey and the Soviet Union); 2,477,000 (18 percent) in Asia; 200,000 (1.5 percent) in Africa; and 74,500 (0.5 percent) in Australia and New Zealand.

Europe

Of the 4,054,000 Jews in Europe, about 2,815,000 are in the Soviet area, including some 2,568,000 in the Soviet Union. More than 1,200,000 are in countries outside the Soviet bloc. France, with a Jewish population currently estimated at 535,000, has the largest Jewish community in Western Europe; the number includes recent arrivals from North Africa. There are 450,000 Jews in Great Britain. Some 110,000 are in Romania, and some 80,000 in Hungary.

305 *World Jewish Population*

TABLE 1
Estimated Jewish population in Europe, by countries

Country	Total population[1]	Jewish population
Albania	1,914,000	300
Austria	7,290,000	12,000
Belgium	9,528,000	40,500
Bulgaria	8,257,000	7,000
Czechoslovakia	14,305,000	18,000
Denmark	4,797,000	6,000
Finland	4,664,000	1,550
France	49,400,000	535,000
Germany	76,000,000	30,000[2]
Gibraltar	22,500	650
Great Britain	55,039,000	450,000
Greece	8,614,000	6,500
Hungary	10,231,000	80,000
Ireland	2,884,000	5,400
Italy	51,962,000	35,000
Luxembourg	333,000	1,000
Malta	317,000	50
Netherlands	12,631,000	30,000
Norway	3,754,000	750
Poland	31,944,000	25,000
Portugal	9,335,000	650
Romania	19,143,000	110,000
Spain	32,140,000	7,000
Sweden	7,869,000	13,000
Switzerland	5,999,000	20,000
Turkey	33,823,000	43,900[3]
USSR	233,200,000	2,568,000[3]
Yugoslavia	19,958,000	7,000
Totals	715,353,500	4,054,250

[1] United Nations, Statistical Office, *Monthly Bulletin of Statistics*, and other sources, including local publications.
[2] Includes East Germany, about 1,300.
[3] Includes Asian regions of the USSR and Turkey.

North, Central, and South America

The Jewish population in the United States was currently estimated at about 5,800,000. Some 270,000 Jews were in Canada, and more than 720,000 in Central and South America and the West Indies. Argentina had 450,000 Jews, Brazil about 140,000. There are 2,000 Jews in Cuba.

TABLE 2

Estimated Jewish population in North, Central, and South America and the West Indies, by countries

Country	Total population[1]	Jewish population
Canada	20,441,000	270,000
Mexico	45,671,000	30,000
United States	199,118,000	5,800,000
Totals North America	265,230,000	6,100,000
Barbados	245,000	100
Costa Rica	1,486,000	1,500
Cuba	8,033,000	2,000
Curaçao	148,000	700
Dominican Republic	3,889,000	400
El Salvador	3,037,000	300
Guatemala	4,575,000	1,500
Haiti	4,485,000	150
Honduras	2,445,000	150
Jamaica	1,839,000	600
Nicaragua	1,715,000	200
Panama	1,329,000	2,000
Trinidad	1,000,000	400
Totals Central America and West Indies	34,226,000	10,000
Argentina	23,031,000	450,000
Bolivia	3,801,000	4,000
Brazil	85,655,000	140,000
Chile	8,750,000	35,000
Colombia	18,620,000	10,000
Ecuador	5,508,000	2,000
Paraguay	2,161,000	1,200
Peru	12,385,000	4,000
Surinam	350,000	500
Uruguay	2,783,000	54,000
Venezuela	9,352,000	12,000
Totals South America	172,396,000	712,700
Totals	471,852,000	6,822,700

[1] See Table 1, note 1.

Asia, Australia, and New Zealand

Of the 2,477,000 Jews in Asia, 2,365,000 are in Israel, 80,000 in Iran, and some 16,000 in India. In no other country of Asia (aside from Turkey and Asian USSR) are there as many as 10,000 Jews. According to available reports, the centuries-old Jewish communities of Aden and Yemen no longer exist; some knowledgeable sources indicate that a very small number of Jews may still be living in Yemen.

TABLE 3

Estimated Jewish population in Asia, by countries

Country	Total population[1]	Jewish population
Afghanistan	15,751,000	800
Burma	25,246,000	200
China	710,000,000	100
Cyprus	614,000	30
Hong Kong	3,836,000	200
India	511,115,000	16,000
Indonesia	107,000,000	100
Iran	25,500,000	80,000
Iraq	8,338,000	2,500
Israel	3,767,000[2]	2,365,000
Japan	99,920,000	1,000
Lebanon	2,460,000	6,000
Pakistan	107,258,000	300
Philippines	34,656,000	500
Singapore	1,956,000	600
Syria	5,450,000	4,000
Totals	1,662,867,000	2,477,330

[1] See Table 1, note 1.
[2] This total includes population under Israeli control, including some 66,000 non-Jews in East Jerusalem and 992,000 non-Jews in areas under military administration.

TABLE 4

Estimated Jewish population in Australia and New Zealand

Country	Total population[1]	Jewish population
Australia	11,751,000	69,500
New Zealand	2,726,000	5,000
Totals	14,477,000	74,500

[1] See Table 1, note 1.

Africa

The Jewish population of Africa continues to dwindle. There are 50,000 Jews in Morocco and 10,000 in Tunisia. Only 2,500 remain in Egypt. Some 500 Jews remain in Libya. Revised figures put the Jewish community of South Africa at 115,000.

TABLE 5

Estimated Jewish population in Africa, by countries

Country	Total population[1]	Jewish population
Algeria	12,150,000	3,000
Congo Republic	15,986,000	400
Egypt	30,147,000	2,500
Ethiopia	23,000,000	12,000
Kenya	9,948,000	700
Libya	1,738,000	500
Morocco	14,140,000	50,000
Republic of South Africa	18,733,000	114,800
Rhodesia	4,530,000	5,500
Tunisia	4,460,000	10,000
Zambia (Northern Rhodesia)	3,881,000	800
Totals	138,713,000	200,200

[1] See Table 1, note 1.

COMMUNITIES WITH LARGEST JEWISH POPULATIONS

The three largest Jewish communities are in the United States, the Soviet Union, and Israel. Together they account for over 78 percent of the Jewish population of the world. Only France, Great Britain, Argentina, and Canada have Jewish populations exceeding 200,000.

TABLE 6

Countries with largest Jewish populations

Country	Jewish population
United States	5,800,000
Soviet Union	2,568,000
Israel	2,365,000
France	535,000
Argentina	450,000
Great Britain	450,000
Canada	270,000

TABLE 7

Estimated Jewish population, selected cities

City	Jewish population	City	Jewish population
Amsterdam	12,000	Manila	300
Antwerp	13,000	Marseilles	65,000
Athens	2,850	Melbourne	35,000
Basel	2,300	Milan	9,000
Belgrade	1,450	Montreal	105,000
Berlin	6,000	Moscow	285,000
Berne	800	Nice	20,000
Bordeaux	6,400	Oslo	600
Brussels	24,000	Paris	300,000
Budapest	65,000	Plovdiv	1,000
Buenos Aires	360,000	Rio de Janeiro	55,000
Casablanca	40,000	Rome	13,000
Cochin	500	Salonika	1,300
Copenhagen	6,000	Santiago	30,000
Florence	1,500	São Paulo	60,000
Geneva	2,650	Sarajevo	1,000
Glasgow	13,400	Sofia	4,000
Guatemala City	1,500	Stockholm	7,000
Haifa	200,000	Strasbourg	14,000
Helsinki	1,100	Subotica	450
Istanbul	38,000	Sydney	28,000
Izmir	4,000	Teheran	30,000
Jerusalem	187,500	Tel Aviv-Jaffa	394,000
Johannesburg	57,700	Toronto	88,000
Kiev	220,000	Toulouse	20,000
Leeds	18,000	Trieste	1,500
Leningrad	165,000	Valparaíso	4,000
London (Greater)	280,000	Vienna	9,250
Luxembourg	850	Warsaw	5,000
Lyons	25,000	Zagreb	1,400
Manchester	28,000	Zurich	6,150

LEON SHAPIRO

JEWISH POPULATION
IN THE UNITED STATES

The Jewish population in the United States is presently estimated at about six million. This shows an increase of three-quarter million in the past thirty years. Among the areas showing the fastest rate of growth are Baltimore and Miami, with an increase of 25 and 90 percent respectively since 1950.

State estimates are based on community estimates, after duplications were eliminated and adjustments made for "unlisted" Jews. Individual community estimates were generally obtained from member federations of the Council of Jewish Federations and Welfare Funds and from the files of the National United Jewish Appeal.

TABLE 8
Estimated Jewish population in the United States

State	Total population[1]	Jewish population	Percent of total
Alabama	3,540,000	9,465	0.27
Alaska	272,000	190	0.07
Arizona	1,634,000	20,485	1.25
Arkansas	1,968,000	3,065	0.16
California	19,153,000	653,585	3.41
Colorado	1,975,000	23,140	1.17
Connecticut	2,925,000	102,930	3.52
Delaware	523,000	8,540	1.63
District of Columbia	809,000	15,000	1.85
Florida	5,995,000	175,620	2.93
Georgia	4,509,000	25,760	0.57
Hawaii	739,000	1,000	0.14
Idaho	699,000	500	0.07
Illinois	10,893,000	283,530	2.60
Indiana	5,000,000	23,610	0.47
Iowa	2,753,000	7,490	0.27
Kansas	2,275,000	3,515	0.15
Kentucky	3,189,000	11,200	0.35

State	Total population[1]	Jewish population	Percent of total
Louisiana	3,662,000	15,630	0.43
Maine	973,000	8,285	0.85
Maryland	3,682,000	177,115	4.81
Massachusetts	5,421,000	257,720	4.75
Michigan	8,584,000	98,345	1.15
Minnesota	3,582,000	33,575	0.94
Mississippi	2,348,000	4,015	0.17
Missouri	4,603,000	80,710	1.75
Montana	701,000	615	0.09
Nebraska	1,435,000	8,100	0.56
Nevada	444,000	2,380	0.54
New Hampshire	686,000	4,260	0.62
New Jersey	7,003,000	362,955	5.18
New Mexico	1,003,000	3,645	0.36
New York	18,336,000	2,520,155	13.74
North Carolina	5,029,000	9,200	0.18
North Dakota	639,000	1,285	0.20
Ohio	10,458,000	160,600	1.54
Oklahoma	2,495,000	6,430	0.26
Oregon	1,999,000	9,045	0.45
Pennsylvania	11,629,000	443,265	3.81
Rhode Island	900,000	21,840	2.43
South Carolina	2,599,000	7,155	0.28
South Dakota	674,000	525	0.08
Tennessee	3,892,000	16,710	0.43
Texas	10,869,000	63,680	0.59
Utah	1,024,000	1,600	0.16
Vermont	417,000	2,330	0.56
Virginia	4,536,000	37,300	0.82
Washington	3,087,000	14,985	0.49
West Virginia	1,798,000	4,760	0.26
Wisconsin	4,189,000	32,295	0.77
Wyoming	315,000	710	0.23
Totals	197,863,000	5,779,845	2.92

[1] These data represent estimates of the total resident population of each state. Members of the Armed Forces abroad are excluded. There is therefore a slight difference between these data and the estimates for the Jewish population since most estimates of the latter include persons in the Armed Forces by civilian residence rather than by military residence.

TABLE 9

Distribution of United States Jewish population by regions[1]

Region	Total population	Percent distribution	Jewish population	Percent distribution
Northeast	48,289,000	24.4	3,723,740	64.4
New England	11,321,000	5.7	397,365	6.9
Middle Atlantic	36,968,000	18.7	3,326,375	57.5
North Central	55,085,000	27.8	733,580	12.7
East North Central	39,123,000	19.8	598,380	10.4
West North Central	15,961,000	8.1	135,200	2.3
South	61,443,000	31.1	590,645	10.2
South Atlantic	29,480,000	14.9	460,450	8.0
East South Central	12,970,000	6.6	41,390	0.7
West South Central	18,993,000	9.6	88,805	1.5
West	33,045,000	16.7	731,880	12.7
Mountain	7,796,000	3.9	53,075	0.9
Pacific	25,249,000	12.8	678,805	11.8
Totals	197,863,000	100.0	5,780,000	100.0

[1] Details may not add to totals because of rounding.

313

NATIONAL
JEWISH ORGANIZATIONS

It is impossible to understand American Judaism without knowing something of its extraordinary solidarity. The following organizations in the United States and Canada are all national in scope and do not include Jewish federations, welfare funds, and community councils of a more local nature.

There is no better commentary on the vitality of Judaism in America than the flourishing character of its nationwide societies, which are often also international in structure. They coordinate every phase of Jewish faith and worship, life and work to a degree unknown in other religious systems.

Along with the organizations are also given the publications for which they are responsible. In many cases, these publications are the mainstay of the groups which sponsor them and have an influence on American (and world) culture far beyond the immediate Jewish membership.

UNITED STATES

Community relations

American Council for Judaism, Inc. (1943). 201 E. 57th St., New York, N. Y. 10022. Seeks to advance the universal principles of a Judaism free of national, civic, cultural, and social integration into American institutions of Americans of Jewish faith. *Brief; Education in Judaism; Information Bulletin; Issues.*

American Jewish Committee (1906). Institute of Human Relations, 165 E. 56th St., New York, N. Y. 10022. Seeks to prevent infraction of civil and religious rights of Jews in any part of the world and to secure equality of economic, social, and educational opportunity through education and civic action; seeks to broaden understanding of the basic nature of prejudice and to improve techniques for combating it; promotes a philosophy of Jewish integration by projecting a balanced view with respect to full participation in American life and retention of Jewish identity. *American Jewish Year Book* (with Jewish Publication Society of America); *Commentary; Insight; Newsletter; Proceedings of Annual Meeting.*

American Jewish Conference on Soviet Jewry (1964). 55 W. 42nd St., Suite 1530, New York, N. Y. 10036. *Ad hoc* group of twenty-five major national Jewish organizations and their local affiliates, seeking to formulate a joint program and policy on behalf of Soviet Jewry. Participating agencies are pledged to lend their resources and personnel to coordinate activities and implement national program, including public education and social action.

American Jewish Congress (1917; reorg. 1922, 1938). Stephen Wise Congress House, 15 E. 84th St., New York, N. Y. 10028. Works to foster the creative religious and cultural survival of the Jewish people; to help Israel develop in peace, freedom, and security; to eliminate all forms of racial and religious bigotry; to advance civil rights, protect civil liberties, defend religious freedom, and safeguard the separation of Church and State. *Congress Bi-Weekly; Judaism.*

———— **Women's Division** (1933). Committed to the preservation and extension of the democratic way of life, and the unity and creative survival of the Jewish people throughout the world.

American Jewish Public Relations Society (1927). 515 Park Ave., New York, N. Y. 10022. Reemphasizes and advances professional status of workers in the public-relations field in Jewish communal service; upholds a professional code of ethics and standards; serves as a clearinghouse for employment opportunities; exchanges professional information and ideas; presents awards for excellence in professional attainments. *Handout.*

Anti-Defamation League of B'nai B'rith (1913). 315 Lexington Ave., New York, N. Y. 10016. Seeks to combat anti-Semitism and secure justice for all citizens alike; through public information, education and community action seeks to achieve greater democratic understanding among Americans. *ADL Bulletin; ADL Christian Friends' Bulletin; ADL Research Reports; Facts; Freedom* pamphlets; *Law; One Nation Library* series; *Rights.*

Association of Jewish Community Relations Workers (1950). 31 Union Sq. W., New York, N. Y. 10003. Aims to stimulate higher standards of professional practice in Jewish community relations; encourages research and training toward that end. Conducts educational programs and seminars; aims to encourage cooperation between community-relations workers and other areas of Jewish communal service. *Community Relations Papers.*

Commission on Social Action of Reform Judaism (1949) (under the auspices of the **Union of American Hebrew Congregations**). 838 Fifth Ave., New York, N. Y. 10021. Develops materials to assist Reform synagogues in setting up social-action programs relating the principles of Judaism to contemporary social problems; assists congregations in studying the moral and religious implications in social issues such as civil rights, civil liberties, Church-State relations; guides congregational social-action committees. *Issues of Conscience.*

Conference of Presidents of Major American Jewish Organizations (1954). 515 Park Ave., New York, N. Y. 10022. Serves as roof organization for twenty-two major American Jewish organizations, as a forum for exchange of information and as coordinating body for its members; deals with American-Israel affairs and problems affecting Jews in other lands.

Consultative Council of Jewish Organizations—CCJO (1946). 61 Broadway, New York, N. Y. 10006. A nongovernmental organization in consultative status with the UN, UNESCO, International Labor Organization, UNICEF, and the Council of Europe. Cooperates and consults with, advises and renders assistance to the Economic and Social Council of the United Nations on all problems relating to human rights and economic and related matters pertaining to Jews.

Coordinating Board of Jewish Organizations (1947). 1640 Rhode Island Ave. N.W., Washington, D. C. 20036. As an organization in consultative status with the Economic and Social Council of the United Nations, represents the three constituents (B'nai B'rith, the Board of Deputies of British Jews, and the South African Jewish Board of Deputies) in the appropriate United Nations bodies with respect to advancing and protecting the status, rights, and interests of Jews as well as related matters bearing upon the human rights of peoples.

Council of Jewish Organizations in Civil Service, Inc. (1948). 380 Lexington Ave., New York, N. Y. 10017. Supports merit system in civil service; promotes professional, social, and cultural interests of its members, cooperates with other organizations in promoting understanding and amity in the community. *CJO Digest.*

Jewish Labor Committee (1933). Atran Center for Jewish Culture, 25 E. 78th St., New York, N. Y. 10021. Seeks to combat anti-Semitism and racial and religious intolerance abroad and in the United States in cooperation with organized labor and other groups; sponsors educational and cultural programs relating to ethical and social values of Jewish labor and "Yiddishist" movements. *JLC News; Point of View.*

———— **Women's Division** (1947). Supports the general activities of the Jewish Labor Committee; maintains child-welfare program in Europe and Israel; participates in educational and cultural activities.

———— **Workmen's Circle Division** (1940). Promotes aims of and raises funds for the Jewish Labor Committee among the Workmen's Circle branches; conducts Yiddish educational and cultural activities.

Jewish War Veterans of the United States of America (1896). 1712 New Hampshire Ave. N.W., Washington, D. C. 20009. Seeks the maintenance of true allegiance to the United States of America; to combat bigotry and to prevent or stop defamation of Jews; to encourage the doctrine of universal liberty, equal rights, and full justice to all men; to cooperate with and support existing educational institutions and establish new ones; to foster the education of ex-servicemen, ex-servicewomen, and members in the ideals and principles of Americanism. *Headquarters Newsletter; Jewish Veteran; Legislative Newsletter.*

National Association of Jewish Center Workers (1918). 15 E. 26th St., New York, N. Y. 10010. Seeks to maintain and improve the standards, techniques, practices, scope, and public understanding of Jewish community center and kindred work. *Annual Conference Paper; Research Reporter; Viewpoints.*

National Bureau of Federated Jewish Women's Organizations. 1 Hemlock Ct., Maplewood, N. J. 07040. Links local women's federations, conferences, and leagues through the mutual exchange of ideas and experiences. *Bureau Facts.*

National Community Relations Advisory Council (1944). 55 W. 42nd St., New York, N. Y. 10036. Consultative, coordinating, and advisory council in Jewish community relations, seeking equal status and opportunity for Jews, full expression of their values as a group and their full participation in the general society. Works with national and local cooperating agencies to reach agreement on policies, strategies, and programs; to formulate and improve techniques, and to plan the most effective utilization of collective resources for common ends. *Guide to Program Planning for Jewish Community Relations.*

National Jewish Commission on Law and Public Affairs (1965). 119 Nassau St., New York, N. Y. 10038. Provides legal and legislative services to Orthodox Jewish organizations and individuals, without charge, by submitting briefs to courts and preparing other legal materials.

World Jewish Congress (1936; org. in U. S. 1939). Stephen Wise Congress House, 15 E. 84th St., New York, N. Y. 10028. Seeks to secure and safeguard the rights, status, and interests of Jews and Jewish communities throughout the world, within the framework of an international effort to secure human rights everywhere without discrimination; represents its affiliated organizations before the United Nations, the Organization of American States, the Council of Europe, and other governmental, intergovernmental, and international authorities on matters which are of concern to the Jewish people as a whole; promotes Jewish cultural interests before UNESCO; organizes Jewish communal life in countries of recent settlement; prepares and publishes surveys on contemporary Jewish problems. *Congress Digest; Folk und Velt;*

Information Series; Information Sheets; Institute of Jewish Affairs Reports; World Jewry.

Cultural

Alexander Kohut Memorial Foundation, Inc. (1915). 3080 Broadway, New York, N. Y. 10027. Furthers original research in the field of Jewish literature, especially Talmudic lore and lexicography.

American Academy for Jewish Research, Inc. (1920). 3080 Broadway, New York, N. Y. 10027. Encourages research by aiding scholars in need and by giving grants for the publication of scholarly works. *Proceedings of the American Academy for Jewish Research.*

American Biblical Encyclopedia Society (**American Torah Shelemah Committee**) (1930). 210 W. 91st St., New York, N. Y. 10024. Fosters Biblical-Talmudical research; sponsors and publishes *Torah Shelemah* (the Encyclopedia of Biblical Interpretation) and related publications; disseminates the teachings and values of the Bible.

American Histadrut Cultural Exchange Institute (1946). 33 E. 67th St., New York, N. Y. 10021. To establish a systematic flow of information between American and Israeli social scientists in the areas of labor, cooperatives, public health, public housing, adult education by means of joint seminars, exchange lectures, and lay participation.

American Jewish Historical Society (1892). 2 Thornton Rd., Waltham, Mass. 02154. Collects and publishes material on the history of the Jews in America; serves as an information center for inquiries on American Jewish history; maintains archives of original source material on American Jewish history. *American Jewish Historical Quarterly.*

American Jewish Institute, Inc. (1947). 250 W. 57th St., New York, N. Y. 10019. Seeks the advancement of Jewish knowledge and culture through the dissemination of data on Jews and Judaism, publication of essential literature, speakers and forum lecturers, and library services. *Current Jewish Thought.*

———— **Jewish Information Bureau, Inc.** (1932). Serves as clearinghouse of information on Jewish subjects. *Index.*

American Jewish Press Association (formerly **American Association of English Jewish Newspapers**) (1943). 390 Courtland St. N.E., Atlanta, Ga. 30303. Seeks the advancement of Jewish journalism, the attainment of highest literary standards for member papers, and the maintenance of an independent weekly press vital to Jewish life in America.

Association of Jewish Libraries (1966) (merger of **Jewish Librarians Association** and **Jewish Library Association**). Yeshiva Univ., 186th St. and Amsterdam Ave., New York, N. Y. 10033. Seeks to promote and improve services and professional standards in Jewish libraries; serves as a center for the dissemination of Jewish library information and guidance; promotes publication of literature in the field; encourages the establishment of Jewish libraries and the choice of Jewish librarianship as a vocation. *Bulletin of the Association of Jewish Libraries.*

Central Yiddish Culture Organization, Inc.–CYCO (1938). 25 E. 78th St., New York, N. Y. 10021. Promotes and publishes Yiddish books; distributes books from other Yiddish publishing houses throughout the world; publishes annual bibliographical and statistical register of Yiddish books and catalogues of new publications. *Zukunft.*

Conference on Jewish Social Studies, Inc. (formerly **Conference on Jewish Relations, Inc.**) (1933). 1841 Broadway, New York, N. Y. 10023. Engages in and supervises scientific studies and factual research with respect to sociological problems involving contemporary Jewish life. *Jewish Social Studies.*

Congress for Jewish Culture, Inc. (1948). 25 E. 78th St., New York, N. Y. 10021. Seeks to centralize and promote Jewish culture and cultural activities throughout the world, and to unify fund raising for these activities. *Bulletin fun Kultur Kongres; Leksicon fun der Nayer Yidisher Literatur; Zukunft.*

——— **World Bureau for Jewish Education** (1948). Promotes and coordinates the work of the Yiddish and Hebrew-Yiddish schools in the United States and abroad. *Bletter far Yiddisher Dertsiung; Bulletin fun Veltsenter far der Yiddisher Shul.*

Hebrew Arts School for Music and Dance (1952). 120 W. 16th St., New York, N. Y. 10011. Chartered by the Board of Regents, University of the State of New York. Provides children with training in instrumental and vocal skills as well as musicianship, combining orientation in Western music with musical heritage of the Jewish people. Adult Division offers instrumental, vocal, and dance classes, music workshop for teachers, and Hebrew Arts Chorale. *Notes and Quotes.*

Hebrew Culture Foundation (1955). 515 Park Ave., New York, N. Y. 10022. Sponsors the establishment of chairs of Judaic and Hebraic studies in institutions of higher learning in the United States.

Histadruth Ivrith of America (1916; reorg. 1922). 120 W. 16th St., New York, N. Y. 10011. Emphasizes the primacy of Hebrew in Jewish life, culture, and education; conducts Hebrew courses for adults; publishes Hebrew books; sponsors the Hebrew-speaking Massad camps, the Hebrew Academy, which serves as a channel for the exchange of research and study among academicians in the field of Hebrew culture, and the Noar Ivri, a youth group on campuses and in cities throughout the United States; sponsors cultural exchange with Israel through organized tours and ulpanim. *Annual of Hebrew Academy; Hadoar; Lamishpaha; Niv; Perakim.*

——— **Hebrew Arts Foundation** (1939). Promotes an understanding and appreciation of Hebrew culture in the American Jewish community through such educational projects as the Hebrew Arts School for Music and Dance, Hebrew Arts Teacher-Training School, and Hebrew Arts Music Publications.

Jewish Academy of Arts and Sciences, Inc. (1927). 46 W. 83rd St., New York, N. Y. 10024. Honors Jews distinguished in the arts and professions; encourages and publishes Jewish achievement in scholarship and the arts by its members and fellows. *Bulletin.*

Jewish Book Council of America (1940) (sponsored by **National Jewish Welfare Board**). 15 E. 26th St., New York, N. Y. 10010. Promotes knowledge of Jewish books. *In Jewish Bookland* (supplement to *JWB Circle*); *Jewish Book Annual.*

Jewish Liturgical Music Society of America (1963). 90-15 68th Ave., Forest Hills, N. Y. 11375. Seeks to advance the standards of American synagogue music; to collect, study, and perform old and new synagogue music; to provide an active musicological forum for all types of synagogue musicians of all branches of Jewish ritual observance. *Annual Bulletin.*

Jewish Museum (1904) (under the auspices of the **Jewish Theological Seminary of America**). 1109 Fifth Ave., New York, N. Y. 10028. Collects, identifies, and exhibits Jewish ceremonial objects of all eras; encourages the design and manufacture of contemporary ceremonial objects; exhibits contemporary art; sponsors lectures and other activities related to the museum's programs.

Jewish Publication Society of America (1888). 222 N. 15th St., Philadelphia, Pa. 19102. Publishes and disseminates books of Jewish interest on history, religion, and literature for the purpose of preserving the Jewish heritage and culture. *American Jewish Year Book* (with American Jewish Committee); *Annual Catalogue; JPS Bookmark.*

Leo Baeck Institute, Inc. (1955). 129 E. 73rd St., New York, N. Y. 10021. Engages in historical research, the presentation and publication of the history of German-speaking Jewry, and in the collection of books and manuscripts in this field; publishes monographs. *Bulletin; LBI News; Year Book.*

Louis and Esther LaMed Fund, Inc. (1939). 19420 Silvercrest, Southfield, Mich. 48075. Fosters the development of Jewish culture by initiating new projects and providing grants and scholarships.

Memorial Foundation for Jewish Culture, Inc. (1965). 215 Park Ave. S., New York, N. Y. 10003. Supports Jewish cultural and educational programs all over the world, in cooperation with universities and established scholarly organizations; conducts annual scholarship and fellowship program.

National Foundation for Jewish Culture (1960). 315 Park Ave. S., New York, N. Y. 10010. Provides consultation, guidance, and support to Jewish communities, organizations, educational and other institutions, and individuals for activities in the field of Jewish culture; awards fellowships and other grants to students preparing for careers in Jewish scholarship as well as to established scholars; encourages the teaching of Jewish studies in colleges and universities; serves as clearinghouse of information regarding American Jewish culture. *Bulletin.*

National Hebrew Culture Council (1952). 426 W. 58th St., New York, N. Y. 10019. Cultivates the study of Hebrew as a modern language in American public schools and colleges. *Bulletin.*

National Information Bureau for Jewish Life (1960). JFK Library for Minorities, Hotel Granada, Ashland Pl. and Lafayette Ave., Brooklyn, N. Y. 11217. Promotes a fuller understanding of the achievements and contributions made by Jews in the fields of American government, business, the performing arts, and sciences; endeavors to depict more dramatically the patriotic roles of Jews in reciting the history of America through a more significant identification of events with personalities and places. *Legislative Newsletter; President's Annual Report.*

National Jewish Music Council (1944) (sponsored by **National Jewish Welfare Board**). 15 E. 26th St., New York, N. Y. 10010. Promotes Jewish music activities nationally and encourages participation on a community basis. *Jewish Music Notes* (supplement to *JWB Circle*).

Society for the History of Czechoslovak Jews, Inc. (1961). 82-34 265th St., Floral Park, N. Y. 11004. Seeks to study the economic, religious, political, social, and cultural history of the Jews of Czechoslovakia and to disseminate information on the subject through the publication of books and pamphlets.

Yiddisher Kultur Farband—YKUF (1937). 189 Second Ave., New York, N. Y. 10003. Publishes a monthly magazine and books by contemporary and classical Jewish writers; conducts cultural forums and exhibits works by contemporary Jewish artists and materials of Jewish historical value. *Yiddishe Kultur.*

Yivo Institute for Jewish Research, Inc. (1925). 1048 Fifth Ave., New York, N. Y. 10028. Engages in Jewish social research; collects and preserves documentary and archival material pertaining to Jewish life, and publishes the results of its findings in books and periodicals. *Yedies fun Yivo—News of the Yivo; Yidishe Shprakh; Yivo Annual of Jewish Social Science; Yivo Bleter.*

Overseas aid

American Committee of OSE, Inc. (1940). 8 W. 40th St., New York, N. Y. 10018. Aims to improve the health of the Jewish people through education in health and hygiene, and by implementing medical and public-health programs, particularly for Jewish children, youth, and migrants. *American OSE Newsletter; Folksgesundt.*

American Council for Judaism Philanthropic Fund (1955). 201 E. 57th St., New York, N. Y. 10022. Maintains programs for the relief and re-settlement of Jewish refugees in Europe and the United States; sup-ports certain institutions in Israel which do not receive funds from United Jewish Appeal or other major fund-raising campaigns.

American Friends of the Alliance Israélite Universelle, Inc. (1946). 61 Broadway, New York, N. Y. 10006. Serves as liaison between Amer-ican Jewry and the educational work in behalf of Jewish children in Europe, Asia, and Africa; familiarizes the public in the United States and other countries in the Western hemisphere with the problems of the Sephardic-Oriental communities in the old world. *Alliance Review; Revista de la Alliance.*

American Jewish Joint Distribution Committee, Inc.—JDC (1914). 60 E. 42nd St., New York, N. Y. 10017. Organizes and administers welfare, medical, and rehabilitation programs and services and distributes funds for relief and reconstruction on behalf of needy Jews overseas. *JDC Annual Report; JDC Overseas Guide; Malben JDC; Statistical Abstract.*

American ORT Federation, Inc.—Organization for Rehabilitation through Training (1924). 222 Park Ave. S., New York, N. Y. 10003. Trains Jewish men and women in the technical trades and agriculture; organizes and maintains vocational-training schools throughout the world. *ORT Bulletin; ORT Yearbook.*

——— **American and European Friends of ORT** (1941). Promotes the ORT idea among Americans of European extraction; supports the Lit-ton Auto-Mechanics School in Jerusalem.

——— **American Labor ORT** (1937). Promotes ORT program of voca-tional training among Jews in labor unions, AFL-CIO, and the Work-men's Circle.

——— **Business and Professional ORT** (formerly **Young Men's and Women's ORT**) (1937). Organizes efforts of all unaffiliated Jews who, through their organizational and social activities, raise funds for the world programs of ORT. *Monthly Calendar; Year Book.*

——— **National ORT League** (1941). Promotes ORT idea among Jewish fraternal *landsmanshaften*, national and local organizations, congre-gations; helps to equip ORT abroad, especially in Israel.

——— **Women's American ORT** (1927). Represents and advances the program and philosophy of ORT among the women of the American Jewish community through membership and educational activities; supports materially the vocational-training operations of World ORT; contributes to the American Jewish community through participation in its authorized campaigns and through general education to help raise the level of Jewish consciousness among American Jewish women. *Highlights; Women's American ORT Reporter.*

A.R.I.F.—Association pour le Rétablissement des Institutions et Oeuvres Israélites en France, Inc. (1944). 119 E. 95th St., New York, N. Y. 10028. Helps Jewish religious and cultural institutions in France.

Conference on Jewish Material Claims against Germany, Inc. (1951). 215 Park Ave. S., New York, N. Y. 10003. Utilized funds received from the German Federal Republic under terms of an agreement with the Conference for the relief, rehabilitation, and resettlement of needy victims of Nazi persecution residing outside Israel.

Freeland League for Jewish Territorial Colonization (1933; in U. S. 1938). 200 W. 72nd St., New York, N. Y. 10023. Plans colonization in some sparsely populated territory for those who seek a home and cannot or will not go to Israel. *Freeland; Oyfn Shvel.*

Jewish Restitution Successor Organization (1948). 215 Park Ave. S., New York, N. Y. 10003. Acts to discover, claim, receive, and assist in the recovery of Jewish heirless or unclaimed property; to utilize such assets or to provide for their utilization for the relief, rehabilitation, and resettlement of surviving victims of Nazi persecution.

United Hias Service, Inc. (1884; reorg. 1954). 200 Park Ave. S., New York, N. Y. 10003. Worldwide organization with offices, affiliates, committees in the United States, Europe, North Africa, Latin America, Canada, Australia, Israel, and Hong Kong. Assists Jewish migrants in preimmigration planning, visa documentation, consular representation, initial adjustment, and reunion of families; carries on adjustment of status and naturalization programs; provides protective service for aliens and naturalized citizens; works in the United States through local community agencies for the integration of immigrants, conducts a planned program of resettlement for Jewish immigrants in Latin America; assists in locating persons abroad for friends and relatives in the United States and overseas; facilitates transmission of funds sent by friends and relatives to families in Israel. *Notes on Immigrant Care; Special Information Bulletin; Statistical Abstract.*

United Jewish Appeal, Inc. (1939). 1290 Avenue of the Americas, New York, N. Y. 10019. Nationwide fund-raising instrument for American Jewish Joint Distribution Committee, United Israel Appeal, and New York Association for New Americans. *Report to Members; Women's Division Record.*

Vaad Hatzala Rehabilitation Committee, Inc. (1939). 132 Nassau St., New York, N. Y. 10038. Assists in immigration and extends aid to needy rabbis, Talmudical scholars, and laymen in Europe and Israel; encourages publication of Talmudical works.

Religious, educational

Academy for Jewish Religion (1954; reorg. 1961). 112 E. 88th St., New York, N. Y. 10028. For training and ordination of rabbis, combining both students and teachers of the Reform, Conservative, and Orthodox groupings.

Agudas Israel World Organization (1912). 471 West End Ave., New York, N. Y. 10024. Represents the interests of Orthodox Jewry on the national and international scenes.

Agudath Israel of America, Inc. (1912). 5 Beekman St., New York, N. Y. 10038. Seeks to organize religious Jewry in the Orthodox spirit, and in that spirit to solve all problems facing Jewry in the United States, Israel, and the world over. *Dos Yiddishe Vort; Jewish Observer.*

——— **Children's Division—Pirchei Agudath Israel** (1925). Educates Orthodox Jewish children in the traditional Jewish way. *Darkeinu; Inter Talmud Torah Boys; Leaders' Guide.*

——— **Girls' Division—Bnos Agudath Israel** (1921). Educates Jewish girls to the realization of the historic nature of the Jewish people as the people of the Torah; to greater devotion to and understanding of the Torah; and to seek solutions to all the problems of the Jewish people in Israel in the spirit of the Torah. *Kol Basya; Kol Bnos.*

——— **Youth Division—Zeirei Agudath Israel** (1921). Educates Jewish youth to the realization of the historic nature of the Jewish people as the people of the Torah; to greater devotion to and understanding of the Torah; and to seek solutions to all the problems of the Jewish people in Israel in the spirit of the Torah. *Leaders' Guide.*

American Association for Jewish Education (1939). 101 Fifth Ave., New York, N. Y. 10003. Coordinates, promotes, and services Jewish education nationally through a community program and special projects. *Jewish Audio-Visual Review; Jewish Newsletter; Our Teacher; Pedagogic Reporter.*

——— **National Council on Adult Jewish Education** (1965). Aims to serve as a national clearinghouse for information in the field of Jewish education; to stimulate community interest in adult Jewish education; and to promote cooperative efforts among organizations engaged in adult Jewish education programs. *Information Bulletin on Adult Jewish Education.*

——— **National Council on Jewish Audio-Visual Materials** (1949). Offers information on and evaluates available audio-visual materials of Jewish interest; publishes these evaluations annually; offers advice and guidance in the planning of new audio-visual materials. *Jewish Audio-Visual Review.*

American Conference of Cantors (1953). 40 W. 68th St., New York, N. Y. 10023. Dedicated to bring to full awareness the best of Jewish musical traditions and to introduce new musical concepts of worship through commissions and competitions for contemporary Jewish composers. *American Conference of Cantors Bulletin.*

Association of Jewish Chaplains of the Armed Forces (1946). 15 E. 26th St., New York, N. Y. 10010. Seeks to promote fellowship among and advance the common interests of all chaplains in and out of the service.

Association of Orthodox Jewish Scientists (1947). 84 Fifth Ave., New York, N. Y. 10011. Seeks to promote the orientation of science within the framework of Orthodox Jewish tradition; to obtain and disseminate information relating to the interaction between the Jewish traditional way of life and scientific developments; to interest and assist Orthodox Jewish youth in the study of science; and to assist in the solution of problems pertaining to Orthodox Jews engaged or interested in scientific pursuits. *Intercom; Proceedings.*

B'nai B'rith Hillel Foundations, Inc. (1923). 1640 Rhode Island Ave. N.W., Washington, D. C. 20036. Provides a program of cultural, religious, educational, social, and counseling content to Jewish college and university students on two hundred sixty-five campuses in the United States, Australia, Canada, England, Israel, the Netherlands, South Africa, Switzerland, and Venezuela. *Clearing House;* Hillel "Little Book" series; *Hillel Newsletter; Inside Hillel.*

B'nai B'rith Youth Organization (1924). 1640 Rhode Island Ave. N.W., Washington, D. C. 20036. Helps Jewish youth achieve personal growth through a program of cultural, religious, interfaith, and intergroup, community service and recreational activities. *BBYO Advisor; Shofar.*

Brandeis Institute (1941). 1101 Pepper Tree Lane, Brandeis (Santa Susana), Calif. 93064. Maintains summer-camp institutes for college students and teen-agers and year-round adult weekend institutes to instill an appreciation of Jewish culture and spiritual heritage and to create a desire for active participation in the American Jewish community. *Brandeis News.*

Cantors Assembly of America (1947). 3080 Broadway, New York, N. Y. 10027. Seeks to unite all cantors who are adherents to traditional Judaism and who serve as full-time cantors in bona fide congregations; to conserve and promote the musical traditions of the Jews; to elevate the status of the cantorial profession. *Annual Proceedings; Journal of Synagogue Music.*

Central Conference of American Rabbis (1889). 790 Madison Ave., New York, N. Y. 10021. Seeks to conserve and promote Judaism and to disseminate its ideas in a liberal spirit. *CCAR Journal; CCAR Yearbook.*

Central Yeshivah Beth Joseph Rabbinical Seminary (in Europe 1891; in U. S. 1941). 1427 49th St., Brooklyn, N. Y. 11219. Maintains a school for the teaching of Orthodox rabbis and teachers. *Ohel Joseph.*

College of Jewish Studies (1924). 72 E. 11th St., Chicago, Ill. 60605. Provides professional training for Hebrew-school, Sunday-school, and nursery-school teachers and Temple administration; grants degrees as bachelor, master, and doctor of Hebrew literature. *Perspectives in Jewish Learning.*

Commission on Status of Jewish War Orphans in Europe. American Section (1945). 47 Beekman St., New York, N. Y. 10038. Seeks to restore Jewish orphans to their former families and to the Jewish faith and environment.

Dropsie College for Hebrew and Cognate Learning (1907). Broad and York Sts., Philadelphia, Pa. 19132. A nonsectarian institution under Jewish auspices; trains scholars in higher Jewish and Semitic learning; offers only postgraduate degrees. *Jewish Quarterly Review.*

———— **Alumni Association** (1925). Fosters Dropsie College interests.

Federation of Jewish Student Organizations (1937). 420 Riverside Dr., New York, N. Y. 10027. Coordinates and acts as clearinghouse for the activities of Jewish student societies in the private universities of New York City.

Gratz College (1895). 10th St. and Tabor Rd., Philadelphia, Pa. 19141. Prepares teachers for religious schools; provides studies in Judaica and Hebraica; maintains a Hebrew high school and a school of observation and practice; provides Jewish studies for adults; community services to Jewish schools of all learnings. *College Bulletin; Gratz-Chats; Telem Yearbook; What's New.*

Hebrew Teachers College (1921). 43 Hawes St., Brookline, Mass. 02146. Educates men and women to teach, conduct, and supervise Jewish schools; to advance Hebrew scholarship and make available to the general public a constructive knowledge of the Jewish spiritual creations and contributions to the world's culture and progress. *Hebrew Teachers College Bulletin.*

Hebrew Theological College (1922). 7135 N. Carpenter Rd., Skokie, Ill. 60076. Maintains Hebrew Theological College, College of Liberal Arts, Teachers' Institute, Graduate School, and College of Advanced Hebrew Studies; offers studies in higher Jewish learning along traditional lines, trains rabbis, teachers, and religious functionaries; confers advanced degrees in Hebrew literature. *Hebrew Theological College Newsletter.*

———— **Liberal Arts College** (1959). Offers two-year junior college course to students of the Hebrew Theological College.

Hebrew Union College—Jewish Institute of Religion of Cincinnati, New York and Los Angeles (1875; 1922; merged 1950; 1954). 3101 Clifton Ave., Cincinnati, Ohio 45220; 40 W. 68th St., New York, N. Y. 10023; 8745 Appian Way, Los Angeles, Calif. 90046. Prepares students for rabbinate, cantorate, religious-school teaching, community service; promotes Jewish studies; maintains libraries and a museum; offers Ph.D. and D.H.L. degrees in graduate department; maintains Hebrew Union College Biblical and Archaeological School in Jerusalem. *American Jewish Archives; Hebrew Union College Annual; HUC–JIR Catalogue; Studies in Bibliography and Booklore.*

———— **Alumni Association** (1889; merged 1949). 1110 Dickinson St., Springfield, Mass. 01108. Aims to promote the welfare of Judaism, of the Hebrew Union College–Jewish Institute of Religion, and of its graduates. *Alumni Bulletin.*

———— **American Jewish Archives** (1947). 3101 Clifton Ave., Cincinnati, Ohio 45220. Assembles, classifies, and preserves Jewish Americana manuscript material and photographs. *American Jewish Archives.*

———— **American Jewish Periodical Center** (1956). Microfilms Jewish newspapers and periodicals, and makes them available on interlibrary loan. *Jewish Newspapers and Periodicals on Microfilm.*

———— **Hebrew Union College Museum** (1913). Collects and preserves art related to Judaism; makes available traveling exhibits of Jewish ceremonial art and extensive pictorial archive on Judaica and Jewish art.

———— **Schools of Education and Sacred Music** (1947). 40 W. 68th St., New York, N. Y. 10023. Trains cantors and music personnel for Orthodox, Conservative, and Reform congregations; trains principals, teachers, and directors of religious education for Reform religious schools.

Herzliah Hebrew Teachers Institute and Jewish Teachers Seminary and People's University (1967) (merger of **Herzliah Hebrew Teachers Institute** and **Jewish Teachers Seminary and People's University**). 515 Park Ave., New York, N. Y. 10022. Hebrew-Yiddish teachers college and school for advanced Jewish studies training men and women for Jewish teaching profession, research, and community service; confers undergraduate and graduate degrees. *Newsletter.*

———— **Graduate School** (1965). Institution for advanced study and research in Jewish culture, history, and the contemporary Jewish community leading to doctor of Jewish literature in Hebrew language and literature, Jewish social studies, or Yiddish language and literature.

———— **Herzliah Hebrew Teachers Institute** (1921). Offers four-year college program in Judaica and teacher education for nationally accredited Hebrew teachers diploma, serving Jewish community without denominational distinction. *Alumni News; Hed Herzliah.*

———— **Jewish Music School** (1964). Offers studies in traditional and contemporary music, religious, Yiddish, secular, and Hebraic; offers diploma and degree programs in Jewish music education, cantorial art, or choral conducting.

——— Jewish Teachers Seminary (1918). Four-year college program toward bachelor of Jewish literature and Yiddish teachers certificate. *Der Seminarist.*

Jewish Ministers Cantors Association of America, Inc. (1910). 236 Second Ave., New York, N. Y. 10003. Seeks to perpetuate the cantorial profession in its traditional form; provides assistance to needy cantors; maintains library of cantorial and Hebrew music. *Kol Lakol Bulletin.*

Jewish Reconstructionist Foundation, Inc. (1940). 15 W. 86th St., New York, N. Y. 10024. Dedicated to the advancement of Judaism as an evolving religious civilization, to the upbuilding of Eretz Yisrael as the spiritual center of the Jewish people, and to the furtherance of universal freedom, justice, and peace; sponsors the Reconstructionist Press. *Reconstructionist.*

——— Federation of Reconstructionist Congregations and Fellowships (1954). Committed to the philosophy and program of the Reconstructionist movement. *Newsletter.*

Jewish Teachers Association—Morim (1926). 1182 Broadway, New York, N. Y. 10001. Promotes the religious, social, and moral welfare of children; provides a program of professional, cultural, and social activities for its members; cooperates with other organizations for the promotion of goodwill and understanding. *JTA Bulletin.*

Jewish Teachers Seminary and People's University (1918). 515 Park Ave., New York, N. Y. 10022. Only Hebrew-Yiddish seminary in America training men and women for Jewish teaching profession, research, and community service, conferring the degrees of bachelor of Jewish literature, bachelor of Jewish pedagogy, and doctor of Jewish literature; also offers courses in Jewish music, camp counseling, and trains trilingual secretaries for Jewish communal service. *Seminary News.*

Jewish Theological Seminary of America (1886; reorg. 1902). 3080 Broadway, New York, N. Y. 10027. Organized for the perpetuation of the tenets of the Jewish religion, the cultivation of Hebrew literature, the pursuit of biblical and archaeological research, the advancement of Jewish scholarship, the maintenance of a library, and the training of rabbis and teachers; maintains the Ramah camps. *Seminary Progress.*

——— American Jewish History Center (1953). Promotes the writing of regional and local Jewish history in the context of the total American and Jewish experience. *Regional History Series.*

——— Department of Radio and Television (1944). Produces radio and TV programs expressing the Jewish tradition in its broadest sense with emphasis on the universal human situation: "Eternal Light," a weekly radio program; "Words We Live By," a summer discussion series; eleven "Eternal Light" TV programs produced in cooperation with the National Broadcasting Company, and eleven "Directions" TV programs in cooperation with the American Broadcasting Company; distributes program scripts and related reading lists.

—— **Institute for Religious and Social Studies** (New York City 1938; Chicago 1944; Boston 1945). Serves as a scholarly and scientific fellowship of clergymen and other religious teachers who desire authoritative information regarding some of the basic issues now confronting spiritually-minded men.

—— **Maxwell Abbell Research Institute in Rabbinics** (1951). Fosters research in Rabbinics; prepares scientific editions of rabbinic works.

—— **Teachers Institute—Seminary College of Jewish Studies** (1909). Offers complete college program in Judaica and teacher education for the degrees of bachelor of Hebrew literature or bachelor of religious education.

—— **University of Judaism, West Coast School of JTS** (1947). 6525 Sunset Blvd., Los Angeles, Calif. 90028. Serves as a center of research and study for graduate students; trains teachers for Jewish schools; serves as a center for adult Jewish studies; promotes the arts through its fine-arts school, art gallery, and theater; through its Earl Warren Institute on Ethics and Human Relations, promotes study of relationship of law to ethics in Western civilization. *Maarav; Register; University News.*

League for Safeguarding the Fixity of the Sabbath (1929). 122 W. 76th St., New York, N. Y. 10023.

Mesivta Yeshiva Rabbi Chaim Berlin Rabbinical Academy (1905). 1593 Coney Island Ave., Brooklyn, N. Y. 11230. Maintains elementary division in the Hebrew and English departments, lower Hebrew division and Mesivta high schools, rabbinical academy, and postgraduate school for advanced studies in Talmud and other branches of rabbinic scholarship; maintains Camp Morris, a summer study camp. *Igud News Letter; Kol Torah; Kuntrasim; Merchav; Shofar.*

Mirrer Yeshiva Central Institute (in Poland 1817; in U. S. 1947). 1791-5 Ocean Parkway, Brooklyn, N. Y. 11223. Maintains rabbinical college, postgraduate school for Talmudic research, accredited high school, and Kollel and Sephardic divisions; dedicated to the dissemination of Torah scholarship in the community and abroad; engages in rescue and rehabilitation of scholars overseas.

National Association of Hillel Directors (1949). c/o Adelphi Univ., Garden City, N. Y. 11530. Seeks to facilitate exchange of experience and opinions among Hillel directors and counselors and promote the welfare of the B'nai B'rith Hillel Foundations and their professional personnel.

National Bar Mitzvah Club (1962). 515 Park Ave., New York, N. Y. 10022. Seeks to enhance meaning of the Bar and Bat Mitzvah ceremonies; to further Jewish education, and to develop personal identification with Israel, through a three-year program which culminates in a summer study tour of Israel. *Israel Calling.*

National Committee for Furtherance of Jewish Education (1940). 824 Eastern Parkway, Brooklyn, N. Y. 11213. Seeks to disseminate the ideals of Torah-true education among the youth of America. *Panorama.*

National Council for Jewish Education (1926). 101 Fifth Ave., New York, N. Y. 10003. Seeks to further the cause of Jewish education in America; to raise professional standards and practices; to promote the welfare and growth of Jewish educational workers; and to improve and strengthen Jewish life and culture generally. *Jewish Education; Sheviley Hachinuch.*

National Council for Torah Education of Mizrachi-Hapoel Hamizrachi (Religious Zionists of America) (1939). 200 Park Ave., New York, N. Y. 10003. Organizes and supervises Yeshivot and Talmud Torahs; prepares and trains teachers; publishes textbooks and educational materials; conducts a placement agency for Hebrew schools; sponsors the National Association for Orthodox Educators. *Bitaon Chemed; Yeshiva Education.*

National Council for Young Israel (1912). 3 W. 16th St., New York, N. Y. 10011. Maintains a program of spiritual, cultural, social, and communal activity toward the advancement and perpetuation of traditional, Torah-true Judaism; seeks to instill in American youth an understanding and appreciation of the ethical and spiritual values of Judaism. Sponsors kosher dining clubs and fraternity houses and an Israel program. *Armed Forces Viewpoint; Newsletter; Women's League Manuals; Young Israel Viewpoint; Youth Department Manuals.*

———— **Armed Forces Bureau** (1939). Advises and counsels the inductees into the Armed Forces with regard to Sabbath observance, Kashrut, and Orthodox behavior; supplies kosher food packages, religious items, and so forth, to servicemen; aids veterans in readjusting to civilian life. *Armed Forces Viewpoint; Guide for the Orthodox Servicemen.*

———— **Employment Bureau** (1914). Helps secure employment, particularly for Sabbath observers; offers vocational guidance. *Viewpoint.*

———— **Eretz Israel Division** (1926). Promotes Young Israel synagogues and youth work in all synagogues in Israel; sponsors Young Israel Mogan Hayeled Home in B'nai Brak.

———— **Institute for Jewish Studies** (1947). Introduces students to Jewish learning and knowledge; helps form adult branch schools; aids Young Israel synagogues in their adult-education programs. *Bulletin.*

———— **Intercollegiate Council—Young Adults** (1950). Provides a program of spiritual, cultural, social, and communal activity for the advancement and perpetuation of traditional Judaism among American college youth; serves as a clearinghouse for information on religious traditions and maintains kosher dining clubs and dorms on college campuses. *Voice.*

National Council of Beth Jacob Schools, Inc. (1943). 115 Heyward St., Brooklyn, N. Y. 11206. Operates Orthodox all-day schools and a summer camp for girls.

National Federation of Hebrew Teachers and Principals (1944). 120 W. 16th St., New York, N. Y. 10011. Seeks to organize Hebrew teachers nationally in affiliated groups and associations; to improve the professional status of Hebrew teachers in the United States; to intensify the study of Hebrew language and literature in Jewish educational institutions. *Yediot Hamerkaz.*

National Jewish Information Service for the Propagation of Judaism, Inc. (1960). 6412½ W. Olympic Blvd., Los Angeles, Calif. 90048. Seeks to convert Gentiles to Judaism and revert Jews to Judaism; maintains College for Jewish Ambassadors for the training of Jewish missionaries and the Correspondence Academy of Judaism for instruction of Judaism through the mail. *Voice of Judaism.*

Ner Israel Rabbinical College (1933). 4411 Garrison Blvd., Baltimore, Md. 21215. Provides full secular and religious high-school training; prepares students for the rabbinate and the field of Hebrew education; maintains a graduate school which grants the degrees of master and doctor of Talmudic law; maintains a branch, the Ner Israel Yeshiva College, in Toronto, Ontario, Canada. *Catalogue.*

P'eylim-American Yeshiva Student Union (1951). 3 W. 16th St., New York, N. Y. 10011. Aids and sponsors pioneer work by American graduate teachers and rabbis in new villages and towns in Israel; does religious, organizational, and educational work and counseling among new immigrant youth; maintains summer camps for poor immigrant youth in Israel; belongs to worldwide P'eylim movement which has groups in Argentina, Brazil, England, Belgium, the Netherlands, Switzerland, France, and Israel; engages in relief work among Algerian immigrants in France, assisting them to relocate and to reestablish a strong Jewish community life. *P'eylim Reporter.*

Rabbinical Alliance of America (Igud Harabbanim) (1944). 156 Fifth Ave., New York, N. Y. 10011. Seeks to promulgate the cause of Torah-true Judaism through an organized rabbinate that is consistently Orthodox; seeks to elevate the position of Orthodox rabbis nationally, and to defend the welfare of Jews the world over. *Perspective.*

Rabbinical Assembly (1900). 3080 Broadway, New York, N. Y. 10027. Seeks to promote Conservative Judaism and to foster the spirit of fellowship and cooperation among the rabbis and other Jewish scholars; cooperates with the Jewish Theological Seminary of America and the

United Synagogue of America. *Conservative Judaism; Proceedings of the Rabbinical Assembly; Rabbinical Assembly Manual.*

Rabbinical College of Telshe, Inc. (1941). 28400 Euclid Ave., Wickliffe, Ohio 44092. College for higher learning, specializing in Talmudic studies and Rabbinics; maintains a preparatory academy including secular high school, a postgraduate department, a teachers' training school, and a teachers' seminary for women. *Pri Etz Chaim—Journal for Talmudic Research; Semi-annual News Bulletin.*

Rabbinical Council of America, Inc. (1923; reorg. 1935). 84 Fifth Ave., New York, N. Y. 10011. Promotes Orthodox Judaism in the community; supports institutions for study of Torah; stimulates creation of new traditional agencies. *Hadorom; Record; Sermon Manual; Tradition.*

Research Institute of Religious Jewry, Inc. (1941; reorg. 1954). 1133 Broadway, New York, N. Y. 10010. Engages in research and publishes studies concerning the situation of religious Jewry internationally.

Sholem Aleichem Folk Institute, Inc. (1918). 41 Union Sq., New York, N. Y. 10003. Aims to imbue children with Jewish values through teaching Yiddish language and literature, Hebrew and the Bible, Jewish history, significance of Jewish holidays, folk and choral singing, and about Jewish life in America and Israel; offers preparation for Bar Mitzvah. *Kinder Journal; Sholem Aleichem Parent's Bulletin.*

Society of Friends of the Touro Synagogue, National Historic Shrine, Inc. (1948). 85 Touro St., Newport, R. I. 02840. Assists in the maintenance of the Touro Synagogue as a national historic site. *Touro Synagogue Brochure.*

Synagogue Council of America (1926). 235 Fifth Ave., New York, N. Y. 10016. Acts as the overall Jewish religious representative body of Orthodox, Conservative, and Reform Judaism in the United States vis-à-vis the Catholic and Protestant national agencies, the United States government, and the United Nations. *Synagogue Council of American Highlights.*

Torah Umesorah—National Society for Hebrew Day Schools (1944). 156 Fifth Ave., New York, N. Y. 10010. Establishes and services Hebrew day schools throughout the United States and Canada; conducts teacher-training institutes, seminars, and workshops for in-service training of teachers; publishes textbooks and supplementary reading material. Conducts educational research and has established Fryer Foundation for research in ethics and character education. Supervises federal-aid programs for Hebrew day schools throughout the United States. *Hamenahel; Jewish Parent; Olomeinu—Our World.*

———— **National Association of Hebrew Day School Administrators** (1960). Seeks to further aims of day-school Torah education through more efficient administration and coordination.

———— **National Association of Hebrew Day School Parent-Teacher Associations** (1948). Acts as a clearinghouse and service agency to PTA's of Hebrew day schools; organizes parent-education courses and sets up programs for individual PTA's. *Day School PTA Handbook; Jewish Parent; National Program Notes; PTA National Bulletin.*

———— **National Conference of Yeshiva Principals** (1956). A professional organization of primary and secondary Yeshivah day-school principals which seeks to make Yeshivah day-school education more effective. *Hamenahel.*

———— **National Yeshiva Teachers Board of License** (1953). Issues licenses to qualified teachers in Torah education.

———— **Samuel A. Fryer Educational Research Foundation** (1966). Serves to improve and strengthen the *middos* (ethics) programs in the three hundred thirty Hebrew day schools in the United States through basic research, experimentation, and demonstration for the development of new definitions, instructional texts, and various teacher-training programs.

Union of American Hebrew Congregations (1873). 838 Fifth Ave., New York, N. Y. 10021. Serves as the central congregational body of Reform Judaism in the Western hemisphere; serves its approximately six hundred sixty-four affiliated temples and membership with religious, educational, cultural, and administrative programs. *Dimensions in American Judaism; Keeping Posted; The Voice.*

———— **Jewish Chautauqua Society, Inc.** (1893) (sponsored by **National Federation of Temple Brotherhoods**). Disseminates authoritative knowledge about Jews and Judaism to universities and colleges in the United States, Canada, and abroad, to Christian church summer camps and institutes, and on television and radio.

———— **National Association of Temple Administrators** (1941). Fosters Reform Judaism; prepares and disseminates administrative information and procedures to member synagogues of UAHC; provides and encourages proper and adequate training of professional synagogue executives; formulates and establishes professional ideals and standards for the synagogue executive. *NATA Quarterly.*

———— **National Association of Temple Educators** (1955). Comprises four hundred sixty Reform temple brotherhoods in the United States, Australia, Canada, and the Union of South Africa; fosters religious, social, and cultural activities; sponsors the Jewish Chautauqua Society. *Brotherhood.*

———— **National Federation of Temple Sisterhoods** (1913). Cooperates with UAHC in the execution of its aims; publishes sisterhood study and program aids, "Sisterhood Topics" in *Dimensions in American Judaism; President's Packet.*

———— National Federation of Temple Youth (1939). Seeks to train Reform Jewish youth in the values of the synagogue and their application to daily life through service to the community and congregation; sponsors study programs, cultural activities, summer-camp sessions and leadership institutes, overseas tours and work programs, an international student exchange program, and community-service projects within the United States. *NFTYMES.*

———— and Conference of American Rabbis: Commission on Jewish Education (1923). Develops courses of study and prepares textbooks and other teaching aids. *Dimensions in American Judaism; Keeping Posted.*

———— and Central Conference of American Rabbis: Commission on Synagogue Administration (1962). Assists congregations in management, finance, building maintenance, design construction, and art aspects of synagogues; maintains the Synagogue Architectural Library consisting of photos, slides, and plans of contemporary and older synagogue buildings. *Synagogue Service.*

———— Central Conference of American Rabbis, and National Association of Temple Administrators: Board of Certification for Temple Administrators (1963). Seeks to establish standards of qualification for Temple administrators and to further opportunities for their training; conducts examinations of candidates and issues certificates of fellowship. *Information Bulletin.*

Union of Orthodox Jewish Congregations of America (1898). 84 Fifth Ave., New York, N. Y. 10011. Serves as the national central body of Orthodox synagogues; provides educational, religious, and organizational guidance to congregations, youth groups, and men's clubs; represents the Orthodox Jewish community in relationship to governmental and civic bodies, and the general Jewish community; conducts the national authoritative U Kashruth certification service. *Jewish Action; Jewish Life; U Kosher Products Directory.*

———— National Conference of Synagogue Youth (1954). Guides and services the youth programs of America's Orthodox congregations through more than three hundred fifty chapters; conducts summer-camp sessions, national and regional conclaves, conventions, encampments, and leader's seminars. *Holiday Manual Series; Jewish Youth Monthly; Keeping Posted with NCSY; Leadership Manual; Mitsvos Maaoiyos Series.*

———— National Organization of Orthodox Synagogue Administrators (1964). Seeks to utilize the experience and knowledge of the synagogue administrator in establishing norms for Orthodox congregations.

———— Women's Branch (1923). Seeks to spread knowledge for the understanding and practice of Orthodox Judaism, and to unite all Orthodox women, and their synagogal organizations into one homogeneous group. *Care and Treatment of Speakers; Chapter Guide; Hachodesh; Holiday Publications; Judy and Jeremy Play and Learn Library; Leaders and Their Training; Manual for Sisterhoods; Newsletter; Speaker's Manual.*

Union of Orthodox Rabbis of the United States and Canada, Inc. (Agudus Harabonim) (1902). 235 Broadway, New York, N. Y. 10002. Seeks to foster and promote Torah-true Judaism in America; assists in the establishment and maintenance of Yeshivot in the United States; maintains committee on marriage and divorce to aid individuals with marital difficulties; disseminates knowledge of traditional Jewish rites and practices and regulates synagogal structure and worship.

Union of Sephardic Congregations, Inc. (1929). 8 W. 70th St., New York, N. Y. 10023. Promotes the religious interests of Sephardic Jews; prepares and distributes Sephardic prayer books and provides religious leaders for Sephardic congregations.

United Lubavitcher Yeshivoth (1940). Bedford Ave. and Dean St., Brooklyn, N. Y. 11216. Organizes and operates Yeshivot in the United States and Israel.

United Synagogue of America (1913). 3080 Broadway, New York, N. Y. 10027. Association of Conservative congregations in the United States and Canada seeking to assert and establish loyalty to the Torah and its historical expositions and to further the observance of the Sabbath and the dietary laws; to preserve in the Service the reference to Israel's past and the hopes of Israel's restoration; to maintain the traditional character of the liturgy, with Hebrew as the language of prayer; to foster Jewish religious life in the home, as expressed in traditional observances; to encourage the establishment of Jewish religious schools; services affiliated congregations and their auxiliaries, in all their religious, educational, cultural, and administrative needs. *Adult Jewish Education; Our Age; Outlook; Synagogue School; Torch; United Synagogue Review.*

———— **Atid, College Age Organization** (1960). 218 E. 70th St., New York, N. Y. 10021. Offers opportunities to the Jewish college-age adult to continue with Judaism; offers a college-age program of Conservative movement, Torah study institute, and encampments; serves congregations and its groups. *Kadimah; Kol Atid; Reaching Your Collegiate Congregant.*

———— **Commission on Jewish Education** (c. 1930). Promotes higher educational standards in Conservative congregational schools and publishes material for the advancement of their educational program. *Igeret; In Your Hands; Our Age; Synagogue School; Your Child.*

———— **Educators Assembly** (1951). Promotes, extends, and strengthens the program of Jewish education on all levels in the community in consonance with the philosophy of the Conservative movement; fosters higher professional standards for school administrators functioning under congregational auspices. *Annual Proceedings; Annual Yearbook; Facts and Trends; Personnel.*

————— National Academy for Adult Jewish Studies (1940). Provides guidance and information on resources, courses, and other projects in adult Jewish education; prepares and publishes pamphlets, syllabi, study guides, and texts for use in adult-education programs; distributes El-Am edition of *Talmud*, kinescopes of "Eternal Light" TV programs on Jewish subjects. *Adult Jewish Education.*

————— National Association of Synagogue Administrators (1948). 3080 Broadway, New York, N. Y. 10027. Aids congregations affiliated with the United Synagogue of America to further aims of Conservative Judaism through more effective administration; advances professional standards and promotes new methods in administration; cooperates in United Synagogue placement services and administrative surveys. *The Synagogue Administrator.*

————— National Federation of Jewish Men's Clubs, Inc. (1929). Maintains a national organization of synagogue-affiliated Jewish men's clubs or brotherhoods dedicated to the ideals and principles of traditional Judaism; seeks to help build a dynamic Judaism through social, cultural, and religious activities and programs. *Torch.*

————— National Women's League (1918). Parent body of sisterhoods of the Conservative movement in the United States, Canada, Puerto Rico, and Mexico; provides affiliates with a program covering religious, educational, social-action, leadership training, Israel affairs, and community projects, and publishes books of Jewish interest; contributes in support of Jewish Theological Seminary and construction of Mathilde Schechter Residence Hall for Women. *Women's League Outlook.*

————— United Synagogue Youth (1951). 218 E. 70th St., New York, N. Y. 10021. Seeks to develop a program for strengthening identification with Judaism, based on the personality development needs and interests of the adolescent. *Advisor's Newsletter; BSB Progress Report; News and Views.*

West Coast Talmudical Seminary Mesivta Beth Medrosh Elyon, Inc. (1953). 851 N. Kings Rd., Los Angeles, Calif. 90069. Provides facilities for intensive Torah education as well as Orthodox rabbinical training on the West Coast; conducts an accredited college preparatory high school combined with a full program of Torah-Talmudic training and a graduate Talmudical division on a college level.

World Union for Progressive Judaism, Ltd. (1926). 838 Fifth Ave., New York, N. Y. 10021. Promotes and coordinates efforts of Reform, Liberal, and Progressive congregations throughout the world; sponsors

seminaries and schools; organizes international conferences of Liberal Jews. *International Conference Reports; News and Views.*
—— **American Board** (1926). Seeks to further the work of the World Union for Progressive Judaism in the United States. *News and Views.*
Yavne Hebrew Theological Seminary, Inc. (1924). 510 Dahill Rd., Brooklyn, N. Y. 11218. School for higher Jewish learning; trains rabbis and teachers as Jewish leaders for American Jewish communities; maintains branch in Jerusalem for Higher Jewish Education-Machan Maharshal and for an exchange-student program. *Yavne Newsletter.*
Yavneh, National Religious Jewish Students Association (1960). 84 Fifth Ave., New York, N. Y. 10011. Seeks to promote religious Jewish education on the college campus, to facilitate full observance of halakhic Judaism, to integrate the insights gained in college students with the values and knowledge of Judaism, to unite Jewish college students everywhere, and to become a force for the dissemination of Torah Judaism in the Jewish community. *Jewish Collegiate Observer; Yavneh Review; Yavneh Studies.*
Yeshiva University (1886). 186th St. and Amsterdam Ave., New York, N. Y. 10033. America's oldest and largest university under Jewish auspices, providing undergraduate, graduate, and professional studies in the arts and sciences and Jewish learning leading to eighteen different degrees and diplomas; with four teaching centers in Manhattan and the Bronx, it offers preparation for careers in education, social work, the rabbinate, medicine, mathematics, physics, psychology, and schools for boys and girls. Yeshiva College for Men, Stern College for Women, Erna Michael College of Hebraic Studies, James Striar School of General Jewish Studies, separate Teachers Institutes for Men and Women, Rabbi Isaac Elchanan Theological Seminary, Bernard Revel Graduate School, Harry Fischel School for Higher Jewish Studies, Cantorial Training Institute, Albert Einstein College of Medicine, Sue Golding Graduate School of Humanities and Social Sciences, Graduate School of Education, Belfer Graduate School of Science. Auxiliary services and special projects include Community Service Division, West Coast Institute of Jewish Studies, Pictorial Mathematics, Psychological and Audio-Visual centers, Israel Institute, National Institute of Mental Health Project, and Teaching Fellowship Program. *Bulletin of General Information; Horeb; Mathematica Press; Scripta Mathematica; Studies in Judaica; Studies in Torah Judaism; Sura; Talpioth.*
—— **Department of Alumni Activities.** Seeks to foster a close allegiance of alumni to their alma mater, by maintaining ties with all alumni and servicing the following associations: Albert Einstein College of Medicine Alumni (1959); Bernard Revel Graduate School of Alumni Association (1955); Rabbinic Alumni Association (1944);

Ferkauf Graduate School of Education Alumni Association (1959); James Striar School of General Jewish Studies Alumni (1963); Stern College Alumnae Association (1958); Wurzweiler School of Social Work Alumni Association (1959); Teachers Institutes Associated Alumni (1942); Yeshiva College Alumni Association (1934). *AECOM Alumni News; Chavrusa; Jewish Social Work Forum; Midrashon; Stern College Alumnae Alon; Wurzweiler School of Social Work Alumni Association Newsletter; Yeshiva College Alumni Bulletin; Yeshiva University Alumni Review.*
——— Society of the Founders of the Albert Einstein College of Medicine (1953). 55 Fifth Ave., New York, N. Y. 10003. To perpetuate the founders' and their families' interests in an association with the Albert Einstein College of Medicine.
——— Women's Organization (1928). Supports Yeshiva University's national scholarship program for students training for the rabbinate, medicine, and other professions, and its expansion and development program. *YUWO Bulletin.*
Yeshivath Chachmey Lublin (1942). 14430 Sherwood, Detroit, Mich. 48237. A religious school and rabbinical seminary. Originally brought students, faculty, and their families from Europe.
Yeshivath Torah Vodaath and Mesivta Rabbinical Seminary (1918). 425 E. 9th St., Brooklyn, N. Y. 11218. Offers Hebrew and secular education from elementary level through rabbinical ordination and postgraduate work; maintains a teachers institute, religious-functionaries department, and a community-service bureau; maintains a dormitory and a nonprofit summer-camp program for boys. *Chronicle; Mesivta Vanguard; Thought of the Week; Torah Vodaath News.*
——— Alumni Association (1941). Promotes social and cultural ties between the alumni and the school; supports the school through fund raising; offers vocational guidance to students; operates Camp Torah Vodaath; and sponsors research fellowship program. *Alumni News; Annual Journal; Hamesivta Torah Periodical.*
——— Beth Medrosh Elyon (Academy of Higher Learning and Research) (1943). 73 Main St., Monsey, N. Y. 10952. Provides postgraduate courses and research work in higher Jewish studies; offers scholarships and fellowships. *Annual Journal.*

Social, mutual benefit

American Federation of Jews from Central Europe, Inc. (1942). 1241 Broadway, New York, N. Y. 10001. Seeks to safeguard the rights and interests of American Jews of Central European descent, especially in reference to restitution and indemnification; sponsors research and publications on the history of Central European Jewry; sponsors a social program for needy Nazi victims in the United States in cooperation with United Help, Inc. *Annual Report; Information Bulletins.*

American Veterans of Israel (1949). 110-23 63rd Ave., Forest Hills, N. Y. 11375. Seeks to maintain contact among American veterans of Israel's War of Independence and the Aliya Bet volunteers who ran the British blockade of Palestine; to foster contacts between America and Israel in pursuance of the ideals that motivated its original members. *Newsletter.*

Association of Yugoslav Jews in the United States, Inc. (1940). 247 W. 99th St., New York, N. Y. 10025. Assists Jews of Yugoslav origin and charitable organizations. *Bulletin.*

Bnai Zion—The American Fraternal Zionist Organization (1908). 50 W. 57th St., New York, N. Y. 10019. Fosters principles of Americanism, fraternalism, and Zionism; fosters Hebrew culture; offers life insurance, Blue Cross hospitalization, and other benefits to its members; sponsors settlements, youth centers, medical clinics, and the John F. Kennedy evaluation center for the mentally retarded in Israel. *Bnai Zion Voice.*

Brith Abraham (1887). 37 E. 7th St., New York, N. Y. 10003. Fosters brotherhood, Jewish ideals and traditions, and concern for welfare of Jews; provides fraternal benefits to members; supports camps for underprivileged children and senior citizens. *Beacon.*

Brith Sholom (1905). 121 S. Broad St., Philadelphia, Pa. 19107. Devoted to service to community, civic welfare, and defense of minority rights. *Brith Sholom News; Community Relations Digest; Peace Tidings.*

Central Sephardic Jewish Community of America (1940). 225 W. 34th St., New York, N. Y. 10001. Seeks to maintain contact between United States Sephardic organizations and Sephardic communities overseas; to raise funds for scholarships for outstanding students in Israel and the United States.

Farband—Labor Zionist Order (1913). 575 Sixth Ave., New York, N. Y. 10011. Seeks to enhance Jewish life, culture, and education in the United States and Canada; supports the State of Israel in keeping with the ideals of labor Zionism; supports liberal causes in the United States and throughout the world; provides members and families with low-cost fraternal benefits. *Farband News.*

Free Sons of Israel (1849). 257 W. 93rd St., New York, N. Y. 10025. Benevolent, fraternal. *Free Son Reporter.*

Hebrew Veterans of the War with Spain (1898). 87-71 94th St., Woodhaven, N. Y. 11421. Social and fraternal; seeks to fight bigotry.

International Jewish Labor Bund (incorporating **World Coordinating Committee of the Bund**) (1897; reorg. 1947). 25 E. 78th St., New York, N. Y. 10021. Coordinates activities of the Bund organizations throughout the world and represents them in the Socialist International; spreads the ideas of Jewish Socialism as formulated by the Jewish Labor Bund; publishes pamphlets and periodicals on world problems, Jewish life, socialist theory and policy, and on the history, activities, and ideology of the Jewish Labor Bund. *Bulletin* (U. S.); *Perspectives* (U. S.); *Unzer Tsait* (U. S.); *Foroys* (Mexico); *Lebns-Fragn* (Israel); *Unser Gedank* (Argentina); *Unser Gedank* (Australia); *Unser Shtimme* (France).

Jewish Peace Fellowship (1941). 251 W. 100th St., New York, N. Y. 10025. Unites those who believe that Jewish ideals and experience provide inspiration for a pacifist philosophy of life; supports efforts to resolve human conflict through pacific methods. *Tidings.*

Jewish Socialist Verband of America (1921). 175 E. Broadway, New York, N. Y. 10002. Promotes the ideals of social democracy among the Yiddish-speaking working people of America. *Der Wecker.*

Mu Sigma Fraternity, Inc. (1906). 140 Nassau St., New York, N. Y. 10038. Sponsors a spirit of brotherhood and fraternalism through organizational, social, and athletic activities; fosters programs of community service. *Lamp.*

Progressive Order of the West (1896). 705 Chestnut St., St. Louis, Mo. 63101. Benevolent. *Progressive Order of the West Bulletin.*

Sephardic Jewish Brotherhood of America, Inc. (1915). 116 E. 169th St., Bronx, N. Y. 10452. Promotes the industrial, social, educational, and religious welfare of its members. *Sephardic Brother.*

United Order True Sister, Inc. (1846). 150 W. 85th St., New York, N. Y. 10024. Philanthropic; fraternal; cancer treatment. *Echo.*

United Rumanian Jews of America, Inc. (1909). 31 Union Sq. W., New York, N. Y. 10003. Seeks to further, defend, and protect the interests of the Jews in Romania; to work for their civil and political emancipation and for their economic rehabilitation; and to represent and further the interests of Romanian Jews in the United States. *Record.*

Workmen's Circle (1900). 175 E. Broadway, New York, N. Y. 10002. Benevolent aid, cultural; educational; fraternal. *Culture and Education; Der Freind; Kinder Zeitung; Workmen's Circle Call.*

————— **English-Speaking Division** (1927). Representing the second and third generations of the Workmen's Circle, it fosters social, cultural, and educational activities within the framework of a Jewish labor and fraternal organization. *Circleite; Point of View* (with Jewish Labor Committee); *Workmen's Circle Call.*

————— **Young Circle League—Youth Section** (1927). Engages children in the program of the Workmen's Circle. *Triangle.*

World Sephardi Federation. American Branch (1951). 152 W. 42nd St., New York, N. Y. 10036. Seeks to promote religious and cultural interests of Sephardic communities throughout the world, assists them morally and materially; assists Sephardim who wish to settle in Israel. *Judaisme Sephardi; Kol-Sepharad.*

Social welfare

American Jewish Correctional Chaplains Associations, Inc. (formerly **National Council of Jewish Prison Chaplains**) (1937). 10 E. 73rd St., New York, N. Y. 10021. (Cooperating with the New York Board of Rabbis and Jewish Family Service.) Seeks to provide a more articulate expression for Jewish chaplains serving the needs of Jewish men and women in penal and correctional institutions, and to make their ministry more effective through exchange of views and active cooperation.

American Jewish Society for Service, Inc. (1950). 120 Broadway, New York, N. Y. 10005. Operates work camps for teen-agers under Jewish auspices and direction.

American Medical Center at Denver (formerly **Jewish Consumptives' Relief Society**) (1904; merged with **Ex-Patients' Sanitarium**, 1966). P. O. Box 537, Spivak, Colo. 80214. Free, nonsectarian, nationwide, medical, and treatment center for cancer, tuberculosis, and chest diseases, clinical and basic cancer research. *Bulletin; For Your Information.*

———— **National Council of Auxiliaries** (1904; reorg. 1936). Provides support for the American Medical Center program by disseminating information, fund raising, and acting as admissions officers for patients from a specific chapter area. *Bulletin.*

Baron de Hirsch Fund, Inc. (1891). 386 Park Ave. S., New York, N. Y. 10016. Supports the Jewish Agricultural Society and aids Jewish immigrants and their descendants to obtain an education and employment by giving grants to agencies active in this field.

B'nai B'rith (1843). 1640 Rhode Island Ave. N.W., Washington, D. C. 20036. Jewish service organization engaged in educational and philanthropic programs in such fields as youth work, community relations, adult Jewish education, aid to Israel, international affairs, service to veterans, and citizenship and civic projects. *ADL Bulletin; B'nai B'rith Women's World; Jewish Heritage; National Jewish Monthly; Shofar.*

———— **Vocational Service** (1938). Conducts occupational and educational research and engages in a broad publications program; also provides direct guidance services through professionally conducted regional offices in many population centers of the country. *B'nai B'rith Vocational Service Newsletter; Catalogue of Publications; Counselor's Information Service.*

———— **Women** (1919). Seeks to advance the highest interests of humanity through cultural, educational, religious, and civic-service programs;

promotes the preservation of Jewish values and responsible community leadership. *B'nai B'rith Women's World.*

City of Hope—A National Medical Center under Jewish Auspicies (1913). 208 W. 8th St., Los Angeles, Calif. 90014. As pilot medical center, seeks to influence medicine and science everywhere, affecting treatment, research, and medical education in catastrophic diseases; is responsible for over five hundred original findings, admits patients suffering from cancer, leukemia, heart and chest diseases, tuberculosis, and blood disorders on a completely free, nonsectarian basis, from all parts of the nation. *Pilot; President's Newsletter; Torchbearer.*

Conference Committee of National Jewish Women's Organizations (1925). 15 E. 84th St., New York, N. Y. 10028. Promotes interorganizational understanding and goodwill among the cooperating organizations; brings to attention of constituent organizations matters of Jewish communal interest for their consideration and possible action.

Council of Jewish Federations and Welfare Funds, Inc. (1932). 315 Park Ave. S., New York, N. Y. 10010. Provides national and regional services to two hundred twenty associated Jewish community organizations in the United States and Canada, aiding in fund raising, community organization, health and welfare planning, personnel recruitment, and public relations programs. *Jewish Communal Services; Jewish Community; Programs and Finances; Yearbook of Jewish Social Services.*

Deborah Hospital (1922). Brown Mills, N. J. 08015. Provides free care for tuberculosis and corrective surgery in cardiac and pulmonary diseases or disabilities.

Hope Center for the Retarded, Inc. (1965). 2250 E. 16th Ave., Denver, Colo. 80206. Provides services for trainable mentally retarded individuals who are not accepted in public schools but who do not require institutionalization. *Hope Center Newsletter Monthly.*

International Council of Jewish Women (1912). 13435 North Park Blvd., Cleveland, Ohio 44118. Seeks to promote cooperation among Jewish women and to advance their status in Jewish and secular law; guides affiliates in developing Jewish education, social-welfare, and volunteer-training programs; acts as consultant to ECOSOC and UNICEF. *Newsletter.*

International Council on Jewish Social and Welfare Services (1961). 200 Park Ave. S., New York, N. Y. 10003. Information and consultative agency for international organizations and governments on Jewish and general social and welfare services, including health, care of the aged, child care, vocational training, migration, resettlement, economic and cultural rehabilitation.

Jewish Agricultural Society, Inc. (1900). 386 Park Ave. S., New York, N. Y. 10016. Helps Jews to settle on farms and aids those already settled in rural communities.

Jewish Braille Institute of America, Inc. (1931). 48 E. 74th St., New York, N. Y. 10021. Seeks to serve the religious and cultural needs of the Jewish blind by publishing prayer books in Hebrew and English Braille; providing Yiddish, Hebrew, and English records for Jewish blind throughout the world who cannot read Braille; maintaining worldwide free Braille lending library. *Jewish Braille Review.*

Jewish Conciliation Board of America, Inc. (1920). 225 Broadway, New York, N. Y. 10007. Adjusts and conciliates disputes involving Jewish individuals and organizations; social-service department settles family problems privately.

Jewish National Home for Asthmatic Children at Denver and Children's Asthma Research Institute and Hospital (1907). 3447 W. 19th Ave., Denver, Colo. 80204. Provides free, national and nonsectarian treatment and care of intractable asthmatic children, integrates clinical and basic research to find causes of asthma and other allergic diseases. *News from the Home Front.*

Jewish Occupational Council, Inc. (1939). 150 Fifth Ave., New York, N. Y. 10011. Acts as clearinghouse and advisory body for all Jewish agencies having programs in vocational guidance, job placement, vocational rehabilitation and training, sheltered workshops, and occupational research. *Program and Information Bulletin; Vocational Abstracts.*

Leo N. Levi Memorial National Arthritis Hospital (1914) (sponsored by B'nai B'rith). 300 Prospect Ave., Hot Springs National Park, Ark. 71901. Maintains a nonprofit national arthritis medical center for men, women, and children regardless of race, creed, or ability to pay.

National Association of Jewish Family, Children's and Health Services (1965). 15 Park Row, New York, N. Y. 10038. Seeks to define the role of and provide a discussion forum for administrators and practitioners in Jewish family, child, and health agencies; formulates programs for the Annual Forum of the National Conference of Jewish Communal Service. *Newsletter.*

National Conference of Jewish Communal Service (1899). 31 Union Sq. W., New York, N. Y. 10003. Discusses problems and developments in the various fields of Jewish communal service on a professional level. *Journal of Jewish Communal Service.*

National Council of Jewish Prison Chaplains, Inc. See **American Jewish Correctional Chaplains Associations, Inc.**

National Council of Jewish Women, Inc. (1893). 1 W. 47th St., New York, N. Y. 10036. Furthers human welfare in the Jewish and general communities, locally, nationally, and internationally; sponsors integrated program of education, service, and social action to provide essential services and to advance human welfare and the democratic way of life. *Council Woman.*

National Jewish Committee on Scouting (1926). Boy Scouts of America, New Brunswick, N. J. 08903. Seeks to stimulate Boy Scout activity among Jewish boys. *Ner Tamid Guide for Boy Scouts and Explorers; Scouting in Synagogues and Centers.*

National Jewish Hospital at Denver (1899). 3800 E. Colfax Ave., Denver, Colo. 80206. Offers nationwide, free, nonsectarian care for needy tuberculosis and chest disease patients, including heart ailments, amenable to surgery; conducts research, education, and rehabilitation. *News of the National.*

National Jewish Welfare Board (1917). 15 E. 26th St., New York, N. Y. 10010. Serves as national association of Jewish community centers and YM–YWHAs: authorized by the government to provide for the religious and welfare needs of Jews in the armed services and in veterans hospitals; member of USO, World Federation of YMHAs and Jewish Community Centers; sponsors Jewish Book Council, JWB Lecture Bureau, National Jewish Music Council. (Represents American Jewish community in USO.) *JWB Circle; Jewish Community Center Program Aids; JWB Year Book.*

———— **Commission on Jewish Chaplaincy** (1940). Represents Reform, Orthodox, and Conservative rabbinates on matters relating to chaplaincy; the only government-recognized agency authorized to recruit, ecclesiastically endorse, and serve all Jewish military chaplains. *Jewish Chaplain.*

World Federation of YMHAs and Jewish Community Centers (1947). 145 E. 32nd St., New York, N. Y. 10016. Fosters YM–YWHA and Jewish community center movement in all countries where feasible and desirable; provides opportunities for training and interchange of ideas and experiences among the national organizations. *Ys of the World.*

Zionist and pro-Israel

American Committee for Boy's Town Jerusalem (1949). 165 W. 46th St., New York, N. Y. 10036. Aids in providing a comprehensive program of academic, vocational, and religious training for more than six hundred Israeli teen-agers. Arranges for faculty transfers to Israel. *Boys Town Jerusalem News.*

American Committee for the Weizmann Institute of Science, Inc. (1944). 515 Park Ave., New York, N. Y. 10022. Supports the Weizmann Institute of Science in Rehovoth, Israel.

American Friends of Religious Freedom in Israel (formerly **League for Religious Freedom in Israel**) (1963). 213 Arcadia Ave., Uniondale, N. Y. 11553. Dedicated to the principle of full religious freedom in Israel through separation of Church and State; seeks to promote public knowledge of religious coercion in Israel, to advise leaders of Israel of critical importance of separation of Church and State, and to rally American Jewish support behind the forces in Israel fighting for this principle.

American Friends of the Hebrew University (1931). 11 E. 69th St., New York, N. Y. 10021. Fosters the growth, development, and maintenance of the Hebrew University of Jerusalem, collects funds and conducts program of information throughout the United States, interpreting the work of the Hebrew University and its significance; under auspices of America Israel University Program, administers American student program and arranges exchange professorships in the United States and Israel. Created and recruited support for Truman International Center for World Peace. *AFHU Bulletin.*

American-Israel Cultural Foundation, Inc. (formerly **American Fund for Israel Institutions, Inc.**) (1939). 4 E. 54th St., New York, N. Y. 10022. Supports projects in fifty Israeli cultural institutions, including the Israel Philharmonic Orchestra, the Habimah theater, and the Inbal dancers, Israel Museum, and Academies of Music; sponsors cultural exchange between the United States and Israel; awards scholarships in all Israel and abroad. *Tarbut.*

American Israel Public Affairs Committee (formerly **American Zionist Committee for Public Affairs**) (1954). 1341 G St. N.W., Washington, D. C. 20005. Conducts public action bearing upon relations with governmental authorities with a view to maintaining and improving friendship and goodwill between the United States and Israel.

American-Israeli Lighthouse, Inc. (1928; reorg. 1955). 30 E. 60th St., New York, N. Y. 10022. Provides education and rehabilitation for the blind in Israel with the purpose of effecting their social and vocational integration into the seeing community. *Tower.*

American Jewish League for Israel (1957). 30 E. 42nd St., New York, N. Y. 10017. Seeks to unite all those who, notwithstanding differing philosophies of Jewish life, are committed to the historical ideals of Zionism; works, independently of class or party, for the welfare of Israel as a whole. *Bulletin of the American Jewish League for Israel.*

American Physicians Fellowship, Inc., for the Israel Medical Association (1950). 1622 Beacon St., Brookline, Mass. 02146. Seeks to foster and aid medical progress in the State of Israel; secures fellowships for selected Israeli physicians and arranges lectureships in Israel by prominent American physicians; aids the Israel Medical Association financially and also contributes medical books, periodicals, instruments, and drugs. *APF News.*

American Red Mogen Dovid for Israel, Inc. (1941). 50 W. 57th St., New York, N. Y. 10019. Purchases medical supplies and ambulances in support of the Mogen Dovid Adom, the Israeli Red Cross Service; helps maintain blood banks and first-aid stations in Israel. *Action.*

American Society for Technion-Israel Institute of Technology, Inc. (1940). 1000 Fifth Ave., New York, N. Y. 10028. Provides financial and technical assistance to Technion-Israel Institute of Technology. *Technion; Technion Yearbook.*

American Zionist Council (1939; reorg. 1949). 515 Park Ave., New York, N. Y. 10022. Coordinating and public-relations arm of the nine national organizations which comprise the American Zionist movement— The American Jewish League for Israel, Bnai Zion, Hadassah, Religious Zionists of America, Labor Zionist Movement, Progressive Zionist League—Hashomer Hatzair, United Labor Zionist Party, United Zionist Revisionists of America, and the Zionist Organization of America; seeks to conduct a Zionist program designed to create a greater appreciation of Jewish culture within the American Jewish community in furtherance of the continuity of Jewish life and the spiritual centrality of Israel as the Jewish homeland.

American Zionist Youth Foundation, Inc. (1963). 515 Park Ave., New York, N. Y. 10022. Sponsors programs for American youth in Israel; Israel Summer Institute, Summer in Kibbutz, Institute for Leaders from Abroad, Year Workshops. *Hora; Maccabean.*

————— **American Zionist Youth Council** (1951). Acts as spokesman and representative of Zionist youth in interpreting Israel to the youth of America; represents, coordinates, and implements activities of the ten Zionist youth movements in the United States: Betar, B'nai Akiva, Dror Hechalutz Hatzair, Ichud Habonim, Hashomer Hatzair, Junior Hadassah, Masada of ZOA, Mizrachi Hatzair, Student Zionist Organization, Young Judaea.

————— **Student Zionist Organization** (1954). Seeks to interpret Israel and Zionism to college students on American and Canadian campuses; carries out action programs in Israel and America. *Echo; SZO Action Bulletin; Zionist Collegiate.*

Americans for a Music Library in Israel (1950). 2451 N. Sacramento Ave., Chicago, Ill. 60647. Seeks to promote and render assistance to musical education in the State of Israel. *AMLI News.*

Ampal—American Israel Corporation (1942). 17 E. 71st St., New York, N. Y. 10021. Seeks to develop and maintain close ties between the United States and Israel through investment, shipping, and export-import business. *Annual Report.*

Bar-Ilan University in Israel (1952). 641 Lexington Ave., New York, N. Y. 10022. Supports growth and development of the American-chartered Bar-Ilan University in Israel; administers American student program and arranges exchange professorships in the United States and Israel. *Bar-Ilan News.*

Dror Hechalutz Hatzair (1948). 2091 Broadway, New York, N. Y. 10023. Fosters Zionist program for youth; maintains leadership seminars and work-study programs in Israel, summer camps in the United States. *Alon Dror; Igeret Dror.*

Federated Council of Israel Institutions—FCII (1940). 38 Park Row, New York, N. Y. 10038. Central fund-raising organization for independent religious, educational, and welfare institutions in Israel not maintained by the UJA and its affiliated agencies. *Annual Financial Report.*

Hadassah, the Women's Zionist Organization of America, Inc. (1912). 65 E. 52nd St., New York, N. Y. 10022. In America helps interpret Israel to the American people; provides basic Jewish education as a background for intelligent and creative Jewish living in America; carries on a project for American Jewish youth; in Israel supports Hadassah's countrywide medical and public-health system, its child-welfare and vocational-education projects; provides maintenance and education for youth newcomers through Youth Aliyah; participates in a program of Jewish National Fund land purchase and reclamation. *Hadassah Headlines; Hadassah Magazine.*

—————**Junior Hadassah, Youth Division** (1920). Conducts education program for creative Jewish living, and public-relations program to help interpret Israel to American youth; in Israel aids varied projects in the fields of nurses' training, child rescue and rehabilitation, land redemption through Jewish National Fund and the kibbutz. *Junior Hadassah World.*

Hagdud Haivri League, Inc. (American Veterans of the Jewish Legion) (1929). 426 W. 58th St., New York, N. Y. 10019. Seeks to uphold the ideals of the Jewish Legion which fought for the liberation of Palestine in World War I and to assist legion veterans in settling in Israel; maintains the Legion House (Bet Hagdudim) which serves as a memorial to the Jewish Legion and as a cultural center for Israeli youth.

Hashomer Hatzair, Inc. 112 Fourth Ave., New York, N. Y. 10003. Affiliation of three principal groups, with different dates of origin.

—————**Americans for Progressive Israel** (1950). Seeks American community support for Israel kibbutz movement; raises funds for Israel, particularly for the pioneer movement; encourages and supports *aliyah* to Israel; participates in the fight for Jewish rights. *Israel Horizons.*

—————**Progressive Zionist League** (1947). Encourages support for a Socialist-Zionist approach to Jewish living in Israel and the United

States; raises funds for Israel, particularly for the pioneer movement; seeks to fight for Jewish rights everywhere.

————— **Zionist Youth Organization** (1925). 150 Fifth Ave., New York, N. Y. 10011. Educates youth toward an understanding of their Jewishness and modern Israel; provides agricultural training for kibbutz life in Israel. *Lamadrich; Niv Haboger; Young Guard.*

Hatzaad Harishon (1964). 515 Park Ave., New York, N. Y. 10022. An organization of white and black Jews concerned with the religious and cultural education of the black Jewish community in the New York area. Seeks to foster better relations between white and black Jews; sponsors and supplies leaders for youth and children's groups; conducts adult-education classes and workshops, and sponsors social activities with other Jewish groups. *Hatzaad Harishon Educational Bulletin; Hatzaad Harishon Newsletter.*

Hebrew University–Technion Joint Maintenance Appeal (1954). 11 E. 69th St., New York, N. Y. 10021. Conducts maintenance campaigns formerly conducted by the American Friends of the Hebrew University and the American Technion Society; participates in community campaigns throughout the United States, with the exception of New York City.

Histadrut. See **National Committee for Labor Israel.**

Israel Music Foundation (1948). 731 Broadway, New York, N. Y. 10003. Supports and stimulates the growth of music in Israel and disseminates recorded Israeli music in the United States and throughout the world.

Jewish Agency–American Section (1929). 515 Park Ave., New York, N. Y. 10022. Represents in the United States the Executive of the Jewish Agency for Israel, Jerusalem, which is recognized by the State of Israel as the authorized agency to work in Israel for development and colonization, the absorption and settlement of immigrants, and the coordination of activities of Jewish institutions and associations operating in these fields. Conducts a worldwide Hebrew cultural program which includes special seminars and pedagogic manuals; disperses information about, and assists in research projects concerning Israel; promotes, publishes, and distributes books, periodicals, and pamphlets concerning developments in Israel, Zionism, and Jewish history; sponsors a radio program "Panoramas de Israel" in the Latin-American countries. *Israel Digest; Israel y America Latina.*

————— **Zionist Archives and Library** (1939). Serves as an archive and information service for material on Israel, Palestine, the Middle East, and Zionism.

Jewish National Fund, Inc.–Keren Kayemeth LeIsrael (1910). 42 E. 69th St., New York, N. Y. 10021. Raises funds to purchase, develop, and reclaim the land of Israel. *Land and Life.*

Keren-Or, Inc. (Jerusalem Institutions for the Blind) (1958). 1133 Broadway, New York, N. Y. 10010. Raises funds for the maintenance of the Jewish Institutions for the Blind in Israel.

Labor Zionist Organization of America—Poale Zion (1905). 200 Park Ave. S., New York, N. Y. 10003. Aids in building the State of Israel as a cooperative commonwealth and national and spiritual home of the Jewish people. Seeks to establish a democratic society throughout the world based on individual freedom and equality and social justice; to strengthen Jewish education and communal life and further the democratization of Jewish community organization in the United States; to promote the welfare of Jews in all lands. *Jewish Frontier; LZOA News Letter; Yiddisher Kemfer.*

——— **Ichud Habonim Labor Zionist Youth** (1935). Fosters identification with pioneering Israel; stimulates study of Jewish life, history, and culture; sponsors community-action projects and ten summer camps in the United States and Canada, work-study programs and three groups for cooperative settlements in Israel. *Furrows; Haboneh; Hamaapil; Hamadrich; Iggeret L'chaverim.*

——— **League for Labor Israel** (1938; reorg. 1961). Conducts labor Zionist educational, youth, and cultural activities in the American Jewish community and promotes educational travel to Israel.

——— **Pioneer Women, the Women's Labor Zionist Organization of America, Inc.** (1925). 29 E. 22nd St., New York, N. Y. 10010. Provides in cooperation with Moetzet Hapoalot, Working Women's Council of Israel, almost half of social services in nearly one thousand installations in Israel where forty thousand women, youths, and children are educated yearly for constructive citizenship. In America, promotes Jewish culture; participates in American civic life. *Pioneer Woman.*

Mizrachi Women's Organization of America, Inc. (1925). 242 Park Ave. S., New York, N. Y. 10003. Conducts social-service, child-care, and vocational-education programs in Israel in an environment of traditional Judaism; promotes cultural activities for the purpose of disseminating Zionist ideals and strengthening traditional Judaism in America. *Mizrachi Woman.*

National Committee for Labor Israel (Israel Histadrut Campaign) (1923). 33 E. 67th St., New York, N. Y. 10021. Provides funds for the social-welfare, vocational, health, and cultural institutions and other services of Histadrut to benefit workers and immigrants and to assist in the integration of newcomers as productive citizens in Israel; promotes an understanding of the aims and achievements of Israel labor among Jews and non-Jews in America. *Histadrut Foto-News.*

——— **American Trade Union Council for Histadrut** (1947). Carries on educational activities among American and Canadian trade unions for health, educational, and welfare activities of the Histadrut in Israel. *Histadrut Foto-News.*

National Young Judaea (1909). 116 W. 14th St., New York, N. Y. 10011. Seeks to orient American Jewish youth to its Zionist heritage and to the service of the Jewish people in America and Israel. *Judaean Leaves; Leaders' Bulletin; Senior; Young Judaean.*

Palestine Foundation Fund (Keren Hayesod), Inc. (1922). 515 Park Ave., New York, N. Y. 10022.

Palestine Symphonic Choir Project (1938). 3143 Central Ave., Indianapolis, Ind. 46205. Seeks to settle cantors and Jewish artists and their families in Israel, and to establish a center for festivals of biblical musical dramas.

Pec Israel Economic Corporation (formerly **Palestine Economic Corporation**) (1926). 500 Fifth Ave., New York, N. Y. 10036. Fosters economic development of Israel on a formally business basis through investments. *Annual Report.*

Poale Agudath Israel of America, Inc. (1948). 147 W. 42nd St., New York, N. Y. 10036. Aims to educate youth to become Orthodox *halutzim;* supports *kibbutzim,* trade schools, and children's homes in Israel. *Achdut; PAI Views; Yediot PAI.*

———— **Ezra-Irgun Hanoar Hachareidi** (1953). Youth organization of the Poale Agudath Israel; aims to give children a religious and agricultural education in order to prepare them to join or build kibbutzim in Israel. *Alonim La Gola.*

———— **League of Religious Settlements—Chever Hakibbutzim** (1951). Seeks to further religious *aliyah* to Israel and to establish homes and kibbutzim for new immigrants.

———— **Women's Division** (1948). 1480 Broadway, New York, N. Y. 10036. Assists Poale Agudath Israel to build and support children's homes, kindergartens, and trade schools in Israel. *Yediot PAI.*

Rassco Israel Corporation and Rassco Financial Corporation (1950). 535 Madison Ave., New York, N. Y. 10022. Has developed investment opportunities in Israel and continues to strengthen economic ties between the United States of America and Israel through its ten thousand investors. *Rassco Reporter.*

Religious Zionists of America. 200 Park Ave. S., New York, N. Y. 10003.

———— **B'nei Akiva of North America** (1934). Seeks to interest youth in religious labor Zionism through self-realization in Israel; maintains training farms, leadership seminars, and summer camps. *Akivon; Hamevaser; La Madrich; Ohalenu; Pinkas.*

———— **Mizrachi-Hapoel Hamizrachi** (1909; merged 1957). Establishes and maintains schools and Yeshivot in Israel and works for its economic and social development; promotes close relations between religious Jewry of the United States and Israel; supports all-day schools and a maximum program of religious education in the United States. *Jewish Horizon; Mizrachi Weg; Or Hamizrach.*

———— Mizrachi Hatzair (1952) (cosponsored by **Mizrachi Women's Organization of America** and **Religious Zionists of America**). A religious Zionist youth organization seeking to instill a love for Torah Judaism and Israel; encourages and educates toward religious *aliyah* as the way to rebuild Israel as a religious society. *Daf l'Chanich; Daf la Madrich; Inyanim.*

———— Mizrachi Palestine Fund (1928). Serves as central financial instrument for work of the Mizrachi-Hapoel Hamizrachi in Israel.

———— Women's Organization of Hapoel Hamizrachi (1948). 45 E. 17th St., New York, N. Y. 10003. Affiliated with the National Religious Women's Organization in Israel; helps support and maintain over one hundred sixty kindergartens, nurseries, girl's homes, and vocational schools. *Menorah Bulletin.*

Society of Israel Philatelists (1948). 40-67 61st St., Woodside, N. Y. 11377. Promotes interest in and knowledge of all phases of Israel philately through sponsorship of chapters and research groups, maintenance of a philatelic library, and support of public and private exhibitions. *Israel Philatelist.*

State of Israel Bond Organization (1951). 215 Park Ave. S., New York, N. Y. 10003. Seeks to provide large-scale investment funds for the economic development of the State of Israel through the sale of State of Israel bonds in the United States, Canada, Latin America, and Western Europe. *B.I.G. News.*

Theodor Herzl Foundation (1954). 515 Park Ave., New York, N. Y. 10022. *Midstream.*

———— Herzl Press. Publishes books and pamphlets on modern Israel, Zionism, and general Jewish subjects.

———— Theodor Herzl Institute. Conducts a Zionist adult-education program through classes, lectures, and academic conferences. Operates Ulpan Center and serves the community through an Extension Service. *Herzl Institute Bulletin.*

United Charity Institutions of Jerusalem, Inc. (1903). 132 Nassau St., New York, N. Y. 10038. Raises funds for the maintenance of eighteen institutions in Israel; helps to support schools, hospitals, kitchens, clinics, and dispensaries.

United Israel Appeal, Inc. (1927). 515 Park Ave., New York, N. Y. 10022. Raises funds for Israel's immigration and resettlement program; chief beneficiary of the United Jewish Appeal campaign; fund-raising representative of all Zionist parties as well as the Palestine Foundation Fund and the Jewish Agency.

United Labor Zionist Party (Achdut Haavodah-Poale Zion) (1920; reorg. 1947). 305 Broadway, New York, N. Y. 10007. Supports a democratic socialist order in Israel and seeks to strengthen the Jewish labor movement in the United States. *Undzer Veg.*

United States Committee for Sports in Israel, Inc. (1950). 147 W. 42nd St., New York, N. Y. 10036. Promotes physical fitness and increased sports participation of world Jewry; sponsors U. S. Maccabiah Team; a junior Maccabiah development program; special projects for coaches, facilities, and training of Israeli personnel; and the Orde Wingate Institute for Physical Education. *Newsletter.*

Women's League for Israel, Inc. (1928). 1860 Broadway, New York, N. Y. 10023. Provides shelter, vocational training, and social-adjustment services for young women newcomers to Israel through its five homes; has built student center, women's dormitories, and cafeteria, and endowed a chair in sociology at the Hebrew University in Jerusalem. *Israel Newsletter; Women's League for Israel News Bulletin.*

World Confederation of General Zionists (1946; reorg. 1958). 30 E. 42nd St., New York, N. Y. 10017. General Zionist world organization, not identified with any political party in Israel; promotes Zionist education and strives for an Israel-centered creative Jewish survival in the diaspora; in Israel encourages private and collective industry and agriculture. *Zionist Information Views.*

Zebulum Israel Seafaring Society, Inc. (1946). 31 Union Sq. W., New York, N. Y. 10016. Encourages sea-mindedness among Jewish youth; assists training schools for seamen in Israel; assists disabled, sick, and old seamen.

Zionist Organization of America (1897). 145 E. 32nd St., New York, N. Y. 10016. Seeks to safeguard the integrity and independence of Israel as a free and democratic commonwealth by means consistent with the laws of the United States; to assist in the economic development of Israel; and to strengthen Jewish sentiment and consciousness as a people and promote its cultural creativity. *American Zionist; House News; Zionist Information Service; ZOA in Review; ZOA Masada Bulletin.*

CANADA

Canada-Israel Securities, Ltd. (1953). 1255 University St., Montreal 2, Que. Parent organization for the sale of State of Israel Bonds in Canada. *Israel Bond Digest.*

Canadian Association for Labor Israel (Histadrut) (1944). 5780 Decelles Ave., Montreal 26, Que. Raises funds for Histadrut institutions, supporting their rehabilitation tasks throughout Canada. *Histadrut Foto-news; Histadrut Review.*

Canadian Friends of the Alliance Israélite Universelle (1958). 5020 Mac-Donald Ave., Montreal 29, Que. Serves as liaison between Canadian Jewry and the Alliance Israélite Universelle.

Canadian Friends of the Hebrew University (1945). 1475 Metcalfe St., Montreal 2, Que. Represents and publishes for the Hebrew University in Canada; serves as fund-raising arm for the university in Canada. *Family Endowment Photo News; Scopus Supplement.*

Canadian Jewish Congress (1919; reorg. 1934). 493 Sherbrooke St. W., Montreal 2, Que. As the reorganized national representative body of Canadian Jewry, seeks to safeguard the status, rights, and welfare of Jews in Canada; to combat anti-Semitism and promote understanding and goodwill among all ethnic and religious groups; cooperates with other agencies to improve social, economic, and cultural conditions of Jews and to rehabilitate Jewish refugees and immigrants; assists Jewish communities in Canada in establishing central community organizations to provide for their social, philanthropic, educational, and cultural needs. *Cercle Juif; Congress Bulletin.*

Canadian Young Judea (1917). 1247 Guy St., Montreal 25, Que. Seeks to imbue its membership with the necessity for the spiritual and physical perpetuation of the Jewish people, emphasizing the centrality of Israel. *Hamagshem; Ha Shachar; Judaean; Machshava; Yedion.*

Canpal-Canadian Israel Trading Co., Ltd. (1949). 1231 St. Catherine St. W., Montreal 25, Que. Promotes trade and finance between Canada and Israel. *Annual Report.*

Federated Zionist Organization of Canada (1967). 1247 Guy St., Montreal 25, Que. The Federated Zionist Organization is the umbrella organization for all Canadian Zionist organizations.

Hadassah-Wizo Organization of Canada (1917). 1500 St. Catherine St. W., Montreal 25, Que. Seeks to foster Zionist ideals among Jewish women in Canada; conducts child-care, health, medical, and social-welfare activities in Israel. *Hadassah Supplement* (in *Canadian Zionist); Orah.*

Jewish Colonization Association of Canada (1907). 493 Sherbrooke St. W., Montreal 2, Que. Promotes Jewish land settlement in Canada through loans to establish farmers; helps new immigrant farmers to purchase farms or settles them on farms owned by the Association; provides agricultural advice and supervision. Contributes funds to Canadian Jewish Loan Cassa for loans to small businessmen and enterprising artisans.

Jewish Immigrant Aid Services of Canada—JIAS (1919). 5780 Decelles Ave., Montreal 26, Que. Serves as a national agency for immigration and immigrant welfare. *JIAS Bulletin; JIAS News; Studies and Documents on Immigration and Integration in Canada.*

Jewish Labor Committee of Canada (1934). 5165 Isabella Ave., Montreal 29, Que. Fights for human rights and against racial discrimination and anti-Semitism; works for strengthening of Jewish life in Canada.

Jewish National Fund of Canada (1902). 1247 Guy St., Montreal 25, Que. Raises funds for Keren Kayemet in Israel. *Bulletin.*

Joint National Committee on Community Services of the Canadian Jewish Congress and Canadian Committee of the Council of Jewish Federations and Welfare Funds (1959). 150 Beverley St., Toronto 2B, Ont. Acts as a field service to aid Canadian Jewish communities in community organization, fund raising, budgeting, health and welfare planning, and the development of regional and national intercity programs.

Keren Hatarbut—Canadian Association for Hebrew Education and Culture (1946). 5234 Clanranald Ave., Montreal 29, Que. Seeks to promote Hebrew education and culture, to stimulate study of the language, and to serve as cultural bridge between Canada and Israel and as a unifying factor in the spiritual and cultural life of Canadian Jewry. Serves as coordinating body for affiliated schools; sponsors Hebrew-speaking Camp Massad. *Egeret Lamechanech.*

Labor Zionist Movement of Canada (1939). 5780 Decelles Ave., Montreal 26, Que. Advances the political, organizational, and educational program of labor Zionism and coordinates the activities of its affiliated organizations. *View-Dos Vort; Viewpoints.*

Mizrachi-Hapoel Hamizrachi of Canada (1915). 5497A Victoria Ave., Montreal 26, Que. Aids *aliyah*, education, social welfare, religious publications in Israel; maintains adult-education programs, religious Zionist youth groups, camps in Canada. *Mizrachi Voice.*

National Council of Jewish Women of Canada (1893). 4700 Bathurst St., Willowdale 473, Ont. Seeks to stimulate individuals and communities to meet human needs and to advance the democratic way of life nationally and internationally through an integrated program of education, service, and social action. *Canadian Council Woman.*

National Joint Community Relations Committee of Canadian Jewish Congress and B'nai B'rith in Canada (1936). 150 Beverley St., Toronto 2B, Ont. Seeks to safeguard the status, rights, and welfare of Jews in Canada; to combat anti-Semitism and promote understanding and goodwill among all ethnic and religious groups. *Congress Bulletin.*

United Jewish Relief Agencies of Canada (affiliated with the **American Jewish Joint Distribution Committee**) (1939). 493 Sherbrooke St. W., Montreal 2, Que. A subsidiary of the Canadian Jewish Congress; federates organizations extending relief to Jewish refugees and other war victims. *Congress Bulletin.*

United Jewish Teachers' Seminary (1945). 5575 Cote St. Luc Rd., Montreal 254, Que. Trains teachers for all types of Jewish and Hebrew schools.

Zionist Organization of Canada (1892; reorg. 1919). 1247 Guy St., Montreal 25, Que. To safeguard the integrity and independence of the State of Israel as a free and democratic commonwealth by means consistent with the laws of Canada. *Canadian Zionist; Etgar.*

JEWISH EDUCATION
IN AMERICA

The current national census of Jewish schools is the latest and most comprehensive in a series of nationwide surveys conducted by the American Association for Jewish Education to determine the size of pupil enrollment in all types of schools, under all kinds of auspices and orientations.

COVERAGE

The sample of this study consisted of 2,070 out of 2,727 known schools, located in 455 communities in the United States. The total Jewish population in the 455 reporting communities was estimated at 5,495,635, of a total of 5,721,000 in the United States. Therefore, it may be assumed that the reporting communities represented about 96 percent of all Jews in the United States.

SUMMARY OF FINDINGS

1 The reported enrollment in all types of Jewish schools was 446,648; the total estimated enrollment, 554,468.
2 About one third of all Jewish children, estimated to be eligible to receive a Jewish education (the 3-through-17 age-group), actually received some form of Jewish education.
3 Nearly seven tenths of all eligible children in the 8-through-12 age-group were enrolled in elementary schools.
4 Close to one seventh of reported Jewish school students received intensive all-day school education. The vast majority of students attended one-day or three-days-a-week schools.
5 More boys than girls were enrolled in Jewish schools (57 percent, compared with 43 percent); boys received a more intensive education than girls.
6 Jewish education was essentially a function of congregational schools.
7 The more intensive the Jewish education, the more Orthodox were the school's auspices and/or orientation.

8 Jewish education was more intensive in Metropolitan New York at all levels, reflecting the large concentration of Orthodox Jews in that area of the country.

9 Close to seven tenths of all students were enrolled in the 13 communities with the largest Jewish population (50,000 or more).

10 Enrollment under Orthodox, Yiddish, and intercongregational auspices was heavily concentrated in New Jersey, New York, and Pennsylvania, while that under Reform, Conservative, and communal-noncongregational auspices was more widely distributed over other areas in the United States.

11 The five communities with the largest Jewish population enrolled proportionately the smallest number of eligible children.

12 Generally, the larger the size of the Jewish population, the smaller the proportion of eligible children enrolled in Jewish schools.

TABLE 10
Enrollment by type of school and auspices

Type of school	Number	Percent	
ORTHODOX			
One-day	11,055	11.5	(5.9%)
Two-to-five-days	38,300	39.8	(19.3%)
All-day school	46,714	48.6	(78.1%)
Totals	96,069	100.0	(21.5%)
CONSERVATIVE			
One-day	47,705	31.2	(25.3%)
Two-to-five-days	101,779	66.5	(51.4%)
All-day school	3,609	2.3	(6.0%)
Totals	153,093	100.0	(34.3%)
REFORM			
One-day	125,061	78.3	(66.3%)
Two-to-five-days	34,587	21.7	(17.4%)
All-day school	13	—[1]	(—[1])
Totals	159,661	100.0	(35.7%)
INTERCONGREGATIONAL			
One-day	723	26.1	(0.4%)
Two-to-five-days	2,040	73.6	(1.0%)
All-day school	11	0.3	(—[1])
Totals	2,774	100.0	(0.6%)

COMMUNAL-NONCONGREGATIONAL
One-day	3,131	10.2	(1.6%)
Two-to-five-days	18,325	59.7	(9.2%)
All-day school	9,231	30.0	(15.4%)
Totals	30,687	100.0	(6.9%)

YIDDISH SCHOOLS
One-day	970	22.2	(0.5%)
Two-to-five-days	3,148	72.1	(1.6%)
All-day school	246	5.6	(0.4%)
Totals	4,364	100.0	(1.0%)

TOTALS ALL AUSPICES
One-day	188,645	42.2	(100.0%)
Two-to-five-days	198,179	44.4	(100.0%)
All-day school	59,824	13.4	(100.0%)
Totals	446,648	100.0	(100.0%)

[1] Less than 0.1 percent.

TABLE 11
Enrollment by type of school and level

Type of school	Nursery-kindergarten			Six-to-seven-year olds		
	Number	Percent		Number	Percent	
PRIMARY DEPARTMENT						
One-day	12,909	42.2	(6.8%)	30,357	80.4	(16.1%)
Two-to-five-days	8,598	28.1	(4.3%)	5,091	13.5	(2.6%)
All-day school	9,065	29.6	(15.2%)	2,311	6.1	(3.9%)
Totals	30,572	100.0	(6.8%)	37,759	100.0	(8.5%)
ELEMENTARY DEPARTMENT						
One-day	107,859	34.8	(57.2%)			
Two-to-five-days	164,338	53.2	(82.8%)			
All-day school	36,636	11.9	(61.2%)			
Totals	308,833	100.0	(69.1%)			
HIGH-SCHOOL DEPARTMENT						
One-day	37,520	54.0	(19.9%)			
Two-to-five-days	20,152	29.0	(10.2%)			
All-day school	11,812	17.0	(19.7%)			
Totals	69,484	100.0	(15.6%)			
TOTALS ALL DEPARTMENTS						
One-day	188,645	42.2	(100.0%)			
Two-to-five-days	198,179	44.4	(100.0%)			
All-day school	59,824	13.4	(100.0%)			
Totals	446,648	100.0	(100.0%)			

358

ANALYTIC INDEX

faith and conduct in, 112-13
fear of classroom influence,
273-76
intolerant of nonadherents, 131
rival of Judaism, 265-67
Christians and Christianity, 281
Church and State
Jewish concepts, 271-76
preoccupation, 276
separation, 274-76
Circumcision, history and ritual,
200-04
Civil marriage, attitude toward,
253
Cohen, Levi, and Israel, divisions
of Jewish nation, 161-62
Cohen, Morris, 258
Cohen, role in redemption of
firstborn, 204-05
Columbus Platform, 105-12
Communal and scheduled prayer,
228-29
Communications media versus
supernatural morality, 138
Community as repository of the
Law, 248-49
Confession of sins
at death, 222-23
Yom Kippur, 178-83
Confirmation services, 169, 207-08
Congregationalism and synagogue
origins in America, 31
Consecration Ceremony, 206
Consensus as normative of
morality, 248-49
Conservatism
concept of God, 125-27
concept of man, 127-28
concept of Torah, 129-31
contraception approved, 220-21
critical of anti-Zionist Reform,
120
divorce customs, 218

fundamental principles, 123-25
human immortality, 128
liaison in American Judaism,
141-43
origin as reaction to Reform,
117-18
origins and development, 49-61
positive-historical Judaism,
121-22
reaction against Orthodoxy,
124-25
Contraception, Jewish approval,
220-21
Conversation at meals, 197
Conversion to Judaism, 250-53
Corech, Passover combining food,
164
Covenant, universality of, 87
Covenant of Abraham, 200
Creation
as process, 126
rabbinic theology of, 80-81
Cremation and embalming, not
traditional, 224
Cremieux, Adolphe, 36-37
Custom contrary to law, 120
Czarist Russia, 50-55

David, Shield of, 232
Davidic ancestry of Messiah, 90-91
Day of Atonement. *See* Yom
Kippur
Day of Kaporos, 179
Days of Omer, 168
Death-bed confession, 222-23
Decalogue
analysis of, 243-45
basis of Jewish morality, 133
Deism and Reform origins, 34
The Deputy, Jewish estimate, 273
Dietary laws
Canadian Reform regulations,
198

Freedom
for community, 269-71
to choose good and evil, 128
Freehof, Solomon B., 254-55
French Revolution and Orthodoxy,
66
Freud, Sigmund
Cabalistic influences, 19
cultural Judaism of, 264
Friedlander, Israel, 122
Frugg, Simon, 41
Fundamental Principles of the
Metaphysics of Morals,
243-44
Funeral eulogy, 224
Funeral hymn, 225
Funeral prayer, 226
Funeral procession, 224
Furtado, Abraham, 65
The Future of an Illusion, 264

Ge-Hinnam, punishment after
death, 84-85
Gemara, analysis of contents, 8-10
Gentiles, salvation of, 83-84
Georgia, Jewish origins, 26
German immigration, history,
35-39
Get, divorce document, 217-18
Ghetto
emancipation and Orthodoxy,
68
of American Judaism, 264-65
Ginzberg, Louis, 67, 122
Girls, naming of, 204
Glazer, Nathan, 259
Gnosticism, origins of Cabala, 18
God
absolute unicity, 74
attributes analyzed, 72-74
attributes in Maimonides' creed,
16
confers grace for the asking, 243

essence and existence in
Maimonides, 73
foreknowledge and human freedom, 71-72
fulfillment in Cabala, 19
in Conservatism, 125-27
in Orthodoxy, 70-75
in Reform, 107
indwelling as lawgiver, 244-45
majesty compared with
creatures, 74-75
recollection of presence, 229-30
rights primary, 240-41
Shekinah presence, 76-77
the Other who demands
obedience, 240
unity as basis for human
solidarity, 126
Gompers, Samuel, 258
Gordin, Jacob, 41
Grace
given in answer to prayer, 243
through prayer, 87-88
The Great Day. See Yom Kippur
Great Hallel at Passover, 165-66
Guide for the Perplexed, divine
attributes, 72-74
Guttmacher, Alan, Jewish approval
of abortion, 222

Ha'am, Ahad, 122
HaCohen, Abraham ben Isaac, 203
Halakoth, Talmud legal code, 6
Hallel, Passover recitation, 165-66
Halvayah, funeral procession, 224
Hammerstein, Oscar, 258
Hanukkah, history and ritual,
173-75
Harahaman, invocation, 203
Haroseth dish, 162
Hasidism
Cabalistic origins, 18
history and practices, 233-36

Latin America, Jewish origins,
22-23
Law
as custom in Reform, 113-18
expression of divine love, 241
interpersonal relations
secondary, 240-41
religious dimension, 240
rights of God primary, 240-41
self-obligation rejected by
Judaism, 244
subject to change and
development, 130
Law of Niddah, history and ritual,
213-15
Laws, six hundred thirteen Mosaic,
75
Laws of the Sons of Noah, 131
Lazarus, Emma, 51-52
L'choh Dodi, Sabbath hymn, 152,
154-56
Leeser, Isaac, 43, 49-50
Lehman, Herbert, 259
Lenin, Jewish collaborators, 51
Levinsky, David, 54-55
Levita, Elijah, 40
Levites for Temple service, 204
Levy, Felix A., 106
Liberty and law, 244-45
Lily of Jacob, 172
Lippmann, Walter, 259
Locke, John, influence on Jewish
freedom, 26
Longfellow on Rhode Island Jews,
26
Lulav, ritual, 170
Luminary, Maimonides' Mishnah
commentary, 14

Magen David, Shield of David,
232
Maggid, Passover narrative of
deliverance, 164

Mahzor Vitri, prayer book, 228
Maimonides, Moses, 13-17
concept of law, 243
creed approved by the people,
249
God's presence and recollection,
229-30
Guide for the Perplexed, 17
laws of Kashrut, 189
Letter of Consolation, 14
Reform origins, 34
regulations on intercourse, 215
resurrection from dead, 88-89
rules of Shehitah, 193
the Chosen People, 277
thirteen articles of faith, 14-16
Man
Conservative concept of, 127-28
Orthodox concept of, 80-89
Reform concept of, 107
Maoz Tzur, Fortress Rock, 174
Maror, Passover eating bitter
herbs, 164
Marranos, history of, 21-23
Marriage
betrothal customs, 209-10
ceremony of glass breaking, 212
contract conditions, 211
divine institution, 210
divorce regulations, 215-18
fertility a divine mandate, 208
history and ritual of Jewish,
208-22
Jew and Christian, 250-51, 253
regulations on intercourse,
213-15
ring ceremony, 211
Talmud on divine origin, 210
Marx, Karl, 37, 95
Mashgiach, meat inspector, 194
Massachusetts, Jewish origins, 26
Matzi, Passover blessing over
bread, 164